A HANDBOOK

OF THE

I0120511

BIRDS OF TASMANIA

AND ITS DEPENDENCIES

BY

FRANK MERVYN LITTLER, F.E.S.

(Member of the Australasian Ornithologists' Union).

1910.

British Library Cataloguing-in-Publication Data
A catalogue record for this book is available from the
British Library

Bird Watching

Bird watching is, very simply, the observation of birds as a recreational activity. It can be done with the naked eye, through binoculars and telescopes, or by listening for bird sounds. Although characterised as 'watching', *bird watching* often involves a significant auditory component, as many bird species are more easily detected and identified by ear than by eye. Recognition of bird vocalizations – *bird listening* is an important part of a birder's toolkit. Many birdwatchers occupy themselves with observing local species (birding in their "local patch"), but may also make specific trips to observe birds in other locales. Birdwatchers partake in many differing activities, including monitoring and conservation, especially taking part in censuses of bird populations and migratory patterns. Such activities are incredibly important, a form of 'citizen science', they assist in identifying environment threats to the well being of birds, thereby raising awareness of environmental issues more broadly. Birding can also be a competitive event, with events encouraging individuals or teams to accumulate large numbers of species within a specified time or area. There is more to bird watching than first meets the eye!

The whole etymology of 'bird watching' is a highly contested area. The first recorded use of the term *birdwatcher* was in 1891, and *bird* was introduced as a verb in 1918. The term *birding* was also used for the practice of *fowling* or hunting with firearms as in

Shakespeare's *The Merry Wives of Windsor* (1602): "She laments sir... her husband goes this morning a-birding." The terms *birding* and *bird watching* are today used by some interchangeably, although some participants prefer *birding*, partly because it does not exclude the auditory aspects of enjoying birds. At the most basic level, the distinction between the two terms is perceived as one of dedication or intensity, though this is a subjective differentiation. Generally, self-described birders perceive themselves to be more versed in minutiae like identification (aural and visual), molt, distribution, migration timing, and habitat usage. Whereas these dedicated *birders* may often travel specifically in search of birds, *birdwatchers* have been described by some enthusiasts as having a more limited scope, perhaps not venturing far from their own yards or local parks to view birds.

Twitching is another common term, of British derivation, used to mean "the pursuit of a previously located rare bird." In North America it is more often called "chasing", though the British usage is starting to catch on there, especially among younger birders. It was originally used in the 1950s, for the nervous behaviour of Howard Medhurst, a British pioneer of the activity. The term *twitcher*, sometimes misapplied as a synonym for birder, is reserved for those who travel long distances to see a rare bird that would then be *ticked*, or counted on a list. Prior terms for those who chased rarities were *pot-hunter*, *tally-hunter*, or *tick-hunter*. The main goal of twitching is often to accumulate species on one's lists, with some participants actively challenging one another to accumulate the longest species list.

The earliest interest in observing birds for their aesthetic rather than utilitarian (mainly food) value is traced to the late eighteenth century in the works of Gilbert White, Thomas Bewick, George Montagu and John Clare. The study of birds and natural history in general became increasingly prevalent in the Britain during the Victorian Era, often associated with collection, eggs and later skins being the artefacts of interest. This was largely due to the contacts of wealthy collectors, with vast swathes of land in the colonies, to obtain specimens from around the world. It was only in the late nineteenth century that the call for bird protection began leading to the rising popularity of observations on living birds. The Audubon Society and the American Ornithologists Union (AOU) were started to protect birds from the growing trade in feathers in the US while the Royal Society for the Protection of Birds began in Britain.

With the turn of the century, the rising popularity of the car also increased the mobility of birdwatchers and this made new locations accessible to those interested in birds. Networks of birdwatchers in the UK began to form in the late 1930s under the British Trust for Ornithology (BTO). The BTO saw the potential to produce scientific results through the networks, unlike the Royal Society for the Protection of Birds (RSPB) which like the Audubon Society originated from the bird protection movement. Increased mobility of birdwatchers also ensured that books like *Where to watch birds* by John Gooders became best-sellers. By the 1960s air-travel became feasible and long distance holiday destinations opened up with the result that by 1965, Britain's first birding tour company, *Ornitholidays* was started by Lawrence Holloway. Travelling far away also led to complications in name usage, British birds like "Wheatear", "Heron" and "Swallow" now needed adjectives to differentiate them in places where there were several related species. The rapidly falling cost of air-travel made flying to remote birding destinations a possibility for an even larger number of people towards the 1980s, and the need for global guides on birds became more pressing.

One of the largest of such projects was the "Handbook of the Birds of the World", started in the 1990s with Josep del Hoyo a country doctor in Catalonia, Jordi Sargatal and ornithologist Andy Elliott. Many birdwatchers have spent their entire lives trying to see all the bird species of the world. Overall, there are about 10,000 species of bird, but only a small number of 'watchers' have seen more than 7000. Some birders have been known to go to great lengths and many have lost their lives in the process. For instance, Phoebe Snetsinger spent her family inheritance travelling to various parts of the world while suffering from a malignant melanoma, surviving an attack and rape in New Guinea before dying in a road accident in Madagascar. She saw as many as

8,400 species. The birdwatcher David Hunt, who was leading a bird tour in Corbett National Park was killed by a tiger in February 1985. More successful efforts have included the amazing 1971 tour of North America by Ted Parker, who saw 626 species in a year. From 2008 the top life-list has been held by Tom Gullick, an Englishman who lives in Spain. In 2012 he became the first birdwatcher to log over 9,000 species. Bird watching is as popular now as it has been in the past, and if anything – it is experiencing a modern day resurgence. The amount of societies, organisations and outings of birders has increased substantially over the last decade. We hope the reader enjoys this book.

PREFACE.

No apology is offered for the appearance of the present modest little volume dealing with the avifauna of our island home. The time appeared ripe for such a book as would deal, in a manner consistent with scientific accuracy, and plain to understand, with our feathered friends. While every endeavour has been made to eliminate errors and to attain as high a degree of accuracy as possible, the author does not claim infallibility. The present volume makes no pretence to be either a "history" or a "monograph" of the various species passed under review.

The sins of omission are both manifold and manifest, and for these kind indulgence is craved. The one most regretted is in connection with the brevity of the field notes under the heading of "Observations." This was imperative in order to compress the subject matter within reasonable limits. Some day it may be the author's privilege, or that of someone more worthy, to write a history of the birds of this garden isle. Until such is done, the hope is expressed that the present effort may to some extent help to bridge the gap. Every endeavour has been made to make the book purely Tasmanian—i.e., to describe from material collected within the confines of Tasmania, and to use only field notes collected in the island. A large amount of success has been achieved in this direction, thanks chiefly to the good offices of various kind friends.

The writings of the author's predecessors and contemporaries have been constantly consulted, and much help obtained therefrom. All measurements taken by the author are expressed in terms of millimeters, as being in his estimation the easiest for comparison, and, now that the decimal system is coming so much into everyday use, the simplest also for the layman.

At the end of the subject matter will be found an extract from the latest Tasmanian *Game Protection Act,* with a complete schedule of the species afforded total protection under the Act.

An asterisk placed against the name of a bird at the beginning of an article denotes that it is protected under the Act.

The Author desires to express his grateful thanks for valuable assistance in material and notes to Mr. H. H. Scott, Curator of the Victoria Museum (Launceston), who kindly placed the entire resources of the Museum at the writer's disposal; to Messrs. H. C. Thompson, H. Stuart Dove, A. L. Butler, R. H. Green, F. D. Barclay, Geo. Russell, Col. Legge, and others who assisted in many ways.

THE AUTHOR.

Launceston, Tasmania.

INTRODUCTION.

TASMANIA and its dependencies consist of the main island of Tasmania, and a number of islands of greater or lesser extent, and groups of islands, chief among which are the Furneaux Group, of which the largest are Flinders, Cape Barren, and Clarke Islands; the Hunter Group includes Robbins Island, Barren Island, Three Hummock Island, and several smaller ones; then King Island, Maria Island, Bruni Island, Schouten Island; the Macquarie Group, consisting of a number of moderate-sized islands; the Kent Group; Hogan's Group; also a number of small islands scattered about Bass Strait in the vicinity of Tasmania.

It is with Tasmania that we are chiefly concerned, and so may to a great extent ignore the islands which are politically joined to her.

Lying as she does at the extreme south of the Australian "region," Tasmania is visited by but few migrants from Arctic and sub-Arctic regions who "winter" in the Southern Hemisphere during the Australian summer. Not only are the species fewer, but the individuals of those species which reach here are considerably less than further north.

Taken as a whole, Tasmania cannot be considered rich in bird-life either as to species or individuals. What birds there are are very irregularly distributed, owing to the very diversified nature of the country, climate, and vegetation.

The only portion of the island where birds may be said to be absolutely scarce is on the West Coast, where the mountains and gullies are densely clothed with forests of myrtle and an almost impenetrable tangle of scrub and undergrowth. About the mountain tops of this portion Hawks, Goshawks, and Falcons may be seen wheeling on facile wing.

The Midlands form the stronghold of such Plovers as are found here. The large amount of clearing that has been going on during the last few years is responsible for a marked decrease in the number of birds in many districts. For not only have the birds been driven to seek other haunts, but those that remained have fallen victims to " pot-hunters " and settlers' cats.

Compared with the resident birds of the Australian mainland, those of Tasmania may be said to show marked melanistic tendencies. Of the species " peculiar " to the island, all save the Lesser White-backed Magpie (*Gymnorhina hyperleuca*) are larger than their nearest allies on the mainland.

A number of species lay four or even five eggs to the clutch, while the same species or related ones on the continent of Australia lay but three. There are also a number of structural differences in the nests of several species as compared with those across the Strait, but this point is not emphasized as much as the preceding ones, nor is it as important.

Some 214 species are glanced at in the succeeding pages. Omitting the orders *Gaviæ* and *Tubinares*, owing to the distribution and economy of certain species included in them not having been fully worked out, the birds may be roughly subdivided as under :—

Position on list challenged	5	species
Occurring on dependencies only	4	,,
" Peculiar " or insular forms	21	,,
Accidental and casual visitors	16	,,
Permanent residents (*circa*)	110	,,

The total number of absolutely authenticated species, including accidentals, casuals, and migrants, of all Orders, for Tasmania and her dependencies may be placed at slightly over 200.

SYSTEMATIC INDEX.

ORDER—ACCIPITRES : BIRDS OF PREY.

SUB-ORDER—FALCONES : FALCONS.

FAMILY—FALCONIDÆ : HAWKS.

SUB-ORDER—PANDIONES : OSPREYS.

SUB-ORDER—STRIGES : OWLS.

FAMILY—BUBONIDÆ : OWLS PROPER.

FAMILY—STRIGIDÆ : BARN OWLS.

ORDER—PASSERIFORMES : PERCHING BIRDS.

SUB-ORDER—PASSERES.

ORDER—PICARIÆ : PICARIAN BIRDS.

SUB-ORDER—CORACIÆ.

SUB-ORDER—HALCYONES.

ORDER—PSITTACI : PARROTS.

ORDER—COLUMBÆ : PIGEONS AND DOVES.

SUB-ORDER—COLUMBÆ : PIGEONS.

ORDER—GAVIÆ : SEA-BIRDS.

FAMILY—LARIDÆ : GULLS AND TERNS.

ORDER—PLATALEÆ.

FAMILY—IBIDIDÆ: IBISES.

ORDER—HERODIONES : HERONS.

FAMILY—ARDEIDÆ: HERONS PROPER.

ORDER—STEGANOPODES : PELICANS.

FAMILY—PHALACROCORACIDÆ: CORMORANTS.

SUB-FAMILY—PHALACROCORACINÆ.

FAMILY—SULIDÆ: GANNETS.

FAMILY—PELECANIDÆ: PELICANS.

ORDER—PYGOPODES : DIVING BIRDS.

FAMILY—PODICIPEDIDÆ: GREBES.

ORDER—IMPENNES : PENGUINS.

ORDER—CHENOMORPHÆ.

SUB-ORDER—ANSERES : GEESE, &c.

FAMILY—ANATIDÆ : DUCKS.

SUB-FAMILY—CYGNINÆ : SWANS.

SUB-FAMILY—ANSERANATINÆ.

SUB-FAMILY—CEREOPSINÆ.

SUB-FAMILY—CHENONETTINÆ.

SUB-FAMILY—ANATINÆ.

SUB-FAMILY—FULIGULINÆ.

SUB-FAMILY—ERISMATURINÆ.

(*For Alphabetical Index see end of book.*)

LIST OF ILLUSTRATIONS.

* I am indebted to the Council of the A.O.U. for the loan of these blocks, through the kind offices of Mr. A. J. Campbell, senior editor of *The Emu.*

A Handbook of the Birds of Tasmania

AND ITS DEPENDENCIES.

ORDER—ACCIPITRES : BIRDS OF PREY.

Sub-Order—Falcones : Falcons.

FAMILY—FALCONIDÆ (11 species).

Sub-Family—Accipitrinæ.

SWAMP-HAWK (ALLIED HARRIER)

(*Circus gouldi*, Bonaparte).

Male.—Upper surface dark brown, not including head and neck, which are reddish-brown; tail ashy-grey to brown, with interrupted bars of dark brown; upper tail coverts white, barred with reddish-brown; breast varies from buffy-white to pale reddish, each feather being striped with dark brown down the centre; legs yellow; beak and claws black; irides bright yellow. Dimensions in mm. :—Length, 603; bill, 35; wing, 420; tail, 252; tarsus, 106.

Female.—Practically same as male, but is generally more bulky.

Young.—Upper surface, including wings, uniform sooty or dark chocolate-brown; upper tail coverts rufous; tail a shade lighter than back and obscurely barred with blackish-brown; chest reddish-brown; abdomen and thighs the same, only brighter.

Nestling.—Covered with buffy-white down; cere and legs yellow.

Nest.—Constructed of dry stalks of docks, thistles, and the like, and lined with grass. The situation usually chosen is among rushes or in a grain field.

Eggs.—Clutch three to five; somewhat oval in shape; texture of shell fairly coarse, and with little lustre; colour white, often nest-stained. Dimensions in mm. of a clutch :—(1) 54 x 30, (2) 51 x 39, (3) 52 x 39.5.

Breeding Season.—September to December.

Geographical Distribution.—Tasmania, King Island, and Aus-

tralia in general; also New Zealand, New Caledonia, Lord Howe
Island, Norfolk Island, and Fiji Islands.

Observations.—This fine Hawk may be seen flying over and
about river flats and marshes almost everywhere in the island.
As far as I am aware, it is nowhere very plentiful, but is in sufficient numbers not to be considered rare. It is somewhat of a
bold nature, openly swooping down on a farmyard and carrying
off sundry chickens during the season.

SPOTTED HARRIER or HAWK
(*Circus assimilis*, Jard. and Selby).

Male.—Crown of the head, cheeks, and ear coverts dark chestnut, each feather having a mark of brown down the centre; back
of the neck, upper part of the back, and chest uniform dark grey;
shoulders, under surface of the wing, abdomen, thighs, and under
tail coverts rich chestnut, the whole of the feathers beautifully
spotted with white, the spots regularly disposed down each web,
and being largest and most distinct on the abdomen; upper tail
coverts brown, barred and tipped with greyish-white; tail alternately barred with conspicuous bands of dark brown and grey.
Length, 19 inches; wing, 16; tail, 10; tarsus, 3⅝" (Gould).

Female.—Similar to male.

Nest.—Situated in a moderately high tree, and composed of
sticks and twigs loosely placed together, with a lining of green
leaves.

Eggs.—Clutch two to three usually; roundish in shape, texture
of shell fairly coarse; surface lustreless: colour bluish-white.
Dimensions in mm. of clutch :—(1) 50 x 40, (2) 49 x 41, (3) 51 x
42.

Breeding Season.—August to December.

Geographical Distribution.—Tasmania and Australia in general;
also Celebes.

Observations.—In no district is this well-marked species at all
plentiful. It is to be found scattered over a wide area, but on
account of its shyness it is not often seen close enough to be readily
identified. The food of this Hawk chiefly consists of lizards, mice,
and other ground game, and, like the Brown Hawk, varying its
diet with beetles and moths. Rarely, if ever, is it a menace to
the farmer's poultry-yard.

*WHITE GOSHAWK
(*Astur novæ-hollandiæ*, Gm.)

Male.—Whole of the plumage pure white; cere and legs yellow;
bill and claws black; irides reddish-brown. Dimensions in mm. :—
Length, 512; bill, 30; wing, 302; tail, 208; tarsus, 79.

Female.—Plumage similar to male; dimensions a little greater.

NEST OF HARRIER.

Photo. by H. C. THOMPSON.

NEST, EGGS, AND YOUNG OF HARRIER.

Photo. by D. LE SOUEF.

From "THE EMU."

Nest.—Composed of fine twigs broken from the extreme tips of dry branches, and lined with a few green eucalyptus leaves; usually situated in a fairly lofty gum.

Eggs.—Two to three usually, four sometimes; roundish oval in shape; texture somewhat coarse; surface almost lustreless; colour bluish-white, more or less smudged and speckled with purplish-brown. Dimensions in mm. of a clutch:—(1) 46 x 38, (2) 48 x 38.5, (3) 46.75 x 37.

Breeding Season.—September to November principally.

Geographical Distribution.—Tasmania, King Island, New South Wales, Victoria, South Australia, and Queensland.

Observations.—Although frequenting many parts of the island, it is by no means common anywhere. One reason for its scarcity is the fact that whenever it appears close to civilization violent efforts are made to shoot it, on account of its handsome appearance. From information received, it appears to be more common in the southern districts than in the northern. From districts other than southern, I have records of it from Launceston, Lilydale, Waratah, Wilmot, Table Cape, Mt. Balfour, Derby, and Gladstone.

GOSHAWK

(*Astur approximans*, Vig. and Hors.)

Male.—Whole of the upper surface blackish-brown; tail barred with blackish; wing coverts outlined with brown, quills barred with blackish; cheeks finely streaked with white; upper throat nearly white; lower throat buffy-white, each feather heavily marked with dark brown; rest of under surface creamy-white, each feather broadly barred with reddish-brown, lighter in shade towards the vent; thighs light reddish, barred with bright reddish; inside of wings creamy-buff, marked and barred with dark brown; under surface of tail silvery-white, the blackish bars showing distinctly. Dimensions in mm.:—Length, 510; bill, 26; wing, 314; tail, 274; tarsus, 76.

Female.—Similiar in plumage to male.

Young.—Male.—Feathers on the upper surface narrowly outlined with reddish-brown; chest creamy-white, each feather heavily marked with blackish; markings on under surface more distinct than in adult. Dimensions in mm.:—Length, 510; bill, 26; wing, 306; tail, 276; tarsus, 76.

Young.—Female.—Upper surface similar to young male; under surface much darker. Dimensions in mm.:—Length, 380; bill, 17; wing, 252; tail, 193; tarsus, 60.

Nest.—A lofty eucalypt is usually chosen, and the nest constructed of sticks and twigs, the lining being leaves.

Eggs.—Clutch two to three usually, four sometimes; in shape stout oval, with one end somewhat sharp; texture fine, with very

little lustre; colour bluish-white, sometimes without markings, at others with spots and blotches of rather pale reddish-brown. Dimensions in mm. of a clutch :—(1) 45 x 35.5, (2) 46 x 34.25, (3) 45 x 35. *Breeding Season.*—August to December. *Geographical Distribution.*—Tasmania, Australia, Norfolk Is., and New Caledonia.
        Observations.—Common compared with the White Goshawk. Like all other Hawks, it is much persecuted on account of its fondness for an occasional chicken. The stomachs of several that I have examined contained only the undigested remains of rats and mice. On farms where there are hayricks, it will stay about day after day on the look-out for its prey, upon which it will swoop down with lightning speed, striking uncalled for terror into the hearts of the farmyard hens and their families, with the result that it pays the extreme penalty. Flying with facile wing, it glides over the grain-fields, keeping a sharp look-out for its prey the while. Lizards and small snakes are not despised when hunger presses.

SPARROW-HAWK

(*Accipiter cirrhocephalus*, Vieillot).

        Male.—Whole of the upper surface, including head, blackish-grey or fawn; tail indistinctly barred with a deeper colour; round the back of the neck a semi-interrupted band of reddish-brown; throat whitish, the feathers obscurely banded with pale reddish; chest and rest of under surface reddish, crossed by numerous bands of white, finest on chest and then widening; thighs distinctly reddish; under sides of wings and tail silver-grey, distinctly barred with dark brown or blackish, very distinct on former. "Irides and eyelashes yellow; cere and gape yellowish-green; base of the bill lead colour, tip black; legs yellow, slightly tinged with green" (Gould). Dimensions in mm. :—Length, 431; bill, 24; wing, 267; tail, 221; tarsus, 71.
        Female.—Similar in plumage to male. Dimensions in mm. :— Length, 445; bill, 24; wing, 283; tail, 203; tarsus, 71.
        Young.—Male.—"Cere and gape olive-yellow; irides and eyelash primrose-yellow" (Gould).
        Nest.—Constructed in the fork of a fairly high tree, and composed of sticks and twigs, and lined with fine roots, leaves, &c. "Frequently the nest of another bird of prey is used" (A. J. Campbell).
        Eggs.—Clutch three usually, four sometimes; roundish, of fine texture, and without lustre; colour white, faintly tinged with blue or green, generally without markings. An example in a clutch in the collection of Mr. F. D. Barclay is somewhat heavily marked with brown at the smaller end. Dimensions in mm. of a clutch :—(1) 41 x 33, (2) 39.5 x 33, (3) 40 x 32.

Photo. by F. E. BURBURY.

WEDGE-TAILED EAGLE.

Breeding Season.—August to November.

Geographical Distribution.—Tasmania, Australia, and New Guinea.

Observations.—With an easy and graceful flight, this elegant winged arrow of a bird skims the hedgerows and trees, and marks down its victim. Of all our Hawks this species is the quickest on the wing, and the most feared by small birds. In the northern parts of the island, at least, it is not as plentiful as either the Goshawk or Brown Hawk.

Sub-Family—Aquilinæ.

WEDGE-TAILED EAGLE
(*Uroaëtus audax*, Latham).

Male.—Upper and under surfaces, except back of the neck, deep brownish-black; feathers on upper back and chest minutely tipped with pale brown; back of the neck pale reddish-brown; head lighter than body; bases of the feathers snow-white. Dimensions in mm. : —Length, 1,091; bill, 62; wing, 598; tail, 433; tarsus, 94.

Female.—Similar in plumage.

As the age of the bird increases, the major wing coverts turn rusty in proportion; the chest takes on a lighter hue.

Young.—Rufous where the adult bird is blackish.

Nest.—A bulky structure of dead sticks, lined with green twigs, grass, and soft bark; placed in the branches of a lofty tree in a commanding position.

Eggs.—Clutch two usually, one or even three sometimes ; round or round oval in shape; texture fairly coarse, and surface almost without lustre ; ground colour brownish-white, more or less heavily marked and blotched with rusty-red and dull purplish. Dimensions in mm. of odd examples :—(1) 73.5 x 60, (2) 73 x 61.

Breeding Season.—August to November.

Geographical Distribution.—Tasmania and Australia in general.

Observations.—Although never as plentiful as in the northern part of the mainland, it is, nevertheless, numerous enough in some districts to justify shepherds keeping a sharp look-out, gun in hand, during the lambing season. Poison is also sometimes employed. For a couple of months during the summer of 1908 five large specimens were seen, day after day, wheeling round the summit and slopes of Mt. Arthur. Only solitary individuals had before been seen in the district. One afternoon in the same summer two fine specimens were seen slowly winging their way over Launceston at a comparatively low elevation. The Lake District is one of its strongholds. The bird above described, and whose measurements are given, had a stretch of 7 feet 6 inches from tip to tip of its wings when alive.

*WHITE-BELLIED SEA-EAGLE

(*Haliaëtus leucogaster*, Gm.)

Male.—"Entire head and neck, with the entire under surface, lesser under wing coverts, under tail coverts, and terminal 3½ in. of the tail, pure white; interscapular region, back, and rump dark cinereous-grey, becoming darker on the upper tail coverts, the white feathers at the lower part of the hind-neck with dark shafts, and the grey hue appearing lower down on each side of them; wing coverts, scapulars, and tertials bluish slate colour, with dark shafts; quills and basal portion of the tail blackish-cinereous; under wing coverts and flank feathers with black shafts. Length to front of cere, 25.2 to 26.5 in.; culmen from cere, 1.98 to 2.0; wing, 21.2 to 22.5; expanse, 71.5 to 78.0; tail, 10.0; tarsus, 3.4 to 3.8" (Col. Legge).

Female.—Plumage similar to male. "Length to front of cere, 27.0 to 27.75 in.; culmen from cere, 2.1; wing, 22.5 to 24.0; expanse, 79 to 80.1; tarsus, 4.0" (Col. Legge).

Young.—"Head buff; upper surface and wings chocolate-brown; chest and abdomen buff-brown" (R. Hall).

A splendid description of the young of this Eagle, from the unfledged nestling onwards, may be found in Col. Legge's "Birds of Ceylon," page 68.

Nest.—A large structure of sticks, usually situated on an isolated rock or in a lofty tree near the coast.

Eggs.—Clutch two usually; oval in shape and coarse of texture; somewhat granulated and faintly glossy; colour dull white, frequently with brownish stains. Dimensions in mm. of a clutch: —(1) 71 x 52, (2) 70 x 51.

Breeding Season.—August and September.

Geographical Distribution.—Tasmania, Australia, Malay Archipelago, Philippines, Northern India, Ceylon, Cape of Good Hope. Friendly Islands, and several other groups of islands scattered about the Pacific Ocean.

Observations.—So far as my observations go, and from the reports of those who know the coast well, this magnificent bird mostly frequents the north and east coasts from Low Head to Cape Pillar. At one or two places along the east coast it is fairly plentiful, but very shy.

Sub-Family—Falconinæ.

BLACK-CHEEKED FALCON

(*Falco melanogenys*, Gould).

Male.—" Head, entire sides of the face, cheeks, and ear-coverts deep black; upper surface blackish-brown; quills blackish, the outer secondaries with white tips; throat creamy; upper breast creamy,

NEST OF WEDGE-TAILED EAGLE.

Photo. by L. C. PITFIELD.

with black stripes; rest of under surface buff-white, with close narrow bars. Thighs transversely barred. Total length, 15 in.; wing, 11.75 in." (R. Hall).

Female.—" Similar, but larger; underneath deep rusty, paler on chest" (R. Hall).

Nest.—The usual situation appears to be a crevice or ledge on a cliff near or on the sea coast; the hollow spout of a tree is also used.

Eggs.—Clutch three; oval in shape; texture fine, with a slight gloss on the surface; ground colour buff, heavily freckled and marked with pinkish-red and rufous-brown. Dimensions in mm. of a clutch:—(1) 50.5 x 38, (2) 51 x 38.5, (3) 50 x 39.

Breeding Season.—August to November.

Geographical Distribution.—Tasmania and Australia in general; also the Moluccas.

Observations.—The range of this bird is somewhat restricted, the southern portion of the island seeming to be mostly favoured. I have seen individuals wheeling round and about Mt. Wellington, but have never met with it in the vicinity of Launceston. At several points along the north-west coast, however, it has been met with. Among other places, I have records of it from Kelso, Lilydale, and the Wilmot district.

LITTLE FALCON (WHITE-FRONTED FALCON)

(*Falco lunulatus*, Lath.)

Male.—Upper surface and wings dark grey; chin and throat buffy-white; remainder of the under surface reddish-brown; thighs distinctly rufous.

Female.—Similar in plumage.

Nest.—Usually an old erection of another Hawk is appropriated and lined with leaves. According to Mr. A. J. Campbell, Mr. A. E. Brent took a nest from the broken spout of a peppermint gum.

Eggs.—Clutch two to three; oval in shape, texture fine, but without lustre; ground colour buff to buffy-white, heavily freckled and blotched with light reddish-brown. Dimensions of a clutch:— (1) 38 x 30, (2) 38 x 29.

Breeding Season.—September to November usually.

Geographical Distribution.—Tasmania and the whole of the mainland.

Observations.—I have never met with this species in the northern portion of the island, but Mr. R. H. Green informs me that he has seen it about Lilydale and Nolands Bay, while Mr. H. Stuart Dove reports it from Table Cape. The latter gentleman writes me that it is the boldest of the Hawks, and one of the swiftest, and is also absolutely devoid of fear. It is irregularly and sparsely distributed over portions of the southern half.

BROWN HAWK

(Hieracidea orientalis, Schlegel).

Male.—Upper surface, including head, wings, and tail, uniform dark brown; the feathers on the lower back, wing coverts, and tail barred with reddish-brown; chin and throat creamy-white to white, varying with age; rest of under surface creamy-white. In some specimens the feathers on the chest and sides are only streaked with black, in others black predominates on the whole of the under surface; thighs brownish-black; under tail coverts silvery-grey. Dimensions in mm.:—Length, 457; bill, 26; wing, 340; tail, 200; tarsus, 62.

Female.—Similar in plumage.

Young.—Male.—Upper surface lighter than adult; under surface white, faintly creamed; feathers on chest and abdomen streaked with brown; sides of body and thighs brown. Dimensions in mm.:—Length, 425; bill, 25; wing, 323; tail, 125; tarsus, 62.

Nest.—Usually situated in the branches of a tall eucalypt, and composed of sticks and twigs, with a lining of leaves and pieces of bark.

Eggs.—Clutch two to three usually; round oval in shape; texture of shell fairly fine and without lustre. Eggs vary much in markings, even those of the same clutch. As a general thing it may be said that the ground colour is buffy-white and the surface much spotted and blotched with reddish to purplish brown; in some eggs the larger end, in others the smaller, is almost entirely covered by the markings; in others, again, the whole egg is smothered. Dimensions in mm. of a pair:—(1) 51.5 x 41, (2) 51 x 39.

A richly-coloured set in Mr. Hubert Thompson's collection is worthy of remark. The upper quarter of (1) is pinkish-white, heavily covered with minute freckles of reddish-brown, with a few large blotches of the same colour about the centre; the rest of the surface is a uniform deep reddish-brown. The upper quarter of (2) is as in (1), but there are a number of various-sized spots scattered about it; the rest of the surface is very heavily blotched with deep reddish-brown and blackish-brown, with the pinkish-red ground colour showing out here and there. The remaining egg (3) is practically a uniform reddish-brown, but the pigment is not as heavily laid on as on the lower quarter of (1)—the extreme upper and lower quarters are slightly paler than the rest of the surface. Dimensions in mm. of this clutch:—(1) 50 x 40, (2) 51.5 x 41, (3) 49 x 40.

Breeding Season.—August to November.

Geographical Distribution.—Tasmania, King Island, and practically the whole of the mainland.

Observations.—Of all the Hawks found in Tasmania this species appears to be the most plentiful. Its food, judging from the contents of the stomachs of a number that I have examined, seems to be chiefly insects, such as grass grub moths, crickets, chafer beetles, grasshoppers, and the like.

On account of its habit of frequenting the vicinity of homesteads, and its comparative tameness, it more often falls a victim to the farmer's gun than any other species. Even if it does take an occasional chicken, it more than pays for it by the number of insect pests destroyed. But then a Hawk is just a Hawk, and nothing more, to the average agriculturist.

KESTREL

(Cerchneis cenchroides, Vig. and Horsf.)

Male.—Head, back, and wing coverts cinnamon-red; the feathers of the head and neck finely streaked with black; tail grey, banded near the extremity with black, and tipped with white; primaries and secondaries dark brown; under surface buffy-white, the feathers very finely streaked with black. Dimensions in mm.: —Length, 301; bill, 17; wing, 248; tail, 158; tarsus, 37.

Female.—Similar in plumage.

Nest.—No proper nest is formed, the eggs being generally laid either in a crevice in a cliff or a hollow spout of a tree.

Eggs.—Clutch four to five usually; roundish, with one end slightly compressed; texture of shell fine and slightly glossed; colour pinkish-white, freckled and blotched with reddish-brown and dark brown, principally on the larger end. Dimensions in mm. of a clutch:—(1) 41 x 35, (2) 40.75 x 34.5, (3) 41 x 34.5, (4) 41 x 35.

Breeding Season.—August to November.

Geographical Distribution.—Tasmania, King Island, and the mainland generally.

Observations.—To the best of my knowledge, this species has not been met with in the northern parts of the island. Col. Legge is of opinion that it is merely a visitor. He informs me that a pair bred in the Sorell district, and also knows of it being observed three times in the vicinity of Cambridge. It does not appear to be at all plentiful on King Island. At the April (1889) meeting of the Royal Society of Tasmania, "the Secretary drew attention to a rare bird that has lately been shot near Muddy Plains. It was commonly known in Australia as the 'Nankeen Kestrel.'" Mr. Morton stated that it was a singular coincidence that in April, 1875, two specimens now in the Museum were shot at Sorell. It was in April, 1873, that the first specimen of this species was obtained, from Clarence Plains.

Sub-Order—Pandiones : Ospreys.

WHITE-HEADED OSPREY
(Pandion leucocephalus, Gould).

Male.—Head and back of the neck white, a few of the feathers streaked with brown; rest of the upper surface dark brown; under surface white, the feathers of the chest and flanks marked with reddish-brown. "Length, 21 to 24 in.; wing, 19 in.; tail, 8½ in." (A. J. Campbell).

Female.—Similar in plumage.

Nestling.—"Covered with down of a sooty-brown colour, except along the centre of the back, along the carpal bend of the wing, and on the breast and flanks, where it is dusky-white; all the feathers of the back are dark brown, with a broad tip of ochraceous-buff; crown and ear coverts blackish; eyebrow and throat white" (Dr. R. B. Sharpe).

Nest.—An immense structure of sticks; the shallow nesting hollow is lined with seaweed. An inaccessible rock on the coast or on an island is usually chosen.

Eggs.—Clutch three to four; in shape roundish oval; shell somewhat granulated and without lustre; colour buffy or yellowish-white, usually heavily blotched with dark purplish-brown, especially about the apex. Dimensions in mm. of odd examples :—(1) 61 x 44, (2) 60 x 42.

Breeding Season.—July to November.

Geographical Distribution.—Tasmania, Australian coast generally, Moluccas, and New Guinea.

Observations.—The Fish-Hawk, as it is frequently called, found in Tasmanian and Australian waters is a sub-species of the one ranging over a wide area in the Old World. Our species is slightly the smaller of the two.

Gould records having shot one in Recherche Bay, but as far as Tasmanian waters are concerned, it is principally to be found about the numerous islets studding Bass Strait. Only an occasional solitary bird, or a pair at most, is to be seen at any time.

Sub-Order—Striges : Owls.

FAMILY—BUBONIDÆ (1 species).

Sub-Family—Buboninæ.

*SPOTTED OWL
(Ninox maculata, Vig. & Horsf.)

Male.—Whole of the upper surface, including head, dark reddish-brown, with numerous white spots; under surface reddish-brown, heavily spotted with white; bill dark horn colour; feet yellowish. Dimensions in mm.:—Length, 290; bill, 21; wing, 203; tail, 123; tarsus, 38.

Female.—Similar in plumage. Dimensions in mm.:—Length, 280; bill, 22; wing, 200; tail, 123; tarsus, 33.

Nest.—A hollow spout of a tree.

Eggs.—Clutch two usually; nearly round in shape; somewhat fine in texture, and slightly glossy; the shell is often a little granulated; colour white. Dimensions in mm. of a pair:—(1) 40 x 34, (2) 40.5 x 34.

Breeding Season.—October to December.

Geographical Distribution.—Tasmania, King Island, New South Wales, Victoria, South Australia, and South Queensland.

Observations.—Whether this or the Chestnut-faced Owl is the more plentiful is hard to say. It is very generally distributed throughout the island. That this the Spotted Owl is the author of the familiar night cry of " Mo-poke " is now firmly established. I myself have had demonstration going far to prove that the cry is not uttered by the Tawny Podargus or Frogmouth.

Some few years ago a Spotted Owl was captured at sea some fifty miles off the Hunter Islands. The skin of this bird I have now in my possession.

FAMILY—STRIGIDÆ (1 species).

*CHESTNUT-FACED OWL (Barn Owl)

(*Strix castanops*, Gould).

Male.—Facial disc chestnut, becoming deeper towards the margin, and encircled with black; upper surface, wings, and tail rufous-brown, irregularly marked with dark brown; a few small spots of white on the head and shoulders; under surface pale brown, with numerous round spots of very deep brown. Dimensions in mm.:—Length, 366; bill, 35; wing, 330; tail, 148; tarsus, 61.

Female.—Similar in plumage, but larger in size.

Nest.—A hole in a tree, or a broken spout in all probability.

Eggs.—Undescribed.

Breeding Season.—Unknown.

Geographical Distribution.—Tasmania, New South Wales, Victoria, and South Australia.

Observations.—Why this handsome Owl should be shot on sight by most country people is hard to understand, considering the good it does in destroying rats and mice. There is hardly a district where this species is not found, but at the same time it is nowhere plentiful. The colour on the under surface varies from dull brownish to dirty-white.

ORDER—PASSERIFORMES : PERCHING BIRDS.

Sub-Order—Passeres.

FAMILY—CORVIDÆ (3 species).

Sub-Family—Corvinæ.

RAVEN

(Corone australis, Gould).

Male.—Whole of upper and lower surfaces black, glossed with purple; bases of the feathers on the neck and throat vary in shade from soiled-white to greyish; bill, legs, and feet black; irides white. Dimensions in mm. :—Length, 535; bill; 65; wing, 368; tail, 200; tarsus, 60.

Female.—Similar in plumage to male. Dimensions in mm. :— Length, 519; bill, 63; wing, 354; tail, 205; tarsus, 59.

Young.—Differ from adults in that the irides are hazel and the bases of the feathers, especially on throat, chest, and neck, are almost snow-white.

Nest.—Large and somewhat deep, constructed of sticks and twigs, and lined with shredded bark, grass, wool, and sometimes horse manure. The topmost bough of a lofty tree is usually chosen.

Eggs.—Clutch, four to five usually; varying in shape from oval to pointed oval; texture fairly fine; surface glossy; colour pale green, spotted and blotched, some very heavily, with blackish-umber and olive. Dimensions in mm. of a clutch :—(1) 41 x 30.5, (2) 44 x 31, (3) 43 x 31, (4) 40 x 30.

Breeding Season.—August to December.

Geographical Distribution.—Tasmania, King Island, and the whole of Australia.

Observations.—After an investigation extending over some years, and examination of specimens from nearly every district in Tasmania, I am forced to the conclusion that the Crow (*Corvus coronoides*) is non-existent in this island. In some works on Australian bird-life the Crow is described as being white-eyed and the Raven hazel-eyed. Ravens are to be procured anywhere here, either white or hazel-eyed. I am of opinion that the irides change with age from hazel to white, similarly to what occurs with the Silver Gull (*Larus novæ-hollandiæ*). One of the chief, if not the chief, distinguishing features between the Crow and the Raven is that the bases of the feathers of the former are snow-white, while those of the latter are dusky. Although a Raven may sometimes be procured whose plumage, especially on the throat and back of the neck, is nearly white at the base, yet the white gradually merges into the black as the tips of the feathers are reached. Now, with the true Crow there is a distinct line of demarcation between the white and the black.

As elsewhere, the food of the Raven varies from lambs' tongues and eyes to fruit, eggs, and grubs. Its melancholy cawing note is too common to be appreciated.

HILL CROW-SHRIKE (BLACK MAGPIE)

(*Strepera arguta*, Gould).

Male.—Upper and under surfaces blackish-brown; in aged examples the under surface becomes grey; tail blackish-brown, all but the two central feathers broadly tipped with white; primaries black, with basal half of inner webs white, extreme tips of some soiled-white; under tail coverts white; irides saffron-yellow; bill legs, and feet black. Dimensions in mm.:—Length, 536; bill, 70.5; wing, 292; tail, 255; tarsus, 68.

Female.—Plumage similar to male, dimensions slightly less.

Nest.—A somewhat rough open structure, composed of sticks and twigs, lined with fine twigs, rootlets, and a little grass. In some localities the nest is placed in a fairly low tree, in others in a lofty one.

Eggs.—Clutch three to four; elongated oval in shape; texture fairly fine; surface slightly rough, but glossy; colour pale vinaceous-brown, blotched all over with purplish-brown, a little light reddish-brown, and a little umber. Dimensions in mm. of a pair: —(1) 44.5 x 29, (2) 44 x 29.5.

Breeding Season.—September to December.

Geographical Distribution.—Tasmania.

Observations.—Parts of the West Coast and the Lake District are the strongholds of this species, but it is to be seen and heard in a number of other places, both north and south. As is well known, Gould likened its note to the sound of a hammer on an anvil, but to my mind the sound more resembles that of a tramway gong, inasmuch as it is a "clanging" note rather than a "clinking" one.

Like the Black Jay, the Black Magpie has developed fruit-stealing propensities, but to a lesser extent. During the depth of winter, in the Lake District and round several mining camps on the West Coast, it becomes very tame, flocking round dwellings and eating any household scraps it can find. It is also much appreciated as an article of diet in these localities during winter, when it becomes very fat. The usual method of securing the bird is to trap it by placing a portion of the inside, say, of a sheep in a small paling enclosure with a piece of strong string attached to one side, the free end some distance away. When a number of birds have gathered inside the enclosure the string is pulled, and down falls a slide, securely entrapping the birds beneath. One of its favourite natural foods is the berry of the "stinkwood" tree.

SOOTY CROW-SHRIKE (Black Jay)

(*Strepera fuliginosa*, Gould).

Male.—Whole of the upper and under surfaces sooty-black, the under surface having a slight tinge of ashy-grey; bases of the inner webs of the primaries white; the outer ones are broadly banded with the same colour, and there is also a narrow edging of white at the tips of some of the secondaries; tail dusky-black, all the feathers with the exception of the two central ones broadly tipped with white; bill, legs, and feet black; irides yellow. Dimensions in mm. :—Length, 455; bill, 57; wing, 255; tail, 173; tarsus, 56.

Female.—Similar in plumage, but smaller in dimensions.

Young.—Small edition of adult.

Nest.—Constructed of sticks and twigs, lined with fine twigs and long, fine rootlets. Altitude of nest greatly depends upon locality.

Eggs.—Clutch two to four; usually more pointed at one end; texture fairly fine; surface moderately glossy; colour rich purplish or dark vinaceous buff, blotched all over with reddish-brown and purplish-brown. Dimensions in mm. of odd examples :—(1) 45 x 32, (2) 42 x 30, (3) 43 x 31.

Breeding Season.—September to December.

Geographical Distribution.—Tasmania, King Island, and several groups of islands in Bass Strait; also Victoria, New South Wales, South Australia, and Queensland.

Observations.—Anyone who has had any experience of the bush cannot but be familiar with this black bird with its conspicuous white tips to its tail feathers and its loud and harsh note. Before orchards came into existence here the food of the Black Jay was almost entirely insectivorous, a few berries being added to give variety. Now, in some of the northern districts, at least, as soon as the apples turn red a marauding band floats down silently from the tree-tops of the surrounding forest and takes toll. A sentinel is always posted on the highest neighbouring tree-top to give the alarm. After land has been scrubbed and burnt, this bird may often be seen in large flocks going carefully over the ground searching for food. After having been shot at a few times it becomes very shy and cunning, and is very careful to give no warning of its presence when near an orchard. When flitting from log to log its tail is jerked up and down, slightly fanned. On the approach of rain or any atmospheric disturbance it is more noisy than at other times. Its cry, which is familiar to most people, is " Killok, killok," varying in tone according to the circumstances under which it is uttered.

FAMILY—DICRURIDÆ (1 species).
*DRONGO
(*Chibia bracteata*, Gould).

Male.—" General colour above black, feathers of the head and sides of the hind-neck tipped with metallic steel-green; rump, upper tail coverts, wings, and tail black, washed with metallic steel-green; all the under surface black, slightly glossed with green; the tips of the feathers of the throat and fore-neck spangled with small spots of metallic steel-green; under wing coverts black, with a rounded spot of white at the tips; bill and legs black; iris red. Total length in the flesh, 12.25 in.; wing, 6.25; outer tail feathers, 5.2; central tail feathers, 4.8; bill, 1.3; tarsus, 0.9" (A. J. North).

Female.—Similar in plumage.

Young.—" Fledglings are blackish-brown above and below; wings and tail black slightly glossed with metallic steel-green " (A. J. North).

Nest.—Situated in a fork at the extremity of a branch of a tree, and composed of rootlets and stalks of climbing plants, lined with thin wiry rootlets.

Eggs.—" Clutch three to four; almost oval in shape; texture of shell fine and thin; surface slightly glossy; colour a light pinkish shade or of a delicate pinkish-blush, sparingly and softly spotted with pinkish-red and purple, also with a few spots of chestnut, all the markings being more numerous about the larger end. Dimensions in inches of a proper clutch :—(1) 1.27 x .85; (2) 1.24 x .83; (3) 1.19 x .83" (A. J. Campbell).

Breeding Season.—October to January.

Geographical Distribution.—Tasmania (accidental), New South Wales, Victoria, Queensland, Northern Territory, and New Guinea.

Observations.—At a meeting of the Royal Society of Tasmania in June, 1888, a communication was read by Colonel Legge regarding the shooting of a Drongo on the East Coast. This was the first record of this species as an accidental visitor to the island. In October of the same year the late Mr. A. Morton exhibited a specimen shot at Stanley and forwarded by Dr. L. Holden. Yet another was shot on the 3rd July, 1900, at Bridport, on the North-East Coast.

FAMILY—PRIONOPIDÆ (2 species).
Sub-Family—Prionopinæ.
*MAGPIE-LARK
(*Grallina picata*, Lath.)

Male.—A broad line over the eye, sides of the neck, upper wing coverts, bases and tips of the secondaries, rump and upper tail coverts, basal half of the tail, and abdomen white; head, back, chin, throat, and chest blue-black. " Total length in the flesh, 10.5 in.; wing, 6.6; tail, 5; bill, 0.85; tarsus, 1.7 " (A. J. North).

Female.—Similar to male, except that in addition the lores, the forehead, and throat are white.

Young.—Similar to adults, but duller in colour.

Nest.—Bowl shape, composed of mud, lined with grass and a few feathers. The favourite situation is on a bare horizontal limb of a tree, in the vicinity of or standing in water.

Eggs.—Clutch three to four; pyriform in shape; texture of shell fine; surface glossy; colour white to pinkish-white, more or less spotted, especially about the apex, where the marks often form a confluent band, with spots of pinkish-red and purple. Dimensions in mm. of a clutch:—(1) 28 x 19, (2) 26 x 20, (3) 26.5 x 19.5, (4) 27 x 20.

Breeding Season.—September to January.

Geographical Distribution.—Tasmania (accidental) and the whole of the mainland.

Observations.—On the 15th July, 1888, Dr. L. Holden shot the first recorded Tasmanian specimen at Stanley.

*WHISTLING SHRIKE-THRUSH (WHISTLING DICK)

(*Collyriocincla rectirostris*, Jard. and Selby).

Male.—Head, rump, upper tail coverts, and tail grey; back, scapulars, and lesser wing coverts brown, striped with olive; greater coverts and quills dark brown, almost black, outer webs grey; lores and an indistinct line over the eye dull white; chin, throat, and fore-neck almost pure white; rest of under surface greyish-white; sides of body and under tail coverts grey; iris dark brown; bill black; legs and feet blackish. Dimensions in mm.:—Length, 251; bill, 24; wing, 124; tail, 107; tarsus, 30.5.

Female.—Eyebrow rufous; feathers of under surface with black shafts; legs and feet greenish-grey; otherwise similar to male. Dimensions in mm.:—Length, 254; bill, 23.5; wing, 123; tail, 104; tarsus, 30.5.

Young.—Male resembles the adult female, save that the sides of the head and upper wing coverts are tinged with rufous; also the under surface is more broadly streaked.

Nest.—The cup-shaped nest is usually composed either of narrow strips of stringy-bark, neatly woven together, or moss, fine rootlets, grass and leaves, with a lining of fine grass. The usual situation is a hollow in a tree or stump.

Eggs.—Clutch three to four; stout oval in shape, with the texture fine; surface glossy; colour pearly-white, more or less spotted and blotched with olive and dull slate. Dimensions in

NEST OF WHISTLING SHRIKE-THRUSH.

Photo. by H. C. THOMPSON.

DUSKY FANTAIL ON NEST.

Photo. by H. C. THOMPSON.

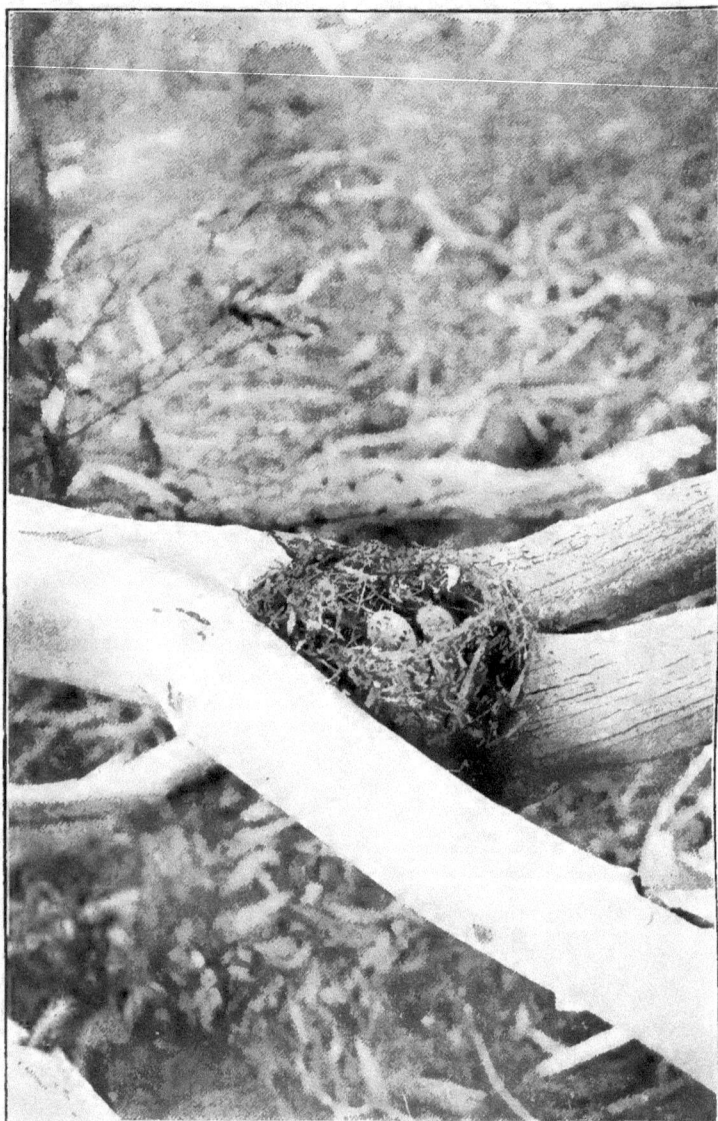

NEST OF SUMMER-BIRD.

mm. of a clutch :—(1) 29 x 20, (2) 28 x 21, (3) 28 x 20.5, (4) 30 x 20.

Breeding Season.—September to December.

Geographical Distribution.—Tasmania, King Island, and Furneaux Group.

Observations.—This cheerful whistler is a favourite with all, wherever found. Many farmers and rough miners would no more think of killing a Whistling Dick than they would a Robin. Its general attitude is one of alertness. Its movements are quick, whether on the ground or on a log or tree. On being flushed when feeding in fairly open ground it generally flies on to the top of the nearest log or stump and looks about as though inquiring why it had been disturbed. It soon becomes very tame round dwellings where it is not disturbed, and if fed with crumbs will soon come every day for some. I have known it fly right into a house and perch on a table when its daily food had accidentally been forgotten. As a destroyer of grubs and similar pests it renders a great service to agriculturists. By means of its powerful bill it is able to strip the bark off eucalypts and other trees to secure its prey. Its loud and melodious whistling note may be heard during all seasons, but, as is usually the case, it is of a better quality during the nesting season.

FAMILY—CAMPOPHAGIDÆ (2 species).

*SMALL-BILLED CUCKOO-SHRIKE (SUMMER-BIRD)

(*Graucalus parvirostris*, Gould).

Male.—Forehead, sides of the face and neck, and the throat jet black; crown of the head, all the upper surface, including centre of the wings, delicate silver-grey; primaries and inner webs of the secondaries black, "the former narrowly and the latter broadly margined with white"; tail grey, passing into deep brownish-black, heavily tipped with white; two centre tail feathers are without white tips and are largely grey; chest and thighs a shade greyer than back; abdomen, under wing coverts, and under tail coverts white; bill black; legs and feet dark brownish-black. Dimensions in mm. :—Length, 327; bill, 21.5; wing, 219; tail, 151; tarsus, 28.5.

Female.—Similar in plumage to male. Dimensions in mm. :— Length, 327; bill, 21.5; wing, 194; tail, 153; tarsus, 25.

Young.—Male.—Only sides of face and neck black; whole of upper surface as in adult; tail similar; throat dusky; chest same as adult; abdomen white, slightly tinged with grey. Bill, legs, and feet as in adults. Full adult plumage is not attained until the following spring.

Nest.—Placed high on a dead horizontal branch of a eucalypt

3

tree; somewhat frailly constructed of fine twigs and fragments of bark matted together with spider's web.

Eggs.—Clutch three to four; oval in shape; texture fine, surface glossy; colour dark green, sometimes heavily and at other times sparingly marked and blotched with various shades of umber; at times the markings are chiefly around the larger end. Dimensions in mm. of a clutch :—(1) 32.5 x 21.5, (2) 32 x 21.5, (3) 30.5 x 22.

Breeding Season.—October to December.

Geographical Distribution.—Tasmania, King and several other of the more important islands in Bass Strait.

Observations.—Some years ago I was under the impression that this bird was a migratory species, as I knew from observation that it forsook certain districts early in autumn and did not return again until August or September. Like several other of our birds, this species is nomadic during autumn and winter. Some winters it is to be found in the bush round Launceston almost every day; other winters not a bird will be seen. The East and North-East Coasts are its favourite winter resorts. After the nesting season is over one hardly ever hears it utter its somewhat plaintive whirring, whistling note, which is uttered both when flying and when at rest; at the latter time the wings and tail are jerked slightly upwards. It has a flight peculiarly its own, progress being made in a series of wave-like motions, the wings being folded against the body when arriving at the crest of a wave and kept motionless for a few seconds and then a few more strokes are again given. So the bird progresses, rising and falling the whole of the time. The "Summer-Bird" is practically the only species that I have seen feeding to any great extent on the small green larvæ of a chrysomelid beetle that is very destructive to silver wattles (*Acacia dealbata*) in many districts. In some parts of the northern end of the island this bird suddenly developed fruit-eating proclivities in 1908—a trait not before known. I have no knowledge of how this Cuckoo-Shrike first received the name of "Summer-Bird," but presume it was on account of its appearing only in some districts to nest and rear its young.

*WHITE-SHOULDERED CATERPILLAR-CATCHER

(*Lalage tricolor*, Swainson).

Male.—Upper surface glossy greenish-black; wing coverts white; rump and upper tail coverts light grey; tail black, the three outermost feathers tipped with white; cheeks, sides of the neck, all the under surface, including under wing coverts and tail coverts, white; bill, legs, and feet black.

Female.—Upper surface brown; tail brown, with lateral feathers tipped with white; chin, throat, and centre of the abdomen dull white; rest of the under surface buffy-white; sides of the breast and abdomen crossed with obscure bars of dusky-brown; bill dark brown; legs and feet greyish-black.

Nestling.—"The under surface boldly shows longitudinal streaks and faint bars upon the flanks. The upper surface, less the rump, shows conspicuous broad marks of black, brown, and white, the blackish-brown marks being subterminal and the white marks terminal" (R. Hall).

Nest.—A shallow structure, loosely constructed of fine stalks, grass, and bark; a layer of cobwebs is usually placed over the whole of the outside. One of the highest forks of a tree or sapling is the favourite situation.

Eggs.—Clutch two to three; round oval in shape; texture fine; surface glossy; colour varies from light to dull warmish green, more or less heavily blotched with bright umber and dull slate. Dimensions in mm. of a clutch:—(1) 45 x 41, (2) 46 x 41.5.

Breeding Season.—September to January.

Geographical Distribution.—Tasmania (accidental) and the whole of Australia, also New Guinea.

Observations.—I am unable to discover how and when this bird first came to be placed on the Tasmanian list.

FAMILY—MUSCICAPIDÆ (9 species).

*DUSKY FANTAIL (CRANKY FAN)

(*Rhipidura diemenensis*, Sharpe).

Male.—Upper surface dark ashy-brown; two central tail feathers black; outermost one on either side pale grey, with outer webs and terminal half of inner white; two next with terminal half of inner webs white, the remainder with only a small terminal tip of dull white; all tail feathers with the exception of the two centre ones with white shafts; median and greater wing coverts tipped with white on the outer webs; secondaries edged with white on the outer webs; a line over the eye, one above the ear coverts, cheeks, and throat white; a black band on lower throat; chest blackish-buff; abdomen ochreous-buff; bill, legs, and feet black. Dimensions in mm. :—Length, 149; bill, 7.25; wing, 7.4; tail, 8.1; tarsus, 15.5.

Female.—Practically similar to male.

Young.—"The young birds of the first year have a white line across the throat above the black throat mark and white spots on the head above the eyes and behind the ears; the remainder of their plumage is grey, except the breast, which is pale buff" (J. R. M'Clymont).

Nest.—Usually situated a few feet from the ground in rather thick scrub, and is saddled on a naked horizontal twig. In shape it resembles a wine-glass with base of the stem broken off; the tail-like appendage extends beneath the twig on which the nest is placed. When a stream is conveniently handy the nest is placed on a twig overhanging it. The materials mostly employed in its construction are fine dry grass, shreds of fine bark, and long, fibrous green moss, the whole being covered exteriorly with matted spider's web, giving it a dirty-grey appearance; the interior lining consists of very fine rootlets, grass, or the long hair from the bases of fern fronds.

Eggs.—Clutch three usually, four rarely; roundish oval in shape; texture fine; surface faintly glossy; colour dirty or buffy white, somewhat heavily spotted and blotched with reddish-brown and grey, especially in the vicinity of the apex, where the spots form a confluent band. Dimensions in mm. of a clutch:—(1) 14 x 10, (2) 14.75 x 10, (3) 15 x 10.25.

Breeding Season.—September to December.

Geographical Distribution.—Tasmania, King and several other islands in Bass Strait.

Observations.—The bump of inquisitiveness seems to be largely developed in this small bird, for it has the habit of following one for hundreds of yards through the bush, just keeping out of reach, and uttering a broken little song the whole of the time. Its flight is weak; its long tail, which is opened fan-wise when flying, seeming too heavy. The name" Cranky Fan," by which it is known to most people, is derived from its curious head-over-heels flight when flitting about the tree-tops or on the edge of scrub. The song is a sweet little run of notes, to be heard to the best advantage during the nesting season. If this little songster can be heard to the accompaniment of a softly babbling stream the effect is greatly enhanced. Almost anywhere in the northern part of the island this species is plentiful, and I am informed the same can be said for the southern.

Much discussion has taken place at various times concerning the utility or otherwise of the wine-glass stem constructed by the members of the genus *Rhipidura* to the bottoms of their nests. Taking everything into consideration, I am quite of Col. Legge's opinion that the stem is placed for the practical purpose of balancing the nest during rough weather. No doubt it is a survival from some very early period, as one often finds a nest in a sheltered situation where no boisterous winds could possibly affect it.

*LEADEN FLYCATCHER

(*Myiagra rubecula*, Latham).

Male.—Head greyish-lead, glossed with steel-green; back and tail also greyish-lead, but very faintly glossed with steel-green; wings blackish, secondary quills edged with ashy-white; neck, throat, and chest blackish, strongly glossed with dull green; rest of under surface white or dull white; bill dark lead, tipped with black; legs and feet black. Dimensions in mm.:—Length, 158; bill, 11; wing, 79; tail, 7.4; tarsus, 16.

Female.—Head dull greyish-lead; back same colour, but tinged with brown; tail brown; wings brown; secondary quills edged with ashy-white; chin and throat pale orange-buff, shading down to dull white on the abdomen and under tail coverts.

Nest.—Almost the only situation chosen in Tasmania by this species for the site of its nest is the extremity of a dead horizontal branch some distance from the ground. The nest is a beautifully neat cup-shaped structure, composed of fine bark and covered with cobwebs and prettily decorated with lichens.

Eggs.—Clutch three; stout oval in shape, with one end decidedly rounded; texture fine; surface glossy; colour whitish; round the upper quarter is a broad belt of umber and purplish-grey, while scattered over the surface are a few spots of the same colours. Dimensions in mm. of a clutch:—(1) 18 x 14, (2) 17 x 14, (3) 17.5 x 14.

Breeding Season.—November to January.

Geographical Distribution.—Tasmania, Australia in general, and New Guinea.

Observations.—To Colonel Legge belongs the honour of being the first to record this Flycatcher for Tasmania. His specimen was procured from near 'Falmouth, in February, 1874. At the present time this species is a regular visitor to the island, arriving and departing about the same time as the other regular migrants, and may be found scattered over a wide area. Among other localities in the northern portion of the island, I have it recorded from Noland Bay, Table Cape, Gladstone, Sprent, and Gunn's Plains. Mr. H. Stuart Dove informs me that it is somewhat scarce on the North-West Coast.

*SATIN OR SHINING FLYCATCHER

(*Myiagra nitida*, Gould).

Male.—Whole of the upper surface glossy blackish-green; throat greenish-black; abdomen white; legs and feet brownish-black. Dimensions in mm.:—Length, 168; bill, 14; wing, 88; tail, 81; tarsus, 16.5.

Female.—Head dark slaty-grey, glossed with greenish-black; back dull slaty-grey; tail brown, as also are the primaries and greater wing coverts; sides of the neck and throat orange-rufous; rest of under surface, including under tail coverts, white.

Nest.—A beautifully formed cup-shaped structure, composed of strips of bark, covered with cobwebs, frequently ornamented with lichens; lined inside with soft shreds of bark and a few fine rootlets. Situated at or near the extremity of a dead horizontal branch of a tall eucalypt.

Eggs.—Clutch two to three; stout oval in shape, with one end distinctly rounded; texture of shell fine; surface glossy; colour pearly-white, with a well-defined belt of dull umber and purplish-grey spots; there are also usually a few spots of the same colour scattered over the rest of the surface. Dimensions in mm. of a clutch :—(1) 18.5 x 14.5, (2) 19 x 14.5.

Breeding Season.—Last week in November to January.

Geographical Distribution.—Tasmania, New South Wales, Victoria, and Queensland.

Observations.—This Flycatcher is both more plentiful and more widely distributed than the Leaden species. It arrives from the mainland towards the end of October, and departs again early in March. Launceston, Kelso, Lilydale, Hobart, Wilmot, Tasman's Peninsula, Noland Bay, Table Cape, Gunn's Plains, and Ross are among the localities frequented by it.

Regarding this species, Mr. H. Stuart Dove writes me :— "Earliest record I have is 22nd September, which was near Launceston, and is early, considering it does not usually build here until last week in November or first in December. Other records are— 3rd November, Launceston district; 10th November, on slopes of Mount Arthur, calling from the top of a dry tree and wagging tail sideways as it did so—the call is like ' Chuee, chuee, chuee, chuee.' Several were building at Russell's Plains on 30th November. They change places frequently when sitting. 5th December one was flying along edge of scrub near Table Cape, backwards and forwards, apparently fly-catching. 16th December a pair came and sat on my verandah-rail at Table Cape, showing to perfection the long, slender shape, the beautiful dark glossy-green of throat and upper surface of male—the female being brownish above, with throat and cheeks orange-rufous. This species is one of my favourites; it is so lively and entertaining in its motions, hardly still for a moment, and the gloss on the upper surface is very beautiful in sunlight."

*SCARLET-BREASTED ROBIN

(*Petrœca leggei*, Sharpe).

Male.—Whole of the upper surface black; forehead white; lesser wing coverts black, secondary and greater white; white also on inner secondaries; lateral tail feathers white, margined with blackish-brown on basal half of inner web and towards the tip of outer web; sides of the head and throat black; breast light scarlet; rest of under surface dull white, all feathers blackish-grey at bases; bill, legs, and feet black. Dimensions in mm. :—Length, 155; bill, 10; wing, 73; tail, 58; tarsus, 19.

Female.—Upper surface brown; white spot on forehead small; white markings on wings as in male; tail feathers also marked as in male; chin and throat greyish white; chest and upper part

NEST OF SCARLET-BREASTED ROBIN.

Photo. by H. C. THOMPSON.

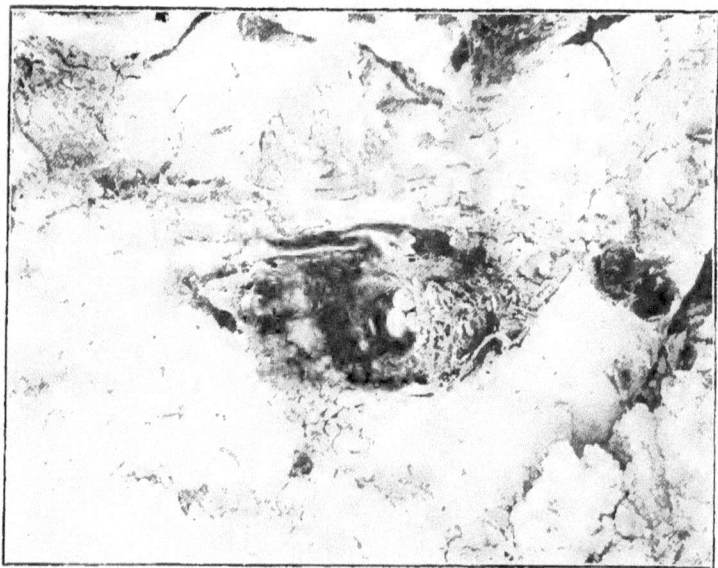

NEST OF FLAME-BREASTED ROBIN
(In the roots of an upturned tree).

Photo. by H. C. THOMPSON.

of abdomen washed with light scarlet; rest of under surface, except under tail coverts, pale brown; under tail coverts dull white.

Young.—Both sexes resemble adult female, save that the under surface is uniform pale grey.

Nest.—Cup-shaped; soft shredded bark, soft grass, and a little moss are its chief constituents; pieces of lichen are frequently stuck on the outside for protective mimicry; the inside lining is usually fur. The forked branches of a tree or sapling in lightly wooded tracts is a favourite situation.

Eggs.—Clutch three to four; stout oval in shape; shell fine and surface somewhat glossy; ground colour light greenish-white, rather heavily spotted and freckled with umber and a little dull grey. In the region of the upper quarter the spots form more or less of a belt. Dimensions in mm. of a clutch:—(1) 17 x 13.5, (2) 17.5 x 13, (3) 16.5 x 13.5.

Breeding Season.—October to December.

Geographical Distribution.—Tasmania, New South Wales, South Australia, and South Queensland.

Observations.—The chief features that distinguish this Robin from the Flame-breasted species are that this has the white mark on the forehead large and the throat black.

The range of this species, as well as its general habits, are practically similar to those of the Flame-breasted Robin. It is, however, less of a nomad than its congener. During the nesting season it is always to be seen in pairs, and it is at that season that its sweet little song is to be heard at its best. At other seasons it consorts in small flocks and mingles with both the Flame-breasted and Dusky Robins. The colour of the breast of the female varies from light to bright red. Somewhat contrary to what occurs with some other birds, the colouration of the female is as bright in the depth of winter as in the height of the breeding season. The amount of colouration on the breast and abdomen of the male also varies, being sometimes merely a broad band of colour on the chest and upper part of the abdomen, while the rest of the under surface is dusky white.

Like the other Robins, its food is procured from off and out of the ground. During winter it often frequents bush homesteads, and will readily pick up any food thrown out to it.

The note of the female is a sharp little " Chip, chip," uttered with a rapid upward flirt of the wings and tail.

*FLAME-BREASTED ROBIN

(*Petrœca phœnicea*, Gould).

Male.—Whole of the upper surface greyish-black; white spot on forehead small; the median and greater wing coverts, also outer webs of inner secondaries, white; tail blackish, with two outer feathers on either side pearly-white; sides of the face and chin blackish; throat, chest, and abdomen orange-scarlet; lower part of abdomen and under tail coverts white; bill black; legs and feet blackish-brown.   Dimensions in mm.:—Length, 153; bill, 10; wing, 76; tail, 57; tarsus, 19.

Female.—Head and back brown; wings and tail dark brown; markings on wings and tail same as in male, only that the white is of a buff shade; spot on forehead small and buffy-white; chin and throat brownish-white; chest and upper part of abdomen brown, rest of under surface dull white.   Dimensions in mm.:— Length, 130; bill, 10; wing, 75; tail, 53; tarsus, 19.

Young.—The males do not attain adult plumage until the second spring season, but they breed while in the dusky plumage.

Nest.—Cup-shaped or flattish and shallow, according to situation.   The choice of situation likewise has much to do with the choice of materials used in construction; fine shreds of bark and soft grass, with which are mixed spider's web, thistle-down, fine rootlets, and a little moss, are chiefly used; fur, fine rootlets, and soft bark are the usual inside lining.   The hollow spout in the broken limb of a fallen tree, a hole in the side of a stump, among the roots of a fallen tree, or under the edge of a bank of a creek are among the sites chosen.

Eggs.—Clutch three usually; stout oval in shape; texture of shell fine; surface almost without lustre; colour bluish or greenish white, spotted more or less heavily, especially about the apex, with umber and dull grey.   Dimensions in mm. of a clutch—(1) 16 x 12, (2) 17.5 x 13, (3) 17 x 12.75.

Breeding Season.—September to December.

Geographical Distribution.—Tasmania, King and several other islands in Bass Strait, New South Wales, Victoria, South Australia, and South Queensland.

Observations.—That this species does not entirely leave the State during the winter months for parts of the mainland has now been proved beyond dispute.   I have records of having seen it during different years (in fact, almost every year) in various parts of Tasmania in the depth of winter.   Some districts are deserted altogether at the first touch of winter; in others the number of birds decreases.   Almost any day any month in winter a few individuals are to be found round Launceston.   According to Mr. H. Stuart Dove the bulk of the birds repair to the coastal regions for the cold months.

The statement made by Gould, and since much copied, to the effect that "it retires to the forests for the purpose of breeding," is somewhat misleading, as a little investigation of the places chosen for nesting will show.   I have found as many nests in open, scrubbed land and round homesteads, where there are only a few prostrate giants and stumps here and there, as I have in forest land.   In some districts this species is extremely plentiful, to the exclusion of the Scarlet-breasted Robin, and *vice versâ*.   In

NEST OF PINK-BREASTED ROBIN.

Photo. by H. C. THOMPSON.

NEST OF DUSKY ROBIN,
Showing egg of Pallid Cuckoo (on right).

Photo. by H. C. THOMPSON.

Gould's " Birds of Australia " (fol., vol. iii., pl. 6), the female is depicted with a reddish breast, and in the letter-press accompanying the plate it is described as having a reddish under surface. This phase of plumage in the female is quite unknown to me.

*PINK-BREASTED ROBIN

(*Petrœca rhodinogastra*, Drapier).

Male.—Whole of the upper surface slaty-white; white spot on forehead small; sides of the head and throat slaty-black; chest and abdomen rose-pink; under tail coverts white; bill black; legs and feet blackish-brown. Dimensions in mm. :—Length, 130; bill, 10; wing, 63; tail, 51; tarsus, 18.

Female.—Upper surface olive-brown; white spot on forehead small; under surface pale brown, except centre of abdomen, which is buffy-white.

Nest.—Cup-shaped; constructed of fine moss, on to which are stuck pieces of lichen and spider's web; inside lining either the hair-like substance from the bases of man-fern fronds or hair. It is usually placed in the forked branches of a low tree in a moist gully or thick scrub.

Eggs.—Clutch three usually, four sometimes; stout oval in shape, with one end somewhat sharply pointed; texture of shell fine and surface fairly glossy; colour greenish-white, finely spotted with umber and grey; the majority of the spots are on the stouter end, where they form a band. Dimensions in mm. of a clutch :— (1) 19 x 14, (2) 18 x 13.75, (3) 19 x 13.75.

Breeding Season.—October to December.

Geographical Distribution.—Tasmania, King and several of the other large islands in Bass Strait, Victoria, and South Australia.

Observations.—This Robin is the rarest of the four species found in Tasmania. In some parts of the island it is called the " Solitary" Robin. The class of country most favoured by this species is among the myrtle forests found in different parts. Round Magnet and Waratah, on the West Coast, it is more plentiful than anywhere else I know of. It is also sparsely distributed on the East, North, North-East, and North-West Coasts. Occasionally a pair is to be seen in the bush round Launceston; also a few in the hilly country between Launceston and Scottsdale. Its note is a low, mournful kind of whistle, not to be confused with that of any of the other Robins.

*DUSKY ROBIN

(*Petrœca vittata*, Quoy and Gaim.)

Male.—Upper surface brown tinged with olive; greater wing coverts blackish-brown tipped with white; quills crossed by a dull white band, except outer primaries; tail brown, three outer feathers

narrowly tipped with white; the outermost one in addition has the
external web white; throat greyish; rest of under surface grey, with
the centre of the abdomen whitish; bill, legs, and feet black.
Dimensions in mm.:—Length, 152; bill, 11.5; wing, 83; tail, 61;
tarsus, 23.5.

Female.—Similar to male.

Young.—Feathers on upper surface brown, broadly streaked
with white; under surface mottled.

Nest.—Somewhat large and loosely built; composed of fine
shredded bark, with which are mixed fragments of grass, spider's
web, and fine rootlets; lined inside with horse-hair or fur; sometimes nothing special beyond the soft bark used to finish off inside
is added.   In the hollow of a stump or in a niche in the bark of a
large tree are the favourite sites.

Eggs.—Clutch three usually; oval in shape; texture of shell
fine; surface glossy; colour olive-green; some eggs are destitute
of markings, others have the apex fawn colour, others again are
pale brownish, darker on the apex, and with a few markings of
fawn colour scattered over the surface.   Dimensions in mm. of a
clutch:—(1) 21 x 15, (2) 20 x 16, (3) 22 x 15.

Breeding Season.—August to December.

Geographical Distribution.—Tasmania, King Island, and Furneaux Group.

Observations.—The Dusky or Stump Robin is a quiet, unemo-
tional kind of bird, frequenting lightly timbered forest land and
cleared tracts.

It is practically voiceless, and pursues its daily round as though
with some load on its shoulders.   On freshly scrubbed and burnt
areas where the young grass is beginning to show it may often
be seen in numbers in company with the Flame-breasted and Scarlet-breasted species eagerly hunting for tiny snails and other
ground food.   Unlike the two other species mentioned, it does
not seek the society of man and eat the crumbs from his table.
One but rarely sees a Dusky Robin perched on the limb of a tree,
logs and dead stumps being practically its only vantage grounds.

*GOULD'S BLUE WREN
(Malurus gouldi, Sharpe).

Male.—"Crown of the head, stripe from the corner of the
mouth below the ears, and a broad crescent on the upper part of
the back metallic ultramarine blue; back of the neck, shoulders,
back, and rump deep velvety black; throat and chest deep blue-
black; under surface greyish-white, becoming brown on the flanks;
tail feathers deep blue with lighter tips; bill black; legs and feet
brown " (Gould).   Dimensions in mm.:—Length, 133; bill, 9;
wing, 55; tail, 67; tarsus, 25.

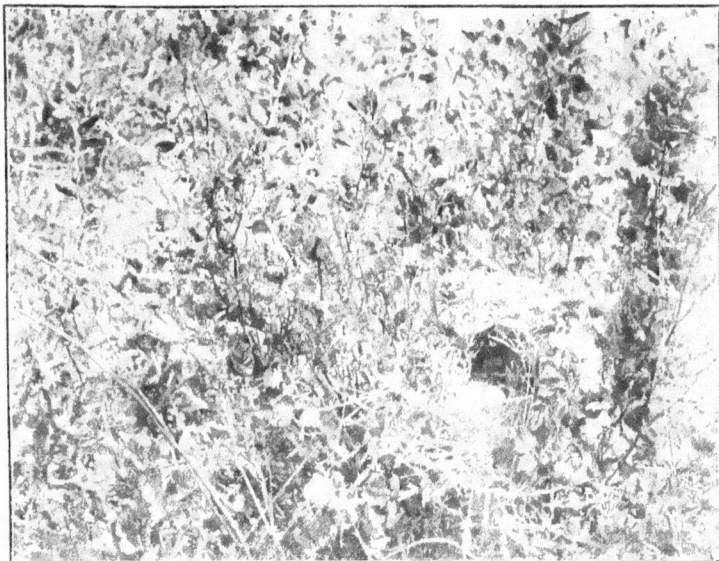

NEST OF GOULD'S BLUE WREN.

Photo. by H. C. THOMPSON.

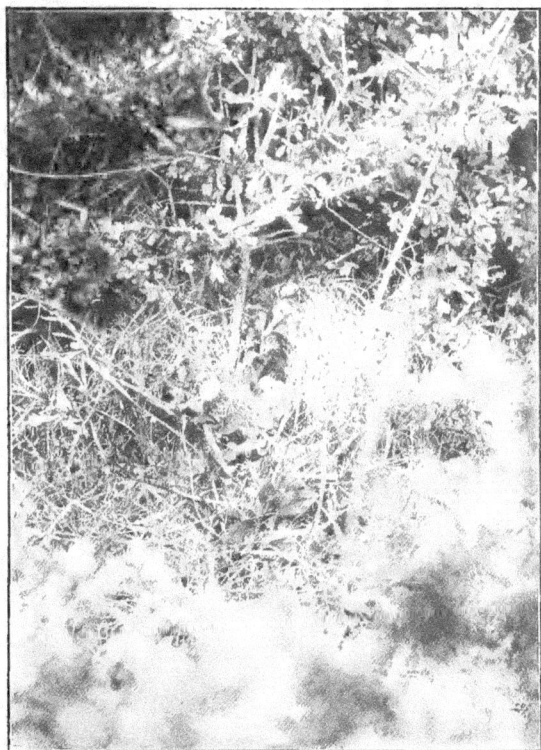

NEST OF GOULD'S BLUE WREN.

(Dimensions in mm. of a typical *M. cyaneus* from Victoria :— Length, 124; bill, 7.75; wing, 53; tail, 57; tarsus, 2.)

Female.—Whole of the upper surface, including wings and tail, brown tinged with rufous; throat and abdomen greyish-white; flanks brownish; bill, legs, and feet reddish-brown.

Male (non-breeding plumage).—Upper surface slightly darker than female; under surface same as female; feathers of tail always distinctly blue; under surface grey, with the exception of the throat, which is whitish.

Female (non-breeding plumage).—Upper surface, including tail, brown; under surface as in male.

Young.—Plumage much lighter in colour than that of the adult female or that of the male in winter dress; upper surface, wings, and tail light brown; under surface dirty-white; irides light brown; legs and feet yellow.

Nest.—Globular or oval shaped, with the entrance on one side near the top; grass, fine rootlets, and shredded bark are mostly employed in its construction, the lining being feathers and thistle-down. It is placed in a variety of situations, such as in black-berry bushes, brier and prickly box bushes, rushes by a river bank, &c.

Eggs.—Clutch four usually; inclined to oval in shape; texture of shell very fine; surface glossy; ground colour white; the mark-ings, which are reddish-brown, vary greatly in individual speci-mens; some are greatly spotted all over, not only with moderate-sized spots, but also with very tiny ones, so as to give the egg quite a pinkish tinge; others, again, have the spots closer together at the stouter end so as to form a belt. Dimensions in mm. of a clutch :—(1) 18 x 12, (2) 18 x 12.75, (3) 19 x 13; (4) 17.5 x 12.5.

Breeding Season.—September to January usually.

Geographical Distribution.—Tasmania and Furneaux Group.

Observations.—Of all birds found in Tasmania the " Blue-cap" or " Cocktail," as it is variously called, is, perhaps the best known. Almost everywhere throughout the island it is very plentiful, the tiny males in their summer livery making spots of colour among the brier and blackberry bushes. There is great irregularity in the moulting of the males. Some rough notes made at different times on this subject read :—" 20th May the male Blue Wrens have lost their summer coats." " 10th July the same year notice the male Blue Wren in summer plumage, it being the first I have seen this spring. Evidently it had only just recently acquired it, as the colouring was not complete, grey feathers not being all moulted out." In the Lilydale district I find that 17th July was the first date on which the male birds were observed to have moulted that year. 1st July the following year I find that " many of the Blue Wrens around Launceston have not moulted at all but still retain their summer plumage." The previous year it was at a much earlier date that they all moulted; in fact, by the 14th of the month the majority of them were regaining their blue coats. " 12th July, the Blue Wren still not moulted." The following year I note that on 5th May a solitary male was still in summer plumage; all others round Launceston had acquired their winter dress. The date of either putting off or on the breeding plumage greatly depends on the climatic conditions. This is the crux of the whole matter.

Much has been written on the subject of the Maluridæ being polygamous or not. At one time I was quite of opinion that our familiar Blue Wren was polygamous, but I have come to modify that opinion, and now hold that it is an uncommon occurrence for this to happen. During the non-breeding season one often sees a male accompanied by a small harem. The young birds of the year more often follow the males than the females when searching for food. Even during the winter the males do not consort much together. One generally, if not always, sees a male (to be distinguished by his distinctly blue tail) accompanied by one, two, or sometimes three females or young birds, forming a little party by themselves. Each little harem keeps to itself; although one may see several groups feeding together, yet there is no indiscriminate mingling. The male does not lose his song entirely in winter, but at the same time it has not the same joyous ring as during the breeding season.

Round homesteads the Blue Wren becomes very tame, hopping about the doorways and even into the passages in search of crumbs, &c.

When in the scrub it prefers to use its legs when moving from place to place. Its powers of running are very great; it is as nimble on its feet as a mouse—in fact, it has the appearance of one when seen a few yards off as it scurries over and under logs and stones. Its flight is rather feeble, and only resorted to when desirous of moving from one locality to another, or when suddenly startled. The song is a weak but rather pleasing run of notes, usually uttered when perched on some elevation.

DARK BLUE WREN

(*Malarus elizabethæ*, Campbell).

Male.—Colouring richer and more intensified than in Gould's Blue Wren. "Length, 5.5 in.; bill, .5 in.; wing, 2.1 in.; tail, 2.5 in.; tarsus, 1.0 in." (A. G. Campbell).

Female.—Differs in plumage from the female of *M. gouldi* in that the tail is tinged with blue. "Length, 5.5 in.; bill, .32 in.; wing, 2.08 in.; tail, 2.3 in.; tarsus, 1.0 in." (A. J. Campbell).

Young.—Similar to female, only that the tail has no bluish tinge.

Nest.—Similar to *M. gouldi.*

NEST OF REED-WARBLER, WITH YOUNG BIRD.

Photo. by H. C. THOMPSON.

Eggs.—Clutch three; "in shape the eggs are roundish oval; texture of shell fine; surface slightly glossy; colour warm or pinkish-white, lightly spotted and splashed with reddish-brown, the markings being thickest about the upper quarter. Dimensions of a clutch in inches:—(1) .7 x .52, (2) .68 x .53, (3) .68 x .52 " (A. J. Campbell).

Breeding Season.—Similar to *M. gouldi.*

Geographical Distribution.—King Island.

Observations.—" This Wren is one of the commonest birds on the island, being found not only in every patch of scrub and timber, but also inhabiting the tall grass and trefoil in the pasture " (A. G. Campbell).

FAMILY—TURDIDÆ (2 species).

Sub-Family—Sylviinæ.

*REED-WARBLER

(*Acrocephalus australis*, Gould).

Male.—Upper surface brown tinged with olive; rump and upper tail coverts lighter, inclined to fawn; primaries and secondaries brown, edged externally with pale olive-brown; throat whitish; rest of under surface tinged with buff; bill dark brown; legs and feet olive-brown. Dimensions in mm.:—Length, 158; bill, 14; wing, 77; tail, 70; tarsus, 23.

Female.—Similar to male.

Nest.—Usually securely fastened to four or five reeds either permanently standing in water or else on the sloping side of a river, where, when the tide is up, the reeds stand in a couple of feet at least of water. It is cup-shaped and deep, and is composed of long and soft pliable stems of aquatic plants and strips of the "leaves " of the reeds, strongly woven together. Occasionally fine roots, cotton threads, and the like are employed. Lining, when present, the flowering tops of the reeds. Instances have come under my notice where the nest has been built some distance away from water.

Eggs.—Clutch three to four; stout oval in shape; texture fine; surface glossy; colour greyish or greenish white, more or less blotched with roundish markings of umber and grey. Dimensions in mm. of a clutch.—(1) 19.5 x 13.5, (2) 20 x 15, (3) 20.5 x 14, (4) 20 x 14.

Breeding Season.—End of September to January.

Geographical Distribution.—Tasmania, New South Wales, Victoria, South Australia; also Lombok (Wallace).

Observations.—This sweet singer usually arrives in Northern Tasmania about the end of the second week or the beginning of the third week in September, and departs at the latter end of March or thereabout. Odd individuals are sometimes to be noted both earlier and later than the dates above indicated.

In the reeds along the banks of the North Esk and the Tamar Rivers this species may be considered common during the breeding season. On account of its shyness and its habit of keeping close among the high reeds, it is seldom seen unless one lays oneself out for that purpose. In the early morning, and also towards dusk, especially when the female is incubating, the sweet notes of the male may be heard floating up in the still air. Not only does it pour forth its tuneful notes during the day, but oftentimes throughout the summer nights.

Its food consists of insects and mollusca gathered from the reeds and from off the mud laid bare by the receding tide.

From observations and information received, I find that this species is very irregularly distributed, there being a number of localities seemingly suited for it in which it is never seen.

Sub-Family—Turdinæ.

*LARGE-BILLED GROUND-THRUSH

(*Geocichla macrorhyncha*, Gould).

Male.—Upper surface olive-brown; the crown of the head has a slight tinge of chestnut; each feather has a crescent-shaped black mark at the tip, the broadest markings being in the centre of the back; upper wing coverts dark brown, margined with olive-brown and tipped with tawny-white; primaries and secondaries brown, margined externally with a warm shade of olive-brown; tail feathers olive-brown, the outermost feather on either side narrowly tipped and margined for two-thirds of an inch on the inner web with white; the next feather on either side has only a tiny tip of white; sides of the neck white, tinged with pale chestnut and tipped with black; chin and throat white, the latter margined with pale chestnut, in addition to which some of the feathers are tipped with black; chest and sides likewise washed with pale chestnut; the feathers are somewhat broadly tipped with black, especially on the sides; centre of the abdomen white; under tail coverts white, a few of the longer feathers narrowly tipped with brownish-black; bill blackish-brown; legs and feet pale brown. Dimensions in mm.:—Length, 305; bill, 26; wing, 144; tail, 124; tarsus, 28.

Female.—Usually differs from the male in that the markings on the under surface are heavier and darker. Dimensions in mm.: —Length, 285; bill, 27; wing, 132; tail, 110; tarsus, 30.5.

Young.—Duller in colour, with the black markings smaller than in the adult stage.

Mr. A. J. North states that after an examination of a large series of skins of the mainland *G. lunulata* and this species, he is convinced they are one and the same species.

NEST OF LARGE-BILLED GROUND-THRUSH.

Photo. by H. C. THOMPSON.

Nest.—The structure is large and open, composed externally of green moss, grass, tiny sticks, and rootlets, the whole being tightly matted together; the inside lining usually consists of grass only. When moss is unobtainable, mud is employed to mat the various materials together with. A sheltered situation among thick scrub is always chosen; a moist, well-wooded gully is a favourite resort. The nest is either placed in the fork of a dogwood, musk, or some similar tree, or else against the base of a bough springing from a horizontal limb. The moss used is the kind that keeps perpetually green as long as there is any moisture in the atmosphere. The egg cavity is often oval instead of round.

Eggs.—Clutch two to three usually, four rarely; elongated oval in shape; texture fine; surface glossy; colour light warmish green, marked all over with fine spots and diffused cloudy markings of reddish or rufous brown. Dimensions in mm. of a clutch :—(1) 39 x 23.5, (2) 35 x 22.5, (3) 37 x 23.

Breeding Season.—July to October or November.

Geographical Distribution.—Tasmania, King Island, Furneaux and Kent Groups in Bass Strait.

Observations.—Moist gullies where there is an abundance of ground food are mostly favoured by this handsomely-marked bird. Owing to the amount of clearing that has been going on in many districts during the past few years, and also to its comparative tameness, it has decreased greatly. Ordinary domestic cats and domestic cats gone wild are its greatest enemies. It seldom flies except when hard pressed, trusting to its legs and similarity of colouring to that of its surroundings to escape from its enemies. Its note is a long-drawn-out whistle, half sweet and half melancholy, mostly to be heard early in the morning and just at dusk. Like the Whistling Shrike-Thrush, when suddenly disturbed it will often jump on to a log or stump, should one be close by, and gaze all round in an inquiring manner before quietly flying a short distance and again settling on the ground. On account of the assiduity with which it searches for " cut-worms " and other caterpillar pests among the farmer's root crops, it should be rigorously protected by him and given every encouragement.

FAMILY—TIMELIIDÆ (12 species).

Sub-Family—Timeliinæ.

*EMU-WREN

(*Stipiturus malachurus*, Shaw).

Male.—Crown of the head light rufous streaked with black; neck and back ash brown, passing into pale chestnut on the rump; all the feathers are centrally streaked with black; primaries and secondaries dark brown, with lighter margins; tail feathers blackish-brown and loosely webbed, outermost feathers shortest;

throat and fore-neck light blue; centre of chest whitish; rest of under surface yellowish-brown, darker on the sides; bill blackish-brown; legs and feet pale olive-brown. Dimensions in mm. :— Length, 153; bill, 8.5; wing, 41; tail (two central feathers), 89; tarsus, 19.5.

Female.—Similar to male save that the head is ashy-brown and the throat and fore-neck are yellowish-brown.

Young.—Duller in colour than adults; no rufous on the crown of the head; feathers on upper surface tinged with ochraceous-brown and very lightly streaked with black; chin and throat very light blue.

Nest.—Resembles somewhat that of the Blue Wren, only that it is very loosely constructed, the mouth takes up practically the whole of the upper part of the nest, and the egg cavity is very shallow, the eggs lying almost on a level with the lip of the opening. Fine, soft grasses are generally used, with a few feathers as lining. A seemingly favourite situation is among grass at or near the foot of a clump of briers; other situations are among a clump of thick grass or in dense scrub.

Eggs.—Clutch three to four; elongated oval in shape; texture of shell very fine and surface glossy; colour pearly white, with markings of rich reddish-chestnut. The amount of markings on eggs in the same clutch varies; in one egg the markings will be evenly distributed, on another those on the stouter end will be more pronounced, and in a third the stouter end alone will be marked. Dimensions in mm. of a full clutch :—(1) 18 x 12.5, (2) 17.5 x 13.5, (3) 18 x 13.5, (4) 18 x 13.

Breeding Season.—September or October to December.

Geographical Distribution.—Tasmania, New South Wales, Victoria, South Queensland, South and Western Australia.

Observations.—This tiny Wren is somewhat rare, only being found in a few districts. Open, plain-like country is its favourite haunt, where the button, band, and cutting grasses grow especially. Its flight is weak and wavering, most of its time being spent on the ground or close to it. In disposition it is very shy, keeping well out of sight should danger, seeming or real, threaten. When flushed it flutters for a few yards and then quickly disappears from sight in a clump of grass.

A few are to be found round Launceston and its vicinity. It is also to be found in suitable localities in various other parts of the island, the class of country mostly favoured being that covered with Epacris and grass-trees in addition to light timber. Of this species Gould says :—" It is a recluse little bird, concealing itself from view by keeping near the ground in the midst of the more dense parts of the grass-beds, and very seldom showing itself. Its extremely short, round wings ill adapt it for flight, and this power is consequently seldom employed, the bird depending for progression upon its extraordinary capacity for running; in fact, when

NEST OF GRASS-BIRD.

Photo. by H. C. THOMPSON.

NESTING HOLE OF YELLOW-TIPPED PARDALOTE.

Photo. by H. C. THOMPSON.

the grasses are wet from dew or rain its wings are rendered perfectly unavailable. On the ground it is altogether as nimble and active, its creeping mouse-like motions, and the extreme facility with which it turns and bounds over the surface, enabling it easily to elude pursuit, and amply compensating for the paucity of its powers of flight. The tail is carried in an erect position, and is even occasionally retroverted over the back.''

Such widely separated places as Kelso, Wilmot, Tasman's Peninsula, Noland Bay, and Smithton are among the localities from which I have it recorded.

*GRASS-BIRD
(*Megalurus gramineus*, Gould).

Male.—Head reddish-brown streaked with dull black; eyebrows dull white; back slightly paler than head; feathers centred with black; rump and upper tail coverts pale fulvous; tail brown margined with fulvous; upper wing coverts similar to back; quills dark brown, outer webs fulvous, innermost secondaries blackish-brown margined with whitish; under surface dull white, washed with fulvous on fore-neck and breast, passing into fulvous-brown on the sides of the body; irides brown; bill olive-brown; legs and feet olive-brown. Dimensions in mm.:—Length, 160; bill, 10; tail, 63; tarsus, 20.

Female.—Similar to male.

Nest.—The commonest type of nest here in Tasmania is that constructed of grass and lined with feathers, placed in the centre of a clump of long tussock-grass in swampy situations; it is slightly domed or hooded.

Eggs.—Clutch three to four; roundish oval in shape; texture very fine; surface slightly glossy; colour light pinkish, sometimes tinged with purplish, spotted all over, at times more heavily on the apex, with purplish-red and dull grey. Dimensions in mm. of a richly marked clutch in Mr. F. Claridge's collection:—(1) 18.75 x 14.25, (2) 17.5 x 14, (3) 17.5 x 14, (4) 18 x 13.75; of a pair in the same collection—(1) 16.5 x 12, (2) 17 x 12.

Breeding Season.—September to the end of the year, generally.

Geographical Distribution.—Tasmania, King Island, and Australia in general.

Observations.—As its name implies, this bird is to all intents and purposes a purely terrestrial species. Most of its time is spent on the ground among the clumps of band-grass on the open areas favoured by it. Rarely does one see it perch on a bush or the like. Its flight is strong and rapid, always close to the ground. In many districts it is fairly common, judging from the frequency with which one can hear its sharp little whistling note issuing from clumps of grass on the edge of flats, creeks, and similar situations.

4

Owing to its rapidity of flight, during which the tail is displayed fanned, and general shyness, one catches but a fleeting glimpse of a bird here and there, even in a locality where it is plentiful.

*GRASS-WARBLER

(*Cisticola exilis*, Vig. and Horsf.)

Male (breeding plumage).—" General colour above golden-buff, the feathers of the back with a slight ashy shade and broadly centred with brownish-black; upper wing coverts like the back, primaries and outermost secondaries brown externally edged with golden-buff, the innermost secondaries blackish-brown margined with golden-buff; tail feathers brownish-black, edged and largely tipped with golden-buff; forehead and sides of the head and neck slightly darker than the crown; all the under surface pale golden-buff, slightly darker on the breast and flanks; under tail coverts pale golden-buff; upper mandible brown, lower mandible flesh colour; legs and feet flesh colour. Total length in the flesh, 3.6 inches; wing, 1.9; tail, 1.2; bill, 0.38; tarsus, 0.72" (A. J. North).

Female (breeding plumage).—Similar to male save that the head as well as the back is broadly striped with black.

Winter Plumage (both sexes).—Practically the same as breeding plumage of female.

Young (both sexes).—Young birds of both sexes resemble the winter plumage of the adult female, but are duller in colour, the feathers on the hind-neck and rump above showing a distinct wash of golden-buff, those on the under surface being dull white, with a faint tinge of yellowish-buff on the neck and golden-buff on the sides of the body" (A. J. North).

Nest.—Generally situated in open grass country or river flats; it is inclined to oval in shape, with entrance near the top; constructed of fine grass, with which are mixed spiders' webs and cocoons; lined with thistle-down or some similar soft material.

Eggs.—Clutch four usually; roundish oval in shape; texture fine and surface lustrous; colour delicate bluish-green, moderately but distinctly blotched with reddish-brown and purplish-brown. Dimensions in mm. of a clutch :—(1) 15 x 11, (2) 14.5 x 10.75, (3) 15 x 10.5, (4) 14.25 x 11.

Breeding Season.—October to December.

Geographical Distribution.—King Island and Australia in general; also " New Guinea Islands, Molucca Islands, Philippines, Formosa, Malayan Peninsula, Further India, and India " (A. J. Campbell).

Observations.—This bird is common among the grassy flats on King Island. So far as I am aware, its existence has not been reported from any of the other large islands lying in Bass Strait, although it is quite possible it frequents more than one.

*TASMANIAN TIT (Brown-tail)

(*Acanthiza diemenensis*, Gould).

Male.—Forehead rufescent; head. and all the upper surface including wings, deep olive-brown; upper tail coverts inclined to chestnut; tail olive-brown, crossed by a band of blackish-brown; cheeks, throat, and chest greyish-white, irregularly streaked with black; rest of under surface greyish-white washed with rufous, deeper on flanks, thighs, and under tail coverts; bill dark brown; legs and feet light brown. Dimensions in mm.:—Length, 100; bill, 11; wing, 51; tail, 45; tarsus, 19.

Female.—Similar to male.

Young.—Similar to adults.

Nest.—Globular in shape, with the top longer than the bottom, entrance at the side near the top; the materials used are fine grasses, moss, leaves, and wool; lined inside with fur and feathers. The nest is almost invariably placed low down in thick scrub; occasionally it is attached to the branches of a young wattle in a thick plantation of these trees.

Eggs.—Clutch three to four; rather oval in shape; texture very fine; .surface glossy; colour pearly-white to faint pinkish-white, fairly freckled all over with reddish and purplish brown; the markings on the outer end form a zone. Dimensions in mm. of a clutch :—(1) 18 x 13.5, (2) 17 x 12.5, (3) 17.5 x 13, (4) 17 x 12.5.

Breeding Season.—August or September to December usually.

Geographical Distribution.—Tasmania and most of the larger islands in Bass Strait.

Observations.—In the northern half of the island, at least, the Tasmanian Tit, Brown-tail, or Badger-Bird, as it is variously called, is very plentiful. Among the eucalypt forests it consorts in small flocks of half a dozen or so individuals.

The food of this species consists of insects of all kinds, especially flies, beetles, caterpillars, and grubs, all of which are obtained on the ground among decaying vegetation or from under the loose bark of the eucalypts. It is a pretty sight to watch a flock of "Brown-tails" scurrying along the limbs of a eucalypt, poking and prying into every crack in the bark in search of food. They are full of energy and animation. It is no uncommon sight to see this species right out on the extreme tips of the twigs of a tree hanging suspended downwards to the leaves picking off spiders and flies from their under surfaces. When searching for food the commonest note is a sharp "Creak, creak" many times repeated with great rapidity; occasionally a double "Creak" is finished up with "Phee, phee," somewhat prolonged. In addition to the above, a few low, unintelligible whistling notes are also uttered. The birds are agile on the wing, darting with great rapidity from tree to tree or from bough to bough when searching for food. Thickly-wooded tracts are mostly preferred as hunting grounds;

insect life being most abundant, and as a natural corollary less labour is required to satisfy the pangs of hunger of self and the little ones at home, if it be nesting season.

EWING'S TIT
(*Acanthiza ewingi*).

Male.—Forehead rufous, feathers faintly edged with black; upper surface brownish-olive, more rufescent on the rump; tail brownish or rufescent olive, broad black subterminal band on all save centre feathers; upper wing coverts like back; primary coverts blackish; bastard wing and primaries almost black; bases of secondaries rufous, then black, with olive on outer webs; chin, cheeks, throat, and fore-neck grey; rest of under surface dull white; flanks dark olive; irides light red; bill brown; legs and feet dark olive-brown. Dimensions in mm.:—Length, 101; bill, 11; wing, 48; tail, 47; tarsus, 19.

Female.—Similar to male.

Nest.—Differs from that of *A. diemenensis* in being smaller and more compactly built; very firm to the touch; sides flat; domed; entrance small and well concealed. Outwardly constructed of grass, moss, cocoons of spiders; inside, very fine grass, neatly woven together, then finally lined with feathers and a little fur. Dimensions in inches:—Top to bottom, 4.25; front to back, 3; across the front, 2.25; diameter of entrance, 1.

Eggs.—Clutch three to four; inclined to oval in shape; texture fine; surface glossy; colour warmish or pinkish white, finely freckled, especially about the apex, with reddish-brown. Dimensions in mm. of a clutch taken near Corra Lynn:—(1) 18 x 13, (2) 18 x 12.75, (3) 17.5 x 12.5.

Breeding Season.—September to December.

Geological Distribution.—Tasmania and King Island.

Observations.—Ewing's Tit was originally figured and described by Gould ("Birds of Australia," fol., vol. iii., pl. 55, 1848), but in his "Handbook" (1865) he places the species as synonymous with the Brown-tail (*A. diemenensis*). It is also omitted from the British Museum Catalogue.

During the 1903 Congress of the Australasian Ornithologists' Union, held at Hobart, the bird was finally and firmly re-established as a distinct species. Specimens were obtained from the slopes of Mount Wellington, and exhibited in the flesh during the progress of the congress. In 1902 Mr. A. J. Campbell shot an *Acanthiza* on King Island which he was doubtful about, and this bird turns out to be *A. ewingi*.

Mr. A. J. North states ("Nests and Eggs," vol. i., p. 274) that an adult female of this species was received at the Australian Museum in July, 1899, having been received from near George

Town. Colonel Legge, in the introduction to his "Systematic List of Tasmanian Birds" (P.R.S. Tas., 1900-1), stated that the re-discovery of this species was very probable, evidently forgetting that in November, 1892, he read a note before the Tasmanian Royal Society entitled "A Note on a Tasmanian Acanthiza." In this note he says (*inter alia*):—"Last December, when visiting an out-of-the-way settlement on the Elephant Hill, near St. Mary's, situated about 1,500 feet above sea level, I met with a solitary bird hopping about the scrub and bushes on the edge of a clearing, and, being attracted by its peculiar note, I procured it, having by chance my gun with me. It proved to be a small Acanthiza, very similar to the common 'Brown-tail' or Tasmanian Acanthiza, but differing in having the forehead pale rufescent-grey instead of rufous and the throat and fore-neck with the markings much less pronounced than in the last-named species—in fact, the colouration of that part is almost uniform, the centres of the feathers also being slightly darker than the rest of the web. At the base of the outer webs of the primaries there is a narrow rufous band, similar to that shown in Gould's figure, which, however, has the markings of the throat more pronounced than in my specimen. Owing to the absence of throat markings, I was inclined to look on the bird as an immature male of the common Brown-tail, particularly as the month was that in which so many young birds are procurable, but the actions and the note of this individual were so totally different from that of the Tasmanian Acanthiza that no doubt is left in my mind as to its distinctness. The common species is gregarious, nearly always being found in small parties, which flit about with great zest and activity, uttering in unison their peculiar little note, which may be syllabilized 'Zit, zit, zit, whoorl,' the latter being somewhat guttural. The note of my new species resembles 'Tit, tit, too, woo,' the latter syllables being soft and melodious. . . . There can be little doubt that this bird is, in reality, the *Acanthiza ewingi* of Gould, which should, therefore, be reinstated in the Tasmanian avifauna."

A *résumé* of the dates of the discovery and re-discovery of Ewing's Tit runs thus:—

1848—First figured and described by Gould.

1854—"List of Birds of Tasmania," by Rev. T. J. Ewing, P.R.S. Tas., August, 1854.

1865—Omitted by Gould from his "Handbook."

1879—Specimen received at Australian Museum from George Town.

1892—Specimen shot by Colonel Legge near St. Mary's.

1902—Specimen shot by Mr. A. G. Campbell on King Island. Examples received by Australian Museum from Waratah.

1903—Several specimens shot on the slopes of Mount Wellington, and the species finally re-identified and reinstated as a valid species.

Briefly described, the habits of this, one might almost say famous, species are to a great extent dissimilar to those of the familiar Brown Tit, for, whereas the latter species consorts in flocks and frequents the open country, the former is either solitary or goes in pairs and resorts to the beds of creeks and moist gullies. This habit has earned for it the name of the " Creek Tit."

The distribution of Ewing's Tit has not yet been fully worked out, but it is known to occur round Hobart and Launceston, on the way to the Lakes, and part of the West Coast.

Mr. H. C. Thompson has furnished me with an interesting note concerning the location of the nest and the nest itself. He states :—" It is always built near a creek, usually in a small bush, near the ground. One nest discovered was in a dry wattle about 15 feet from the ground ; the tree was in thick scrub near water. The nest is much smaller than that of the Brown-tail, and is very compact; it is oval in front, with flat sides ; entrance very small, and often closed when the bird is not laying, making it difficult to find. It is constructed of dead grass, rootlets, and moss, and lined with feathers and fur. I have seen the egg of the Bronze-Cuckoo built into the lining of this nest."

LARGE-BILLED TIT

(*Acanthiza magnirostris*, Campbell).

Male.—" Upper surface olive-brown; forehead cinnamon-brown, each feather having a crescent-shaped mark of a brighter colour at the extremity, and tipped with dark brown; upper tail coverts reddish or rufous brown; tail marked with a band of dark brown near the extremity ; cheeks, throat, and chest whitish, each feather centred and edged with dark brown or black; rest of the under surface light olive-brown, darker on the flanks and under tail coverts; bill dark brown; feet brownish or fuscous. Length, 4.25 in. ; culmen, .45 ; wing, 2.0 ; tail, 1.6 ; tarsus, .7 " (A. J. Campbell, *Emu*, ii., p. 202).

Female.—Similar to male.

Nest.—Unknown

Eggs.—Unknown.

Breeding Season.—In all probability similar to that of the rest of the genus.

Geographical Distribution.—King Island.

Observations.—This Tit was discovered by Mr. A. G. Campbell during a visit to King Island towards the end of 1902. The discoverer of this species records that it frequents more the shorter scrub of the island, away from the watercourses. So far as I am aware, its nest and eggs are still *desiderata*.

*YELLOW-RUMPED TIT (YELLOW-TAIL)

(*Acanthiza chrysorrhoa*, Quoy and Gaim.)

Male.—Forehead black, each feather tipped with white; upper surface, including wings, olive-brown; rump and upper tail coverts bright citron-yellow; base of tail feathers yellowish-white, central portion blackish-brown, then a short tip of greyish-white; chest and under surface yellowish-white, passing into light olive-brown on the flanks; bill, legs, and feet blackish-brown. Dimensions in mm.:—Length, 106; bill, 9.75; wing, 59; tail, 46; tarsus, 17.

Female.—Similar to male.

Nest.—A bulky, elongated structure, divided into two parts. The nest proper is closed in, with a spouted side entrance; above this is a semi-nest, open back and front. Dry grasses and wool are usually the chief materials employed; the lining is either wool alone or wool and feathers, a thick layer being used. The situation varies, but as a general thing the drooping boughs of a moderately low to low tree, or near the centre of a gorse bush, is chosen.

Eggs.—Clutch three to four or even five; long oval in shape; texture very fine; surface glossy; colour pure white, without markings, but sometimes a few tiny spots of dull red appear on the apex. Dimensions in mm. of a clutch:—(1) 18 x 12.5, (2) 18.5 x 13, (3) 18.25 x 13, (4) 18 x 12.5.

Breeding Season.—August to December.

Geographical Distribution.—Tasmania, New South Wales, Victoria, Queensland, South and Western Australia.

Observations.—This bird is popularly known to most under the name of Yellow-tail. It is widely distributed throughout the island, and is perhaps the commonest of the *Acanthizæ*. It is also very common during certain seasons of the year in suburban gardens. This more particularly applies to the winter months, when its natural food is running short and competition is very keen among its feathered congeners for anything in the shape of provender. The object of the upper or false nest has been the subject of much discussion. Many and varied opinions and theories have been advanced from time to time as to its real object and utility. The most generally accepted theory is that it serves as a roosting-place for the male at night while its mate is engaged in the task of incubation. Another theory is that it acts as a blind to enemies, for, on finding an empty space, they naturally conclude that the nest is vacant, and so do not investigate further. Yet another theory is that it serves as a shelter for the young when grown too big for the nest proper but not yet able to shift for themselves. Often have I found a nest containing the first clutch of eggs of the season and the upper apartment showing signs of having been used. I do not see any reason why the three theories should not dove-tail one into the other, and the upper structure come in for all three purposes—viz., a blind to enemies, shelter for the parent bird, and a refuge for the young fledglings. It is no uncommon sight to see the birds assembled in flocks of 30 or 40 in winter, running over the ground picking up any stray scrap of food, in addition to the usual diet of insects and seeds. As I have above mentioned, the bird does not confine itself to bush-land, but comes right into gardens in the larger towns in search of food. It is often to be seen swarming over the fruit trees in search of codlin moth and other grubs; it is not averse to picking off mussel scale where thick.

When flushed from the ground, the Yellow-tail utters a sharp, high-pitched note, and only flies a few yards before again alighting. It is quite possible to go within a few yards of a flock without the birds taking flight. When flying a short distance it moves in a jerky, wavy manner. The song of this species is a very pretty little run of notes—not loud, but very sweet; it is usually uttered when the birds are feeding together in a flock on the ground. This species is about the earliest of our birds to nest. One mild June I saw a parent bird carrying food to its young. For a completed nest to be discovered in July is no rare occurrence.

Mr. H. Stuart Dove writes me:—"On 29th September, 1909, I found in a prickly wattle at Flowerdale a two-chambered nest, lower part of which contained an egg and three unfledged young; upper part had an unfinished dome, with a depression on one side like a roosting-place. On 24th December this nest was found to be triple; the lowest compartment contained one freshly-laid white egg; the next compartment had three eggs, partly incubated; the third compartment was empty, but had been used for shelter, and was not so well covered as the other two. There was also a sort of shallow depression on top at right-hand side (the so-called 'cock's nest'). Looked at again after New Year, the three eggs in middle compartment were hatched, but single egg in lowest room remained the same."

*WHITE-BREASTED SCRUB-TIT

(*Acanthornis magna*, Gould).

Male.—Crown of the head, lower back, and rump deep brownish-olive; upper back olive; tail blackish-brown, outer webs lighter, sub-terminal band black; wings black, first five primaries narrowly edged on terminal half of outer webs with white; greater wing coverts edged with white; lores and a stripe over the eyes white; ear coverts and cheeks slate-black; throat white, becoming pale yellow on the abdomen; flanks and under tail coverts deep brownish-olive; irides light yellow; bill blackish; legs and feet brownish. Dimensions in mm.:—Length, 109; bill, 13; wing, 53; tail, 44; tarsus, 21.

Female.—Colouration in general browner; throat tinged with yellow.

SCRUB-TIT AND NEST.

Photo. by A. J. CAMPBELL.   *From "* THE EMU."

Young.—Dull brownish-olive; patch of dull yellow on each side of the chest; centre of abdomen white.

Nest.—According to Mr. A. L. Butler, the position of the nest varies according to the nature of the scrub in which it is found. He says :—" I have found them as low as 3 inches from the ground and as high as 9 feet, in grass and ferns, and then again in the dead fronds of the tree-fern." The nest is globular in shape, with a side entrance, and is composed of strips of bark, rootlets, and a little green moss, the lining being fern down, feathers, and fur.

Eggs.—Clutch three; inclined to oval in shape; texture of shell fine ; surface glossy ; colour pearly-white, more or less blotched with reddish-brown and purplish-brown, and, as is often the case, the markings are heaviest about the stouter end. Dimensions in mm. of a clutch :—(1) 18 x 13, (2) 19 x 13, (3) 18.5 x 12.5.

Breeding Season.—October and November principally.

Geographical Distribution.—Tasmania.

Observations.—On account of the nature of the country it frequents, combined with its shyness, this interesting Scrub-Tit is but rarely seen unless one lays oneself out to specially search for it. Of its habits Mr. Butler says :—" With its mouse-like move-ments, it will fly to the base of a tree-fern, run rapidly to the top and down the other side, just pausing long enough to grasp an unwary beetle, or some such small object, then off again to another tree, and repeat the performance. Whilst it is feeding its note is a short 'Cheep, cheep,' but at times you will hear it trilling out a little song something like the *Calamanthus* (Reed-Lark), but not so full or sustained as that bird's note."

Regarding the distribution of this Tit, it has been found round Piper's River in the north, Penguin in the north-west, and Waratah in the west. I expect there are other places where it is present. Mr. Butler has found it at the Huon, Carnarvon, North-West Bay River, Glenorchy, Bismarck, New Norfolk, in addition to different places about the base of Mount Wellington.

*BROWN SCRUB-WREN

(*Sericornis humilis,* Gould).

Male.—Crown of the head, back, and wings dark olive-brown ; rump and tail dark olive-brown tinged with reddish; " spurious wing blackish-brown, each feather margined with white; throat greyish-white spotted with blackish-brown " (Gould); chest dark grey, passing into brownish-yellow on abdomen; chest obscurely marked with blackish-brown; flanks rufous-brown. Dimensions in mm. :—Length, 130; bill, 13; wing, 62; tail, 54; tarsus, 25.

Female.—Similar to male, except that the lores are slate instead of black.

Nest.—Somewhat large for the size of the bird; inclined to globular in shape, with the entrance at the side; composed of fine rootlets, leaves, grass, and moss, lined with fur and feathers. When not built right on the ground at the foot of a thick shrub or a clump of broad-leaved cutting-grass, it is placed a little way up. In some districts the nest has been found in a clump of black-berries.

Eggs.—Clutch three to four; somewhat stoutish oval; texture fine; surface fairly glossy; colour light purplish-buff, marked, especially about the apex, with umber and purplish-brown. Dimensions in mm. of a clutch :—(1) 21.5 x 17, (2) 21 x 15.5, (3) 21 x 16, (4) 21.5 x 16.5.

Breeding Season.—August or September to the end of the year.

Geographical Distribution.—Tasmania, King Island, Furneaux and Kent Groups.

Observations.—Although it may be stated that as a general rule the Sombre Sericornis frequents localities clothed with dense to moderately dense undergrowth, yet in some districts where the only cover is among the blackberry and gorse hedges the species is surprisingly plentiful. I may instance the Scottsdale district in this respect. Its diet consists almost exclusively of insects, which are gathered from among the fallen leaves and branches, and from under the bark of the trees strewn about its haunts. It seldom ascends to the top of the scrub, preferring to remain among the undergrowth. Its progress through the thickets is "on foot," and it displays a marvellous nimbleness. During certain seasons the male utters a series of rather pretty low and sweet notes.

*SPOTTED GROUND-BIRD (Ground-Dove).

(*Cinclosoma punctatum*, Lath.)

Male.—Upper surface brown to rufous-brown, the feathers on the back with distinct black centres; on the other parts the black is somewhat obscure; upper wing coverts glossy black tipped with white; primaries and outer secondaries brown, the former margined externally with ashy-grey to whitish, the inner series of the latter chestnut, broadly striped with black on the outer web; two central tail feathers greyish-brown, rest black broadly margined with grey on their inner webs and tipped with white; "stripe over the eye, a nearly circular spot on the side of the neck, and the centre of the abdomen white" (Gould); throat and a narrow band across the chest glossy black; chest ashy-grey; flanks and under tail coverts reddish-buff; each feather has a broad stripe of black down the centre; bill black; legs and feet pale flesh colour. Dimensions in mm. :—Length, 278; bill, 16; wing, 114; tail, 130; tarsus, 31.

Female.—Upper surface lighter than in male; throat greyish-white; spot on the neck rufous; no pectoral band.

Nest.—Bowl-shaped; rather loosely constructed of strips of bark, leaves, and a little grass; lined with similar materials, only finer. Usually situated under the shelter of a log or a large stone on the ground.

Eggs.—Clutch two to three or even four; somewhat lengthened oval in shape; texture of shell fine; surface glossy; colour white; spotted and blotched, especially about the stouter end, with umber and dull grey. Dimensions in mm. of a clutch :—(1) 37 x 24, (2) 36 x 24, (3) 36.5 x 25.

Breeding Season.—August to September.

Geographical Distribution.—Tasmania, New South Wales, Victoria, South Australia, and South Queensland.

Observations.—The distribution of this species is fairly general in Tasmania, being the most plentiful in those districts best suited to its habits. But in no locality is it as plentiful as it was before the country was opened up as it is now. Lightly timbered slopes are greatly favoured by this species, but it also may be found in heavily timbered tracts. It keeps almost exclusively to the ground, although occasionally it may be seen perched on a bough some distance from the ground. Its powers of flight are nowise strong, and are seldom used except when the bird requires to traverse any unusual distance. Great agility is displayed in running along fallen trees and over the ground when searching for food, which consists of insects, seeds, and small berries. When suddenly disturbed it rises from the ground with a whirring noise very much like that made by a quail; only a short distance is traversed, as it quickly descends and is lost to sight in the scrub. A somewhat long-drawn whistling note is practically the only sound uttered by this bird.

In Gould's day this species was extremely plentiful, and he mentions having seen large numbers exposed for sale in Hobart shops. Under the *Game Act* of 1907 this bird is afforded total protection.

STRIATED FIELD-WREN

(*Calamanthus fuliginosus*, Vig. and Horsf.)

Male.—Upper surface greenish-olive, all the feathers centred with black; tail feathers olive-brown, the central pair streaked with black along the shafts; on the rest a subterminal band of black, except on the extreme outer webs, which are pale ashy-brown, as also are the extreme tips; primaries and secondaries blackish-brown; the outer primaries are margined externally with ashy-white, and the remainder of the quills with greenish-olive; chin and throat white, streaked with black; centre of abdomen white to buffy-white; rest of under surface yellowish-buff, streaked with black; bill brown, tip blackish. Dimensions in mm. :—Length, 142; bill, 11; wing, 58; tail, 54; tarsus, 23.

Female.—Similar to male, except that the chin and throat are dull yellow or buff instead of white. Dimensions in mm. :—Length, 135; bill, 10.5; wing, 58; tail, 48; tarsus, 22.5.

Nest.—Roundish, more or less domed or hooded; constructed outwardly of grass, leaves, moss, &c., then a layer of fine grass, finally feathers and hair. The usual situation is either on or close to the ground in a clump of long grass, rushes, gorse, or briers. When young are in the nest the entrance is opened out, so that it takes on a bowl-shaped appearance.

Eggs.—Clutch three to four; roundish, with one end distinctly pointed; texture fine; surface glossy: colour vinaceous-buff; round the apex is a broad belt of reddish or purplish brown. Dimensions in mm. of a clutch :—(1) 20 x 16, (2) 20 x 15.5, (3) 19.75 x 16, (4) 20.5 x 15.75.

Breeding Season.—August to December.

Geographical Distribution.—Tasmania, New South Wales, and South Australia.

Observations.—When searching for food among tussock-grass and similar light growth favoured by this Field-Wren, its tail is carried in a line with its body, and not erect like Gould's Blue Wren. The means by which a person observing this bird quietly feeding, and who had not before seen it, could tell it belonged to the erect-tailed Wrens would be by the narrowness of the tail at the base, and the manner in which the feathers fold over one another. As soon as the bird comes out into the open the tail is erected and kept so. After coming to rest on a branch or post, the tail is jerked backwards and forwards several times. On the ground it is a quick runner on occasions, but when searching for food it progresses with a hopping motion. Open grassy country, studded with band-grass and cutting-grass, is mostly favoured. When flushed in the open it flies with rapid motion, just clearing the ground, only rising sufficiently to clear any obstacle, and quickly drops on the ground out of sight. Rarely does it perch on a bush at the end of its flight after being flushed. On account of its strong odour it is known to quail-shooters as the "Stink-Bird." Sporting dogs will often set to it in mistake for their proper quarry. During the breeding season especially it has a very sweet little song, which is most frequently uttered when perched on the top of a brier or gorse bush. The rest of the year it is practically voiceless.

*WHITE-FRONTED CHAT

(*Ephthianura albifrons*, Jard. and Selby).

Male.—Forehead, sides of the head, cheeks, and throat white; crown of the head and nape black; rest of the upper surface dull grey; upper tail coverts black; tail feathers dark brown, central pair uniform, rest tipped with white on the inner web; primaries and secondaries dark brown; "chest crossed by a broad crescent of deep black, the points of which run up the sides of the neck and join at the back of the occiput" (Gould); remainder of the under surface white; flanks tinged with grey; bill, legs, and feet black. Dimensions in mm.:—Length, 118; bill, 11; wing, 71; tail, 40; tarsus, 17.

Female.—All the upper surface, including head, wings, and tail, greyish-brown; the white spot on the tip of the inner webs of the lateral tail feathers indistinct; throat and under surface buffy-white; crescent on chest narrow and less distinct than in male.

Young.—Resembles adult female, but a little more dusky in hue.

Nest.—Cup-shaped; the favourite situation appears to be the centre of a tussock or clump of band-grass, when the nest is composed of fine grass-stems and lined with horse-hair.

Eggs.—Clutch three usually; roundish oval in shape; texture of shell fine; surface fairly glossy; colour white, spotted and freckled, especially on the larger end, with reddish-brown and purplish-brown. Dimensions in mm. of a clutch:—(1) 18 x 14, (2) 17.5 x 13.5, (3) 18 x 13.5.

Breeding Season.—August to October generally, November sometimes.

Geographical Distribution.—Tasmania, King and several other Bass Strait Islands, New South Wales, Victoria, South Queensland, South, Western, and North-Western Australia.

Observations.—By many people this species is known as the "Moony" on account of the crescent-shaped band on its chest. The range and numbers of the White-fronted Chat have increased greatly during the last few years. Not so long ago it was restricted to a few districts, and rare in these; now it is a plentiful species in many. It appears to have been first noted in the southern end of the island, and, after having spread over a wide area, gradually advanced up north by way of the midland districts. As a rule open grassy country is mostly favoured, where it may be seen busily engaged searching for seeds and insects among the grass. On the North-West Coast it may frequently be seen in fairly large flocks on the sea shore about high water mark, eagerly searching among the *débris*. The muddy edges of lagoons, clay-pans, and the like are resorted to. When rising from the ground with rapid flight, sharp and distinctly metallic notes are uttered, dissimilar to those of any other bird I know of. This bird is distinctly nomadic in its habits, suddenly appearing in a district for a longer or shorter time, and then as suddenly disappearing.

FAMILY—LANIIDÆ (5 species).

Sub-Family—Gymnorhinæ.

*LESSER WHITE-BACKED MAGPIE

(*Gymnorhina hyperleuca,* Gould).

Male.—Head, scapulars, primaries and secondaries, terminal half of tail, and entire under surface, save under tail coverts, glossy black; hind-neck, back, upper and under tail coverts, basal half of tail, shoulders, wing coverts, and basal half of outer webs of primary coverts pure white; irides yellowish-brown; bill bluish-horn colour, tip black; legs and feet black. Dimensions in mm. :— Length, 365; bill, 46; wing, 240; tail, 140; tarsus, 55.

Female.—Back greyish-white; under surface greyish-black without gloss.

Young.—Male.—Upper surface ashy-grey; wing coverts parti-coloured, black and white; under surface more grey than black; irides hazel; bill lead-coloured; legs and feet black.

Nest.—Open and bowl-shaped; sticks, twigs, and strips of eucalypt bark constitute the main items in its composition; the inside lining consists principally of grass and shredded bark. The situation usually chosen is in the forked branches of a eucalypt, generally some distance from the ground. Although the same nest is but rarely if ever used during successive seasons, the same tree is frequently resorted to year after year.

Eggs.—Clutch three to four; oval in shape; texture fine; surface glossy; colour light greenish, blotched and marked all over with rather dark umber. In some clutches both the ground colour and the markings vary a good deal, but the above description may be taken as typical. Dimensions in mm. of a clutch :—(1) 36 x 26, (2) 37 x 25.5, (3) 36 x 25.5, (4) 37 x 26.

Breeding Season.—August or September to December.

Geographical Distribution.—Tasmania.

Observations.—Although this species is one of the best known birds in many districts in Tasmania, yet there are parts where it is almost if not quite an absolute stranger. It is only within the last few years that it has extended its range to any extent on the West Coast, and I am given to understand that even now in the more densely timbered and moist localities it is unknown. The male bird is by far the handsomer of the two, especially during the breeding season, when the contrast between the white upper surface and the black under surface is very pronounced. To Tasmania belongs the privilege of being the first State to recognize the Magpie as being of economic value, and to extend protection to it. In 1879, under the *Game Protection Act,* 42 Vict., No. 24, it was decreed that whosoever killed the birds or destroyed their eggs would be liable to a penalty not exceeding £1. In 1885 this Act was extended, under 48 Vict., No. 35, so that persons could not buy, sell, or offer for sale birds of this species. Notwithstanding this, large numbers of young birds are taken annually from their nests and sold in the towns for garden pets. Very entertaining and useful ones they are, too. Because this bird may often be seen busy in a field of sprouting grain, some farmers labour under the impression that it is the grain it is after, but a little time spent in investigation would show that it is the pests affecting the crops that the Magpie so diligently searches for.

A most lamentable number of Magpies are destroyed every year through the careless and indiscriminate laying of poison for rabbits and Sparrows. There are a certain number of agriculturists who cannot, or will not, see any good in birds, and who consider that even their total annihilation would have no effect on the many " pests " with which they are plagued.

The food of this species is almost entirely insectivorous ; in the winter seeds and any stray grains are added to the *menu.* Grass-grubs are greatly sought after.

When not engaged in seeking food most of the time is passed among the branches of lofty trees. It moves in flocks of, say, six to a dozen individuals, although occasionally larger companies may be seen. The largest I have seen round Launceston consisted of 47 birds. Round Conara (the native name of the Magpie) and other midland districts even larger flocks may be seen. This bird is of a somewhat pugnacious disposition, always quite willing to cross swords with one of its own species or any other bird ; or, if tame, it does not scruple to try conclusions with a cat or dog. Hawks are its pet aversion, not an opportunity being lost to harass every one that comes near. On one occasion a Hawk was too clever for its tormentors. Some half-dozen Magpies were chasing one away from a tree which contained a nest and young birds. Suddenly the Hawk doubled, and, darting straight for the tree, plucked a young bird from out of the nest and sailed triumphantly away.

A Magpie makes an entertaining pet, though after a while it becomes very mischievous, and delights in pulling up freshly-set plants.

This bird is one of our best songsters, its voice being both very powerful and pleasing. Early on a summer's morning nothing is more delightful than to hear a number of Magpies pouring forth their melodious song while swaying on the topmost bough of some lofty tree. Morning and evening are the times when most singing is done, but it is no uncommon thing to hear the birds burst into song in the middle of some bright moonlight night.

The wing power of this bird is very great ; it can dash through the air with marvellous rapidity. Long distances (comparatively) speaking) are traversed without perceptible movement of the outstretched wings.

GREY BUTCHER-BIRD (Jackass)
(*Cracticus cinereus*, Gould).

Male.—Head, ears, and back of the neck black; rest of the upper surface, including shoulders, grey, with a faint tinge of bluish; tail black, tipped, principally on the inner webs, with white, except the two centre feathers, which are wholly black; upper tail coverts white; space between the eyes and the bill, middle of the secondaries, and throat white; rest of the under surface greyish-white; primaries black; bill bluish lead colour, with black tip; legs black. Dimensions in mm. :—Length, 326; bill, 40; wing, 154; tail, 121; tarsus, 34.

Female.—Whole of the upper surface, including head and shoulders, ashy-grey; tail brownish, tipped like male, only obscurely so; secondaries also brown, edged with white; throat dirty-white; rest of under surface greyish-white, more grey than white; bill and legs same as male. Dimensions in mm. :—Length, 285; bill, 36; wing, 137; tail, 109; tarsus, 31.

Young.—"An adolescent male had the marginal wing coverts tipped with buff and the median wing coverts tipped with olive; the feathers of the mantle had brownish-olive tips. Iris light brown " (J. R. M'Clymont).

Nest.—Somewhat large and open; composed of long, thin twigs compactly woven together and lined with long, fine grass. It is placed among the branches of a tree at no very great distance from the ground; a she-oak is a favourite tree. Dimensions of a typical nest :—Over all, 7 in.; egg cavity, 5 in.; depth of same, 2½ in.

Eggs.—Clutch three to four; roundish oval in shape; texture fine; surface glossy. The eggs of a clutch vary considerably. In a clutch before me one egg is pale green with only a broad band of reddish-brown and purplish-brown round the larger end; another is fawn colour, spotted and blotched all over with reddish-brown; a third is warmish green, banded at the larger end and the rest of the surface spotted with both reddish-brown and purplish-brown; the fourth is a little more green, densely spotted, especially about the stouter end, with small reddish-brown spots. Dimensions in mm. of a clutch :—(1) 31.5 x 24, (2) 32.5 x 24, (3) 32.25 x 24, (4) 33 x 22.

Breeding Season.—August to November principally.

Geographical Distribution.—Tasmania.

Observations.—The distribution of the " Jackass," as it is familiarly called, is fairly general throughout the island, though in some districts it is much more plentiful than in others. Properly speaking, this bird is merly a sub-species of the mainland Butcher-Bird (*Cracticus destructor*), the chief point of difference being its larger bill.

This so-called " Jackass " is a very familiar bird, either to dwellers in town or country. Its favoured haunts are moderately

NEST AND YOUNG OF GREY BUTCHER-BIRD.

Photo. by H. C. THOMPSON.

thickly timbered tracts, where it can find an abundance of both insect and animal life to satisfy its wants. It is a familiar bird round bush dwellings, where, with its loud and discordant notes, it strikes terror into the hearts of chickens and cage-birds. So far as my observations go, the autumn and winter months are when the Grey Butcher-Bird is most frequently seen about town gardens. A "Jackass" is much in favour as a pet, being either caged or allowed the run of the garden, where it does good work among many noxious insects. A young bird may, by dint of perseverance, be taught to whistle scraps of airs with a certain degree of accuracy. The food of this species consists of large insects, mice, and small birds. Also, during winter, it may often be observed picking scraps of fat off sheep and other skins hanging on farm fences. Like its English cousin, our Butcher-Bird often impales its victims on long thorns. In many instances each bird has its particular bush which it uses as a larder, and this is usually near its nest. Recently I came across a larder which contained two callow nestlings of some small bird, the remains of a mouse, and a number of large beetles. On another occasion a couple of Sparrows were found impaled. The Butcher-Bird does not at first kill its victims, but impales them alive, for it knows well that dead bodies soon decay, and as a rule it does not like its game "high." Its notes are hard to describe, they being rather "a jumble of discordant sounds." Nevertheless, the vocal efforts of a number of these birds singing in the early morning, or of two rival males courting the same female, are far from being unpleasant. The notes are very loud, and can be heard for some considerable distance.

<h2 style="text-align:center">Sub-Family—Pachycephalinæ.</h2>

<h3 style="text-align:center">*WHITE-THROATED THICKHEAD</h3>

(Pachycephala gutturalis, Lath.)

This species is included by Colonel Legge in his "Systematic List." I have two records of it by a good field observer from different localities, nevertheless I do not feel justified in listing it as a Tasmanian species.

<h3 style="text-align:center">*GREY-TAILED THICKHEAD</h3>

(Pachycephala glaucura, Gould).

Male.—" Crown of the head, lores, space beneath the eye, and a broad crescent-shaped mark from the latter across the breast deep black; the throat within the black is white; back of the neck, a narrow line down each side of the chest behind the black crescent, and the under surface yellow; back and wing coverts yellowish-olive; wings dark slate margined with grey; tail entirely

5

grey; under tail coverts white, or very slightly washed with yellow; irides yellowish-brown; bill black; feet dark brown " (Gould). Dimensions in mm.:—Length, 173; bill, 12; wing, 100; tail, 84; tarsus, 25.

Female.—Upper surface olive-brown; under surface pale brown.

Young.—When newly fledged both surfaces are greyish, washed with chestnut; this changes to a plumage closely resembling the adult female's. The young males do not attain full plumage until the second year.

Nest.—Comparatively bulky; constructed of fine twigs and bark, a few leaves being often added; the inside lining usually consists of fine grass and rootlets or fine twigs. A low bush or tree in thick scrub is very frequently chosen as a situation, with the nest placed at the end of a thin bough.

Eggs.—Clutch two to three usually; inclined to oval in shape; texture fine; surface glossy; colour light yellowish-white, darker towards the apex, which is thickly freckled with small spots of umber and dull slate, the latter colour appearing as though beneath the surface; a few spots of the same colours are scattered over the rest of the surface. Dimensions in mm. of a clutch:—(1) 23 x 17, (2) 24 x 17.

Breeding Season.—October to December.

Geographical Distribution.—Tasmania and several of the larger islands in Bass Strait.

Observations.—This sweet-voiced bird is fairly plentiful nearly everywhere in the island where the conditions are suitable for it. It is somewhat shy, however, and is more often heard than seen. Moderately well timbered country is mostly favoured, where it may be seen busily engaged in searching for insects on and under the bark of the eucalypts, also among the foliage; it is also very adroit at catching its prey on the wing.

For its size the Grey-tailed Thickhead has a wonderfully deep voice, which is to be heard to the best advantage when the males are challenging one another from the tree-tops at the commencement of the breeding season.

Mr. H. C. Thompson informs me that he has frequently seen birds in immature dress sitting on eggs or tending young, so that he is convinced that, like the Flame-breasted Robin, this species breeds while yet in adolescent plumage.

*OLIVE THICKHEAD

(Pachycephala olivacea, Vig. and Horsf.)

Male.—Head slate-grey; upper surface, including tail, olive-brown; primaries and secondaries slaty-black, narrowly margined with olive-brown; throat white, freckled with dark grey; upper chest grey, rest of under surface light brown; bill black; legs and feet dark brown. Dimensions in mm. :—Length, 200; bill, 14.25; wing, 99; tail, 92.5; tarsus, 30.25.

Female.—Head olive-brown; upper surface, including tail, chestnut-olive; primaries and secondaries dark brown, narrowly margined with a lighter shade; throat white, freckled with dark grey; no grey as in male on upper chest, but a short extent of fawn, lighter in colour than rest of under surface. Dimensions in mm. :—Length, 200; bill, 14; wing, 98; tail, 92; tarsus, 29.15.

Nest.—Cup-shaped and moderately large; constructed of fine twigs and bark, the inside lining being principally fine grass. The situation usually chosen is a low tree in thick scrub.

Eggs.—Clutch three to four usually; oval in shape, with both ends pointed; texture of shell fine; surface fairly glossy; colour light yellowish or creamy white, more or less spotted and blotched, especially about the apex, with chestnut and dull grey. Dimensions in mm. of a clutch :—(1) 28.5 x 21, (2) 29 x 21, (3) 29 x 20.75.

Breeding Season.—September to December.

Geographical Distribution.—Tasmania, King and several other islands in Bass Strait; also New South Wales, Victoria, and South Australia.

Observations.—As far as my experience goes, I have found this Thickhead less plentiful than the Grey-tailed species. It also favours denser country, and is quicker than that species.

Launceston, Lilydale, Waratah, Penguin, Hobart, Sandford, Tasman's Peninsula, Table Cape, Gladstone, Gunn's Plains, and Ross are among the places for which I have it recorded. A note by Mr. H. Stuart Dove runs :—"A pair of these fine birds made their appearance in my garden at Table Cape in the middle of May one year, and stayed the winter with me, hopping quietly about in the open or among the bushes, looking for insect food. At this period they were very silent, but in the spring their peculiar notes resounded among the trees. The call to mate during winter months is a hissing note, finishing smartly; and a somewhat similar call is used in summer, but during the latter season the well-known bold, melodious whistle, somewhat like the words ' I'll *wet* you,' is the more frequent."

FAMILY—CERTHIIDÆ (2 species).

Sub-Family—Certhinæ.

WHITE-THROATED TREE-CREEPER

(*Climacteris leucophæa*, Lath.)

Male.—Head brown, feathers centred with black; back olive-brown; upper tail coverts greyish; tail brownish-black, tip paler; wings dark greyish-brown, crossed by a band of dull buff; chin white; centre of abdomen soiled-white; sides of body and flanks dark brownish, the feathers conspicuously centred with white; bill black; legs and feet blackish-brown.   Dimensions in mm.:— Length, 145; bill, 16; wing, 81; tail, 63; tarsus, 18.

Female.—Similar to male.

Young.—Differs from adult in having the forehead slightly rufescent; rump and upper tail coverts distinctly rufous; abdomen washed with rufous.

Nest.—Within a hollow limb or tree trunk; composed of fine bark, grass, and moss, and lined with fur or feathers.

Eggs.—Clutch three usually; roundish in shape; texture fine; surface slightly glossy; colour white, sparsely blotched on the stouter end with reddish-brown and purplish-brown.   Dimensions in mm. of a pair:—(1) 21 x 16, (2) 20.5 x 16.

Breeding Season.—September to December.

Geographical Distribution.—Tasmania, New South Wales, Victoria, Queensland, and South Australia.

Observations.—The right of this species to appear on the permanent Tasmanian list has now been practically settled, for, although no specimens have been secured, I have seen it in the big forests in the north-east of the island; Col. Legge feels sure he has seen it in the myrtle forests at the back of Quamby Bluff and on the track to the Great Lake; and Miss J. A. Fletcher is practically certain of it being among the big timber in the Wilmot district.

BROWN TREE-CREEPER
(*Climacteris scandens*, Temm.)

At one time I was under the impression that this Tree-creeper, in addition to the White-throated species, was a frequenter of our forests; now I am convinced I made an error in identification.   At the same time I am induced for several reasons to include it, at least provisionally, among the birds of Tasmania.

FAMILY—MELIPHAGIDÆ (11 species).
Sub-Family—Zosteropinæ.
*WHITE-EYE (SILVER-EYE)
(*Zosterops cœrulescens*, Lath.)

Male.—Crown of the head olive-green; circle of short white feathers round the eye; back green tinged with brown; upper tail coverts brownish; tail greenish-black; wings similar, outer webs of quills greenish-yellow; chest greyish; centre of abdomen and under tail coverts white; sides of the breast brown; irides brown; bill blackish; legs and feet pale brown.   Dimensions in mm.:— Length, 110; bill, 10; wing, 60; tail, 47; tarsus, 15.5.

Female.—Similar to male.

Young.—Practically similar to adults at an early age.

Nest.—Cup-shaped; composed of fine grass-stems, with which are mingled scraps of wool, moss, and cotton (if built near a habitation); usually lined with long horse-hairs; suspended by the rim in almost any kind of thick bush or low tree. In suburban gardens the pear is a favourite tree.

Eggs.—Clutch three to four; roundish oval in shape; texture very fine; surface slightly lustrous; colour uniform light bluishgreen. Dimensions in mm. of a clutch:—(1) 16 x 11, (2) 15 x 10, (3) 14.5 x 11, (4) 15 x 11.

Breeding Season.—September to December.

Geographical Distribution.—Tasmania, King and several other islands in Bass Strait, New South Wales, Victoria, Queensland, South Australia; also New Zealand, Chatham Islands, New Caledonia, New Hebrides, and Fiji.

Observations.—The majority of growers of small fruits consider this bird a pest, and use every endeavour to diminish its numbers. Although during the fruit season it does a fair amount of damage, it more than pays for the fruit taken by the quantity of blight destroyed during the autumn and winter months. It usually moves in flocks varying in numbers from half a dozen birds to many dozens. Its movements are quick and eager. During both autumn and spring its song is very sweet, and exhibits a considerable range. The White-eye is not at all particular as to the class of country it frequents, it being equally at home in heavily timbered tracts, light open country, or suburban gardens. It is principally during the autumn and winter months that the birds congregate in any number; often flocks of from 12 to 50, if not more, may be seen hunting for food in garden or field. During the summer months it moves in pairs or in very small flocks at most. Food of this species consists of insects of all descriptions, seeds, small berries, and fruit. It is very fond of the berry-like seeds of the grass-palm. During the fruit season the White-eye is considered a very great pest by horticulturists, especially those who grow small and soft fruits, such as currants, cherries, gooseberries, and grapes. The greatest havoc is generally wrought in those orchards which are planted right up to the edge of thick scrub. It is not so much the quantity of fruit actually eaten, but the quantity only pecked and half eaten, which makes this bird so obnoxious to orchardists. But to the credit of its account must be put the good done by the destruction of vast quantities of noxious insects during the remaining months of the year. The movements of this bird are very rapid when insect-hunting; it seems animated with the desire to devour as many as possible in the shortest time. Suburban growers of chrysanthemums and roses have a lot to thank it for; but for its assistance it would often be a difficult task to bring these plants to perfection. In the early autumn, when food is becoming somewhat scarce, it turns its attention to the pear-slugs, destroying numbers of them when they are full grown and are thinking of descending and turning to pupæ in the ground. This bird is often kept in captivity, either a young one that has been taken from the nest or an old one that has been wounded. During the summer the song of the White-eye is somewhat feeble and uninteresting, but the opposite is the case during the colder months. I have often been astonished at the power and sweetness of its notes. The flight of this species is fairly strong; it sometimes may be seen flying in flocks at a great altitude.

Sub-Family—Myzomelinæ.

*SPINEBILL

(*Acanthorhynchus tenuirostris*, Lath.)

Male.—I have carefully compared typical Tasmanian examples with Gould's description of both *A. tenuirostris* and *A. dubius*, and find the birds tally exactly with neither, but are a compound. Crown of the head shining greenish-black; space between the bill and the eye, ear coverts, lunulated band on the sides of the chest, primaries, and six middle tail feathers black; the remainder of the tail feathers black at base, rest white; back of the neck rufous-chestnut, passing into chestnut-brown on the upper part of the back; secondaries, greater wing coverts, and rump greenish-grey; throat, cheeks, and chest white, the first with a patch of chestnut-brown in the centre; abdomen, flanks, and under tail coverts light chestnut-brown; bill and feet black. Dimensions in mm.:— Length, 140.5; bill, 21; wing, 59.5; tail, 58; tarsus, 20.

The dimensions of the above bird tally with Gould's *A. dubius* except that the bill is slightly shorter.

Female.—Similar in plumage to male.

Young.—" Differs from the adult in being without the crescentic mark on the chest; the throat and chin are uniformly sandy-grey; the rest of the under surface is orange-brown; head and back olive-brown; upper surface of wings glossy greyish-black (plumbaginous), under surface of wings grey; tail feathers, 10 in number, black, except three, which are white for about the half or one-third their length, reckoned from the tip. Iris brown tipped with red; tarsus lead-coloured; upper mandible brown, lower mandible yellow" (J. R. M'Clymont).

Nest.—Cup-shaped and deep; neatly constructed of moss and strips of bark, and lined with grass, then feathers. The situation chosen is usually either the centre of a thick bush or the top of a tea-tree.

Eggs.—Clutch two to three; shape varies from oval with one end somewhat pointed to stoutish oval; texture fine; surface a little glossy; colour pale buff, darker on the apex, sparsely spotted, especially about the apex, with rich brown and a little purplish-grey. Dimensions in mm. of a clutch:—(1) 20.5 x 14.5, (2) 19 x 13, (3) 19.5 x 14.

Breeding Season.—October to December.

Geographical Distribution.—Tasmania, King Island, Furneaux Group, New South Wales, Victoria, South Australia, and Queensland.

Observations.—When hovering Humming Bird-like in front of a flower, the tail is widely spread, plainly displaying the white tail feathers on either side. This Honey-eater is one of if not the most plentiful of its kind in many parts of the island. It is one of the species that most frequently visit the suburban gardens and pay attention to the blossoms of salvia, abutilon, fuchsia, and flowers of a like nature. Its vocal capacities are practically restricted to one note, which is uttered slowly at first then increases in rapidity and volume until it becomes decidedly shrill. For some reason this species is known to boys as the " Painter."

Sub-Family—Meliphaginæ.

*STRONG-BILLED HONEY-EATER
(*Melithreptus validirostris*, Gould).

Male.—Crown of the head, ear coverts, and back of the neck black; a band of white traverses the occiput, terminating at each eye; back, including rump, yellowish-olive; tail brownish-olive; wings brown; chin black; throat white; rest of under surface greyish-brown; bill black; feet pale brown. Dimensions in mm.:
—Length, 148; bill, 15.5; wing, 76; tail, 63; tarsus, 19.

Female.—Similar in plumage to male. Dimensions in mm.:
Length, 148; bill, 14.5; wing, 81; tail, 63; tarsus, 19.

Young.—" In the young bird of this species the mantle is tinged with greenish-olive; the cheeks, lunar mark behind the head from eye to eye, and the centre of abdomen are light yellow, and the bill, cere, and legs are straw-yellow in colour, the black head, ear coverts, and throat remaining prominent " (A. G. Campbell).

Nest.—Cup-shaped and deep; composed of strips of soft bark, wool, and grass-stems; the inside lining is usually the soft flowering heads of grasses. The top of a sapling is very frequently chosen as a site.

Eggs.—Clutch three usually; approximately oval in shape; texture of shell fine; surface without lustre; colour fleshy-pink, more or less spotted and blotched with reddish-brown and dull purplish-brown, the majority of the markings being in the region of the apex. Dimensions in mm. of a clutch:—(1) 22 x 17, (2) 22 x 16, (3) 21 x 17.

Breeding Season.—August to December.

Geographical Distribution.—Tasmania and King Island.

Observations.—In a number of districts this fine Honey-eater is fairly plentiful. The denser portions of the scrub are almost always resorted to, it being seldom that one sees this species out in the open the same as almost any of the Honey-eaters. Its manner of feeding during the autmun and winter months reminds one of a Tree-creeper. The agility with which it runs up and down the perpendicular stems of the trees, poking its bill into the crevices of the bark and detaching loose pieces, is wonderful. I have seen them so plentiful in a belt of thick scrub that the noise of their beaks and feet on the loose dry bark sounded like the pattering of dogs on dry leaves. While feeding a somewhat sharp whistling note is frequently uttered, in addition to which a fair amount of quarrelling is continually going on.

*BLACK-HEADED HONEY-EATER

(*Melithreptus melanocephalus,* Gould).

Male.—Head black; upper surface greyish or brownish olive tail blackish, outer fringes greyish; wings slightly more brown than the back; lower throat and chest almost pure white; breast and abdomen greyish-white; sides of the body greyish; bill black; legs and feet pale brown. Dimensions in mm.:—Length, 142; bill, 12; wing, 76; tail, 61; tarsus, 19.

Female.—Slightly duller in colouration, but otherwise similar.

Young.—Head and upper surface brownish; cheeks and throat brownish-black; bill brownish.

Nest.—Usually placed at the end of a slender horizontal branch of a peppermint, white gum, or sometimes stringy-bark; a thick clump of leaves is chosen, so that the nest is practically invisible from the ground. It is cup-shaped and somewhat deep; sometimes it is placed high, at others low; the vicinity of a creek is nearly always chosen. Wool is the chief constituent; scraps of green moss are woven into the outside to make it harmonize with its surroundings.

Eggs.—Clutch three, sometimes with the addition of one of the Pallid Cuckoo; roundish oval in shape; texture fine; surface slightly glossy; colour pale fleshy-pink, only moderately spotted and blotched with reddish-brown and purplish-brown; most of the markings are about the apex. Dimensions in mm. of a clutch:—(1) 20.5 x 14.5, (2) 20 x 13, (3) 19 x 14.

Breeding Season.—November to end of December. Frequently three broods are reared.

Geographical Distribution.—Tasmania, King Island, and Furneaux Group.

Observations.—From my own experience and that of other observers, this species does not appear to be as plentiful in the northern portion of the island as in the southern. In its general habits it strongly resembles the Strong-billed Honey-eater.

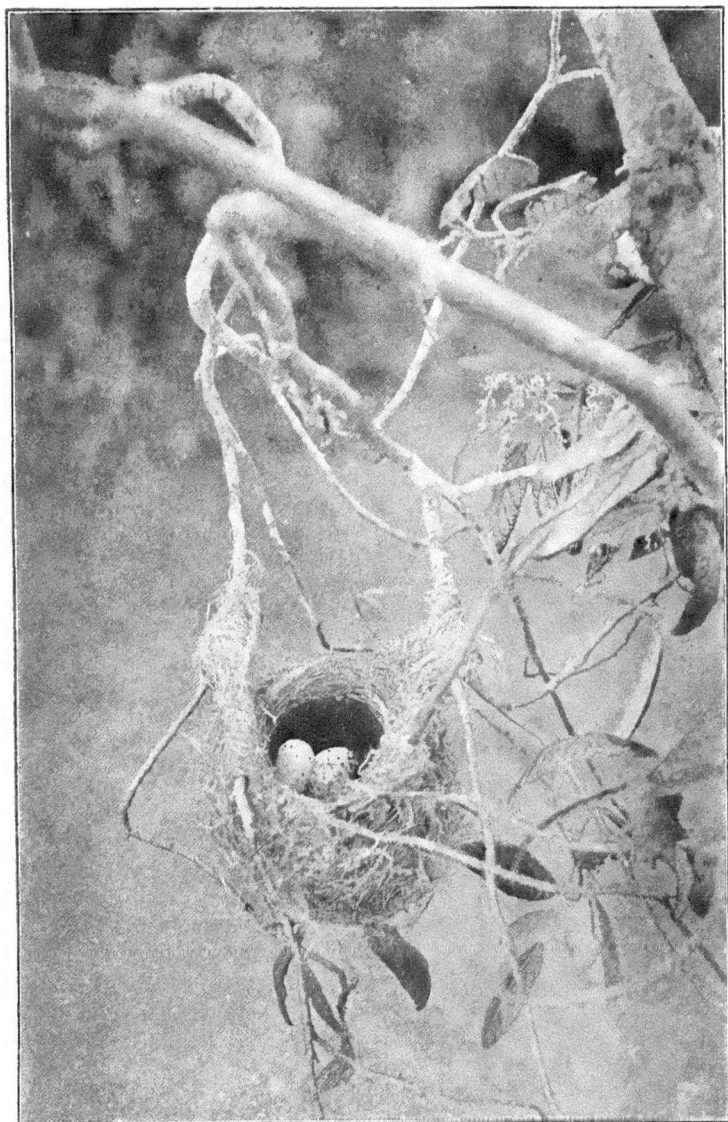

NEST OF BLACK-HEADED HONEY-EATER.

Photo. by H. C. THOMPSON.

YELLOW-THROATED HONEY-EATER
(Nest under leaves on left of picture).

Photo. by H. C. THOMPSON.

A rather curious trait that has been observed by all who have had anything to do with the taking of this species' nest, and which was first recorded by Mr. A. E. Brent, is the manner in which the female bird clings to the nest when the tree in which it is built is being felled and has even crashed to the ground.

*FULVOUS-FRONTED OR TAWNY-CROWNED HONEY-EATER

(Glycyphila fulvifrons, Lewin).

Male.—Crown of the head tawny; eyebrow white; a line of brownish-black commences at the base of the bill, passes through the eye down the sides of the neck to the breast; back dark brown, shafts of the feathers greyish-white; wings and tail dark brown, inner webs of quills edged with fulvous; throat, breast, and abdomen white; sides of body and flanks ashy-brown; irides light brown; bill blackish-brown; legs and feet brown. Dimensions in mm.:—Length, 155; bill, 16.5; wing, 81; tail, 70; tarsus, 23.

Female.—Similar to male.

Young.—A prominent patch of yellow on the throat, which disappears when the birds put on adult plumage.

Nest.—Cup-shaped and deep; usually constructed of pieces of soft bark and grass-stems; a few spiders' cocoons are often added; lined inside with soft grass, and then wool or cow-hair. A favourite situation is in a low bush in open country. At both Kelso and Bridport nests have been taken from the centre of a grass-tree (*Xanthorrhœa*).

Eggs.—Clutch two usually; inclined to oval in shape; texture fine; surface fairly glossy; colour white, faintly tinged with pink and sparingly spotted with chestnut or purplish brown or black. Dimensions in mm. of a clutch :—(1) 21 x 14, (2) 20.5 x 14.

Breeding Season.—August to December.

Geographical Distribution.—Tasmania and Kent Group; also New South Wales, Victoria, South and Western Australia.

Observations.—Open, sandy, heath-clad country is mostly favoured by this Honey-eater, which is not at all plentiful in the island. Its flight is the most rapid of any of our Honey-eaters.

I have but few records of this species in Tasmania beyond the two localities above given, they being Lilydale, Waratah, Wilmot, and the country lying about St. Helens.

*YELLOW-THROATED HONEY-EATER

(Ptilotis flavigularis, Gould)·

Male.—Head and cheeks blackish-grey; ear coverts greyish-white; upper surface, including wings and tail, dark yellowish-olive; throat gamboge-yellow; chest blackish-grey; abdomen pale grey tinged with olive-green; bill black; legs and feet deep blackish-brown. Dimensions in mm.:—Length, 192; bill, 14; wing, 93; tail, 95; tarsus, 24.

Female.—Similar in plumage to male.

Young.—Upper and under surfaces greyish; no yellow on throat.

Nest.—A warmly constructed cup-shaped structure; outwardly composed of soft bark, twigs, grass, and spiders' web; the inside lining being usually fur, wool, hair, and the like. Although the usual situation is in a low bush, yet at times the centre of a clump of band-grass is chosen. Then, again, another nest was in a tea-tree bush overhanging a river and some 10 feet from the surface of the water.

Eggs.—Clutch two to three; somewhat oval in shape; texture fine; surface slightly glossy; colour a delicate pinkish-white, sparingly spotted with reddish-brown and purplish-grey; the majority of the markings are frequently concentrated in an open zone round the larger end. Dimensions in mm. of a clutch:—(1) 25 x 17, (2) 25.5 x 16.75, (3) 24 x 16.5.

A clutch from Flinders Island differs in three respects from the above one—viz., the ground colour is deeper; there is no zone, but the spots are somewhat thickly scattered over the stouter end; and the purplish-grey predominates. Dimensions in mm. of this clutch:—(1) 26 x 19, (2) 27 x 19, (3) 26 x 19.5.

Breeding Season.—August to December.

Geographical Distribution.—Tasmania, King and several other islands in Bass Strait.

Observations.—The Yellow-throated Honey-eater is fairly well distributed over the island. In some districts it is very plentiful, while in others, where the nature of the country does not suit it, it is rare, if not altogether wanting. It favours fairly heavily timbered country, from whence it procures its food, when flowering trees and shrubs are not plentiful, which consists of various kinds of insects obtained from under the bark of the trees of its haunts, as well as flies, &c. The vocal powers of the species are practically limited to a loud whistle-like call note, often repeated. The favourite position when uttering this call note is on the topmost bough of some tree or sapling.

In several districts in Northen Tasmania where " small fruit " growing is rather extensively gone in for, this Honey-eater is considered a perfect pest during the spring and summer months, owing to the ravages it makes among the cherries, currants, and gooseberries. Its local name in these districts is the "Green Cherry-Picker."

*CRESCENT HONEY-EATER (Tasmanian Honey-eater)

(*Meliornis australasiana*, Shaw).

Male.—Upper surface, including head, dusky-black; tail brownish-black, fringed with golden-yellow at the base; two outermost feathers with a large and the third with a medium-sized oval

CRESCENT HONEY-EATER AND NEST.

From "The Emu."

Photo. by A. H. E. Mattingley.

spot of white on the inner webs at the tip; wings blackish-brown, primaries and secondaries margined externally, especially at their bases, with golden-yellow; a black stripe passes from the base of the bill through the eye, and a lunar-shaped mark of the same colour traverses each side of the chest and nearly meets in the middle; a narrow stripe above the eye, one behind the lunar-shaped mark, and the throat and chest white; a narrow streak of brown traverses the centre of each feather on the latter; centre of the abdomen also white; flanks and under tail coverts dusky grey; bill, legs, and feet black. Dimensions in mm.:—Length, 155; bill, 15.5; wing, 77; tail, 81; tarsus, 22.5.

Female.—Both upper and lower surfaces are nearly uniform dusky-brown; no stripe over the eye, nor white spots on the lateral tail feathers; golden-yellow on the wings reduced to a tinge only; lunar-shaped mark on chest practically absent; throat pale brownish-grey. Dimensions in mm.:—Length, 152; bill, 15; wing, 70; tail, 62; tarsus, 22.

Nest.—A stout and deep cup-shaped structure, composed of strips of bark and twigs; the lining consists of soft grass and the flowering stalks of certain mosses. It is placed either among bracken ferns or else in the centre of a clump of sword-grass. Occasionally the nest is ornamented on the outside with tiny clumps of moss of the colour of its surroundings.

Eggs.—Clutch three generally, four sometimes; roundish oval in shape; texture fine; surface slightly glossy; colour delicate fleshy-pink, spotted and blotched round the apex with reddish-brown and dull purplish-brown. Dimensions in mm. of a clutch: —(1) 19 x 14.5, (2) 19 x 14, (3) 19.25 x 14.

Breeding Season.—August to December.

Geographical Distribution.—Tasmania, King and several other islands in Bass Strait, New South Wales, Victoria, South Australia, and South Queensland.

Observations.—Not only is this species fairly plentiful on open heath (*Epacris*) and honeysuckle (*Banksia*) clad country, but also among tea-tree scrubs, where its sharp whistling notes are very frequently to be heard, especially during the breeding season. Its movements are quick, as also is its flight. In disposition it is fairly tame, allowing one to approach to within a short distance before taking flight.

Even during the spring and summer months, when flowering plants are plentiful, it is an adroit pursuer of flies and the like. During the autumn and winter months it lives almost entirely on insect diet. Like the Spinebill, it is often a common object in suburban gardens, feeding on the nectar from various flowering shrubs, and making its presence known by its loud and sharp (slightly metallic) whistle, which is almost invariably uttered from the top of a tree or bush. The Tasmanian Honey-eater is perhaps the commonest and most noisy species of Honey-eater that frequents suburban gardens, though the Spinebill runs it close.

*WHITE-BEARDED OR NEW HOLLAND HONEY-EATER

(*Meliornis nova-hollandiæ*, Latham).

Male.—May be briefly described as being black, white, and yellow. Detailed description:—Crown of head and cheeks black, with minute white feathers on the forehead round the base of the upper mandible; a superciliary stripe and a small patch on either side of the lower mandible white; upper surface brownish-black, with a little white showing on upper back; tail brownish-black, tipped on inner webs with white, except the three centre feathers, which are wholly black; wings black, the outer edges of the quills tinged with rich yellow; throat black, with fine white bristle-like feathers in centre; rest of under surface white, striped with black; irides white; bill black; legs and feet brown. Dimensions in mm.: —Length, 176; bill, 19; wing, 78; tail, 80; tarsus, 23.

Female.—Similar to male.

Young.—" In an adolescent male and an adolescent female the malar tufts of the adult were absent; the small projecting white feathers on each side of the base of the lower mandible of the adult were also absent, but there were a few small buffy-white feathers which extended from the base of the lower mandible to the ears; the hair-like feathers on the chin were darker in colour than the corresponding feathers of the adult; the heads were not black but brownish-black, and the colours of the breast-feathers were not markedly contrasted. The feathers of the mantle of the adult are black, with white edges; those feathers of the adolescent birds were uniform dusky-brown; the bills were brown, blended with horn colour " (J. R. M'Clymont).

Nest.—Cup-shaped; composed of bark, fine twigs, grass, and wool; inside lining usually the flowers of the native " flax " or fur and wool. Placed not far from the ground, in a thick bush.

Eggs.—Clutch two to three usually, four rarely; oval and of fine texture; surface slightly glossy; colour pinkish-buff; the spots, which are principally reddish-chestnut, are concentrated round the stouter end, giving that part a decidedly pinky tinge. Dimensions in mm. of a clutch:—(1) 21 x 15, (2) 21 x 15.25; (3) 20.75 x 15.

Breeding Season.—August to December.

Geographical Distribution.—Tasmania and a number of islands in Bass Strait; also New South Wales, Victoria, South Australia, and part of Queensland.

Observations.—In many localities throughout Tasmania this Honey-eater is decidedly plentiful.

The Spinebill, the Crescent, and this species are frequently found in close company. *Banksia* and *Epacris* country is mostly favoured. Suburban gardens are often visited for what they contain in the way of salvia, daphne, and abutilon bushes. Soft fruits, such as grapes and ripe pears, are readily eaten if placed within reach. Its movements on the ground remind one much of

NEST OF NEW HOLLAND HONEY-EATER.

Photo. by H. C. THOMPSON.

the English Magpie. When moving among the branches of a bush, either in search of insects or for the purpose of extracting honey from the blossoms, its actions are somewhat slow—it has not the bright alertness of either the Spinebill or the Crescent Honey-eater. On being approached when feeding, instead of taking alarm and at once flying away, it will dodge the observer round the tree or bush, taking care to keep as far away as possible.

*MINER

(*Myzantha* (*Manorhina*) *garrula*, Lath.)

Male.—Forehead greyish-white; crown of the head, ear coverts, and base of the jaws black; hind-neck grey, narrowly barred with whitish; back dark grey, slightly washed with yellow, with black shaft-streaks to feathers; rump and upper tail coverts a little lighter; tail feathers brownish-grey, black on the inner webs; the centre ones have the extreme outer webs yellow; all are broadly tipped with white; wing coverts same colour as back, lesser series fringed with yellow; primaries brownish-black, greyish-white on the outer webs; secondaries brownish-black on inner webs, greyish on outer, which are broadly fringed with yellow; chin and throat blackish down the centre; lower throat, sides of the neck, and upper breast greyish, with sub-terminal crescent-shaped marks of dark brown; lower breast with dark shaft-streaks on terminal half of feathers only; abdomen grey; under tail coverts white; bill yellow; legs and feet yellowish flesh colour.   Dimensions in mm. :— Length, 280; bill, 24.5; wing, 134; tail, 133; tarsus, 33.

Female.—Resembles male. Dimensions in mm. :—Length, 277; bill, 16.5; wing, 150; tail, 128; tarsus, 33.

Young.—Closely resemble adults.

Nest.—Cup-shaped and open; very frequently frailly con-structed, but sometimes the opposite is the case; fine twigs, grass-stems, shreds of bark, and rootlets play the chief part in its composition; a varied assortment of substances is used for lining, such as horse-hair, grass-stems, bark, feathers (rarely), wool, &c. The forked branches of a tree or sapling are chosen as a resting place for the structure. As a rule the nest is never placed very high up, though often it is difficult of access.

Eggs.—Clutch three to four; oval to round oval in shape; texture fine; surface glossy; the ground colour is pinky-white, spotted and blotched all over with reddish-chestnut and purplish-grey; in boldly marked specimens there is a large patch of reddish-chestnut at the apex. Other specimens are very thickly and evenly spotted all over with small spots of colouring matter. Dimen-sions in mm. of an average clutch :—(1) 28.5 x 20, (2) 26.5 x 20, (3) 28 x 20.5, (4) 29 x 19.75.

Breeding Season.—August to December.

Geographical Distribution.—Tasmania, New South Wales, Victoria, South Australia, and South Queensland.

Observations.—For some reason almost if not quite impossible to determine, this species is very irregularly distributed over the island. From many districts where other Honey-eaters are plentiful it is entirely absent. Cultivated and semi-cultivated tracts are its favourite haunts. It is, perhaps, the noisiest of any of our birds; it keeps up an almost unceasing chatter in a scolding voice. Should one happen to be stalking some other bird or animal, and a Miner be in the vicinity, it will speedily give warning of one's presence by loud cries of alarm. It often associates in flocks 20 to 30 strong Though appearing to court the company of other species, it is nevertheless of a quarrelsome disposition, continually engaging in heated argument over nothing in particular. The food of this species consists principally of the honey from eucalypt and honeysuckle blossoms. All descriptions of insects are also consumed. A large proportion of its insect food is procured on the ground from among the grass and on cultivated fields. When feeding in the trees many curious antics are performed as it clings by its feet to the extreme tips of the twigs. The flight is very laboured, and progress slow. By the way in which the wings are used one would imagine great speed was being evolved; it is altogether an ugly flier.

WATTLE-BIRD

(*Acanthochæra inauris*, Gould).

Male.—Crown of the head and back of the neck striped with black and grey, each feather being centred with black and fringed with grey; back and shoulders dusky-brown; primaries blackish-brown, tipped with white; outer webs greyish-white; two centre tail feathers dark grey, rest blackish-brown, all broadly tipped with white, giving the under side of the tail a graduated appearance; chin white; neck blackish-grey, feathers obscurely tipped with silvery-grey; feathers on chest grey and lanceolate, narrowly centred with black; breast and flanks buffy-grey, the feathers with broad black centres; centre of abdomen rich yellow; bill black; legs and feet light flesh colour; bare skin round the ear, and upper extremity of long, pendulous wattle, which hangs from below the ear, white, gradually deepening into rich orange. Dimensions in mm.:—Length, 397; bill, 21; wing, 160; tail, 235; tarsus, 33.

Female.—Similar to male.

Nest.—Flattish; sometimes bulky; constructed of twigs and grass, and lined with soft grass and fur or wool; usually situated in low to moderate-sized trees.

Eggs.—Clutch two to three; elongated oval in shape; fine of texture; surface glossy; colour salmon-pink, sometimes tinged with buff, moderately spotted and blotched with chestnut-brown and purplish-grey. Dimensions in mm. of a clutch :—(1) 37 x 23, (2) 35 x 24, (3) 36 x 24.

Breeding Season.—August to December.

Geographical Distribution.—Tasmania and King Island.

Observations.—On the mainland the place of this species, whose correct vernacular designation is that of the Yellow Wattle-Bird, is taken by the Red Wattle-Bird (*A. carunculata*). Only certain favourable districts are frequented by the Wattle-Bird—favourable both as regards climate and food. Altogether the species is very irregularly distributed through the island. It is among the most highly esteemed of our game birds. Owing to the great slaughter that had taken place during former years, and fearing that the species was in danger of extinction, it was decided in 1901 to afford the species two years' absolute protection. This was enforced during 1902-3.

During the seasons in which flowering eucalypts are plentiful the birds become very fat and weigh at least 6 ozs. During the winter its food consists of the honey from eucalypt blossoms and honey-suckle cones. In summer, as the honeysuckles alone are in flower, insects, especially beetles, are added to its diet. In some districts the eucalypts flower one year and in others the next; the consequence is that the Wattle-Bird moves from one district to another in search of food. I have known it to be very plentiful one season and the next hardly a bird was to be seen or heard. In summer it resorts to the mountain slopes, returning to the plains as winter approaches. The harder the winter frosts, the more plentiful is the bird expected to be. The thickly-wooded plains are warmer than the mountain slopes. It soon becomes very wild after being shot at, and is therefore difficult to approach, giving the alarm and taking flight at the least sign of danger. I have heard of it when feeding in honeysuckles (*Banksia*) allowing one to approach really close, but have had no experience of this personally, for my dealings with the species have always been among the topmost twigs of lofty eucalypts. It moves in flocks, which vary greatly in numerical strength. I do not know whether as a rule the Wattle-Bird sleeps at its feeding ground, but at the first glimpse of daylight it can be heard among the tree-tops. I have watched large flocks leaving their feeding ground at dusk, and moving further into the bush. The voice of this species is most remarkable, and once heard is not easily forgotten or mistaken for that of any other bird. The cry is loud and harsh, and is between a cough and a scolding voice suffering from a cold in the throat. Its discordant nature is most in evidence when two or more birds are quarrelling.

*BRUSH WATTLE-BIRD

(*Acanthochæra mellivora*, Lath.)

Male.—Upper surface dark brown, shafts streaked white; feathers on lower back, rump, and upper tail coverts tipped with white; the last-mentioned feathers are greyish; tail brown tipped with white, fringes olive, shafts black; greater and lesser wing coverts greyish, tipped with white; primaries, basal three-quarters of inner webs chestnut, outer webs and terminal quarter of inner blackish-brown; secondaries blackish-brown, fringed with olive; chin, throat, and fore-neck greyish-black, tipped with white; feathers of chest and sides of neck lanceolate, basal half grey, terminal black, shaft-streaks white; breast and abdomen brownish, broadly centred and tipped with white; from each side of the upper edge of the breast springs a small tuft of semi-decomposed white feathers, which project slightly when the bird is excited; under tail coverts whitish; bill black; legs and feet brown. Dimensions in mm.:—Length, 329; bill, 23; wing, 135; tail, 158; tarsus, 28.

Female.—Plumage similar to male save that the tufts on the side of the breast are absent.

Young.—Similar to adults, only the markings are less pronounced.

In no work of reference can I find any mention of the breast-tufts, which resemble those on the sides of the throat of the Tui or Parson-Bird of New Zealand, only smaller and nearly straight instead of incurved. In cabinet skins and mounted specimens the feathers lie down flat on the breast and are indistinguishable from the others unless searched for.

Nest.—Flattish and moderately well built; constructed of fine twigs and lined with fine shredded bark. Usually situated in the fork of a tree or bush.

Eggs.—Clutch two usually. Shape varies from oval to long oval; texture of shell fine; surface moderately glossy; ground colour usually salmon-pink, fairly well blotched and spotted, especially about the apex, with reddish-brown and dull purplish-grey. Dimensions in mm. of a clutch:—(1) 27 x 19, (2) 26 x 19.5.

Breeding Season.—September to December.

Geographical Distribution.—Tasmania, Victoria, New South Wales, South Australia, and South Queensland.

Observations.—The same class of country is frequented as by the Wattle-Bird, with the difference that it will continue to feed among the honeysuckles no matter how scarce the flowering cones, whereas the Wattle-Bird will readily forsake the banksias for eucalypts well out in flower. Such has been my experience; of course, in different districts it might develop other traits. At no time does one see large flocks of this species. In disposition it is very noisy and quarrelsome, in some respects being an exact counterpart of the Miner. Its note is very disagreeable, being very harsh and guttural.

" The Brush Wattle-Bird is a bold and spirited species, evincing a considerable degree of pugnacity, fearlessly attacking and driving away all other birds from the part of the tree on which it is feeding; and there are few of the Honey-eaters whose actions are more sprightly and animated. During the months of spring and summer the male perches on some elevated branch and screams forth its harsh and peculiar notes, which have not inaptly been said to resemble a person in the act of vomiting, whence the native name of ' Goo-gwar-ruck,' in which the natives have endeavoured to imitate this very singular note. While thus employed it frequently jerks up its tail, throws back its head, and distends its throat, as if great exertion was required to force out these harsh and guttural sounds" (Gould).

FAMILY—DIC/EID/E (3 species).

*YELLOW-TIPPED PARDALOTE (Diamond-Bird)

(Pardalotus affinis, Gould).

Male.—" Forehead black; crown of head black, with a stripe of white down the centre of each feather; a stripe of yellow commences at the base of the upper mandible and runs above the eye, where it is joined by a stripe of white, which leads nearly to the occiput; back of the neck and back greyish olive-brown; rump and upper tail coverts yellowish olive-brown; wings blackish, each of the primaries having a fine round spot of white near the tip, and the third externally edged with white, the secondaries margined with white and rufous, and the tips of the spurious wing yellow; tail blackish-brown, each feather having a transverse mark of white at the tip; ear coverts and cheeks grey; throat yellow; middle of chest and abdomen light yellow intermixed with white; flanks yellowish olive-brown; bill black; feet brown " (Gould). Dimensions in mm. :—Length, 102; bill, 7; wing, 71; tail, 34; tarsus, 19. (I have compared the above description by Gould with specimens from various parts of the island, and as they tally exactly I did not see the utility of redescribing the bird.) The dimensions, however, are taken from a bird selected at random from a series from different districts.

Female.—Similar to male.

Nest.—Although a hole in the side of a tree, either some distance up or close to the ground, is usually chosen as a site, yet sometimes the nest will be placed in a hole in the side of a bank, notably the sandy cliffs at Berriedale. The nest itself is constructed of fine pieces of bark and grass, with a warm lining of feathers.

Eggs.—Clutch four to five; stout or roundish oval in shape; texture fine; surface glossy; colour pure white. Dimensions in

6

mm. of a clutch :—(1) 17.5 x 13, (2) 18 x 14, (3) 19 x 13.5, (4) 19 x 14, (5) 18 x 14.

Breeding Season.—September to January.

Geographical Distribution.—Tasmania, King and some other islands in Bass Strait, New South Wales, Victoria, South Australia, and South Queensland.

Observations.—When all else is still in the bush the monotonous " Sleep, baby " cry of this Pardalote may be heard issuing from the tops of the loftiest eucalypts. In some districts it is a very plentiful species, and may be seen in small flocks moving from tree-top to tree-top. Occasionally it descends into the low scrub and may be observed busily searching the under sides of the boughs and leaves for insects. I have never observed it descend in heavily timbered country, but always in light-wooded tracts. In addition to insects, it feeds on seeds of various descriptions. Small flocks sometimes come out of the bush and visit the trees in suburban gardens, especially during autumn and winter.

*SPOTTED PARDALOTE (DIAMOND-BIRD)
(*Pardalotus punctatus*, Temm.)

Male.—"Crown of the head, wings, and tail black, each feather having a round spot of white at the tip; a stripe of white commences at the nostrils and passes over the eye; ear coverts and sides of the neck grey; feathers of the back grey at the base, succeeded by a triangular-shaped spot of fawn colour, and edged with black; rump rufous-brown; upper tail coverts crimson; throat, chest, and under tail coverts yellow; abdomen and flanks tawny; bill black; feet brown " (Gould). Dimensions in mm. of an average bird from the Launceston district :—Length, 87; bill, 6; wing, 56; tail, 33; tarsus, 18.

Female.—Upper surface differs from that of the male in that the feathers on the crown of the head are tipped with pale yellow and edged with black; throat and chest whitish, instead of yellow; rest of plumage as in male. Dimensions in mm. :—Length, 97; bill, 6; wing, 58; tail, 34; tarsus, 20.

Young.—Fully fledged, each and every feather on the upper surface and head tipped with a beautiful golden-orange.

Nest.—Almost invariably if not invariably the nest is placed in a hollow cavity at the end of a tunnel varying in length from 1 foot to 3 feet drilled in the side of a railway cutting, sand-pit, or almost any bank at all suitable. I have found nests in a low bank at the side of a road along which much daily traffic passed. The tunnel is always drilled in a slightly upward direction. The nest is spherical in shape, and composed of fine and soft strips of bark, with a lining of grass and feathers. A nest containing five fully fledged young birds was composed entirely of fine grasses.

Eggs.—Clutch four to five; fairly round in shape; texture fine; surface slightly lustrous; colour pure white. Dimensions in mm.

of a clutch:—(1) 16.5 x 13, (2) 16 x 13, (3) 15.75 x 13, (4) 16 x 12.75, (5) 16 x 13.

Breeding Season.—August to December.

Geographical Distribution.—Tasmania and some of the larger islands in Bass Strait; also New South Wales, Victoria, South and Western Australia, and Queensland.

Observations.—Unlike any of the other Pardalotes, this species mostly frequents heavily scrubbed country, and but seldom goes into the tops of the gums in search of food. Its time is spent either on the ground or among the thick undergrowth, where it finds an abundance of insect food. In disposition it is shy, and very quick to take flight; its movements among the trees are quick and eager. Like the Fire-tailed Finch (*Zonæginthus bellus*), the Spotted Pardalote has almost disappeared from several districts where it was at one time plentiful, owing to the great clearing operations that have been going on during the past few years.

*FORTY-SPOTTED PARDALOTE (Diamond-Bird)
(*Pardalotus quadragintus*, Gould).

Male.—" Crown of the head and all of the upper surface bright olive-green, each feather obscurely margined with brown; wings brownish-black, all the feathers except the first and second primaries having a conspicuous spot of white near their extremities; tail blackish-grey, the extreme tips of the feathers being white; cheeks and under tail coverts yellowish-olive; throat and under surface greyish-white, passing into olive on the flanks; bill blackish-brown; feet brown" (Gould). Dimensions in mm.:—Length, 94; bill, 7; wing, 56; tail, 32; tarsus, 17.

Female.—Similar to male.

Nest.—A hole in the side of a lofty eucalypt is the usual site chosen for the nest, which is constructed of fine shredded bark and grasses.

Eggs.—Clutch four; somewhat roundish in shape; texture fine; surface slightly glossy; colour pure white. Dimensions in mm. of a clutch:—(1) 16 x 12.5, (2) 15.5 x 12.5, (3) 16 x 13, (4) 15.75 x 13.

Breeding Season.—September to January.

Geographical Distribution.—Tasmania and King Island.

Observations.—The southern portion of the island is the stronghold of this little Pardalote. So far as I am aware, it has not yet been seen in any of the northern districts. Like the Yellow-tipped species it spends most of its time among the tops of lofty eucalypts, where, on account of its coat assimilating in colour to that of its surroundings, it is seldom seen unless specially searched for. Mr. A. L. Butler writes me that in addition to Hobart he has seen the Forty-spotted Pardalote on the East Coast above Swansea, and further down the coast, and also at Port Esperance. I have found it in a few localities on the North-East Coast.

FAMILY—HIRUNDINIDÆ (3 species).

*SWALLOW

(*Hirundo neoxena*, Gould).

Male.—Frontal band deep brick-red, extending from above each eye; head, ear-coverts, and back glossy blue; tail blackish, slightly glossed with green, the tip of the outer web of all save the two centre feathers and the outermost on each side with a small round spot of white; wing coverts and quills blackish-brown, externally washed with steel-blue; cheeks and throat brick-red; remainder of under surface mouse-brown; bill, legs, and feet black. Dimensions in mm. :—Length, 145; bill, 7.5; wing, 111; tail, 70; tarsus, 9.5.

Female.—Similar to male.

Nest.—Composed of small pellets of mud or clay, built up line upon line, mingled with short lengths of grass or straw to give greater adherence to the structure; in shape it resembles a shallow bowl. Many and varied are the places chosen to cement the structure to, some such being the side of a cave, a cliff, inside a hollow tree, under a bridge, pier, wharf or culvert, on the rafters inside any class of building, and under the eaves; or, in fact, in any nook or angle where it is possible to attach a nest. There are a number of records of " freak " situations being chosen. A pair of birds will return to the same nest year after year, a little more material being added to the outside each succeeding season. The length of time the construction of a nest takes depends greatly on the distance to be traversed for suitable material. With mud and clay of the proper consistency close at hand, three days will see the outside wall well on towards completion. The structure is very warmly lined with feathers.

Eggs.—Clutch four generally; stout oval in shape; texture very fine; surface glossy; ground colour warm or pinky white, freckled with numerous small spots of reddish-brown and umber or slate. The markings are heavier about the larger end. Dimensions in mm. of a clutch :—(1) 18 x 13.5, (2) 18 x 13, (3) 19 x 13, (4) 17.75 x 13.25.

Breeding Season.—September to December or January, when two to three broods are raised.

Geographical Distribution.—Tasmania, King Island, and Australia in general.

Observations.—It is impossible to fix exact dates for the arrival and departure of the Swallow. From observations ranging over a number of years, the date of arrival of the vanguard varies from the first week in July to the first week in September. The date of departure also varies greatly, a number of birds often remaining well into April. It often happens that individual birds remain the winter through in some districts; this frequently happens on the North-West Coast, and several instances have come under my notice here in Launceston. During the winter of 1909 a small flock of five remained throughout the winter in this city. When the time approaches for the winter migration, hundreds of Swallows may be seen in the early part of almost any autumn round Low Head, at the mouth of the River Tamar. Migration usually takes place towards dusk. Its note is sweet, but weak; when on the wing it often utters a short, shrill cry. The general habits of this species are too well known to enlarge upon.

*TREE-MARTIN
(*Petrochelidon nigricans*, Vieill.)

Male.—Frontal band pale brick-red, extending to corner of each eye; ear coverts blackish; head and upper back deep steel-blue; lower back and rump whitish-brown, slightly washed with greyish-red; tail feathers dusky-brown; lesser wing coverts deep steel-blue; the remainder, also the quills, dusky-brown; innermost secondaries narrowly tipped with white; sides of neck sandy-buff, streaked with dull black; throat whitish, tinged with buff, the feathers having blackish shafts; neck, chest, and sides of body pale sandy-rufous; chest and abdomen whitish, tinged with pale sandy-rufous; under tail coverts deep sandy-rufous; bill, legs, and feet pale brown. Dimensions in mm.:—Length, 133; bill, 6.5; wing, 112; tail, 55; tarsus, 11.

Female.—Similar to male.

Young.—No frontal band; upper surface dusky-brown blotched with blue; under surface buffy-white.

Nest.—Generally a hollow broken limb or a hole in an elbowed limb is chosen, and a lining of eucalypt leaves placed therein. Mr. H. C. Thompson has come across instances where this species has routed Swallows out of their homes, and, after making some alterations, put a lining of leaves in and laid.

Eggs.—Clutch three to five; stout oval to oval in shape; texture of shell fine; surface glossy; colour pearly-white, more or less very finely freckled with pale reddish. Dimensions in mm. of a stout oval clutch:—(1) 17 x 13, (2) 17.5 x 13, (3) 18 x 12.5, (4) 17 x 12.5. A beautiful clutch in Mr. H. C. Thompson's collection differs from the usual type in that three of the four eggs are somewhat heavily freckled and spotted, especially about the apex, with rich chestnut, the fourth egg being quite normal. Dimensions in mm. of this clutch, which is elliptical in shape:—(1) 21 x 14, (2) 20 x 14, (3) 19.5 x 13.5, (4) 21 x 13.5.

Breeding Season.—September to December.

Geographical Distribution.—Tasmania, King Island, Australia in general; also New Zealand, Aru Islands, New Briton, New Guinea, and Ke Islands.

Observations.—It is usually late September or early October before this species puts in an appearance. Semi-cleared areas with lofty trees are its usual haunts. Although when on the wing it resembles the Welcome Swallow, it may be distinguished from that species by its bright-coloured rump and absence of red on the throat. As a general rule it flies high among and over the tree-tops; it also may frequently be seen in small flocks gliding gracefully among the tree-stems at no great height. Occasionally it even descends to the ground to gather food. The range of this species cannot be defined exactly as far as this island is concerned, but there are a number of localities in various parts where it is never seen. In disposition it is shy, but should nothing occur to disturb it when it has taken up its abode near a habitation it will become comparatively tame, but not as much so as the Welcome Swallow. By the end of April every Tree-Martin has disappeared.

FAIRY MARTIN
(*Petrochelidon ariel*, Gould).

Male.—Crown of the head rust-red; nape of the neck dark blue, edged with rufous; upper back and shoulders dark blue; lower back and rump creamy-white, tinged with pale dusky-brown; tail feathers dusky-brown, outer webs glossed with blue; sides of face and ear coverts dusky-brown; cheeks and throat white; neck, sides of body, and flanks sandy-brown; the feathers on the throat and neck have dark shafts; breast and abdomen white; under tail coverts white, with a dusky tinge; "bill blackish-grey; legs and feet olive-grey; iris blackish-brown" (Gould). Dimensions in mm.:—Length, 116; bill, 6.5; wing, 93; tail, 48; tarsus, 10.

Female.—Similar to male.

Young.—Crown of head, also nape, dull brick-red; upper back and shoulders blackish-brown, with obscure sandy edges to the feathers; lower back and rump creamy-white, faintly tinged with pale sandy; upper tail coverts blackish-grey; tail feathers blackish-brown; greater wing coverts and quills blackish-brown; the secondaries and greater wing coverts are tipped, the former narrowly and the latter broadly, with pale sandy; cheeks and throat whitish; neck, sides of body, and flanks very pale sandy; feathers on throat and neck have dark shafts as in adult; breast and abdomen creamy-white.

Nest.—"The long, bottle-shaped nest is composed of mud or clay, and, like that of the Common Martin (of Europe), is only worked at in the morning and evening. These birds appear to work in small companies, six or seven assisting in the formation of each nest, one remaining within and receiving the mud brought by others in their mouths. In shape these nests are nearly round, but vary in size from 4 to 6 or 7 inches in diameter, the spouts of some being 8 or 9 inches in length. When built on the sides of rocks, or in the hollows of trees, they are placed without any

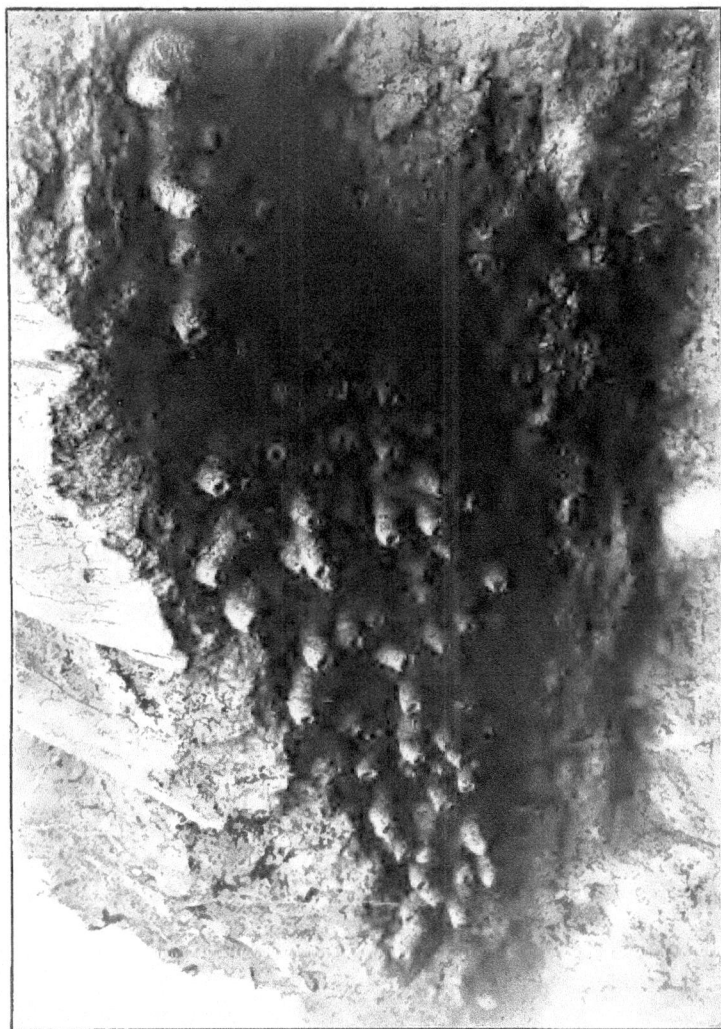

NESTS OF COLONY OF FAIRY MARTINS.

Photo. by C. A. BARNARD.   *From* " THE EMU."

regular order in clusters of thirty or forty together, some of the spouts inclining downwards, others at right angles, &c." (Gould).

Eggs.—" Clutch four to five; lengthened in form or oval; texture of shell very fine; surface glossy; colour white, but occasionally faintly freckled, especially about the apex, with light yellowish-brown. Dimensions in inches :—(1) .7 x .48, (2) .7 x .48, (3) .7 x . 48 " (A. J. Campbell).

Breeding Season.—August to October.

Geographical Distribution.—Tasmania (occasional) and Australia in general.

Observations.—According to Mr. A. J. Campbell, " Mr. S. H. Wintle, geologist, was the first observer to direct attention (*Victorian Naturalist*, February, 1887) to the fact that the Fairy Martin should be placed on the Tasmanian list of avifauna, because he had found the bird breeding at Bridport the season of 1883 and other years." No birds of this species were visible at that place when I visited it during the breeding season on two occasions. Dr. W. Macgillivray is reported by the same authority to have seen individuals about Launceston in October, 1893. I have no personal knowledge of this species in Tasmania, nor have Messrs. Arthur Butler, H. C. Thompson, H. Stuart Dove, or several other observers from whom I inquired.

FAMILY—MOTACILLIDÆ (1 species).

GROUND-LARK (Pipit)

(*Anthus australis*, Vig. and Horsf.)

Male.—Head distinctly blackish, striped with fawn-buff; upper back fawn-buff, the feathers largely centred with black; shoulders, lower back, and rump more uniform fawn-buff; upper tail coverts tawny; tail feathers blackish-brown, edged with fulvous; outer feathers entirely white save for an oblique mark of brown half-way down the inner web; penultimate white on the outer web, tip, and inner half of inner web; shaft and outer three-quarters of inner web dark brown ; median and greater wing coverts blackish, edged with tawny-buff; primaries dark brown, the inner quills having a very slight whitish tip; secondaries blackish-brown, broadly margined with tawny-buff; lores and a distinct eyebrow while, tinged with fulvous; cheeks pale fulvous; ear coverts pale fulvous, mottled with blackish-brown; throat dull white; fore-neck and chest fulvous, the feathers with broad blackish-brown centres; breast pale buff; abdomen and under tail coverts whitish; sides of body light tawny-buff; the feathers have shaft-streaks of blackish-brown; bill blackish on upper mandible and on terminal half of lower, pale yellowish-brown on basal half; legs and feet pale brown. Dimensions in mm. :—Length, 175; bill, 12; wing, 90; tail, 67; tarsus, 26.5.

Female.—Head, neck, back, tail, and wings more distinctly tawny-buff than male; centres of feathers on fore-neck, chest, and sides of body lighter and narrower than in male. Dimensions in mm. :—Length, 173; bill, 13; wing, 85; tail, 65; tarsus, 26.

Young.—Upper surface more tawny-buff than female; under surface white to creamy-buff; markings on chest and sides of body somewhat indistinct; penultimate feathers of tail with less white than in adults.

Nest.—Circular and moderately deep; constructed of dead grass, and placed either in a slight depression under the shelter of a tuft of grass or a large stone in open grass lands, or else in the centre of a tuft of band-grass. When built in the first-mentioned situation the rim of the nest is usually on a level with the ground. In the second situation I have on occasions found a " colony " of nests in a small area.

Eggs.—Clutch three to four; oval in shape; texture fine; surface more or less glossy; usual ground colour greyish, freckled and marked all over, some specimens more heavily than others, with umber and dull grey. Dimensions in mm. of a clutch :—(1) 24 x 17, (2) 23 x 16, (3) 22.5 x 16.5, (4) 23 x 17.

Breeding Season.—August to January.

Geographical Distribution.—Tasmania, King and a number of other islands in Bass Strait; also the whole of the mainland.

Observations.—Some observers have expressed the opinion that this species is migratory. This is incorrect; but at the same time the bird is nomadic in its habits. There are a number of districts from which it entirely disappears during the autumn and winter months, and others where it is most plentiful during these months. Doubtless the food question plays an important part in its distribution during the various seasons of the year. In addition to open, grassy tracts, cultivated fields are much favoured by this species, for it is there that the bulk of its food is obtained. Its flight is of an undulatory character; occasionally it will soar to a considerable height and trill its pretty little song, reminding one strongly of the English Lark. When on the wing its tail is spread, displaying the white webs on the outer feathers. Its running powers are great, and are frequently used, save when hard pressed or when wishing to pass from place to place. During the breeding season it goes about in pairs, at other times in small flocks.

FAMILY—ARTAMIDÆ (1 species).

*WOOD-SWALLOW

(*Artamus sordidus*, Lath.)

Male.—Whole of upper surface chocolate-brown, lighter on head and neck, darker on lower back and rump; tail feathers black, tipped with white, except the two centre ones, which are

WOOD-SWALLOW'S NESTING SITE.

Photo. by A. H. E. MATTINGLEY. From "THE EMU."

NEST OF BALD-COOT.

Photo. by H. C. THOMPSON.

entirely black, only outer extremity of inner webs of outer feathers tipped with white; wings slate; external webs of second and third primaries and extreme fringe of web of fourth white; under surface chocolate-brown, slightly rufescent on abdomen and flanks; under wing coverts white; bill blue, tipped with black; legs and feet black; iris brown. Dimensions in mm.:—Length, 178; bill, 16; wing,. 130; tail, 75; tarsus, 17.

Female.—Similar to male. Dimensions in mm.:—Length, 170; bill, 15; wing, 125; tail, 73; tarsus, 17.5.

Young.—Upper surface as in adults, but the feathers streaked with soiled-white; under surface lighter than adults; feathers more obscurely streaked than on upper surface; scapulars tipped with greyish-white; extreme tips of primaries edged with soiled-white.

Nest.—Open and somewhat shallow; constructed of fine twigs, and generally lined with fine rootlets. A low banksia is a favourite nesting tree, but other low trees and bushes are also chosen.

Eggs.—Clutch three to four; stout oval in shape; texture fine; surface fairly glossy; colour yellowish or dull white (eggs of both colours sometimes appear in the same clutch) spotted and blotched with umber and smoky-grey; the markings usually form a band round the centre or else the stouter end of the eggs. Yellowish-white eggs are frequently more heavily spotted all over than the dull white ones; also a much greater number of spots appear as though beneath the surface. Dimensions in mm. of a clutch:—(1) 21 x 15.75, (2) 21.5 x 15, (3) 22 x 16.

Breeding Season.—September or October to the end of the year.

Geographical Distribution.—Tasmania, King and several other islands in Bass Strait; also practically the whole of the mainland.

Observations.—In some districts this species is fairly plentiful, but there are great areas in which it is hardly if ever seen. Almost any class of country, as long as there is a fair quantity of standing timber, is suitable for it. Mr. A. J. Campbell, in his "Nests and Eggs," states that he was always under the impression this species was stationary in Tasmania; Gould states to the contrary; and I, from long-extended observations, feel sure that the species is strictly migratory. It is quite possible that some individuals remain all the winter. I have never yet either heard of or seen a single specimen during the winter months. The date of arrival varies considerably, much depending on the climatic conditions. Some years it arrives early in August, and others not until mid-September. From the end of March to the middle of April migration is proceeding; by the end of the latter month there is hardly one to be heard or seen. This species has the peculiar habit of occasionally hanging in clusters, like a swarm of bees, on the under side of a bough.

Its food consists of insects, most of which are captured while on the wing. In some localities the Wood-Swallow has a bad reputation as a destroyer of bees. Doubtless some are destroyed, but I am of opinion more false bees or "drone-flies" are destroyed than honey-bees. The movements of this bird when on the wing are graceful in the extreme. Its broad pinions are eminently suited for sailing over and among the trees of its haunts. Occasionally it ascends to a great height, until it becomes a tiny speck in the sky. Even when almost out of sight in the air, its not unpleasant reedy notes can be distinctly heard. When at rest it has the curious habit of every now and then flicking its tail with a quick movement from side to side.

FAMILY—PLOCEIDÆ (1 species).

Sub-Family—Viduinæ.

*FIRE-TAILED FINCH

(*Zonæginthus bellus*, Lath.)

Male.—Narrow frontal band, lores, and feathers round the eyes black; upper surface brown, vermiculated with very fine blackish cross lines, those on the head, mantle, sides of face, ear coverts, and sides of neck so fine as to be almost invisible, back, scapulars, and wing coverts more distinct; lower rump and upper tail coverts bright crimson; terminal half of centre tail feathers black, basal half barred with light brown, fringes dull crimson; rest of feathers blackish, barred with light brown on outer webs; greater wing coverts and secondaries distinctly barred with black; primaries blackish-brown, outer webs light brown; under surface silvery-grey, distinctly vermiculated with black; cross bars fine on throat and fore-neck; abdomen and under tail coverts black; bill crimson, base of upper mandible paler; legs and feet very pale brown. Dimensions in mm.:—Length, 122; bill, 10; wing, 57; tail, 47; tarsus, 17.

Female.—Similar to male.

Young.—"Much browner and more dusky than the adults; the head uniform brown; the black on the lores and base of forehead scarcely indicated; under surface of body browner, with indistinct vermiculations of blackish cross lines, but no distinct cross barring as in the adult; bill dusky " (B. M. Cat.)

Nest.—A large bottle-shaped structure with a side entrance, constructed of grass chiefly, lined with a little fur and a few feathers, usually situated in a thick-foliaged tree, such as a musk or tea-tree.

Eggs.—Clutch four to seven; somewhat elongated oval in shape; texture fine; surface without gloss; colour pure white. Dimensions in mm. of a clutch:—(1) 18 x 12.5, (2) 18 x 12, (3) 17 x 12.75, (4) 17.5 x 12.5, (5) 18 x 12, (6) 17.5 x 12.5.

Breeding Season.—September to January.

' *Geographical Distribution.*—Tasmania and the principal groups in Bass Strait; Victoria, New South Wales, South Australia, and South Queensland.

Observations.—Owing to the extensive clearing of large areas of undergrowth and heavy timber, this species has entirely disappeared from some localities, and is much reduced in numbers in others. The Fire-tailed Finch prefers fairly heavily timbered country, where among the fallen leaves and grass it obtains the bulk of its food. Although shy in disposition, it speedily becomes tame when not molested. During the early morning hours in any suitable locality small flocks may be seen searching through the grass for tiny snails and the like. It is very quick on the wing, and has a somewhat plaintive whistling note. As a cage-bird it is very much sought after, notwithstanding its being on the totally protected list, on account of its hardiness.

ORDER—PICARIÆ : PICARIAN BIRDS.

Sub-Order—Coraciæ.

FAMILY—CYPSELIDÆ (2 species).

Sub-Family—Cypselinæ.

WHITE-RUMPED SWIFT

(Micropus pacificus, Lath.)

Male.—" Upper plumage dark blackish-brown with a greenish gloss, the feathers narrowly edged with whity-brown, these edges becoming more indistinct if the birds are quite adult; a band across the rump pure white, with narrow brown shaft-streaks; chin and throat white with brown shaft-streaks; remainder of the lower parts, under wing coverts, and under tail coverts brown, with white edges and blackish subterminal bars to the feathers in all stages; ' iris brown; bill black; feet pinkish; claws dark brown ' (Oates). · Total length, nearly 7 in. ; wing, 7 to 7.3; lateral rectrices, 3.3; central, 2.1; tarsus, 0.45 " (B. M. Cat.)

Female.—Similar in plumage.

Nest.—" The nest consists of a few straws and feathers cemented with saliva " (R. Hall).

Eggs.—" Clutch two usually; oval in shape, while others are exceedingly elongated and bluntly pointed at the smaller end; texture of shell fine; surface has a faint trace of gloss; colour pure white. Dimensions in inches of a proper clutch :—(1) 1.01 x .66, (2) 1.0 x .6; of a more oval example, .95 x .7 " (A. ·J. Campbell).

Breeding Season.—(?).

Geographical Distribution.—Tasmania (rare visitor), Australia in general; also Mongolia, Baikal, Amoor, Cachar, Burmah, Assam, Japan, and China.

Observations.—The records concerning the visits of this Australian Swift, as it is sometimes called, are but few. The reason is not far to seek, for it is usually in company with the Spine-tailed species, whose powers of flight are well known. It is almost if not quite a matter of impossibility to distinguish one species from another, unless they are flying low and passing and repassing in front of the observer. The first record I made of the White-rumped Swift was during the autumn of 1902, when a number were seen in company with a large flock of Spine-tails, the whole flying low down. This was late one afternoon. In February, 1896, Colonel Legge observed several examples among a large flock of Swifts "dashing" about the homestead at Cullenswood.

Sub-Family—Chæturinæ.

*SPINE-TAILED SWIFT

(*Chætura caudacuta*, Lath.)

Male.—Forehead generally wholly white; crown, nape, and sides of ⁻the head blackish-brown, with metallic gloss; back, shoulders, and rump pale brown, lightest in centre of back; wings and tail black, glossed with greenish and steel blue; inner webs of innermost secondaries mostly white; chin, throat, and under tail coverts white; rest of under surface sooty-brown; lower flanks glossy bluish-black, with white tips; bill blackish; legs and feet blackish-brown.   Dimensions in mm.:—Length, 200-202; bill, 7.75-78; wing, 195-210; tail, 51-57; tarsus, 14.5-15. It will be noted from the above measurements that individuals vary somewhat considerably in certain parts.

Female.—Similar to male.

Young.—Practically no white on forehead; brownish spots on under tail coverts.

Nest.—Mr. D. Le Souëf (*Emu*, vol. vii., p. 73) describes the nest, as seen by him under the Kegan Waterfall, in Japan, as being large and made of mud, evidently of two or three colours, and built on a sloping wall of rock well under cover.   "The nest is about a foot in depth externally by about 4 inches across on the top; the cup or egg cavity was evidently shallow, as the sitting bird was well exposed."

Eggs.—So far as I am aware, they are still undescribed.

Breeding Season.—(?).

Geographical Distribution.—Tasmania and Australia; also Mongolia, Eastern Siberia, China, and Japan.

Observations.—This projectile of a bird usually first appears in Tasmania about the second week in February, and the last one for the season about the end of March. I have records, however,

NESTING SITE OF SPINE-TAILED SWIFT.

Photo. by D. LE SOUEF. *From "* THE EMU."

of having seen the first bird during the first week in February, and the last right at the latter end of April. So far as my observations for Launceston are concerned, which have extended over a number of years, the bird has always come from over the south to south-eastern horizon and disappeared north to north-west. The times of appearance vary from noon to dusk; the majority, however, have been well on in the afternoon. Prior to a storm seems to be a favourite time for putting in an appearance. A calm evening with a clear atmosphere is also a favourite condition for this Swift. The style of flight varies from a projectile-like speed with a swish, swish of wings, now dashing close to the earth, now soaring high in the air, to a slow circular flight very high in the sky. The number appearing at one time varies from a few individuals to a few hundreds. I am informed that occasionally in the midland districts a flock numbering thousands may be seen streaming northwards. The problem of where they come from is one I am afraid will never be solved. We know where they breed, but where did those many hundreds of birds come from that I and others have seen appearing over the southern horizon and disappearing over the northern? There are but few absolutely authentic records of this Swift having been seen perching. Mr. G. E. Shepherd (*Emu*, vol. ii., p. 31) mentions having seen a Spine-tailed Swift circling round a tall eucalypt just at dusk one evening. The bird dashed into a clump of thick leaves near the top, and although Mr. Shepherd stayed round for a quarter of an hour he did not see the bird come out. It is quite possible, however, the bird slipped out on the side where Mr. Shepherd was not looking.

The following extract from the "Nature Notes" in a recent *Argus* may not be without some interest :—

"That Swifts perch and pitch more frequently than was supposed is shown by the notes of observers. Mr. J. Harrison (Maldon) says that Mr. Campbell, a resident of the New England district, New South Wales, saw them on the Macleay River perching in considerable numbers on the cliffs of Wellington's Lookout. Mr. Arthur Scott, Omeo, remembers seeing Swifts pitch upon the ground between Cape Clear and Western Creek, in the Ballarat district, 35 years ago. They appeared to be picking up sand or grit.

"Miss M. Anderson, Romsey, mentions a curious experience : —' Some years ago, on a stormy November morning, with rain just beginning to fall, I heard a babel of strange bird cries, and went out to see what caused it. I found the air thick with Swifts, which were literally hurling themselves on to the trunk and large bare limbs of an old gum-tree in the yard. They clapped themselves perfectly flat against the bark, touching one another, and covering the tree-trunk almost from the ground to top. The tree is over 100 feet high, so it can be imagined how numerous the birds were. A curious circumstance was that they only clung on to the parts of the tree facing to the south, from which quarter the wind was blowing a gale. The rain, which was about the heaviest I have ever seen, came down in torrents, and lasted for about 20 minutes, during which I could not see the birds, but when it cleared a little they were seen still clinging closely to the tree. When the rain ceased they threw themselves into the air in much the same fashion as they had pitched, and went their way.' "

FAMILY—PODARGIDÆ (2 species).

Sub-Family—Podarginæ.

*TAWNY FROGMOUTH (Mopoke)

(Podargus strigoides, Lath.)

Male.—Upper surface grey, the feathers with black shaft-streaks and shaded with brown, many tipped with white; forehead paler than crown; tail irregularly banded with brown, grey, and buff, small subterminal spot of black; shoulders and wings more or less tawny; primaries dusky-black, outer webs conspicuously spotted with white and tinged with tawny; inner webs with irregular bands of pale buff; secondaries likewise banded; under surface grey, paler and tinged with tawny on abdomen, all feathers with black shaft-streaks; bill black; legs and feet brownish-black. Dimensions in mm.:—Length, 470; bill, 30; wing, 260; tail, 215; tarsus, 38. Much difference in colouring exists in different individuals, especially as regards the tawny tinge. A specimen now before me is distinctly ferruginous on the whole of the upper surface.

Female.—Similar to male.

Nest.—A somewhat frail platform of twigs, with a few fine rootlets and pieces of grass. Usually placed in the fork of a horizontal limb of a tree in open forest country.

Eggs.—Clutch two usually; elliptical in shape; a little coarse in texture; surface somewhat glossy and very minutely pitted; colour white. Dimensions in mm. of a clutch:—(1) 48 x 34, (2) 47 x 33.5.

Breeding Season.—September to December.

Geographical Distribution.—Tasmania, New South Wales, Victoria, South Australia, and Queensland.

Observations.—For some unknown reason this bird is generally credited with uttering the cry that has been translated into the words "More Pork," on which account the bird is often known under the names of "More Pork," "Mopoke," or "Mope-hawk." But, as I have already pointed out, it is the Spotted Owl (*Ninox maculata*) that utters the weird cry. This can easily be verified by anyone who takes the trouble. The Tawny Frogmouth is distributed over nearly the whole of the island. In some districts it is

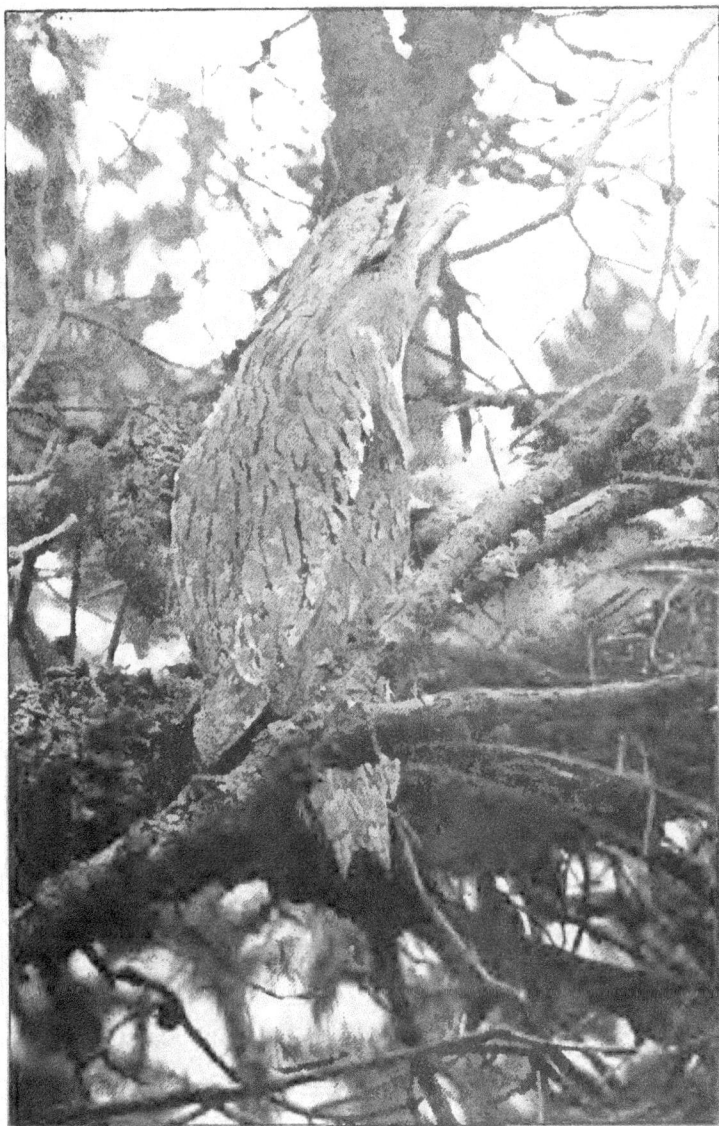

FROGMOUTH BY NEST WITH YOUNG.

Photo. by J. SEARS.   From "THE EMU."

fairly common, but not so in others. It is animated only during the night, at which time it sallies forth on noiseless wings and feeds on moths and other nocturnal insects. During the day it sits in an upright attitude on the dead limb of a tree. The bird is a wonderful example of protective mimicry. The reason that a dead, weather-beaten limb is selected is on account of the colour of the bough, as imitating very closely the prevailing colour of the bird. It matches so exactly that in broad daylight Hawks and other enemies, including man, pass the bird by as being only part of the tree. As a rule it sits close in to where the limb springs from the main stem. Occasionally, however, I have seen it sitting fully exposed on a bough. The whole day is passed in a state of apparent slumber. When disturbed it will fly a short distance, then perch and go to sleep, as though nothing had happened. But as soon as the shades of night fall the bird arouses itself and becomes keen-eyed and alert, sallying forth from its resting-place in search of prey.

Sub-Family—Ægothelinæ.

*OWLET-NIGHTJAR (Little Nightjar)

(*Ægotheles novæ-hollandiæ*, Lath.)

Male.—Head deep brown, with two longitudinal stripes and two crescents on the hinder part light grey; rest of upper surface, including wing coverts, dusky, finely marked with pale grey; tail dusky, barred on the inner webs with whitish-grey; quills dusky, outer webs paler; sides of head pale grey, tinged with rufous; under surface grey to pale grey, vermiculated with blackish-brown; bill blackish; legs and feet yellowish. Dimensions in mm.:—Length, 225; bill, 8.5; wing, 130; tail, 115; tarsus, 23.

Female.—Similar in plumage.

Nest.—A hole in the side of a tree or in the hollow spout of a broken limb, which is usually lined with eucalypt leaves.

Eggs.—Clutch three to four; roundish in shape; texture fine; surface glossy; colour white. Dimensions in mm. of a clutch:— (1) 25.5 x 21, (2) 25 x 21.5, (3) 25 x 22, (4) 25.5 x 21.

Breeding Season.—September to the end of the year.

Geographical Distribution.—Tasmania and Australia in general.

Observations.—Owing to its small size and nocturnal habits the Owlet-Nightjar is a bird about whose habits but little is known. I have records of it from over a large area, showing that it is to be found in every suitable stretch of forest country where it can find favourable nesting-places and where it can procure an abundance of food. It is a very timid species, for, should there be any disturbance close to the tree in which it is resting during the day it will immediately fly out. Its call at night consists of a fairly loud double note, which Mr. A. J. Campbell vocalizes as "Chirk-chirk."

Sub-Order—Halcyones.

FAMILY—ALCEDINIDÆ (2 species).

Sub-Family—Alcedininæ.

*BLUE KINGFISHER

(*Alcyone azurea*, Lath.)

Male.—Head and upper surface bright blue; line in front of the eyes yellowish-buff; tail feathers blackish-brown; wings blackish-brown, with a little blue on the tertiaries; throat buffy-white; rest of under surface rufous; sides of breast washed with lilac; bill black; legs and feet yellow-brown. Dimensions in mm. :—Length, 183; bill, 49; wing, 79; tail, 33; tarsus, 10.

Female.—Similar to male.

Young.—" Similar to adult, but not so brilliant blue, the shoulders and lateral breast patch black, only slightly washed with blue; the neck stripe orange-buff; head blackish, banded with blue " (B. M. Cat.)

Nest.—A tunnel drilled into the side of a bank of a creek or river, and a cavity hollowed out to receive the eggs.

Eggs.—Clutch five to seven; round in shape, with one end compressed; texture fine; surface glossy; colour pearly-white. Dimensions in mm. of a small clutch :—(1) 24 x 19, (2) 23 x 18.5, (3) 24 x 18.

Breeding Season.—October to December.

Geographical Distribution.—Tasmania, New South Wales, Victoria, South Australia, and Queensland.

Observations.—I have seen and have records of this scarce Kingfisher from various parts of the island. Owing to its retiring habits it is but seldom seen by the casual observer, even about the rivers it haunts.

Duck River was once a favourite resort, but now, so I am informed on good authority, the species is as rare there as elsewhere.

*SACRED KINGFISHER

(*Halcyon sanctus*, Vig. and Horsf.)

Male.—Head greenish-blue outlined from each side of the gape with blackish-green; back and wings, except primary feathers, dull green; primaries blackish-green, margined externally with dull green; tail bluish-green; collar and whole of under surface buffy-white. Dimensions in mm. :—Length, 210; bill, 47; wing, 95; tail, 63; tarsus, 14.

Female.—Similar in plumage to male.

Young.—According to Gould, the young have the back more

brown, the wing coverts margined with buff, and the feathers of the breast margined with dark brown; also a shorter bill.

Nest.—As a general rule a hole is drilled into a decayed place in the trunk of a tree, or else into a decayed elbow of a dead limb.

Eggs.—Clutch four to five; round in shape, with one end somewhat contracted; texture fine; surface glossy; colour pure white. Dimensions in mm. of a clutch:—(1) 25 x 22, (2) 25.5 x 22, (3) 25.5 x 21.5, (4) 25.25 x 21.

Breeding Season.—October to December.

Geographical Distribution.—Tasmania, King Island, whole of Australia; also Solomon Islands, New Guinea, New Hebrides, New Caledonia, Java, Lombok, Sumatra, Celebes, and Moluccas.

Observations.—I have never yet met with this summer visitor to our shores anywhere in the northern part of the island. Mr. A. L. Butler mentions (*Emu*, vol. vii., p. 89) having noted it several times on the Derwent, once as early as the 4th August. He also mentions having seen one dive into the water and catch fish after the manner of the Azure Kingfisher.

In May, 1873, a specimen of the Sacred Kingfisher, freshly shot, was presented to the Hobart Museum. It was at the time stated that this specimen was the first record for Tasmania.

I can find no record of the eggs of this species having been taken here.

Sub-Order—Coccyges.

FAMILY—CUCULIDÆ (6 species).

Sub-Family—Cuculinæ.

*PALLID CUCKOO

(*Cuculus pallidus*, Lath.)

Male.—Upper surface ashy-brown, faintly glossed with green; lateral tail coverts with indistinct white margins; two centre tail feathers same colour as back, rest blackish, all tipped and notched on both webs with white, giving the appearance of bars; wing coverts slightly lighter than back, with obscure white edges; quills blackish-brown, barred on their inner webs with white; under surface uniform stone colour, becoming almost white on abdomen and under tail coverts; thigh coverts somewhat obscurely barred with dusky; under wing coverts almost white; irides brown; bill black; legs and feet yellow. Dimensions in mm. :—Length, 330; bill, 21; wing, 201; tail, 175; tarsus, 21.

Female.—Similar to male.

Young.—" White predominates in its plumage, in many places tinged with buff and brown, resembling the colour of sealskin. Brown and white intermingle on the head; the feathers of the mantle are brown, with buff tips; the body feathers on the back

7

are white, with brown centres; the upper tail coverts are brown, with whitish edges, lanceolate in shape and ornamental in character, the ends of the barbs being unconnected; the tail feathers are sooty-brown and deeply toothed with whitish. The throat is like the head; towards the lower part of the under surface the brown gradually disappears, and on the abdomen all the feathers are white; primaries dark brown, toothed with white on the outer webs, and having buff spots on the margins of the inner webs; secondaries similar to primaries but without buff spots; wing coverts brown, or brown with buffy tips; lower surface of wings and tail grey, toothed with white, except the lower wing coverts, which are grey with wavy brown markings; axillaries white, tinged with buff; iris brown; feet horn-coloured; bill yellowish-brown " (J. R. M'Clymont).

Eggs.—Somewhat oval in shape; texture fine; surface glossy; colour flesh-pink, very sparsely spotted with reddish. Dimensions in mm. of odd examples:—(1) 24 x 17, (2) 24.5 x 17.

Breeding Season.—September to November or December.

Geographical Distribution.—Tasmania, King Island, and the whole of Australia.

Observations.—The Pallid Cuckoo, which is a moderately common species in most districts, usually arrives during the early part of September and departs during March or April. The note of this species, which is a melancholy one, may often be heard sounding through the bush when all other birds are silent.

Why Cuckoos should foist the responsibility of rearing their families on to other birds is beyond comprehension. There must be some reason, and a good one too, if we could but find it out, for in nature there is a reason for everything—nothing, not even the most insignificant trifle, being left to chance.

At one time there was great diversity of opinion as to how Cuckoos managed to deposit their eggs in nests whose openings are barely large enough to admit their heads. With regard to the Pallid Cuckoo, however, it will be observed from the list which comes later that open nests are the rule. Nevertheless, with this species as well as the others found there, it has been proved beyond doubt that the eggs are first laid on the ground and then carried in the bill of the parent bird to be placed in the nest. It sometimes happens that the Pallid Cuckoo lays its egg in a nest either before it is quite finished or the rightful owners have laid theirs. It is no very uncommon occurrence to find the egg of this Cuckoo either built into the lining of a nest or else the nest deserted and containing an addled egg of this species.

Regarding the ejection of the rightful occupants of the nest by a young, blind, and naked Cuckoo, and what precisely causes the Cuckoo to effect the ejection, many theories have been advanced. Mr. A. H. E. Mattingley (*Emu*, vol v., pp. 145-152) is of opinion that the action is purely automatic and governed by external stimuli. Mr. C. L. Barrett (*Emu*, vol. vi., p. 59) holds the belief " that the process is referable to hereditary instinct or sub-conscious memory aided by dawning reason." The arguments employed by both writers are equally strong in their own way, and have much to commend in them. The whole subject is both extremely interesting and intricate, and much remains to be learnt before we can say we have unravelled the ins and outs and the why and wherefore of the parasitical habits of the Cuckoos. Concerning the method of ejectment Mr. C. L. Barrett says (*Emu*, vol. v., p. 22):—'' Struggling desperately until it succeeded in getting the feebly resisting Wren into the hollow of its back, and balancing it there with extended embryo wings, the young Cuckoo, with head bowed between its strong legs, which, with claws firmly fixed in the sides, were straddled across the nest, worked its way gradually to the entrance, and on this being reached suddenly raised the head and with a sharp upward lift of the body pushed the unfortunate nestling over the edge. His work accomplished, the young usurper gave a final shrug of the body, as if to make certain his burden was gone, and subsided exhausted to the bottom of the nest.''

The young of the Pallid Cuckoo is very voracious, but perhaps not more so than the young of other species. After it is fully fledged it may be seen chasing its unfortunate foster-parents round, calling lustily for food the while. It is very amusing to watch a great hulking Cuckoo being assiduously attended by some tiny bird who is in a continual fluster endeavouring to satisfy the wants of its huge foster-child.

The following list of the foster-parents of the Pallid Cuckoo is compiled from my own observations and those of a number of other Tasmanian observers, and is, as far as I can make it, a complete one :—

> Dusky Robin (*Petrœca vittata*)
> Leaden Flycatcher (*Myiagra rubecula*)
> White-fronted Chat (*Ephthianura albifrons*)
> Grey-tailed Thickhead (*Pachycephala glaucura*)
> Whistling Shrike-Thrush (*Collyriocincla rectirostris*)
> Spinebill (*Acanthorhynchus tenuirostris*)
> Yellow-throated Honey-eater (*Ptilotis flavigularis*)
> Black-headed Honey-eater (*Melithreptus melanocephalus*)
> Strong-billed Honey-eater (*Melithreptus validirostris*)
> New Holland Honey-eater (*Meliornis novæ-hollandiæ*)
> Miner (*Myzantha garrula*)
> Wattle-Bird (*Acanthochœra inauris*)
> Brush Wattle-Bird (*Acanthochœra mellivora*)
> Wood-Swallow (*Artamus sordidus*).

The above remarks concerning the sources of the lists of foster-parents of the Pallid Cuckoo apply with equal force to the other species.

*FAN-TAILED CUCKOO
(*Cacomantis flabelliformis*, Lath.)

Male.—Upper surface blue-grey; upper tail coverts similar, with white edges to outer feathers; tail blue-black, all feathers tipped and notched with white, greater on outer feathers, forming incomplete bars; scapulars and wing coverts slightly glossed with green; patch of white on pinion joint; "quills dark brown, with a white patch on their inner webs, forming a diagonal white bar" (B. M. Cat.); sides of the head and chin grey, becoming rufous on the throat; rest of under surface similar, only slightly paler; under wing coverts rufous-buff; irides pale brown; bill black, save base of lower mandible, which is yellowish; legs and feet yellowish. Dimensions in mm.:—Length, 280; bill, 16; wing, 145; tail, 155; tarsus, 20.

Female.—Upper surface similar to male; lower surface paler; narrow faint dusky bars on throat and breast. Dimensions in mm.: —Length, 275; bill, 16; wing, 143; tail, 151; tarsus, 20.

Young.—Upper surface dark brown, mottled with rufous; upper tail coverts tipped with rufous; tail feathers notched with rufous-buff on outer webs and white on inner; wings rusty; throat and chest dusky-white, shaded with rufous; rest of under surface lighter, barred with dark brown.

Eggs.—Stout oval in shape; texture fine; surface glossy; colour dull white, thickly freckled with minute specks of reddish-brown and purplish-brown; round the upper quarter is a distinct band of similar markings. Dimensions in mm. of odd examples:—(1) 21.5 x 17, (2) 22.5 x 17.5.

Breeding Season.—September to December.

Geographical Distribution.—Tasmania, King Island, and the whole of the mainland.

Observations.—This bird is, perhaps, the most plentiful species of Cuckoo frequenting our shores. Its rather mournful whistling notes may be heard almost everywhere from early spring to late autumn. It is the first to come and the last to go—in fact, on several occasions I and other observers have seen individuals during the depth of winter. One July I had a specimen brought me, which on skinning proved to be very fat; its stomach was full of the remains of hairy caterpillars. When perching the Fan-tailed Cuckoo may be observed moving its tail, more or less spread, up and down every few seconds.

The foster-parents of this Cuckoo, as far as I know, are:—

Tasmanian Tit (*Acanthiza diemenensis*)
Scrub-Tit (*Acanthornis magna*)
Blue Wren (*Malurus gouldi*)
Brown Scrub-Wren (*Sericornis humilis*)
Black-headed Honey-eater (*Melithreptus melanocephalus*)
Wood-Swallow (*Artamus sordidus*)
Dusky Robin (*Petræca vittata*).

Mr. A. J. Campbell records the fact that Mr. A. E. Brent once found in a Brown-tail's nest two eggs of that species and one each of the Fan-tailed, Bronze, and Narrow-billed Bronze Cuckoos.

*NARROW-BILLED BRONZE-CUCKOO
(Chalcococcyx basalis, Horsf.)

Male.—Upper surface brown glossed with metallic green; outer webs of quills narrowly margined with dusky-white; two centre tail feathers brown washed with metallic gloss; rest of feathers with terminal white spot on inner webs and a subterminal blackish bar; outer feather blackish broadly barred and notched with white, next three pairs with basal three-fourths rufous, rest greenish-brown, with two white spots on inner webs; a broad white streak on sides of head form an extended eyebrow; under surface white, shaded and mottled with brown on throat and sides; sides of breast barred with brown; under wing coverts white, barred with brown; bill black; legs and feet blackish-brown. Dimensions in mm. :—Length, 158; bill, 12; wing, 100; tail, 74; tarsus, 17.

Female.—Similar to male.

Eggs.—Oval in shape; texture fine; surface slightly glossy; colour pinkish-white, finely freckled all over with pinkish-red. Dimensions in mm. of odd examples :—(1) 17 x 13, (2) 17 x 13.5.

Breeding Season.—September to December.

Geographical Distribution.—Tasmania, King Island, the whole of Australia, Timor, Lombok, Java, Flores, and the Aru Islands.

Observations.—To all intents and purposes the general habits of this species and those of the Bronze-Cuckoo may be said to be very similar. In common with other species, the Narrow-billed Bronze-Cuckoo arrives early in September and departs towards the end of March. Its food consists of insects of various descriptions gathered from off the ground and from the leaves and branches of trees. One very good trait that it and the Bronze species has lately developed to some considerable extent is that of feeding on the larvæ of a chrysomelid beetle very common wherever the silver wattle grows. These larvæ are responsible for the defoliation and subsequent destruction of very many wattles, especially young ones, every year.

So far as my knowledge goes, the following are the foster-parents of the Narrow-billed Bronze-Cuckoo in Tasmania :—

Scarlet-breasted Robin (*Petrœca leggei*)
Yellow-rumped Tit (*Acanthiza chrysorrhoa*)
Tasmanian Tit (*Acanthiza diemenensis*)
Blue Wren (*Malurus gouldi*)
Emu-Wren (*Stipiturus malachurus*)
White-fronted Chat (*Ephthianura albifrons*)
Striated Field-Wren (*Calamanthus fuliginosus*)
White-eye (*Zosterops cœrulescens*)
New Holland Honey-eater (*Meliornis novæ-hollandiæ*).

*BROAD-BILLED BRONZE-CUCKOO

(*Chalcococcyx lucidus*, Lath.)

Some doubt exists as to whether this species is really found in Tasmania. Mr. A. J. Campbell states that a specimen of this Cuckoo is in the Australian Museum, Sydney, labelled as from Tasmania. This specimen, he states, is more bronzy-brown than either the Bronze or Narrow-billed Bronze-Cuckoos. But I have found this bronzy-brown appearance rather constant in all specimens of Tasmanian-taken Bronze-Cuckoos I have examined.

In the proceedings of the Royal Society of Tasmania, October, 1870, it is recorded that a specimen of this species of Cuckoo shot at Kangaroo Bottom had been presented to the Museum. Mr. Arthur Butler informs me that at the present time there is no specimen of this Cuckoo in the Hobart Museum. He also states that at one time it was the custom down South to call the Bronze-Cuckoo the Broadbill; he is of opinion this is how the error arose. The stronghold of the Broad-billed Bronze-Cuckoo is New Zealand.

*BRONZE-CUCKOO

(*Chalcococcyx plagosus*, Lath.)

Male.—Upper surface violet-brown, with a strong metallic gloss; forehead partially mottled with white; upper tail coverts same as back, outer webs of outer feathers barred with white; tail metallic coppery with green reflections, dark subterminal spot on each feather, also white spot on inner web of all except centre feathers; "outer pair of feathers with broad white ends and four or five partial white bars, the next pair having two rufous blotches on the inner web" (B. M. Cat.); wing coverts like back; quills brown glossed with copper; sides of the head and neck whitish, mottled with brown; rest of under surface white, distinctly barred with coppery-bronze, showing green reflections in some lights; under wing coverts white, narrowly barred with coppery-bronze; under surface of quills dusky, with broad white bases to inner webs, forming oblique band across the wing; under surface of tail ashy-white instead of metallic; bill black; legs and feet blackish-brown. Dimensions in mm. :—Length, 160; bill, 13; wing, 101; tail, 72; tarsus, 15.

Female.—Similar to male.

Eggs.—Elliptical in shape; texture fine; surface glossy; colour uniform bronzy or olive. Dimensions in mm. of odd examples :— (1) 17 x 12.5, (2) 17.5 x 12.

Breeding Season.—September to November or December.

Geographical Distribution.—Tasmania, King Island, whole of Australia; also several islands and groups of islands in the South Pacific Ocean.

Observations.—Owing to the great similarity in colouring of this species and the Narrow-billed Bronze-Cuckoo, some difficulty frequently arises when endeavouring to identify the two species, especially when they are perched a little distance away. It is somewhat hard to say whether this species or *C. basalis* is the more plentiful, one species being frequently found in a district while the other is absent.

The foster-parents of the Bronze-Cuckoo are :—

Yellow-rumped Tit (*Acanthiza chrysorrhoa*)
Tasmanian Tit (*A. diemenensis*)
Blue Wren (*Malurus gouldi*)
Scarlet-breasted Robin (*Petrœca leggei*)
White-fronted Chat (*Ephthianura albifrons*)
Tawny-crowned Honey-eater (*Glycyphila fulvifrons*).

*CHANNEL-BILL

(*Scythrops novæ-hollandiæ*, Lath.)

Male.—Head and neck uniform pearl-grey ; rest of upper surface darker olive-grey; all the feathers of the back and wings have broad brownish-black ends, giving these parts a mottled appearance ; tail has a broad subterminal bar of brownish-black and is tipped with white ; under surface greyish-white, paler on the throat, with more or less indistinct broad bands on sides of body, thighs, and under tail coverts ; tail pale olive-grey with alternate broad markings of white and black on the inner webs ; bill yellowish-brown ; legs and feet olive-brown. Dimensions in mm. :—Length, 635, bill, 100 ; wing, 355 ; tail, 280 ; tarsus, 42.

Female.—Similar to male.

Eggs.—" Inclined to oval in shape ; texture of shell somewhat coarse ; surface slightly glossy ; colour vinaceous-buff, dully blotched with chestnut or umber and purplish-brown. Much resembles those of the Hill Crow-Shrike (*Strepera arguta*) of Tasmania. Dimensions in inches :—(1) 1.66 x 1.13, (2) 1.63 x 1.26 '' (A. J. Campbell).

Geographical Distribution.—Tasmania (accidental), Australia in general ; also a number of islands in the Austro-Malayan region.

Observations.—A specimen shot at Clarence Plains in November, 1867, and exhibited at a meeting of the Tasmanian Royal Society in the same month, was the first specimen of this species to be recorded for this island. I do not think any others have been procured since. In some parts of the mainland this bird, which is the largest of the Australian Cuckoos, is called the " Flood-Bird.''

ORDER—PSITTACI : PARROTS.

FAMILY—LORIIDÆ (3 species).

BLUE-BELLIED LORIKEET

(*Trichoglossus novæ-hollandiæ*, Gm.)

Male.—Head blue; nape yellowish-green; back, tail, and wings green; breast yellow, more or less stained with red, except on the sides; also some faint, narrow blue cross-bars on breast; middle of the abdomen blue; flanks green, bases of feathers yellow stained with red; under wing coverts red; bill red tipped with yellow; legs and feet dark brown to blackish. Dimensions in mm.:—Length, 302; bill, 17; wing, 167; tail, 137; tarsus, 13.

Female.—Practically similar to male.

Young.—Resemble the adults save that the yellow-green band on the nape is scarcely visible; also the red stains on the yellow breast are practically absent.

Nest.—Within a hole in a branch or the trunk of a tree.

Eggs.—Clutch two; round in shape, with one end somewhat compressed; texture fairly fine; surface almost without lustre; colour white. Dimensions in mm. of odd examples:—(1) 27.5 x 24, (2) 27 x 23.5, (3) 26.5 x 23.

Breeding Season.—October to December.

Geographical Distribution.—Tasmania and practically the whole of the mainland.

Observations.—From New Norfolk, in 1871, came the first record of this handsome Lorikeet for Tasmania. Both in March and October of that year were specimens procured from the same district. The Blue-bellied Lorikeet does not take up a permanent abode in any locality except where the food supply is constant. As a rule it moves from district to district, following the lines of the flowering eucalypts. It is only when its natural food becomes scarce that it turns its attention to fruit, &c.

It is a fine sight to see a flock of this species wheeling and flashing in the bright sunshine. Both when on the wing and when feeding it is very noisy.

I cannot obtain any particulars of the eggs of this species ever having been taken here.

MUSK-LORIKEET

(*Glossopsittacus concinnus*, Shaw).

Male.—General colour green; forehead, lores, and ear coverts red; crown of the head distinctly tinged with blue; hind-neck and upper part of the back olive-brown; inner webs of the quills blackish; sides of the breast more or less yellow; bill blackish-brown,

orange at tip; legs and feet blackish.   Dimensions in mm. : —
Length, 220; bill, 15; wing, 118; tail, 90; tarsus, 13.

Female.—Save that the blue on the head is less distinct, the
plumage is similar to that of the male.

Nest.—Within a hole in a living or dead tree.

Eggs.—Clutch two to four; roundish oval in shape; texture
fairly fine; surface without gloss; colour white.   Dimensions in
mm. of a clutch : —(1) 24.5 x 20, (2) 25 x 20.5, (3) 24.5 x 21.

Breeding Season.—September to December.

Geographical Distribution.—Tasmania, New South Wales, Victoria, South Australia, and Queensland.

Observations.—Of the Lorikeets and Parrakeets found in Tasmania this is the most plentiful and therefore the best known.
Well-timbered tracts of eucalyptus country are mostly favoured,
for it is there that it obtains its food.   When changing its feeding
ground it generally leaves in large flocks and with much screeching.   During the summer of 1898 this species proved a perfect
nuisance in the gardens around Launceston.   It was that summer
that bush-fires raged so fiercely in so many districts, causing great
mortality among many species of birds.   Apples and pears hung
thickly on the trees in suburban gardens.   One day flocks of the
Musk-Lorikeet " came down like a wolf on the fold," settled on
the laden trees, and commenced a fierce onslaught.   Guns were
brought into requisition, and great slaughter ensued, but, nothing
daunted, the Lorikeets returned to the charge again and again.   It
was not so much the actual fruit eaten as the quantity destroyed
and partly eaten or knocked on to the ground by the hustling birds.
Not only in Tasmania was damage done by this species that
summer, but also in New South Wales at least; for a Sydney paper
remarked : —" For some time past complaints have been made in
different parts of the colonies of the ravages made by a small green
Parrakeet.   This bird is known vernacularly by the name of the
Musk-Lorikeet.   Immense flocks of these Lorikeets have devas-
tated entire orchards, and many thousands have been killed in the
Richmond River, the Hawkesbury, Illawarra, and Monaro districts,
but still there is no apparent diminution in their numbers as long
as there is any fruit left to feed upon.   So tame were these birds
in the latter localities that numbers of them were knocked down
with sticks or caught by the hands while feeding in the fruit trees.
Shooting does not seem to deter or frighten them away, for many
will remain in the same tree from which probably ten or a dozen
have just been killed or have fluttered wounded and screeching to
the ground.   But this pest is not confined to the country districts,
for in the suburbs a few miles out of Sydney they freely enter
gardens and devour all soft fruit, principally at the present time
plums and pears.   Numbers, too, are snared by boys by the aid of
horse-hair nooses on the forked end of a long pole and the vocal
allurements of a captive call-bird.   Unhappy birds! a hard fate is

theirs; cramped into a small cage, improperly or insufficiently fed, death soon puts an end to their miserable existence, for but comparatively few survive the following winter."

The natural food of this species consists of the honey extracted from the flowers of various species of eucalypt; frequently when just shot while feeding on the gum blossoms a wounded bird will disgorge a quantity of liquid honey.

LITTLE LORIKEET

(*Glossopittacus pusillus*, Shaw).

Male.—General colour green; face red; hinder neck and shoulders olive-brown, inner webs of lateral tail feathers red at base, becoming yellow towards the tip; bill black; legs and feet blackish-brown. Dimensions in mm.:—Length, 167; bill, 11; wing, 104; tail, 60; tarsus, 9.

Female.—Practically similar to male.

Nest.—Placed within a small hole of a branch or in the elbow of a limb of a tree.

Eggs.—Clutch four; roundish to round oval in shape; texture fine; surface without gloss; colour white. Dimensions in mm. of a clutch:—(1) 19 x 15, (2) 18.5 x 15, (3) 18.5 x 16, (4) 19 x 15.5.

Breeding Season.—September to December.

Geographical Distribution.—Tasmania, New South Wales, Victoria, South Australia, and Queensland.

Observations.—This chubby little Lorikeet is less plentiful, generally speaking, than the preceding species. It frequents the same class of country, and is sociable in its habits, for it may often be seen feeding in the gum-trees with the Musk and Swift Lorikeets. Owing to this sociable habit its presence is often overlooked in a district. In addition to feeding on honey from the eucalypt blossoms, it may often be seen performing strange antics among the branches of the parasitical *Loranthus*, as it feeds on the berries. Like all Lorikeets it favours well-timbered tracts, moving from one belt of eucalypts to another, as they come out into blossom.

FAMILY—CACATUIDÆ (4 species).

Sub-Family—Cacatuinæ.

*BLACK COCKATOO

(*Calyptorhynchus funereus*, Shaw).

Male.—Brownish-black, slightly glossed with green; feathers of upper back and wings narrowly margined with brown tinged with olive; ear coverts dull yellow; tail darker than back; all the feathers save the two centre ones pale yellow, irregularly freckled with black on inner webs for basal two-thirds; extreme tips of all

EUCALYPT BARK RIPPED BY BLACK COCKATOOS.

Photo. by A. H. E. MATTINGLEY.   *From* "THE EMU."

feathers brownish-olive; under surface slightly browner than upper; feathers of chest and breast edged with brownish-olive; abdomen more or less tinged with olive; bill black; legs and feet brownish-black. Dimensions in mm.:—Length, 590; bill, 48; wing, 375; tail, 23.5; tarsus, 28.

Female.—Similar to male.

Young.—Ear coverts bright yellow; feathers of under surface somewhat broadly marked with yellow; yellow on tail heavily freckled with brown; bill whitish, tipped with black.

Nest.—Within a hole in the trunk of a lofty tree, usually far removed from civilization.

Eggs.—Clutch two; roundish oval in shape; texture coarse; surface slightly glossy; colour white. Dimension in inches of an odd example, according to Mr. A. J. Campbell:—1.9 x 1.5.

Breeding Season.—I can neither find any record nor hear of any eggs being taken prior to the end of December.

Geographical Distribution.—Tasmania, King and other of the larger islands in Bass Strait, New South Wales, Victoria, South Australia, and South Queensland.

Observations.—Mountainous and heavily timbered tracts are mostly favoured by this species, which has, perhaps, a wider distribution throughout the island than the White Cockatoo. It is in such regions that it can best obtain its food of insect larvæ from the giant eucalypt and other forest trees.

On account of its nesting so far from the ground, and in such extremely difficult positions, records of the taking of the eggs of this Cockatoo are somewhat scarce. Messrs. A. E. Brent, Percy Grubb, and Leo Burbury have all taken eggs at different times. An interesting note by the first-named gentleman is given by Mr. A. J. Campbell; it runs:—'' For about three weeks, when the female is sitting, I discovered that the male would go to the nest three times a day—at morn, noon, and night—and was most regular. I would find myself standing watch in hand looking for him every day for several days, and found that his times never varied more than seven minutes. To ascertain his reasons, I went to the nest at night, and crept, without disturbing the sitting bird, to a spot where I could see all that went on, and waited. After some time, the old bird's cry would be heard in the distance, and at the same time the female's head would appear at the hole, and she would answer him with a small scream, and would repeat in answer to him as he drew near. As soon as he appeared in sight she would fly out and settle on a dry branch, meeting him there, and after the usual greeting he would sit and feed her for fully ten minutes just as if she had been a young bird. After this she would sit and preen her feathers for a time, and then return to the nest, always entering the hole tail first. This performance I witnessed for several days.''

In some districts the Black Cockatoo is regarded as an unfailing herald of rain, for it then flies very near to the earth and keeps up a continuous screeching as it slowly proceeds through the thick forests to the lowlands. Not only during actual rainy weather does it fly low and screech continuously, but also, at times when to an ordinary individual no rain seems imminent, it instinctively seems to know that a change is pending, and the wet almost invariably comes within the next twenty-four hours. Usually during stormy weather the highlands are deserted for the low. Occasionally during rough weather I have seen small flocks pass over Launceston low down.

When flying in flocks it straggles a great deal, sometimes forming a " Chinamen's procession." It is naturally a noisy bird, but when a large flock gets together on a good feeding ground the din is deafening. The fat white grubs to be found beneath the bark of eucalypt and other trees form its favourite diet. It is a sight worth watching to see a large flock at work on the bark of, say, stringy gums. In a few minutes the trees have the appearance of having been well worked with strong rakes. The bark hangs in long shreds and strips everywhere; pieces are even bitten out of the limbs in search of the succulent morsel. Honeysuckle (*Banksia*) cones are also in some request. The strong outside covering presents no difficulties to the powerful bill of the Black Cockatoo.

*GANG-GANG COCKATOO

(*Callocephalon galeatum*, Lath).

Male.—General colour slate-grey; crown of the head, crest, and cheeks scarlet; upper and under surfaces, shoulders, and wing coverts narrowly margined with greyish-white, somewhat indistinct on under surface; bill horn colour; legs and feet black. Dimensions in mm. :—Length, 340; bill, 31; wing, 250; tail, 135.

Female.—General colour slate-grey; crest grey; quills and tail feathers barred with light grey; feathers of under surface margined with sulphur-yellow and dull red; under tail coverts barred with dull yellow.

Young.—Males.—" Like the females, but with dull red narrow bars on the pileum; back, uropygium, and upper tail feathers, wing coverts, scapulars, and secondaries with sulphur-yellow bars " (B. M. Cat.)

Nest.—Within a hole in a tall forest tree.

Eggs.—" Clutch four to five; round oval in shape; texture of shell somewhat coarse; surface without gloss; colour pure white. Dimensions in inches :—1.31 x 1.08. According to Le Souëf—(1) 1.28 x .92, (2) 1.25 x 94 " (A. J. Campbell).

Breeding Season.—In all probability similar to that of the other species.

Geographical Distribution.—Tasmania (?), King Island, New South Wales, Victoria, and South Australia.

Observations.—A certain amount of doubt exists as to whether this species has ever really been found here in Tasmania; but it is moderately plentiful on King Island. Even to this day the nesting habits of this Cockatoo have not been fully worked out, much still remaining to be known.

WHITE COCKATOO
(*Cacatua galerita*, Lath.)

Male.—Entire plumage white, save for the crest, which is deep sulphur-yellow, and the under wing coverts and under tail coverts, which are tinged with yellow; bill black; legs and feet blackish. Dimensions in mm.:—Length, 530; bill, 49; wing, 370; tail, 250; tarsus, 26.

Female.—Similar to male.

Nest.—Within a hole in a tall tree usually.

Eggs.—Clutch two to three; lengthened oval in shape; texture fairly coarse; surface glossy; colour white. Dimensions in mm. of odd examples:—(1) 47 x 30, (2) 47.5 x 31.

Breeding Season.—August to November.

Geographical Distribution.—Tasmania, King Island, and the whole of the mainland.

Observations.—There are some districts in the island where I have never seen or heard a White Cockatoo, but the Black species has been most plentiful, and *vice versâ*. Sometimes this bird is spoken of as the Great Sulphur-crested Cockatoo. It is hard to say which is the more noisy, this or the Black Cockatoo. If anything *C. galerita* has the more harsh, discordant screech. There is hardly a prettier sight than to see some forest giant, one perhaps gaunt and leafless, covered with the snowy forms of this species. In some agricultural districts the bird does a great deal of damage to the grain crops, and is in consequence much detested by farmers. Some miles past Cressy I have seen the fields almost white with Cockatoos intent on feeding on and destroying the grain. When they were disturbed the din was terrific. Nearly, if not always, there is a sentinel bird perched on a limb or a fence close by to give warning at the slightest menace of danger.

ROSE-BREASTED COCKATOO (GALAH)
(*Cacatua roseicapilla*, Vieillot).

Male.—Crown of the head pale rosy-pink; upper surface grey, deepening into brown at the extremity of the quills and becoming nearly white on the rump and upper tail coverts; neck and all the under surface from below the eyes and smaller under wing coverts rich rosy-red; under tail coverts grey; tail grey, darker below; irides deep rosy-red; bill white; legs and feet dark brown. Dimensions in mm. :—Length, 355; bill, 25; wing, 255; tail, 131; tarsus, 21.

Female.—Similar to male.

Nest.—A hollow within a tree, generally near water.

Eggs.—Clutch four or five; roundish oval in shape; texture of shell fairly fine; surface slightly glossy; colour pure white. Dimensions in mm. of odd examples :—(1) 34 x 25, (2) 35 x 25.5, (3) 35 x 25.25.

Breeding Season.—July to February or later.

Geographical Distribution.—Tasmania (accidental) and Australia in general.

Observations.—On the 5th May, 1908, Mr. J. Adams, of the Lower Piper, shot two Galahs, which turned out to be a pair, at Jerusalem Plains. Both specimens were forwarded to the Launceston Museum, but it was found that only one was in a fit condition to be set up, and it is now in the Tasmanian ornithological section.

A few days after securing the above birds another of the same species was observed by Mr. Adams in the farmyard with his poultry.

FAMILY—PSITTACIDÆ (6 species).

Sub-Family—Platycercinæ.

GREEN OR YELLOW-BELLIED PARRAKEET

(*Platycercus flaviventris*, Temm.)

Male.—Forehead crimson; cheeks blue; crown of the head, back, and sides of the neck greenish-yellow, varying in intensity among fully adult birds from different localities; back and shoulders dark olive, approaching black in some individuals, each feather edged with green; upper tail coverts dark green, tipped with pale yellow; middle of wing blue, varying in intensity; primaries blue on external edges for basal half, blackish-brown for remainder; two central tail feathers green, remainder dark blue for two-thirds and light blue for the remaining third; whole of under surface jonquil-yellow; irides dark brown; bill horn coloured; legs and feet black. Dimensions in mm. :—Length, 335; bill, 18; wing, 183; tail, 188; tarsus, 19.

Female.—Slightly less in bulk than male, mandibles also a little less stout. No variation of moment in plumage.

Young.—According to Gould, the young of the year are greenish-olive, with a faint tinge of blue on the cheeks, wings, and outer tail feathers, and a faint indication of the red mark on the forehead.

Nestling.—When first hatched they are covered with long white down and present the appearance of round balls of white cotton wool (Gould).

Nest.—A hole in the side of a lofty eucalypt is the usual site.

Eggs.—Clutch four to six usually; elliptical in shape; texture of shell fine; surface glossy; colour pure white. Dimensions in mm. of a clutch:—(1) 27.5 x 21, (2) 27 x 21, (3) 27 x 21.5, (4) 28 x 22.

Breeding Season.—October to December.

Geographical Distribution.—Tasmania, King and several other of the principal islands in Bass Strait.

Observations.—I suppose, next to the Rosella (*Platycercus eximius*), the Green Parrakeet, or, as it is more commonly called, the Green Parrot, with its cry of "Cossack, cossack," is the most familiar of the Psittaci in Tasmania. It is widely distributed, there being but few districts where it is not found. All classes of country are frequented by it; its natural home is, however, among well-wooded hills and gullies. Owing to certain changes that have taken place in its diet, it is now very frequently to be seen in open cultivated districts, where at certain seasons it can obtain a plentiful supply of food. It is owing to this change in diet, or more correctly speaking the development of a catholic taste, that the species is held in much disfavour by farmers, who do not appreciate toll being levied on their cereal crops. In addition to seeds, insects and their larvæ, gum blossoms or what they contain are fed on to a limited extent. The flight of this Parrakeet is fairly powerful, the bird progressing in long undulations.

So far as I am aware this species has not yet developed any strong fruit-eating proclivities. I have seen a flock settle on the ground among well-laden apple trees and busily search in the grass for terrestrial food, paying no attention to the fruit on the trees close by. I hardly think the same would happen were ground food scarce.

ROSELLA

(Platycercus eximius, Shaw).

Male.—Crown of the head, back of the neck, chest, and under tail coverts scarlet; cheeks extending down to the fore-neck white; feathers of the back black, broadly margined with yellow; rump and upper tail coverts pale green, faintly tinged with yellow; centre of the abdomen yellow, towards the vent pale green; shoulders and middle of the wing intense blue; external edges of the primaries blue, remainder dark brown; two central tail feathers bluish-green, other tail feathers dark blue, passing into light blue; bill horn colour; feet blackish-brown. Dimensions in mm.:—Length, 340; bill, 19.5; wing, 157; tail, 190; tarsus, 21.

Female.—Resembles male in plumage. Dimensions in mm.:—Length, 335; bill, 19; wing, 159; tail, 186; tarsus, 21.

Nest.—Placed within the trunk of a tree, or in the end of a hollow spouted limb, at a varying distance from the ground, in moderately heavily timbered country.

Eggs.—Clutch six to nine; oval to round oval in shape; texture fine as a rule; surface slightly glossy; colour pure white. Dimensions in mm. of a clutch :—(1) 27 x 22, (2) 26 x 22, (3) 26 x 21, (4) 26.5 x 21.5, (5) 27 x 22, (6) 26 x 21.

Breeding Season.—October to December.

Geographical Distribution.—Tasmania, New South Wales, Victoria, South Australia, and South Queensland.

Observations.—The irregular manner in which the Rosella is distributed in Tasmania is somewhat puzzling. There are portions of districts to which it is either an entire stranger or only an occasional visitor whose topographical features do not in any appreciable manner differ from those where the bird is most plentiful. However, taking everything into consideration, this species may be considered plentiful.

As a rule lightly timbered and open tracts are resorted to, where it frequently may be seen in large flocks. On account of the quantity of freshly sown grain it steals in agricultural districts, it is much disliked by farmers, and its ranks thinned by means of poison and shot-guns. In disposition it is fearless, and does not hesitate to come round bush habitations in search of food.

As is doubtless well known, the Rosella was first called the Rosehill Parrakeet, on account of it having first been found there. As a cage-bird it is a great favourite, both on account of its brilliant plumage and its tractability. In addition to these qualities, it is hardy and lives to a great age.

BLUE-WINGED GRASS-PARRAKEET
(*Neophema venusta*, Temm.)

Male.—" A conspicuous bar of deep indigo blue across the forehead, bordered above by a narrow edging of light metallic blue; lores and a stripe above and behind the eye rich yellow; crown of the head, back, rump, upper tail coverts, throat, chest, and flanks brownish olive-green; shoulders and wing coverts deep blue; primaries black, the outer edges of the first three or four slightly tinged with green; centre of the abdomen and under tail coverts yellow; four middle tail feathers greenish-blue, the basal portions of the remainder beautifully blue on their outer edges, and largely tipped with fine yellow; bill and feet brown " (Gould). Dimensions in mm. :—Length, 220; bill, 13.5; wing, 112; tail, 131; tarsus, 15.

(The above description by Gould tallies precisely with Tasmanian examples examined. The dimensions, however, are the average of a number of specimens.)

Female.—Similar in plumage to male.

Young.—According to Mr. R. Hall's correspondent, Mr. Graham, published in the *Victorian Naturalist* (1898), the birds when they first leave the nest are grey, yellowish about the head and the tail feathers. Later the body and wings become greenish, with a little grey on the head. In a fortnight all trace of grey disappears.

Nest.—Within a small hole in a tree or in a hollow log or stump.

Eggs.—Clutch five to seven; roundish in shape; texture fairly fine; surface glossy; colour white. Dimensions in mm. of a clutch: —(1) 22 x 18, (2) 21.5 x 18, (3) 22 x 17.75, (4) 21.5 x 17.5, (5) 22 x 18.

Breeding Season.—September to January.

Geographical Distribution.—Tasmania, King and several other islands in Bass Strait, New South Wales, Victoria, and South Australia.

Observations.—This extremely elegant Parrakeet was observed by Gould in various places both in the north and the south of the island. He was very much charmed with the species, about which he says:—". . . for whether perched on a small dead branch of a low bush, or resting on the stronger grasses, there is grace and elegance in all its actions. It runs over the ground and threads its way among the grasses with the greatest facility, and the little flocks are usually so intent upon gathering the seeds as to admit of your walking close up to them before they will rise; the whole will then get up simultaneously, uttering a feeble cry, and settling again at a short distance, or flying off to some thickly foliaged tree, where they sit for a time and again descend to the ground."

To my knowledge this bird is found during certain months about such widely separated localities as Lilydale, Tasman's Peninsula, Cleveland, and the country about Noland Bay, and other places. Mr. Arthur Butler observed three pairs in June, 1909, on the North-West Coast. I have seen odd birds in July in different years in the country lying round the foot of the Western Tiers.

ORANGE-BELLIED GRASS-PARRAKEET

(*Neophema chrysogastra*, Lath.)

Male.—Frontal band blue, margined with light blue; crown of the head and the rest of the upper surface green; two central tail feathers bluish-green; the next on either side similarly coloured, but with inner web margined with black; shoulders, wing coverts, outer webs of primaries, and under wing coverts deep blue; lores, cheeks, and breast yellowish-green, becoming greenish-yellow on the abdomen, in the centre of which is a large patch of orange; under tail coverts yellow; iris black; bill bluish-black; legs and feet greyish-white. Dimensions in mm. :—Length, 215; bill, 12; wing, 106; tail, 109; tarsus, 14.

Female.—Similar to male, but duller in colouring.

8

Young.—" Much duller than the adult; the blue frontal band but faintly indicated; the under parts more olive; the orange spot on the abdomen very small; the tail more greenish; some-times some of the quills have a white spot on the inner web " (B. M. Cat.)

Nest.—Within a hollow of a limb of a fallen tree.

Eggs.—Clutch four to six; round in shape; texture fine; surface almost without lustre; colour white. Dimensions in mm. of a clutch :—(1) 20 x 17, (2) 19 x 16.5, (3) 19.5 x 17, (4) 20 x 16.75.

Breeding Season.—November to January.

Geographical Distribution.—Tasmania, New South Wales, Victoria, and South Australia.

Observations.—The stronghold of this Parrakeet appears to be the southern portion of the island. In Gould's day it was to be found about Hobart and New Norfolk, and was very abundant on the Actæon Islands, at the entrance of D'Entrecasteaux Channel. He wrote :—" These small and uninhabited islands are covered with grasses and scrub, intermingled with a species of barilla, nearly allied to *Atriplex halimus* (a salt-bush), and almost the only land bird that enlivens these solitary spots is the present beautiful Parrakeet. I frequently flushed small flocks from among the grass, when they immediately alighted upon the barilla bushes around me, their sparkling orange bellies forming a striking con-trast with the green of the other part of their plumage and the silvery foliage of the plant upon which they rested. I made many unsuccessful attempts to discover their breeding-places. As, however, these islands are destitute of large trees, I am induced to believe that they lay eggs in holes on the ground, or among the stones on the shore."

I am given to understand that it is still almost if not quite as plentiful as when Gould wrote about it. So far as the northern parts of the island are concerned, the species is somewhat rare, but I have records of it from various places scattered over a wide area.

Like the Blue-winged species, this one obtains the greater part of its food from off the ground, from whence it may be flushed in small flocks. On the ground it is a swift runner. It is interest-ing to watch a flock scurrying along with short, quick steps through the grass in search of its favourite food-seeds. It arrives towards the end of September, and departs about the end of February. During a visit to Ninth Island, lying off the North-East Coast of Tasmania, during the latter part of September, 1909, a pair, then six birds, of this species were observed migrating to Tasmania. They made a stay of very short duration on the island—just long enough to gather a little food.

SWIFT LORIKEET

(*Nanodes discolor*, Shaw).

Male.—General colour green; forehead, front part of cheeks, throat, and under wing coverts scarlet; centre of the crown deep blue; sides of the head and ear coverts bluish; lores and a band bordering the red of the cheeks and throat yellow; tail red-brown tipped with blue, three outer tail feathers on each side almost entirely blue; tips of shoulders dark red; upper wing coverts green; outer coverts blue; primary coverts blue-black; primaries black, narrowly edged with greenish-yellow on outer webs; secondaries green on the outer web, red mark on inner webs; under surface green tinged with yellowish; under tail coverts scarlet, with greenish-yellow edges; bill yellowish-brown; legs and feet light brown. Dimensions in mm. :—Length, 255; bill, 13.5; wing, 126; tail, 127; tarsus, 13.

Female.—Similar to the male but duller.

Young.—Similar to adults, but has the under tail coverts yellowish-green, only the larger ones stained with red.

Nest.—Within a hollow in the dead branch of a tree.

Eggs.—On the mainland two or three form a clutch, whereas in Tasmania Mr. A. E. Brent is quoted by Mr. A. J. Campbell as having taken many clutches of from four to six; roundish in shape; texture fine, surface glossy; colour white. Dimensions in mm. of odd examples :—(1) 23 x 20, (2) 24 x 20.5, (3) 23.5 x 20.

Breeding Season.—November to December.

Geographical Distribution.—Tasmania, New South Wales, Victoria, South Australia, and South Queensland.

Observations.—This elegant Lorikeet may frequently be seen feeding with other species in the flowering eucalypts. In some districts it is moderately plentiful during the early summer and part of the autumn months. As regards the general habits of the species, I cannot do better than quote from Gould, as his remarks accurately describe them. He wrote :—" During September and the four following months it is not only abundant in all the gum forests of Van Diemen's Land, but is very common in the shrubberies and gardens at Hobart Town, small flights being constantly seen passing up and down the streets and flying in various directions over the houses. They approach close to the windows, and are even frequently to be seen on the gum-trees bordering the streets, and within a few feet of the heads of the passing inhabitants, being so intent upon the gathering of honey from the fresh-blown flowers, which daily expand, as almost entirely to disregard the presence of the spectator. The tree to which they are so eagerly attracted is the *Eucalyptus gibbosus*. Their plumage so closely assimilates in colour to the leaves of the trees they frequent, and they moreover creep so quietly yet actively from branch to branch, clinging in every possible position, that were it not for their movements and the trembling of the leaves it would be difficult to perceive them without a minute examination of the tree upon which they have alighted.''

*GROUND-PARRAKEET

(*Pezoporus formosus*, Lath.)

Male.—General colour green; forehead orange, somewhat in-clined to red; feathers of crown and nape of neck centrally streaked with black; remainder of upper surface irregularly banded with black and yellow; four central tail feathers green, narrowly barred with yellow; lateral feathers yellow, barred with deep green; quills brown, with outer webs greenish; fore-neck sparsely spotted with black; breast, abdomen, and under tail coverts greenish-yellow, somewhat heavily bordered with black; under surface of quills grey, with a yellow band; " bill horn; feet bluish flesh colour; iris black, with a fine ring of light grey " (Gould). Dimensions in mm. :—Length, 315; bill, 16; wing, 130; tail, 192; tarsus, 23.

Female.—Similar to male.

Young.—No orange band on forehead.

Nest.—A hollow in the ground under the shelter of a clump of band-grass, button-grass, or even thistles; the hollow usually has a lining of fine grass.

Eggs.—Clutch three to four; round in shape; texture fine; surface glossy; colour pure white. Dimensions in mm. of a clutch : —(1) 25.15 x 21, (2) 25 x 20.5, (3) 26 x 21.

Breeding Season.—September to November.

Geographical Distribution.—Tasmania and some of the larger islands in Bass Strait, New South Wales, Victoria, South and Western Australia.

Observations.—The range of this species in the northern part of the island is somewhat wide, but nowhere is it at all plentiful. It consorts in small bands of about half a dozen individuals. In various localities along the North and North-East Coast it is more plentiful than in inland districts.

Although epacris and grass-tree covered country, such as is to be found about Falmouth and George's Bay, are its favourite haunts, yet I have seen it equally at home in paddocks thickly covered with Scotch thistle some miles past Cressy and towards the Lakes. The Ground-Parrakeet is purely a terrestrial species, it seeming incapable of perching like others of the Parrot family. When flushed it will fly for a few yards, then drop on to the ground again, seeking to elude its pursuer by running swiftly and hiding itself among the undergrowth.

ORDER—COLUMBÆ: PIGEONS AND DOVES.

Sub-Order—Columbæ : Pigeons.

FAMILY—TRERONIDÆ (2 species).

Sub-Family—Ptilopodinæ.

*PURPLE-CROWNED FRUIT-PIGEON

(*Ptilopus superbus,* Temm.)

Male.—" Pileum purple-violet; occiput and sides of the head olive-green; sides and back of the neck bright rufous; back, rump, upper tail coverts, scapulars, and wing coverts green, with an olive-brown tinge; scapulars, inner greater wing coverts, and inner secondaries with deep blue spots near the tip; small wing coverts near the bend of the wing deep blue; quills black, primaries with narrow outer edges yellow; secondaries and greater wing coverts green on the outer web and edged with yellow; chin and greater part of the cheeks pale grey; breast grey, with the base of the feathers purple; below the breast a broad black band more or less tinged with blue or green; abdomen white; flanks green, with two white bands; under tail coverts white, with a longitudinal green spot on the inner web and tinged with pale yellow at the apical edge; under wing coverts greyish-green; quills underneath dark grey; tail above green, with a greyish-white band at the tip; tail below dark grey, with a white band at the tip " (B. M. Cat.) Dimensions in mm.:—Length, 245; bill, 18; wing, 125; tail, 80; tarsus, 17.

Female.—" Upper parts, including the pileum and hind-neck, green; a deep blue spot on the occiput; blue spots on the scapulars and inner secondaries less distinct than in the male; no blue patch on the smaller wing coverts near the bend of the wing; lower part of the throat and breast grey and green, without the purple colour at the base of the feathers; no transverse black band below the breast " (B. M. Cat.)

Nest.—A frail platform, composed of a few twigs, and placed in a small tree or in scrub a few feet from the ground.

Eggs.—Clutch one; elliptical in shape; texture fairly fine; surface glossy; colour faintly creamy-white. Dimensions in mm.: —29 x 21.

Breeding Season.—September to February.

Geographical Distribution.—Tasmania (accidental), New South Wales, Queensland, and Northern Territory; also New Guinea and a number of adjacent islands.

Observations.—The late Sir Richard Dry shot the first specimen of the Purple-crowned or Superb Fruit-Pigeon in September, 1872, at Quamby, after a heavy northerly gale.

I have no knowledge of any specimen having been obtained since then.

Sub-Family—Carpophaginæ.

*TOPKNOT-PIGEON

(*Lopholæmus antarcticus*, Shaw).

Male.—" Crest over the nostrils, sides of the head, neck, breast, and under surface silvery-grey, the feathers of the neck and breast being hackled, admitting the darker colouring of their bases to be perceived through the interstices; elongated crest at the occiput rust-red; from the eye to the occiput beneath the crest a line of black, which, meeting behind, is continued for a short distance down the back of the neck; all the upper surface dark slate-grey; primaries, secondaries, and edge of the wing black; tail light grey at the base, black for the remainder of its length, crossed by an irregular hand of buffy-grey about an inch from the extremity; irides fiery orange, surrounded by a lash of pink red, and seated in a bare mealy space of the same colour, but hardly so bright; bill bright rose-red, inclining to lilac at the tip; fleshy part covering the nostrils-and at the base of the lower mandible greenish lead colour in the male and lead colour in the female; feet purplish-red; back of the tarsi and soles of the feet greyish-brown" (Gould). Dimensions in mm.:—Length, 380; bill, 15; wing, 265; tail, 153; tarsus, 32.

Female.—Similar to male.

Young.—" Crest shorter and tail band narrower and less defined " (B. M. Cat.)

Nest.—A platform of stoutish twigs placed in a fairly lofty tree.

Eggs.—Clutch one; oval in shape, with both ends somewhat pointed; texture roughish; surface glossy; colour pearly-white. Dimensions in mm.:—41 x 30.

Breeding Season.—October to December.

Geographical Distribution.—Tasmania (casual), New South Wales, Victoria, and Queensland.

Observations.—This bird is included by the Rev. T. J. Ewing in his " List of the Birds of Tasmania," read before the Tasmanian Royal Society, August, 1854.

The only records I can find relating to this casual visitor refer to two individuals shot in July, 1907, on the North-East Coast.

FAMILY—PERISTERIDÆ (2 species).

Sub-Family—Phabinæ.

BRONZE-WING PIGEON

(*Phaps chalcoptera*, Lath.)

Male.—Forehead tinged with fulvous; dull purple band across the crown; hind-neck and back brownish-grey, with lighter edges; two centre tail feathers brownish-grey, remainder bluish-grey, browner towards the base, with a broad subterminal band of blackish-brown; wings same as back; on the outer web of the wing coverts a broad spot of rich coppery-red or golden bronze-green; on outer webs of inner secondaries are green metallic spots with steel-blue reflections; lores black; a line over the ear coverts white; cheeks, ear coverts, and sides of the neck grey; throat white; breast vinous; abdomen grey; under tail coverts grey; sides brownish; axillaries and under wing coverts cinnamon; bill blackish; legs and feet carmine-red. Dimensions in mm. :— Length, 355; bill, 17; wing, 190; tail, 142; tarsus, 24.

Female.—Generally duller than male; forehead grey; purple band on occiput wanting; breast greyish, like abdomen.

Young.—Closely resembles female.

Nest.—A slight platform of twigs, just sufficiently concave to prevent the eggs rolling out; usually placed in the fork of a horizontal limb not far from the ground.

Eggs.—Clutch two; roundish to oval in shape; texture fine, except the smaller end, which is slightly granular; surface glossy; colour pure white. Dimensions in mm. of a clutch :— (1) 36 x 25, (2) 38 x 26.

Breeding Season.—September or October to January.

Geographical Distribution.—Tasmania and Australia in general.

Observations.—Shooting season begins 1st March and ends 31st July. As a game bird this fine Pigeon is held in high esteem by all true sportsmen, but unfortunately its numbers are far from being on the increase. Two factors are responsible for this, the first being the opening up of the country, and the second the increase in domestic cats in localities where not long since they were rare, owing to the increase in settlers. During the early morning and evening hour the gentle cooing note of the Bronze-wing Pigeon travels a long way on the still air from its feeding ground or waterhole. The seeds of the blue climbing berry, so plentiful in some districts, are much sought after. In disposition it is very shy, and does not willingly allow of a close approach. Should one be so fortunate as to approach close to a small flock feeding on the ground, to which he has been guided by the cooing notes, and which will have stopped before he is within some thirty yards of the birds, he will see them cautiously walking about, craning their necks in all directions in their endeavours to locate the enemy. Should the observer venture closer the·birds will rise with a sharp whirr as their strong wings beat the air, and will fly swiftly and erratically for a short distance before pitching on to the ground. There are times when one will flush the bird from almost under one's feet. The rapid and erratic flight makes the bird a difficult mark for all but old hands with the gun. Heavily to moderately heavily timbered country seems to be its favourite haunts, but it frequently may be found in very lightly timbered tracts. As an aviary bird it does well and breeds moderately well.

BRUSH BRONZE-WING PIGEON

(*Phaps elegans*, Temm.)

Male.—Forehead yellowish; crown of the head grey; a broad chestnut band commences behind the eyes and unites at the occiput; hind-neck and upper back chestnut; lower back, rump, upper tail coverts, and scapulars olive-grey; centre tail feathers olive-grey, basal half of next two pairs brownish-chestnut, rest grey; all the lower feathers have a subterminal band of blackish; upper wing coverts olive-grey, outer ones tinged with chestnut; inner median and greater wing coverts metallic green on outer webs, tips grey; quills brown; a black line on the lores; upper cheeks and upper ear coverts whitish; lower cheeks and under surface olive-grey; a triangular spot of chestnut on the throat. Dimensions in mm.:—Length, 330; bill, 15; wing, 160; tail, 115; tarsus, 24.

Female.—Very similar to male.

Young.—Greyish-brown.

Nest.—A platform of twigs similar to the Bronze-wing, but usually placed in a shady gully.

Eggs.—Clutch two; elliptical in shape; texture fine; surface glossy; colour white. Dimensions in mm. of a clutch:—(1) 31 x 24, (2) 32 x 25.

Breeding Season.—October to December, or even January.

Geographical Distribution.—Tasmania, King and several other Bass Strait islands; also Australia in general.

Observations.—The advance of civilization is responsible for the appreciable decrease in the numbers of the Brush Bronze-wing Pigeon during the last decade. To a certain extent the same localities as are favoured by the Bronze-wing Pigeon are frequented by this species; the difference lies in the fact that the former often frequents lightly timbered tracts, but the latter rarely, if ever, does so. The Brush Bronze-wing is somewhat of a melancholy, retiring nature; it has not the dash and vigour of the Bronze-wing. It contents itself with quietly wandering in the

NEST OF BRUSH BRONZE-WING PIGEON.

Photo. by H. C. THOMPSON.

scrub and searching for food. Often one may find it in close proximity to bush homesteads, always providing there · is an abundance of cover available under which it can hide when danger threatens. This proclivity has been fatal to many birds in more than one district, the domestic cats being responsible for the damage done. It is said that this bird sometimes does no little damage to freshly planted seeds in settlers' gardens. Seeds of all descriptions, small berries, especially those of the native cherry (*Exocarpus*), and insects form its stable food.

ORDER—GALLINÆ : GAME BIRDS.

Sub-Order—Alectoropodes.

FAMILY—PHASIANIDÆ (3 species).

STUBBLE QUAIL

(*Coturnix pectoralis*, Gould).

Male.—Crown of the head blackish-brown, all the feathers tipped with reddish-brown; a pale buff stripe down the centre of the head and mantle sandy, each feather with a broad buff shaft-stripe tapering to a point; also on one or both webs there is a wide black blotch; scapulars, rump, back, and upper tail coverts very similar in colour to mantle, but with narrow wavy bars of reddish-white; wing coverts light brown, with narrow shaft-streaks and transverse bars of buff; quills blackish-brown, outer webs of primaries brown; sides of head, chin, throat, and fore-neck uniform dull brick-red; a black patch in the middle of the chest; sides of chest, breast, and abdomen whitish, with a black stripe down the centre of each feather; sides and flanks reddish-buff, with wide shaft-streaks of white; bill black; legs and feet pale flesh colour. Dimensions in mm.:—Length, 190; bill, 10.5; wing, 107; tail, 35; tarsus, 22.

Female.—Upper surface resembles male, save that the hind-neck and mantle are more sandy-buff; sides of the head and throat whitish-buff, spotted with black; "feathers of the chest and breast with a black curved subterminal bar on either side of the shaft, not confluent at the extremity but separated by a wide buff isthmus " (B. M. Cat.) Bill, legs, and feet as in male. Dimensions in mm.:—Length, 192; bill, 10.5; wing, 103; tail, 37; tarsus, 22.

Young.—Male.—The dull brick colour on the sides of the head and throat not distinct; black breast-patch almost absent.

Nest.—Frequently the nest is in a furrow in a crop, in which case the depression is lined with straw; thick herbage is also chosen, in which case the lining is grass.

Eggs.—Clutch seven to eleven generally; in shape roundish oval, with the texture somewhat coarse and the surface glossy; the ground colour, which is dirty-yellow, is heavily blotched and smudged with dark olive-green. Dimensions in mm. of a clutch : —(1) 29 x 22, (2) 31 x 23, (3) 30 x 21, (4) 32 x 21, (5) 31 x 23, (6) 29 x 22, (7) 30 x 24, (8) 28 x 22, (9) 29 x 21.

Breeding Season.—Somewhat irregular, but may be roughly stated to be from October to January or February.

Geographical Distribution.—Tasmania, New South Wales, Victoria, Queensland, South and Western Australia.

Observations.—Shooting begins 1st May, ends 30th June. Practically every district that has been cultivated holds this fine game bird in greater or lesser numbers. Areas that have been down with cereal crops are preferred to mere grass-lands, as they provide a far better supply of food. Gould remarks :—" Open grassy plains, extensive grass-flats, and the parts of the country under cultivation are situations favourable to the habit of this bird. In its economy and mode of life it so closely resembles the Quail of Europe that a description of one is equally descriptive of the other. Its powers of flight are considerable, and when flushed it wings its way with arrow-like swiftness to a distant part of the plain ; it lies well to a pointer, and has from the first settlement of the State always afforded considerable amusement to the sportsmen. It is an excellent bird for the table, fully equalizing in this respect its European representative."

Through this bird nesting in grain crops, numbers of eggs are destroyed every year. On account of the irregularity of the nesting season, which sometimes extends right into early autumn, young birds may frequently be met with when the shooting season opens. This fact causes some sportsmen to complain that the " season " opens too early, yet there are others again who say it opens too late. But while Quail continue to nest so irregularly there will always be young birds about, no matter when the " season " is.   •

" The chief food of this species consists of grain, seeds, and insects ; the grain, as a matter of course, being only procured in cultivated districts, hence the name of ' Stubble ' Quail has been given to the bird by the colonists of Tasmania, from the great numbers that visit the fields after the harvest is over " (Gould).

As a game bird this species is much appreciated by gourmets. Owing to the straightness of its flight it is easier to shoot than the other species. To a certain extent Quail are nomadic in their habits ; they move about from district to district or one part of a district to another. Their movements are largely dependent on the amount of food available. After having obtained all available food from the stubble fields they scatter over the grassy pasture lands, and pick up what they can.

BROWN QUAIL

(*Synœcus australis*, Temm.)

Male.—Forehead and throat greyish-white tinged with buff; all the upper surface irregularly marked with grey, black, and chestnut, each feather with a distinct narrow white stripe down the shaft; wings marked with obscure lines of grey, brown, and black; all the under surface buffy-grey ('' pale rufous-buff ''— Hall), each feather having numerous zig-zag markings of black, and many with a fine stripe of white down the centre; bill blackish-brown; legs and feet flesh-colour. Dimensions in mm.:—Length, 205; bill, 15; wing, 106; tail, 48; tarsus, 24.

Female.—'' Differs from male in having the black markings and patch on the upper and under parts much coarser; the centres of the feathers are not grey, and the shaft-stripes, which are much wider than in the male, are pale buff '' (B. M. Cat.)

Young.—Closely resembles adult female.

(According to Mr. W. R. Ogilvie-Grant, the old males are nearly uniform in colour, the cross bars and shafts almost entirely disappearing.)

Nest.—A variety of situations are chosen by different birds; they vary from in the centre or under the shelter of a clump of tussock-grass or rushes to a furrow in a green paddock. The nest itself is a flimsy structure of grass and leaves.

Eggs.—Clutch seven to eleven; roundish, but sharply compressed at one end; somewhat coarse in texture; surface glossy; colour dull to bluish white, finely freckled with olive or light brown. Dimensions in mm. of a small clutch:—(1) 32 x 23, (2) 34 x 24, (3) 33 x 23, (4) 34 x 23, (5) 31 x 22, (6) 31 x 23, (7) 33 x 24.

Breeding Season.—November to January.

Geographical Distribution.—Tasmania, including many of the Bass Strait islands, Australia in general, and New Guinea.

Observations.—Shooting begins 1st May, ends 30th June. Among sportsmen there is a diversity of opinion as to whether this species or the Stubble Quail is the better sporting bird. The Brown Quail rises quickly and speeds on a strong wing in a fairly straight line, offering a good mark to a quick, straight shot.

Moist grassy flats and swampy localities are mostly favoured, but it may also be found among ''root'' crops and in situations favoured by the Stubble Quail. The stomachs of a number of birds of the species under discussion were examined and found to contain grass in ½-inch lengths and dock seeds. Some few years since an effort was made by a number of sportsmen to have Quail in general totally protected for at least a couple of seasons, for it was argued that the birds were becoming woefully scarce. Nothing came of the agitation, however, several sports-

men who were opposed to the proposal stating that in their opinion
native cats and domestic cats run wild were responsible for more
havoc than shooters, for they (the cats) destroyed birds all the
year round. From my own experience I know there is much
truth in this assertion. The Brown Quail is fairly well distributed
throughout Tasmania and some of the Bass Strait islands, where
it is very plentiful some years.

As an aviary bird this species does well, breeding freely, and
is fairly easy to rear.

GREATER BROWN QUAIL (SWAMP-QUAIL)

(*Synœcus diemenensis*, Gould).

Male.—Resembles *S. australis* save that the rufous on the
upper parts is more distinct. Altogether the species is brighter
and more distinctly marked than the preceding one. Furthermore,
it is looser feathered, having a somewhat fluffy appearance. The
dimensions are also greater, but I am unable to give figures, as
my skins met with a mishap.

Female.—Resembles the female of *S. australis*, but is slightly
larger, and more distinctly marked.

Nest.—A hollow lined with grass, &c., usually in thick herbage
or under the shelter of a grass-tussock in marshy localities.

Eggs.—Seven to thirteen; roundish oval in shape; texture
somewhat coarse; surface glossy; colour greenish-yellow, spotted
with olive-green. Dimensions in mm. of a portion of a clutch:—
(1) 32 x.24, (2) 31.75 x 24, (3) 32 x 24.25, (4) 32.5 x 25, (5) 32 x
24.75, (6) 31.75 x 25, (7) 32.25 x 24.5.

Breeding Season.—October to January or later.

Geographical Distribution.—Tasmania and Victoria.

Observations.—Shooting begins 1st May, ends 30th June.
The Swamp-Quail, or Silver Quail, as Mr. A. J. Campbell
states it is called in Victoria, is not recognized by the British
Museum authorities as a valid species. But then they have not
had the opportunity of seeing it in its native haunts and standing behind a gun to it, but have only the evidence of "skins,"
which as substitutes for the live birds leave very much to be
desired. Very much the same localities are frequented as by
the Brown Quail, with the difference that the Swamp-Quail very
seldom finds its way to cultivated fields. I have frequently found
it in the proximity of a river where the soil was sandy and grew
practically nothing but sedges.

ORDER—HEMIPODII : HEMIPODES.

FAMILY—TURNICIDÆ (1 species).

PAINTED QUAIL

(Turnix varia, Lath.)

Male.—Crown of the head, nape, and forehead dark brown, spotted with buffy-white; back, rump, and upper tail coverts transversely marked with chestnut-red and black; wings reddish, each feather spotted with white and marked with black; primaries brown; chest buff, the feathers irregularly spotted with grey; abdomen yellowish-white. Dimensions in mm. :— Length, 192; bill, 14; wing, 101.5; tail, 40; tarsus, 22.

Female.—Principally differs from male in that it has a bright rufous nuchal collar, more or less clearly defined, the chest is grey, the shaft of each feather outlined with pale buff, widening into a broad mark near the tip, and the bill is stouter.

Nest.—" Simply a hole in the ground " (J. D. MacLaine). Sometimes the slight depression has a scanty lining of grass or leaves. The nest is generally under the shelter of a tussock or stone.

Eggs.—Clutch four; roundish in shape, with one end somewhat compressed; texture fine; surface glossy; colour whitish, heavily freckled with fine spots of cinnamon-brown and umber; interspersed with which are markings of dark purple and bluish-grey. Dimensions in mm. of a clutch :—(1) 26 x 22, (2) 27 x 21.5, (3) 27.5 x 22, (4) 26 x 21.

Breeding Season.—October to December.

General Distribution.—Tasmania, King Island, and Australia in general.

Observations.—Shooting begins 1st May, ends 30th June. The Painted Quail is somewhat of a scarce species in Tasmania, very few brace in a season falling to the gun of any sportsman, no matter how keen. As a matter of fact, its existence as a game bird is to all intents overlooked

Dry, sandy tracts are mostly resorted to by this species. On several *Epacris* and *Banksia* covered areas on the North-East Coast it is no uncommon occurrence to flush a small covey of Painted Quail. When pursued it runs along the ground as far as possible; then, when absolutely forced to fly, it takes wing with a wavering flight that makes shooting difficult.

Gould says of this species :—" Among the Game Birds of Australia the Varied Turnix plays a rather prominent part, for, though its flesh is not so good for the table as that of the little Partridge Quail, it is a bird which is not to be despised when the game bag is emptied at the end of a day's sport, for it forms an acceptable variety to its contents. Although it does not

actually associate with either of the birds mentioned above, it
is often found in the same districts, and all three species may
be procured in the course of a morning's walk in many parts of
New South Wales, Victoria, and South Australia, where it frequents sterile, stony ridges, interspersed with scrubby trees and
moderately thick grass. It is also very common in many parts
of Tasmania suitable to its habits, hills of a moderate elevation,
and of a dry, stony character being the localities preferred. It
is also numerous on the sandy, sterile islands in Bass Strait. It
runs very quickly, and when flushed flies low, its pointed wings
giving it very much the appearance of a Snipe or Sandpiper.
When running or walking over the ground the neck is stretched
out, and the head carried very high, which, together with the
rounded contour of the back, gives it a very grotesque appearance.''

ORDER—FULICARIÆ.

FAMILY—RALLIDÆ (8 species).

*SLATE-BREASTED RAIL (Lewin's Rail)

(*Hypotænidia brachypus*, Swain.)

Male.—Crown of the head and hind-neck dull chestnut,
streaked with black; back, shoulders, and tail olive-brown,
streaked with black centres to the feathers; the majority of the
wing coverts are black or olive-brown and black, all tipped and
barred with white; quills blackish-brown, external webs olive-
brown; lower sides of neck olive-brown; throat white; breast
olive-brown to ashy-grey; lower breast and abdomen " isabelline'';
sides of the body and flanks mostly barred with white or yellowish-
white; bill brownish-red; legs and feet flesh colour or pale brown.
Dimensions in mm.:—Length, 208; bill, 36; wing, 104; tail, 48;
tarsus, 32.

Female.—Similar to male.

Young.—'' Similar to the adults, but much duller on the
upper surface, the vinous colour of the head and neck being
absent; throat whitish, remainder of under surface dark ashy;
centre of the breast whitish; the sides of the body with a few
black feathers barred with white '' (B. M. Cat.)

Nest.—Situated in a swamp or on swampy ground by the side
of a rivulet, and composed of rushes and fine grass. The rushes
among which it is placed are usually drawn together overhead
to form a covering. Leading to the nest is a staging, always
placed some distance above the water.

Eggs.—Clutch four to five; roundish oval in shape; texture
of shell fine; surface glossy; colour pinkish-white, somewhat

heavily marked with pinkish-red and purple. Dimensions in mm. of a clutch:—(1) 34 x 25, (2) 34.5 x 25, (3) 35 x 24.5, (4) 34.5 x 25.

Breeding Season.—September to December.

Geographical Distribution.—Tasmania, King Island, New South Wales, Victoria, South Australia, South Queensland, and Western Australia; also New Zealand.

Observations.—Lewin's Rail is fairly plentiful in some localities, but, owing to its great shyness, it is difficult to make observations as to its habits. Low, swampy situations are its favourite haunts, for it is in such places that it can find sufficient food and build its nest. Its food consists of insects of all descriptions, captured both in and out of the water; also molluscs, such as are usually found in damp localities. When disturbed this Rail will dive under the water instantly, only reappearing again at some considerable distance. An interesting note from Mr. A. E. Brent is given by Mr. A. J. Campbell, which is well worth quoting. It runs:—" Both Spotted Crake and Lewin's Rail have the stage or track leading up to the nest, but much larger in the latter, on account of the great height of some of the positions from the ground, as compared with those of the Crake, which are low down. I have found the nest of the Rail as high as 3 feet from the ground, whereas I have never seen the other more than 1 foot high. The nest of the Rail is more compact, rounder, and deeper, with the fine grass and rushes overhead laced together and formed into a kind of dome-shaped basket-work covering. I should like to draw your attention to the fact that this little bit of workmanship does not occur until such time as the bird is sitting, when she seems to amuse herself by reaching up her long neck and bill and pulling the rushes down. The nest of the Crake is not like the Rail's, being composed of dry bits of rushes and aquatic weeds, carelessly made, with a slight attempt at an overhead covering. When sitting, the nest-stage and eggs are mostly plastered with a thick coating of mud; in fact, you cannot tell if the latter are eggs or stones. I find I have omitted to say the nest of the Rail is composed of fine band-grass (dry), beautifully put together, with a track of the same material, which has the appearance of being gathered up by the end and carried in as far as the nest by the bird, where the end is tucked in, and the remaining part, which is generally long, left lying where the bird entered. By this means the nest is formed. In the case of the Crake, she carries nothing for her stage, but simply makes use of the rushes and grass at hand, and with her fine long toes she must tread it into position."

*PECTORAL RAIL

(*Hypotænidia philippinensis*, Linn.)

Male.—Crown of the head olive-brown spotted with black; lores dusky-brown, becoming rufous on the sides of the neck; distinct white eyebrow; hind-neck ferruginous, with black centres to the feathers; feathers of the back black, with ochraceous edges and spangled with white spots; lower back, rump, and tail ochraceous-brown, with black centres to the feathers; wing coverts similar colour to back, no spots of white on lesser and median series, but large ones on greater series; primary coverts rufous, tipped with olive-brown and banded with black; quills also rufous, but tipped as well as banded with black; secondaries blackish, tipped with ochraceous-brown; cheeks and fore-neck ashy-grey, washed with brown; throat white; remainder of under surface white, barred with black; flanks barred black and white; across the breast a broad zone of reddish-buff; under wing coverts black, edged with white; bill pale reddish-brown; legs and feet greyish-brown. Dimensions in mm.:—Length, 295; bill, 33; wing, 147; tail, 66; tarsus, 39.

Female.—Similar to male.

Young.—"The colours generally are duller, the pectoral band is reduced to a mere wash of yellowish-brown, and the bars on the under parts of the body are far less conspicuous than in the adult" (Buller).

Nestling.—"Covered with glossy black down" (Buller).

Nest.—Composed of dry grass and leaves placed in a depression among herbage in the vicinity of water.

Eggs.—Clutch five to eight usually; roundish oval in shape; texture fine; surface fairly glossy; colour pinkinsh-white, with a few bold, round blotches of reddish-brown, purple, and purplish-grey. Dimensions in mm. of a clutch:—(1) 35 x 25, (2) 36 x 25, (3) 35.5 x 24.75, (4) 35 x 25.5, (5) 36 x 26, (6) 36 x 25.

Breeding Season.—September to December.

Geographical Distribution.—Tasmania, Australia in general, New Zealand, many of the Pacific Islands, and right up to the Philippines.

Observations.—The Land Rail, as this bird is frequently termed, is but a summer visitor, arriving about August and departing about February. Unfortunately, I have not sufficient data to determine with certainty the exact dates of arrival and departure. In very few, if any, localities in Tasmania is this Rail even comparatively plentiful. On account of its shy, retiring disposition, it is but seldom seen unless specially searched for. It escapes observation by running rapidly through the thick vegetation of its haunts; only when hard pressed does it take flight. The localities mostly favoured by this species are grassy flats between hills, whence there is always an abundant supply of water; marshy ground where a river flows through low-lying country, and any other place where there is moisture and a dense growth of vegetation. Its food consists chiefly of a miscellaneous assortment of insects and molluscs gathered in the marshes and swamps of its hunting ground.

*SPOTTED CRAKE
(*Porzana fluminea*, Gould).

Male.—Forehead dark slaty-grey; crown of the head and back olivaceous-brown, the feathers having dusky centres; wing coverts same colour as back, but less spotted; bastard wing, primary coverts, and quills olivaceous-brown; the feathers of the bastard wing are edged with white, as is the first primary; innermost secondaries spotted with white; throat and breast dark slaty-grey; abdomen white; sides of body black, with white bars; edge of the wing white; under wing coverts blackish, edged with whitish; bill bright orange at base, passing into olive-green; legs and feet dark olive-green. Dimensions in mm. :—Length, 172; bill, 20; wing, 102; tail, 54; tarsus, 29.

Female.—Similar to male.

Nest.—Situated in a clump of grass or rushes growing in a swampy locality, and composed of green weeds and lined with soft grass. A staging connects the nest with the water.

Eggs.—Clutch four to five; roundish oval in shape; texture fine; surface glossy; colour brownish-olive, blotched and marked, especially about the stouter end, with red and purplish-brown. Dimensions in mm. of a clutch :—(1) 32 x 22, (2) 31 x 21.5, (3) 31.5 x 22, (4) 32 x 22.

Breeding Season.—September to the end of the year.

Geographical Distribution.—Tasmania, New South Wales, Victoria, and South Australia.

Observations.—Owing to the reclamation of certain lagoons and semi-swamps, places where it was once abundant know it no more. At no time and in no place are the habits of aquatic birds easy of study, and now that some of their breeding places have gone for ever the task of ascertaining new facts concerning their life-history, &c., is rendered very much more difficult. Like the rest of the family, the Spotted Crake is of a very retiring disposition. Its grey and brown plumage so assimilates with its surroundings as to prove a defence that makes detection difficult. On account of its habit of keeping close to its natural haunts—reed-beds and swampy ground generally—much difficulty is experienced in gathering satisfactory notes of its general habits.

When forced to take refuge in flight, which it does only when very hard pressed, its wing power is somewhat feeble, the flight being rather low and laboured, with much flapping of the rounded

9

wings. As may be expected, its food consists of insects captured in and out of the water, and molluscs generally found in the herbage of swampy localities.

*LITTLE CRAKE

(Porzana palustris, Gould).

Male.—Head brown, streaked with darker colour; back dark brown, spotted with white, feathers edged with rusty-brown; tail feathers dark brown, with lighter edges; throat and chest pale ashy-grey; centre of abdomen white; flanks blackish-grey, barred with white; bill, legs, and feet olive-brown. Dimensions in mm. :— Length, 154; bill, 16; wing, 82; tail, 40; tarsus, 24.

Female.—Similar to male.

Nest.—Composed of short portions of rushes and aquatic plants, loosely woven together, and concealed in rushes, &c., growing in shallow water. There are two entrances to the nest, one at the back and another in front.

Eggs.—Clutch four to eight; oval in shape; texture fine; surface glossy; colour brownish-olive, freckled or spotted all over with dark brownish-olive. Dimensions in mm. of a clutch :—(1) 28 x 19, (2) 27.5 x 18, (3) 27 x 19, (4) 28 x 18.5, (5) 27.5 x 17.5.

Breeding Season.—October to January.

Geographical Distribution.—Tasmania, New South Wales, Victoria, South Australia, Western Australia, and South Queensland.

Observations.—The dense, rank vegetation of some of our swamps and lagoons is the favourite haunt of this Crake. In some districts this species is fairly plentiful, but, owing to its general habits, it is difficult to ascertain with any degree of certainty as to its rarity or not.

*SPOTLESS CRAKE

(Porzana tabuensis, Gmelin).

Male.—Crown of the head and neck blackish-brown; back chocolate-brown; rump, upper tail coverts, and tail blackish; wing coverts similar to back; primary coverts and quills dusky-brown, first primary edged with whitish; innermost secondaries chocolate-brown; under surface slaty-grey; throat paler; under tail coverts black, barred with white; bill black, legs and feet dull red. Dimensions in mm. :—Length, 162; bill, 13; wing, 78; tail, 40; tarsus, 26.

Female.—Similar to male.

Young.—Upper surface resembles that of the adult; under surface nearly white, throat white.

Nest.—Composed of dry grass, placed on the ground under the shelter of a clump of rushes or band-grass, in the proximity of water.

NEST OF NATIVE-HEN, WITH CHICK.

Photo. by H. C. THOMPSON.

Eggs.—Clutch four usually; lengthened oval in shape; texture fine; surface glossy; colour greyish-white, mottled with chestnut. Dimensions in mm. of a clutch:—(1) 27 x 20.5, (2) 27.5 x 21, (3) 26.75 x 20, (4) 28 x 21.5.

Breeding Season.—October to December, perhaps January.

Geographical Distribution.—Tasmania, New South Wales, South and Western Australia, Queensland; also New Zealand, and many islands in the South Pacific, up to the Philippines.

Observations.—To the best of my knowledge this is the rarest of the Rails and Crakes in Tasmania; as a matter of fact, in none of its habitats is it at all plentiful. Frequently this species is known as the Tabuan Water Crake. In its general habits and food it much resembles the other species previously discussed.

" Its compressed form enables it to thread its way among the close-growing reed-stems with wonderful celerity; and although its low purring note (resembling that of a brood hen) may sometimes be heard on every side, it is extremely difficult to obtain a glimpse of the bird. Its body weighs only two ounces; and its attenuated toes are well adapted for traversing the oozy marsh in search of its food, which consists of small fresh-water molluscs, insects, seeds of aquatic plants, and the tender blades of various grasses. It seldom takes wing, and then only for a very short distance; but it runs with rapidity, swims very gracefully, and often dives to escape its enemies " (Sir W. Buller).

NATIVE-HEN

(*Tribonyx mortieri*, Du Bus).

Male.—Upper surface greyish-olive, lightly washed with chestnut-brown on the crown of the head and back of the neck, and distinctly tinged with the same colour on the back, rump, and upper tail coverts; tail black; wing coverts greenish-grey, tinged with olive, the median series tipped with white; primary coverts and quills blackish-brown, edged with reddish-brown; under surface bluish-slate, becoming blackish on the abdomen and under tail coverts; conspicuous patch of white on the flanks; sides of the body brownish; thighs purplish-grey; irides ruby; bill yellowish-green; legs and feet yellowish. Dimensions in mm.:—Length, 500; bill, 39; wing, 190; tail, 95; tarsus, 77.

Female.—Similar to male save that the chestnut-brown on the back is less pronounced. Dimensions in mm.:—Length, 445; bill, 39; wing, 190; tail, 95; tarsus, 77.

Nest.—Flat and shallow; a variety of substances enter into its composition, depending largely on its situation. When it is half afloat, either in a swamp or under shelter of a bank of a creek, it is composed of grass or aquatic herbage; when on the bank of a river or stream at the base of a tree or among briers, leaves, twigs, and grass are used.

Eggs.—Clutch four to nine; varying in shape from stout oval to long oval; texture of shell coarse; surface fairly glossy; ground colour grey or greenish-stone, marked with moderate-sized spots of reddish-brown and purplish-brown, many minute spots of the latter colour appearing as though under the surface. Clutches from different localities often differ in size, shape, and the number and intensity of the markings. Dimensions in mm. of an average clutch:—(1) 53 x 40, (2) 54 x 39, (3) 54 x 38, (4) 56 x 39, (5) 51 x 36, (6) 54 x 40, (7) 54 x 38. Of a selected pair:—(1) 62 x 39, (2) 65 x 37.

Breeding Season.—August to January.

Geographical Distribution.—Tasmania.

Observations.—There are very few dwellers in the country, at least, who do not know this bird, if not by sight at least by sound. In some districts it is extremely plentiful, but, owing to its shy disposition, it is always difficult to obtain an idea of its numbers unless one lays oneself out for the express purpose of watching for it. Although as a general rule the nest is placed well out of sight and away from habitations, I know of more than one instance where the nest was constructed in the open by the side of a creek not more than two hundred yards from a dwelling. Along the edges of rivers that overflow their banks at times, and where there is a quantity of *débris* washed up against the roots of the willows and briers, no true nest is formed, but only a semblance of one, for sticks, leaves, and other vegetable matter are raked together and formed into an apology for a nest. Swampy places, creeks, and rivers, where there is a sufficiency of cover on the banks, are the favourite haunts of this bird. During the middle of the day it generally remains hidden among the undergrowth of its retreats, but early in the morning and just about sundown it sallies forth in search of food. It is at such times that one is made painfully aware of the harsh, grating voice of this bird, which can be heard for a considerable distance. A chorus of some half-dozen or more is rather excruciating, especially when heard at close quarters, as I have often found when lying watching their habits. Each and every bird seems to commence on a different key, so that the discord may be imagined. The noise of sharpening a saw or cutting through galvanized iron is music in comparison. The Native-Hen is a very swift runner, and will give most dogs a good " go " over a short distance. From practical experience I know that this bird cannot be domesticated, even when the eggs are taken from the nest and brought out under a farmyard hen. A peculiar habit of the bird is that of bobbing its tail constantly up and down as though the appendage were on a spring. When not in motion it is carried erect like that of the ordinary domestic fowl. In some agricultural districts where the haunts of the Native-Hen are in close proximity to grain fields, farmers are very vehement in their accusations against the bird, for they allege it does great damage to the grain just when it sprouts, and also when in the ear. It is not so much the amount of grain consumed as the quantity destroyed that is objected to, for a small party of birds will trample down a large patch in the course of a night, and make it look as though an elephant had been rolling there. The places trampled down are often circular in shape, as though they had been used as play-grounds. When a small flock or even a pair of birds are feeding in or about a grain field, one bird is always on the watch, and gives a short cry of alarm should danger threaten. As a natural result of its mischievous traits, a relentless war with poison and gun is waged on this unfortunate fowl. In several instances that have come under my notice the charges brought by farmers have been fully sustained. When not engaged in purloining forbidden grain, the food of this species consists of a certain quantity of aquatic vegetation and a miscellaneous assortment of insects gathered on land and out of the water, admixed among all of which is always more or less gravel, used as an aid to digestion. Owing to the weakness of the muscles of the chest and wings, the Native-Hen is almost, if not quite, incapable of rising about the surface of the ground. On the other hand, the leg and thigh muscles are well developed. As an article of diet this bird is despised by all except Chinamen, who, I am given to understand, use it for making certain dishes of which they are very fond.

BALD-COOT
(*Porphyrio melanonotus*, Temm.)

Male.—Face, back of the head, centre of the abdomen, and thighs sooty-black; back of the neck, breast, and flanks rich indigo blue; upper surface, tail, and wings shining black; outer webs of primaries indigo blue; under tail coverts pure white; iris brown; frontal plate and bill crimson; legs and feet salmon-pink, joints black. Dimensions in mm.:—Length, 515; bill, 74; wing, 278; tail, 110; tarsus, 92.

Female.—Similar to male.

Young.—"Pretty black creatures, resembling at a distance Langshan chickens" (Miss J. A. Fletcher).

Nest.—A somewhat carelessly put together structure of reeds, rushes, or aquatic plants; placed in a swamp or lagoon among the growth there.

Eggs.—Clutch four to seven generally; oval or elliptical in shape; texture somewhat coarse; surface slightly glossy; colour greyish-brown or greenish-stone, spotted and blotched with reddish-brown (the most frequent colour), purplish-brown, and dull grey. The markings are bolder and more reddish than those on Coots' eggs. Dimensions in mm. of a clutch:—(1) 53 x 36, (2) 56 x 36, (3) 55 x 35, (4) 52 x 34, (5) 54 x 35, (6) 55 x 33.

Breeding Season.—September to December usually.

Geographical Distribution.—Tasmania, King Island, New South Wales, Victoria, South Australia, Queensland, Northern Territory; also New Zealand, Norfolk and Lord Howe Islands.

Observations.—In many parts of Tasmania the Bald-Coot is more or less plentiful, but, taking it altogether, it is not as plentiful as the Native-Hen. Nearly every swamp, lagoon, and river flat supplies its quota. It is said that this bird becomes easily domesticated and will live quite contentedly among poultry. Like the previous species, it is very destructive to sprouting grain, so much so that farmers in affected districts have occasionally been forced to organize a regular battue. It has a rather extraordinary method of eating its vegetable food. It seizes the food between the hind claw and sole of one foot, holding it up, and rapidly devouring it in small pieces. Like the Native-Hen, it is a very swift runner, and makes use of this power to escape from its enemies, fancied or real. Only when hard pressed does it take to flight. Early morning and evening are the best times to see this bird, for it is at such times that it sallies out in search of food, which is similar to that of the preceding species. Down the River Tamar, where it is frequently secured by shooting parties, it has developed great cunning, for often the heads of the birds may be seen peering over the tops of the long reeds, which they have climbed to see if danger threatens. As soon as they know they are perceived they drop out of sight and scurry away.

COOT

(Fulica australis, Gould).

Male.—Head and neck black; whole of the upper surface bluish to greyish black; under surface black; irides red; bill bluish-grey; legs and feet blackish. Dimensions in mm.:—Length, 370; bill, 36; wing, 177; tail, 51; tarsus, 47.

Female.—Similar to male except that the under surface is greyish and the feathers are very narrowly margined with whitish.

Young.—"The young in down are black, having yellow hair-like tips, the down thickest about the face and neck; bill cream colour" (A. J. Campbell).

Nest.—A bulky structure, partly submerged: composed of broken reeds and other aquatic plants, the top not coming more than a few inches above the surface of the water. It is placed in a swamp or a lagoon.

Eggs.—Clutch seven to nine; oval in shape; texture of shell somewhat coarse; surface slightly glossy; colour dull or buffy-white, or else stone colour, spotted and freckled with small spots of dark purplish-brown, many appearing as though below the surface. Dimensions in mm. of a clutch:—(1) 51 x 36, (2) 52 x 35, (3) 52 x 34, (4) 51 x 33, (5) 49 x 33, (6) 50 x 34, (7) 51 x 35.

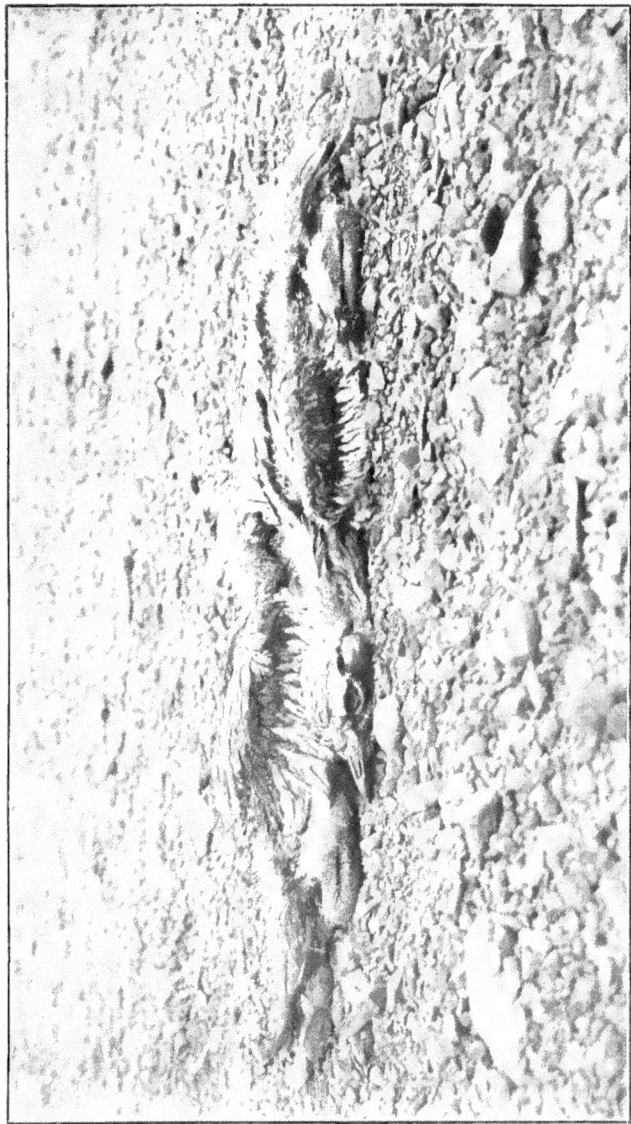

YOUNG STONE-PLOVERS "PLANTING."

Photo. by H. BURRELL.

From "THE EMU."

Breeding Season.—September to December.

Geographical Distribution.—Tasmania, King Island, and Australia in general.

Observations.—The Coot is not as generally distributed throughout the island as either of the two preceding species. On some of the lakes and larger lagoons it is, however, fairly numerous. Of late years its numbers have diminished, owing to Duck-shooters taking heavy toll, as it is considered by many very palatable. It is quite a sight to see large flocks of this species feeding in the water, and when suddenly disturbed scuttling off as fast as they can to take shelter in the reeds. Diving is often resorted to when feeding; the birds give a slight upward spring and then disappear for a short space, returning with some food plucked from below. In addition to vegetable stuffs, the usual insects and molluscs found in and about lakes and lagoons are devoured.

ORDER—LIMICOLÆ : PLOVERS, &c.

FAMILY—ŒDICNEMIDÆ (1 species).

*STONE-PLOVER (LAND CURLEW)
(*Burhinus (Œdicnemus) grallarius*, Lath.)

Male.—Crown of the head and hind-neck ashy-grey, streaked with blackish; shoulders and back also streaked, but more heavily; lower back and rump ashy-grey, with blackish shaft-streaks; tail feathers crossed by numerous narrow and irregular bars; the outer ones are broadly tipped with black; there is also a broad subterminal bar of white; lesser wing coverts dark brown; median series dull white, with black shaft-streaks; greater series dark ashy-brown; primary coverts and quills black, first four primaries broadly banded with white; secondaries white towards base of inner web; eyebrow white; band below the eye black; ear coverts brown; cheeks reddish-brown, streaked with black; throat and under surface white, tinged with tawny and streaked with black; under tail coverts pale cinnamon-buff; bill black; legs yellowish-olive; feet brownish. Dimensions in mm. :—Length, 520; bill, 49; wing, 270; tail, 155; tarsus, 116.

Female.—Similar to male.

Young.—" The prevailing colour of the young in down is a light grey, with a darker marking in the shape of an oval line extending from the head to near the end of the back; dark lines also extend from the wings towards the tail " (A. J. Campbell).

Nest.—None formed, the eggs being laid on the bare ground.

Eggs.—Clutch two usually; inclined to oval in shape; texture fairly fine; surface slightly glossy; colour pale buff, blotched all over with umber and dull slate. Dimensions in mm. of a clutch from Victoria :—(1) 58 x 39, (2) 57 x 38.5.

Breeding Season.—August to December.

Geographical Distribution.—Tasmania (accidental) and Australia in general.

Observations.—The first record we have of this species in Tasmania is contained in the proceedings of the Royal Society, 1894-5 report. We there find that a bird was obtained at Spring Bay, April, 1895, and another at Swansea in the following July. In *The Emu* (vol. vii., p. 36) Mr. T. Hurst, Caulfield (Vic.), reports having seen a flock of fully 30 "feeding contentedly in a stubble paddock" some twelve miles down the west bank of the River Tamar. This was Easter, 1907. I have grave doubts as to the birds seen being correctly identified. Personally I have never met with this species in Tasmania, nor can I ascertain any undoubted record of it being seen by anyone else since the birds of 1895 were shot.

The Stone-Plover favours grassy plains and uplands with outcrops of broken stones, where it can hide with ease when danger threatens. Like all Plovers, it resorts to strange devices in its endeavours to lure an intruder from the vicinity of its eggs or young. Its flight, though rapid, has an appearance of being laboured. It does not remain in the air for long, but soon drops to the ground. In disposition it is very shy; very rarely does it allow one to approach to within anything like close quarters. When on the ground it runs with great rapidity, and should real or imaginary danger threaten, rather than fly it will squat down among the stones and remain practically invisible. The colour of the young bird matches more closely the stones of their haunts than does that of the parent bird. They (the young birds) will remain crouched among the stones until almost trodden on. Stone-Plover usually move about their feeding and breeding grounds in pairs or small bands of four or six birds. Sometimes, however, at certain seasons of the year, they congregate in larger flocks. I believe that it is at night time that this bird moves from one district to another or wings its way to more southerly regions. At the approach of evening the air resounds with its loud, harsh cries. Its food consists of insects and seeds found on the ground among the stones of its haunts.

FAMILY—CHARADRIIDÆ (24 species).

Sub-Family—Arenariinæ.

TURNSTONE

(*Arenaria interpres*, Linn.)

Male (breeding plumage).—General colour of upper surface black mixed with chestnut; lower back and rump white; upper tail coverts black; tail feathers black, with white bases, all but centre feathers tipped with white; lesser wing coverts blackish; median coverts chestnut mottled with black; greater coverts blackish, tipped with white; primary coverts black, innermost with white tips; primaries black, with white shafts; secondaries mostly white, with blackish tips; crown of the head and hind-neck white, streaked and mottled with black; " base of forehead and narrow frontal line black, followed by a band of white, which unites with a broad eyebrow, and is extended over the ear coverts " (B. M. Cat.); lores and cheeks white; a patch of black beneath the eye, which is connected with the sides of the neck, fore-neck, and sides of the breast, all of which are black interspersed with white; throat and abdomen white; iris hazel; bill black; legs and feet deep orange-red. Dimensions in mm.:—Length, 200; bill, 23; wing, 154; tail, 57; tarsus, 24.

Female (breeding plumage).—Chestnut markings less conspicuous.

Male and Female (winter plumage).—Upper surface, including head, dusky-brown, feathers edged with ashy-brown; sides of face brown; sides of neck light brown.

Young.—Upper surface dusky-brown, feathers edged with sandy-buff; crown of head dark brown, streaked with sandy-buff; lower throat, fore-neck, sides of neck, and sides of breast mottled with dusky centres to the feathers; rest of plumage very similar to adults.

Nest.—According to Dr. R. B. Sharpe, the nest is constructed in a slight depression in the ground, and lined with a few dead leaves. It is generally concealed behind a bush, or under some broad-leaved plant or a tuft of herbage.

Eggs.—Clutch four; pyriform in shape; texture fine; surface glossy; colour greenish-stone, boldly blotched and daubed with umber; there are also some underlying spots of purplish-grey. Dimensions in inches, as given by Dr. Sharpe:—1.5-1.7 x 1.05-1.2.

Breeding Season.—June to (?).

Geographical Distribution.—Tasmania, Australia in general; also practically the whole of the rest of the world.

Observations.—The Turnstone is but an infrequent visitor to our shores during the summer months from the Polar regions, from whence it arrives in winter or non breeding plumage.

Writing of this species, Dr. Sharpe says:—" This handsome little Plover is by no means shy, and in autumn the young birds may be approached within easy distance of observation. I have seen them at this latter period of the year resting, at full tide, on the green herbage just beyond the high water mark in some of our southern harbours. When sitting on the shingle, however, their plumage so completely harmonizes with the surrounding stones that they are not discovered until they fly up with a sharp note. It is essentially a bird of the sea-coasts, and is very seldom seen inland, although it is said to move across country in its migra-

tions. The name of ' Turnstone ' is derived from its curious habit
of turning over pebbles to look for the insects underneath, and
Colonel Fielder has in his possession a slab of stone several inches
square which he saw turned over by one of these birds. Edward,
the Banffshire naturalist, noticed three of them engaged upon moving the body of a fish, which, as they could not overturn it, they
undermined, and were then enabled to reach the insects which
were underneath the body. Mr. E. W. Nelson also says that the
species feeds upon the larvæ of the insects which are found upon
the tens of thousands of seal carcasses strewn about the Seal
Islands in North-Western America. ' The call note of the Turnstone,' writes Mr. Seebohm, ' is a clear, loud, shrill whistle,
having some resemblance to the call notes of the Golden and Grey
Plovers, which may be represented by the syllable ' Ko ' or
' Keet.' It has also a double note, which may be represented by
the syllables ' Kitter '; and not infrequently the single note is
added, making a treble note, ' Kitter keet.' In spring, during the
breeding season, it is said that these notes are often so rapidly
uttered that they form a trill.' ''

Sub-Family—Hæmatopodinæ.

*PIED OYSTER-CATCHER

(*Hæmatopus longirostris*, Vieill.)

Male.—Head, neck, back, wings, and chest sooty-black; rump,
under tail coverts, and abdomen pure white; irides crimson; legs
light brick colour. Dimensions in mm. :—Length, 493; bill, 74;
wing, 265; tail, 105; tarsus, 54.

Female.—Plumage similar to male; bill longer by 15-17 mm.
and more slender.

Young.—Head black; neck, back, tail, wing, and chest
brownish-black, the feathers margined with pale rufous; rump and
upper tail coverts white, streaked with brownish-black; breast and
the rest of the under surface pure white; bill yellowish, tip black;
legs and feet flesh colour.

Nest.—The only semblance of a nest is a shallow circular depression scratched in the sand near the sea shore.

Eggs.—Clutch two; somewhat elliptical in shape; texture somewhat coarse; surface glossy; ground colour light stone-grey,
spotted and blotched with umber; obscure markings of bluish-grey
appear as though under the surface. Dimensions in mm. of a
clutch :—(1) 64 x 41, (2) 63 x 40.

Breeding Season.—September to December.

Geographical Distribution.—Coasts of Tasmania and several of
its larger dependencies, whole of the mainland; also New Zealand, New Guinea, and Moluccas.

Observations.—About the sea-shore around the coasts of Tas-

mania and the majority of the islands in Bass Strait, the Pied
Oyster-catcher is fairly common, but very shy. When disturbed
the bird utters a cry which, as Mr. A. J. Campbell tells us, has
caused a southern tribe of aborigines in Western Australia to call
it " Quickham," for so the alarm notes may be translated.
Its flight is rapid and strong; frequently when on the wing
it will utter its loud call notes, as though endeavouring to attract
the attention of others of its species. As a general thing it moves in
pairs, but occasionally a small flock of some half-dozen birds may
be seen busily searching among the *débris* and stones left exposed by the tide for small crustaceans, molluscs, and the like.
The late Sir Walter Buller wrote :—" During the nuptial season
it is curious to watch the male bird paying his addresses to the
mate of his choice; elevating his back and lowering his bill till
it nearly touches the ground, he struts or runs round her with a
loud quivering note, no doubt expressive of his undying attach-
ment; and when there are two rival males thus performing in
concentric circles before the same shrine of devotion, it is amusing to watch with what perfect indifference the object of this
demonstration appears to receive the attentions of her rival suitors.
When once, however, her affections are secured, she appears to
remain faithful to her mate, and the pair continue together, if
not for life, certainly long after the breeding season, with all its
cares, has passed by. Even when consorting together, as they
frequently do, in small flocks, each pair seems to maintain its
individuality ; and when at rest on the sands the party may be seen
disposed in couples, at short distances apart from the rest."

SOOTY OR BLACK OYSTER-CATCHER

(*Hæmatopus unicolor*, Wagler).

Male.—Entire plumage sooty-black; iris red; round the eye is
a fleshy circle of coral-red; bill coral-red; legs and feet coral-pink;
nails yellow. Dimensions in mm. :—Length, 470; bill, 75; wing,
288; tail, 127; tarsus, 53.

Female.—Plumage similar to male; bill longer by 15-17 mm.,
and more slender. The difference in the length of the bills is the
only external distinguishing mark of the sexes.

Young.—Small editions of the adults.

Nest.—As Mr. J. D. MacLaine remarks, the eggs are laid
among the seaweed, well above high water mark, or on the mesem-
bryanthemum in the clefts of the rocks.

Eggs.—Clutch two; somewhat elliptical in shape; texture
fairly coarse; surface glossy; colour stone-grey, marked and
spotted with irregular shaped and sized blotches of umber and
dark brown, a few markings of dull greyish appearing as though
under the surface. Dimensions in mm. of a clutch :—(1) 66 x 42,
(2) 68 x 45.

"The eggs are similar to those of the Pied Oyster-catcher, but are larger in size, darker in the ground colour, and the character of the markings as a rule is not so uniformly roundish in shape" (A. J. Campbell).

Breeding Season.—August to December.

Geographical Distribution.—Coast of Tasmania, a number of islands in Bass Strait, and Australia; also New Zealand.

Observations.—This species is generally to be seen in company with the preceding one, but there are some islets in Bass Strait where the Black Oyster-catcher is the only species seen. In its economy it is a counterpart of the Pied species. During the breeding season it moves in pairs, at other times in small bands. Very rarely does one see it further inland than the extreme edge of the rocks, where it will allow itself to be splashed time and again by the rollers without moving out of the reach of the water. Even when flying from one part to another of the rocky shore of its haunts, it prefers flying over the water to taking a short cut inshore. Its sharp cry is usually uttered when on the wing, but sometimes when at rest, especially should danger threaten. When with eggs or young, many strange antics are performed in an endeavour to entice intruders away. In general disposition the bird is very shy.

Sub-Family—Lobivanellinæ.

SPUR-WINGED PLOVER

(*Lobivanellus lobatus*, Lath.)

Male.—Crown of the head black, also back of the neck, and extending backwards to meet a broader band across the hind-neck as far as a black patch on the sides of the upper breast; back of the neck and rump brown, tinged with olive; sides of the rump and upper tail coverts white; tail white, with a broad band of black at the tip, the outer feathers tipped on extreme ends with white; wing coverts like the back; primaries, coverts, and quills black; lores, sides of face, and ear coverts, as well as the entire under surface, white, including the under wing coverts and axillaries; bill pale yellow, tip darker; legs and feet purplish-red; wattles yellow. Dimensions in mm. :—Length, 380; bill, 34; wing, 247; tail, 104; tarsus, 75.

Female.—Similar to male.

Young.—"Collar round the neck and underneath part white; forehead, crown of the head, rest of upper surface mottled black and brownish-grey" (A. J. Campbell).

Nest.—No proper nest is constructed, but the eggs laid in a depression in the ground by the side of a swamp or the edge of marshy country; on occasions a few dead stalks are placed in the nesting hollow.

NEST OF SPUR-WING PLOVER.

From "The Emu."

Photo. by H. Burrell.

Eggs.—Clutch, three to four usually; pyriform or nearly so in shape; texture fairly fine; surface glossy; colour rich warmish green, somewhat boldly marked with different shades of olive. Dimensions in mm. of a clutch:—(1) 50 x 36, (2) 48 x 35, (3) 49 x 36, (4) 48 x 35.5.

"Eggs show a marked tendency to correspond with the colouration of their environment" (Col. Legge).

Breeding Season.—August to the end of the year.

Geographical Distribution.—Tasmania, several of the larger islands in Bass Strait, New South Wales, Victoria, South Australia, and Queensland.

Observations.—Shooting begins 1st February, ends 30th June. This fine bird mostly confines itself to open, swampy localities bordered by grassy uplands. Except during the immediate breeding season it moves in flocks, which vary greatly in size. On the mainland two broods are said to be reared in a season; in all probability the same applies to Tasmania. The note of the Spur-winged Plover is a harsh cry, which grows very loud and discordant when the bird is alarmed. The ordinary cry is uttered when on the wing. It moves from one feeding ground to another very often under the cover of darkness. On moonlight nights I have on many occasions heard flocks passing over Launceston, calling loudly as they flew. Sometimes one flock can be heard calling to another, which answers in quite a different key. I do not know whether they have any special time for moving; I have heard them at all times from 9 p.m. until midnight. This Plover is a very courageous bird when there are young or eggs to be defended. Although naturally very shy, it becomes bold and daring in the extreme when real or imaginary danger threatens. In addition to feigning lame or wounded, and doing all in its power to lure the intruder away from its nest, it will boldly attack sheep-dogs and predaceous birds. Not only does it fly screaming round them, but right into their faces to turn them from its nest. It does not hesitate to attack man should occasion arise. Its food consists of insects and the like gathered from off the ground of its haunts.

Sub-Family—Charadriinæ.

BLACK-BREASTED PLOVER

(*Zonifer tricolor*, Vieill.)

Male.—Crown of the head and nape glossy black; back brown, glossed with purplish-bronze; sides of rump and upper tail coverts white; basal half of tail white, terminal half black with the extreme tips of the feathers white; wing coverts like the back, median series tipped with white; there is also a subterminal bar of black; greater coverts white; primary coverts and quills black; behind the eye a broad streak of white; cheeks and throat white,

" encircled with a broad band of black, which extends from the
base of the bill, below the eye, and across the ear coverts down
the sides of the neck on to the fore-neck and breast, where it
widens and forms a very broad pectoral band "; rest of under
surface, also under wing coverts, white; bill yellow, tipped with
black; legs and feet blackish-brown; iris yellow; wattle deep red,
base bright yellow. Dimensions in mm. :—Length, 285; bill, 24;
wing, 200; tail, 94; tarsus, 49.5.

Female.—Plumage similar to male. Dimensions in mm. :—
Length, 275; bill, 22; wing, 183; tail, 85; tarsus, 44.

Nestling.—" Sandy-brown, with black markings; a white
collar round the hind-neck; under surface white, with a broad
black collar on the breast" (B. M. Cat.)

Nest.—A slight indentation in a fallow field or open grass run
is lined with a small collection of pieces of dead herbage.

Eggs.—Clutch four; pyriform in shape; texture of shell fine;
surface slightly glossy; colour light olive-stone, usually spotted
and blotched all over with small markings of brown. Dimensions
in mm. of a clutch :—(1) 46 x 30, (2) 44 x 31, (3) 45.5 x 31, (4)
45 x 30.

Breeding Season.—September to December.

Geographical Distribution.—Tasmania, New South Wales,
Victoria, Queensland, South and Western Australia.

Observations.—Shooting begins 1st February, ends 30th June.
The Black-breasted Plover is more familiar to most people than
the species previously discussed, as it is the one more frequently
exposed for sale during the open season, and also it resorts to
cultivated land in the vicinity of homesteads. Whereas the Spur-
winged Plover is hardly ever found away from more or less marshy
ground, the species now under review frequents grass lands and
cultivated fields impartially. In some districts at certain times
of the year it is rather common, moving in fairly large flocks. It
seems rather a remarkable thing that two prominent writers, when
dealing with Australian ornithology, should persistently overlook
the fact that this species and the previous one are found in this
island.

During the shooting season the Black-breasted Plover becomes
very wild, often not allowing one to approach to within gunshot.
Shooters, if they can obtain a wounded bird, make it cry out; by
doing this others are attracted back, when one or two shots can be
obtained. It moves over the ground very fast. When feeding it
will run a short distance, stop, then hurry on a little further. On
several occasions I have been to within a few yards of a flock of
this species, and no notice has been taken of me. Certainly, I
was without a gun, on the road, and the birds feeding in a field
close to the dividing fence.

It resorts to many of the same devices as the previous one in
order to lure intruders from its nest. It is not, however, as

courageous as the Spur-wing. Sometimes a number will nest close together in a field, for common safety, perhaps.

As may be expected, its food consists of all kinds of insects and their larvæ, gathered in the open country and cultivated fields.

GREY PLOVER
(*Squatarola helvetica*, Linn).

Male (breeding plumage).—General colour of upper surface, including scapulars and wing coverts, mottled with bars of black and ashy-white; lower back and rump dusky-brown, spotted and fringed with white; upper tail coverts and tail white, barred with black; quills black, inner webs white; crown of the head like back, but with more black; forehead and eyebrow white, extending down the sides of the neck to the upper breast, where it forms a large patch; lores, sides of the face, ear coverts, and under surface black, except abdomen and under tail coverts, which are white; axillaries black; iris dark hazel; bill, legs, and feet black. Dimensions in mm. :—Length, 263; bill, 33; wing, 201; tail, 74; tarsus, 45.

Female (breeding plumage).—Similar to male, save that the upper surface is less spangled with black and the under surface less uniformly black.

Male and Female (winter plumage).—Black on face and breast absent; upper surface ashy-brown, edged with whitish; throat and under parts white.

Young.—Resemble adults in winter dress, but are spangled with golden-buff on the upper surface; axillaries black.

Nest.—"Was a hollow, evidently scratched, perfectly round, somewhat deep, and containing a handful of broken, slender twigs and reindeer moss " (Seebohm and Harvie-Brown). The nest was situated on "one of the dry, tussocky ridges intersecting the bog." This was on the tundra in the valley of the lower Petchora, Kassia.

Eggs.—Clutch four. "Intermediate in colour between those of the Lapwing and the Golden Plover, and subject to variations, some being much browner and others more olive; none quite as olive as typical Lapwings' eggs or as buff as typical ones of the Golden Plover, but the blotching is in every respect the same. The underlying spots are equally indistinct; surface spots are generally large, especially at the larger end, but occasionally very small and scattered, and sometimes taking the form of thin streaks. They vary in length from 1.9 to 2.2 inches, and in breadth from 1.45 inch to 1.4. Only one brood is reared in the year " (Seebohm).

Breeding Season.—Messrs. Seebohm and Harvie-Brown found eggs in June and July.

Geographical Distribution.—Tasmania, Australia in general,

New Guinea, South Africa, and the Indian Peninsula, breeding
in the high north in Siberia, Russia, and Alaska.

Observations.—The true home of this globe-trotting bird is
within the Arctic Circle, where it breeds during the summer,
wandering far southward during the winter, arriving here in small
flocks during the beginning of our summer.

All writers on the Grey Plover state it is essentially a shore-
loving bird, never venturing far inland, yet the only locality from
which I have records of it for Tasmania is in the Lake district.
Doubtless it also frequents the Low Head district, in company
with the Lesser Golden Plover, as the country is more suitable
for it.

LESSER GOLDEN PLOVER
(*Charadrius dominicus*, Mull.)

Male (breeding plumage).—Upper surface, including head,
lower back, rump, and upper tail coverts, mottled with black,
golden-buff, and ashy-white markings; scapulars and wing coverts
with more gold and buff than back; tail feathers brown, barred
with pale golden, outer ones notched with white on outer webs;
frontal band and eyebrow white, extending down the sides of the
neck and joining the white on the sides of the body; sides of face,
ear coverts, and throat smoky-black; centre of fore-neck, breast, and
abdomen deep black; thighs black; under tail coverts white; axillaries smoked-brown; iris dark hazel; bill black; legs and feet lead-
grey to nearly black.   Dimensions in mm.:—Length, 260; bill,
24; wing, 170; tail, 65; tarsus, 40.5.

Female (breeding plumage).—Similar to male, but with black
on breast patchy.

Male and Female (winter plumage).— Black on face and breast
wanting; axillaries always smoked-brown.

Young.—Resemble adults in winter plumage, but with more
golden on upper surface and slightly more brownish on lower.

Nest.—"Merely a hollow in the ground upon a piece of turfy
land, overgrown with moss and lichen, and lined with broken
stalks of reindeer moss" (Seebohm).

Eggs.—Clutch three to four; pyriform in shape; texture fairly
fine; surface glossy; colour varies from rich clay-brown to light
stone-grey, mottled all over with blotches of black, the underlying
blotches and spots being reddish-brown. Dimensions as given by
Dr. Sharpe are:—1.85-2.05 in. x 1.27-1.35 in.

Breeding Season.—Similar to preceding species.

Geographical Distribution.—Tasmania, Australia in general,
New Guinea, New Zealand, many islands in the Pacific, India, and
South America, breeding in the far north of the old and new
worlds.

Observations.—Here we have another bird whose globe-trotting propensities are at least as great as those of the Grey Plover.

It only visits us in small flocks and in company with other species. Gould obtained specimens along the banks of the Derwent and vicinity; he also shot it on one of the islands in Bass Strait. I have received specimens from Low Head, where small flocks were feeding in company with other birds along the sea-beach.. It is also to be found about the Great Lake district. According to Mr. A. J. Campbell, this species arrives in the Australian "region" towards the end of October. What time it arrives at Low Head I am unable to definitely ascertain. I have seen it on the opposite side of the river in December. The middle to the latter end of May is the latest it has been seen at Low Head. Very often this bird is known under the name of the Asiatic Golden Plover.

*DOUBLE-BANDED DOTTREL

(*Ochthodromus* (*Ægialitis*) *bicinctus*, Jard. and Selby).

Male (*breeding plumage*).—A broad stripe of white across the forehead, above which a band of black; rest of head and whole of upper surface pale brown; primaries blackish-brown; throat white, surrounded by a narrow line of black, which commences above the upper mandible and continues down the sides of the neck and across the chest in a broad band; across and down the centre of the abdomen a broad band of bright chestnut; rest of under surface white; two central tail feathers greyish-brown, next paler, outside ones white; bill yellowish, tipped with black. "Dimensions:—Length, 6¾ in.; bill, ⅝; wing, 4⅝; tail, 2⅜; tarsus, 1⅛" (Gould).

Female (*breeding plumage*).—Similar to male.

Male and Female (*winter plumage*).—The chestnut band becomes considerably reduced, but does not altogether disappear.

Young.—"Upper parts diffused with rust-red, each feather having a narrow margin of that colour; forehead, throat, and under parts white, with a slight tinge of rufous; a broad zone of dark mottled grey encircles the fore-neck, but there is no indication of the pectoral band of chestnut" (W. Buller).

Young "in down resemble little brownish puffs, being of a bright sandy-yellow, mottled with dark brown on the upper surface, changing to yellowish-white on the under parts" (A. J. Campbell).

Nest.—None formed, eggs being laid in a slight hollow.

Eggs.—"Clutch three; inclined to pyriform in shape; texture of shell fine and thin; surface without gloss; colour of a greenish tinge, or light green stone (but sometimes greyish-stone), spotted and fancifully streaked fairly over with sepia or black. In some specimens the markings form patches about the obtuse end. Dimensions in inches:—1.4 x .98, (2) 1.37 x 1.0" (A. J. Campbell).

10

Breeding   Season.—According to the late Sir W. Buller, August to December.

Geographical   Distribution.—Tasmania and several of its dependencies, Australia, New Zealand, New Guinea, and several other islands in the Pacific.

Observations.—So far as I am aware the eggs of this species have not yet been found either in Tasmania or Australia, its breeding stronghold being New Zealand. Gould observed large numbers in the vicinity of George Town during the month of May; they were on migration. The late Mr. Ronald Gunn stated that the species was plentifully dispersed along the northern shores of the island. Colonel Legge is of opinion that the Double-banded Dottrel breeds òn some of the islands in Bass Strait. This may be so, but, taking into consideration the attention that the various groups have received during the past few years, it is strange that if the bird really does breed on any of them its eggs have not been found. The late Sir W. Buller, the well-known authority on New Zealand birds, says :—"In location of the nest itself there is very little attempt at concealment, the bird apparently trusting more for protection to the assimilation of colouring; but after the young are hatched out the old birds (and particularly the female) manifest considerable solicitude for the safety of their offspring, and feign lameness or a damaged wing for alluring intruders away—a device which very often succeeds. The young bird runs the moment it quits the shell, and is not slow to second its parent in the art of self-preservation. Its sandy colour makes it almost indistinguishable when squatting on the ground, and it has the instinct to remain perfectly motionless the moment it hears the note of alarm, even allowing itself to be handled without betraying a sign of vitality."

The following interesting note was forwarded by Mr. H. Stuart Dove :—" On the afternoon of 16th July, 1909, which was warm and sunny, about 30 of this species were feeding in a swampy paddock at East Devonport. The flock was wary, and would not allow me near enough to make out the bands; but it is my own opinion, and that of a distinguished ornithologist to whom I referred the matter, that the party was of this species. As the conspicuous black band pales to ashy-brown in winter, it is not remarkable that this was not to be made out at a distance without glasses, and the chestnut band would not be very conspicuous either under these conditions. Upper surface appeared brownish, under surface white, with whitish patch at rump when on wing. The wings were somewhat curved, and a pretty effect was produced when they all wheeled together before alighting. This species is not infrequent along East Devonport sands." Under date of 6th December he again writes :—" It may interest you to know that I have seen the Double-banded Dottrel several times this spring on our beaches, although it is supposed to go to southern New

Zealand to breed. A pair was observed on 15th September, and on 30th October two pairs were seen, in company with the Red-capped species, which is always here."

*RED-CAPPED DOTTREL
(*Ægialitis ruficapilla*, Temm.)

Male.—Crown of the head and back of the neck rich rusty-red; between the forehead and the crown of the head is a crescent-shaped line of black; a line of the same colour extends from the corner of the mouth to the eyes, and down the sides of the head; upper surface and wings light brown, each feather tipped with yellowish; four central tail feathers dark brown, remainder white; primaries blackish-brown, with edges of outer webs white, forehead and under surface white; irides brown; bill black; legs and feet blackish. Dimensions in mm.:—Length, 158; bill, 15; wing, 103; tail, 40; tarsus, 25.

Female.—Similar to male, save that the rusty-red colour is pale.

Nest.—A slight depression in the sand a little distance above high water mark, occasionally ornamented with a few pieces of seaweed, but at other times quite plain.

Eggs.—Clutch two, pyriform in shape; texture fine; surface without gloss; colour usually stone, blotched and spotted with dark brown and sepia. Dimensions in mm. of a selected clutch from the mouth of the Tamar:—(1) 30 x 23, (2) 28 x 22.

Breeding Season.—September to October or January.

Geographical Distribution.—Tasmania, King Island, the whole of Australia, also New Guinea.

Observations.—The Red-capped Dottrel is, perhaps, the most plentiful of the Dottrels, or Sand-Plovers, to be seen round our coasts. It is in addition the smallest species. It does not congregate in flocks as large as some of the other species.

A note on this species, taken while on a visit to Kelso, at the mouth of the Tamar, may not be without interest:—"The first birds to attract my attention were Red-capped Dottrels. These pretty little birds were very numerous on all sides, some busily fishing in the shallow pools; in one small pool nearly a dozen were counted; some engaged in play, mimic combats, and running hither and thither in sheer exuberance of spirits; others resting on the dry sand; others, again, flying on rapid wing from one part of the beach to another. The rapidity with which they run is surprising; one can hardly follow their slim little legs as they twinkle over the sand. The flight is very rapid, and generally not far from the surface of the water or the ground. Both when on the wing and on the ground they utter their sharp little cry. These birds have a curious habit, the same as I have noticed in the Silver Gulls—*i.e.*, of now and then running sideways for some yards as though blown by a strong breeze—no satisfactory explanation for which is forthcoming from observation. From the intentness with which the parties in the pools were fishing, substantial results must have been crowning their efforts. Many were engaged in turning over dead 'sea-urchins' and scraps of seaweed scattered about. Turning my glasses inshore, my attention was arrested by the suspicious movements of one of these birds; it ran down the beach to a pool, pottered round for some time as though unable to decide on its next movements, then ran slowly up the beach, dodging among the piled-up heaps of kelp, until at last it arrived at a spot a little distance above high water mark, then, apparently satisfied that the coast was clear, squatted on the sand. After keeping the spot under observation for some little time, I walked slowly up to where the bird appeared to have stopped—it, of course, had fled at my first movement—but could find no semblance of a nest. After searching round for some little time I slowly retraced my steps, examining carefully every foot of the ground; not many yards had been traversed before I suddenly espied, right at my feet, a pair of the prettily marked eggs of this species lying on a shallow depression in the bare sand. The nesting hollow was not more than the size of a crown piece, and quite destitute of lining save for a few broken scraps of grass-roots lying against one side. The nest was some three or four yards above high water mark. Subsequently I watched another bird sneak above high water mark, come to a standstill, and squat down. But owing to its distance from where I lay concealed, and the similarity of the surroundings, I was unable to locate the exact spot."

BLACK-FRONTED DOTTREL

(*Ægialitis melanops*, Vieill.)

Male.—Forehead, a stripe commencing at the eye, passing over the ear coverts and round the back of the neck, and a broad band across the chest extending a short distance downwards black; a stripe of white passes over each eye and continues round the back of the neck, separating the black band from the crown; crown, back, and middle of the wings brown; shoulders deep chestnut; tips of greater wing coverts white, forming an obscure band across the wing; primaries black; whole of the under surface, save for the black band, white; two middle tail feathers brown, tipped with black; next three on each side white at the base, passing into blackish-brown tipped with white; remainder entirely white; bill orange, tipped with black. Dimensions in mm. :—Length, 164; bill, 15; wing, 106; tail, 56; tarsus, 25.

Female.—Similar to male.

Nest.—Merely a slight hollow in a river bed or on a sandy ridge.

Eggs.—Clutch three; pyriform in shape; texture fine; surface without gloss; colour light stone, marked all over with fine spots

NEST AND EGGS OF RED-CAPPED DOTTREL.

Photo. by H. C. THOMPSON.

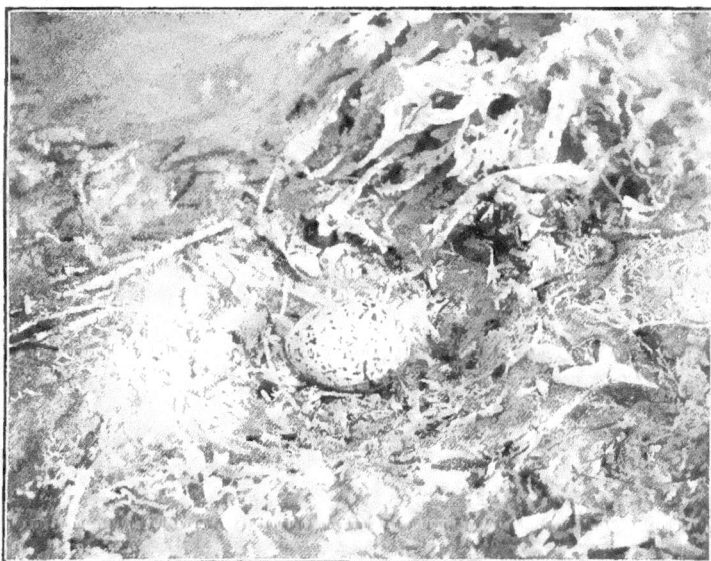

NEST AND EGG OF HOODED DOTTREL.

Photo. by H. C. THOMPSON.

and lines, chiefly of umber. Dimensions in mm. of odd examples:
—(1) 29 x 20, (2) 28.5 x 21.

Breeding Season.—August to the end of the year.

Geographical Distribution.—Tasmania (accidental) and Australia in general.

Observations.—The first record, so far as I am aware, of this species being found in Tasmania was by Mr. W. L. May, of Sandford, in 1896, who shot a specimen. As to whether this species has succeeded in establishing itself here I do not know. Personally I have never met with it in the flesh.

Unlike other Dottrels, the Black-fronted species does not frequents the exposed sea-beaches, but prefers the shores of inland lagoons and lakes.

*HOODED DOTTREL

(*Ægialitis cucullata,* Vieill.)

Male.—Head, fore-neck, and a band across the upper part of the back sooty-black; back of the neck and under surface white; back and shoulders greyish-brown; centre of the wing white, rest black; two middle tail feathers black; the next three on each side white at the base and tip, black in the centre; remainder of feathers white; bill orange, tipped with black. Dimensions in mm.:—Length, 206; bill, 19; wing, 130; tail, 63; tarsus, 25.

Female.—Resembles the male save that the head is mottled with white.

Young.—Crown of the head, back, and upper tail coverts light grey, each feather being narrowly margined with black; semicircular band of black on nape of neck; neck, throat, and whole of under surface white; primaries black; secondaries black, narrowly tipped and margined with white; bill black.

Nest.—Just above high water mark a slight circular depression is made in the sand, in which are sometimes placed a few scraps of seaweed.

Eggs.—Clutch two to three; somewhat pyriform in shape; texture fine; surface without gloss; ground colour soft stone-grey, spotted and marked all over with irregularly shaped marks of blackish-brown. Dimensions in mm. of a clutch:—(1) 38 x 26.5, (2) 37 x 27, (3) 38 x 26.5.

Breeding Season.—September to January.

Geographical Distribution.—Tasmania, some of the larger Bass Strait islands, New South Wales, South and Western Australia, and South Queensland.

Observations.—The Hooded Dottrel is plentiful practically everywhere round the coasts of Tasmania. Being very graceful in all its movements, it is very pretty to watch it running over the sands with short, quick steps. When running very fast its legs fairly twinkle, if one may be pardoned for using the term. It is very entertaining to watch a small band feeding at low water when the tide is just on the turn. As the waves retreat the birds run down as far as they can and hunt about in the wet sand with great energy. As the waves come tumbling shorewards back the birds scurry as fast as their legs will carry them, only to hurry down the sandy beach again in the wake of the retreating breakers.

Unless hard pressed this bird does not take readily to flight, preferring to trust to its legs to carry it out of danger.

Sub-Family—Himantopodinæ.

*WHITE-HEADED STILT
(*Himantopus leucocephalus*, Gould).

Male.—Back of the neck, back, and wings glossy greenish-black; rest of plumage pure white; bill black; legs flesh colour. Dimensions in mm.:—Length, 370; bill, 56; wing, 223; tail, 77; tarsus, 105.

Female.—Similar to male.

Young.—Crown of the head, back, wings, and tail dull black, tinged with brown; under surface pure white.

Nest.—Constructed of grass, twigs, and aquatic herbage, and placed some inches above the water in a shallow swamp.

Eggs.—Clutch four; pyriform in shape; texture of shell fine; surface fairly lustrous; colour yellowish-olive, heavily marked with sepia and dull greyish-black. Dimensions in mm. of a clutch:—(1) 44 x 29, (2) 43 x 28, (3) 44 x 30, (4) 43.5 x 29.

Breeding Season.—Erratic. According to Mr. A. J. Campbell, August or September, or even as late as April or May.

Geographical Distribution.—Tasmania, Australia in general; also New Guinea and Moluccas.

Observations.—The first notice of this species being found in Tasmania was a communication to the Tasmanian Royal Society, July, 1852, when it was reported that a specimen had been shot at South Arm in April of that year.

Its appearance in certain localities depends greatly upon climatic conditions. During a wet season, when there is an abundance of water in swamps and lagoons, it is sure to be found in greater or lesser numbers. The White-headed Stilt is very graceful in all its actions; but for its delicate proportions its long legs would appear incongruous. It associates in small flocks along the margins of inland swamps and lagoons, where its long legs are of great use in allowing it to wade among the aquatic plants and search for its food.

The late Sir Walter Buller says of this species:—" Notwithstanding the extraordinary length of its legs, this bird is most graceful in all its movements; it is a very pretty sight to watch a flock of them on the edges of a lagoon stalking about in the

shallow water in search of their food, which consists of aquatic
insects and small molluscs, and displaying their well-balanced
bodies in a variety of artistic attitudes. When on the wing the
legs are trailed behind with a slight swaying motion, as if to
preserve the equipose, and the bird utters a sharp, quick-repeated
note like the yelping of a small cur."

*BANDED STILT
(*Cladorhynchus leucocephalus*, Vieill.)

Male.—Whole of the upper surface, including head, neck, and
tail, white; chest crossed by a broad band of chestnut; wings and
centre of abdomen black; bill black; legs flesh colour ("red "—
Gould; "yellowish "—A. J. Campbell). Dimensions in mm. :—
Length, 439; bill, 72; wing, 198; tail, 90; tarsus, 82.

Female.—Similar to male.

Young.—"Entirely white below " (R. Hall).

Nest.—None formed, the eggs being laid on the bare ground
usually, or should a slight depression be formed it is ornamented
with a few scraps of herbage.

Eggs.—Clutch four; inclined to pyriform in shape; texture
fine; surface slightly glossy; colour rich olive-stone, marked and
blotched with sepia and umber. Dimensions in mm. of odd
examples :—(1) 45 x 30, (2) 42 x 29.5.

Breeding Season.—According to Mr. A. J. Campbell, between
the months of April and November in the interior.

Geographical Distribution.—Tasmania, New South Wales,
Victoria, South, Western, and North-West Australia.

Observations.—In certain favourable localities it may be seen
in small numbers in company with other waterfowl wading about
in the mud at the mouths of estuaries, in swamps and lagoons. It
does not visit us until near the end of the year, and again departs,
after a short stay of a few months, for the interior of the mainland.
As may be expected from the nature of its haunts, its food consists
of all manner of molluscs and insects gathered in and about the
lagoons and mud-flats it frequents.

Its note may best be described as somewhat similar in sound
to the barking of a pup.

*RED-NECKED AVOCET
(*Recurvirostra novæ-hollandiæ*, Vieill.)

Male.—Head and upper part of the neck chestnut; middle of
the wings, primaries, and part of the shoulder feathers black; rest
of the plumage white. " Length, 18½ in.; bill, 3⅜; wing, 8¾; tail,
3½; tarsus, 3½ " (Gould).

Female.—Similar to male.

Nest.—The eggs are laid on the bare ground, usually near water.

Eggs.—" Clutch four; long oval in shape; texture of shell

somewhat coarse; surface lustreless; colour a shade of deep stone, or stone colour with an olive tinge, moderately marked over the surface with blotches and large spots, mostly roundish in form, of dark brown; also some duller markings of a slaty-chocolate appear under the shell's surface. Dimensions in inches of a clutch:—(1) 2.04 x 1.34, (2) 2.03 x 1.4, (3) 1.92 x 1.28 " (A. J. Campbell).

Breeding Season.—September to December.

Geographical Distribution.—Tasmania, Australia in general; also New Zealand.

Observations.—This species cannot be said to be a regular visitor to our shores, and when it does come it is in small numbers only. In appearance it greatly resembles a Stilt, but its bill is very much upturned. The Avocet frequents the shores of lakes and estuaries.

Speaking of the European representative of this species, Mr. Seebohm says:—" Like the Stilt, the Avocet haunts the margins of the water, running daintily along the wet, shining sands, or exploring the black mud-banks in the shallow lakes. It is not particularly shy, but if alarmed will mount into the air, its long legs stretching behind in a line with its bill, and fly round and round, uttering its alarm note, which resembles the syllables ' Tut, tut, tu-it, tu-it.' If one of the birds is wounded its companions fly round overhead, incessantly uttering their notes, as if bewailing its fate. At all seasons of the year the Avocet is sociable, and may be observed in large or small parties. It is a very beautiful sight to watch a party of these birds, when their nesting grounds are invaded, daintily run along before you, their brilliant plumage contrasting strongly with the mud or sand. . . . The food of the Avocet is captured principally on the mud and in marshy places. It is chiefly composed of worms, small crustaceans, and vast quantities of aquatic insects. Their prey is searched for as the bird moves its long, slender bill from side to side across the surface of the sand or mud, or in the shallows. The Avocet never appears to probe in the soft ground with its bill, but always uses it in a side direction. A small quantity of gravel is swallowed to aid digestion. Sometimes the bird captures the little gnats and other insects as they flutter over the water, or flit by on the land.''

Sub-Family—Totaninæ.

*CURLEW

(*Numenius cyanopus*, Vieill.)

Male.—The whole of the upper and lower surfaces are varying shades of brown and greyish-buff, heavily striated with dark brown; legs bluish lead colour. Dimensions in mm. :—Length, 530; bill, 177; wing, 305; tail, 110; tarsus, 83.

Female.—Similar in plumage to male. Dimensions in mm. :—
Length, 600; bill, 188; wing, 315; tail, 118; tarsus, 89.
Nest and Eggs.—Unknown.
Breeding Season.—Unknown.
Geographical Distribution.—Tasmania, King Island, and doubt-
less other of the larger islands in Bass Strait; Australia in general,
New Zealand, New Guinea; migrating to Eastern Siberia, where it
breeds.
Observations.—The Curlew is a fairly familiar bird about the
mouth of the Tamar and various other localities on the North,
North-East, and North-West Coasts towards the latter end of the
year, arriving in September. I cannot speak with any degree of
certainty concerning the Southern Coast. A note of mine made
one December at the mouth of the Tamar reads :—" Away on a
small bank by the edge of the water was a long-billed, long-legged
bird whose identity puzzled me for some short while, but when
at last it flew to join some companions, before unnoticed on the
edge of a channel slightly to my left, I found the party to consist
of Curlews. With slow and stately walk they marched about,
searching the shallow pools with long, inquiring bills for their
breakfast. I noticed that when on the wing the neck is sometimes
constricted after the manner of the White-fronted Heron (*Notophoyx novæ-hollandiæ*)."
In common with other migratory species, the Curlew at the
approach of autumn wings its way to Siberia, where spring is
fast approaching, and there breeds. Gould was of opinion it
would be found breeding in the highlands of Tasmania, but, as
is well known, such is not the case.
Some years a few individuals remain all the winter, they being,
in all probability, non-breeding birds.

*WHIMBREL

(*Numenius variegatus*, Salvad.)

Male (breeding plumage).—Upper surface nearly uniform dark
brown; feathers of mantle and upper back marked with ashy-
brown; lower back and rump very thickly mottled with bars and
spots of brown; tail ashy-brown, tipped with white and crossed
by regular bars of dark brown; wing coverts like the back;
primaries blackish-brown, notched with white on inner webs;
secondaries brown, with white marks on both webs; centre of
crown streaked with brown, remainder of crown dark brown, forming two broad bands; sides of face and neck pale brown, with
darker streaks; chin and upper throat white, sparsely spotted with
brown; lower throat, breast, and sides of body pale reddish-buff,
streaked with dark brown; abdomen and under tail coverts white,
the latter with brown marks; axillaries white, with broad and
numerous bands of brown; iris dark brown; bill blackish; legs and

feet deep lead colour. Dimensions in mm.:—Length, 385; bill, 75; wing, 225; tail, 95; tarsus, 54.

Female (breeding plumage).—Similar to male.

Male and Female (winter plumage).—Lower back perfectly white; under surface less distinctly streaked; otherwise similar to summer plumage.

Young.—Upper surface much mottled, the feathers spotted on both webs with whitish or pale reddish buff; under surface practically similar to adults.

Nest and Eggs.—Unknown.

Breeding Season.—Unknown.

Geographical Distribution.—Tasmania, Australia in general, New Guinea, through the Malay Archipelago to Japan and Eastern Siberia.

Observations.—So far as my observations go, this species is a somewhat rare visitor to our shores. When it does straggle down here it is with the other migratory waders, in whose company it may be seen; its food and general habits are also very similar. The Australian Whimbrel is very closely allied to the species found in Europe—in fact, some authorities go so far as to consider them one and the same. In general appearance this bird is very similar to the Curlew, but smaller.

*BARRED-RUMPED GODWIT

(*Limosa novæ-zealandiæ*, Gray).

Male (breeding plumage).—Upper surface blackish, mottled with pale rufous and cinnamon; lower back and rump dusky, feathers with white edges; tail feathers greyish-brown, barred and tipped with white; wing coverts dark brown, feathers edged with white and some tinged with chestnut; primary coverts and quills blackish, primaries lighter brown on inner webs; secondaries edged with white and with subterminal white mark on inner webs; crown of head chestnut, streaked with black; eyebrow chestnut; lores and side of face chestnut, the former spotted with black; under surface chestnut, streaked with black on upper breast; under wing coverts thickly mottled with dusky bases to the feathers; axillaries distinctly barred with dusky-brown; iris brown; bill, tip blackish, base reddish; feet blackish-brown. Dimensions in mm.:—Length, 376; bill, 86; wing, 224; tail, 74; tarsus, 55.

Female (breeding plumage).—Similar to male, but less distinctly marked.

Male and Female (winter plumage).—Upper part of back rusty-brown, mottled with white; lower back greyish-white, varied with brown; rump and upper tail coverts barred with brown; tail feathers brown, barred and tipped with white; wing coverts brown, more or less tipped with white; primaries brown; secondaries light rust-brown; crown and sides of the face dusky-brown; throat white; breast and sides of the body creamy-white, tinged with grey; abdomen and under tail coverts white.

Young.—Resemble adults in winter plumage, but more reddish on both upper and under surfaces; tail distinctly barred with dusky-brown and buffy-white.

Nest and Eggs.—Unknown.

Breeding Season.—Unknown.

Geographical Distribution.—Tasmania, Australia in general, New Zealand, the other Oceanic islands, the Malayan Archipelago, up through China and Japan to Eastern Siberia.

Observations.—This species is the Eastern representative of the Bar-tailed Godwit (*L. limosa*) of Europe. The two species breed in almost but not quite the same regions. The European bird nests principally in Finland and Lapland, only going as far east as the Yenesei Valley, while the Australian species favours chiefly the eastern portion of Siberia. It is generally considered that the Taimyr Peninsula forms the dividing line between the two species. Their general habits are to all intents similar. The vicinity of the sea-shore, and on the sand-banks and mud-flats, are the favourite haunts of the Barred-rumped Godwit. In addition to these places it is not infrequently found on flooded lands, swamps, and lagoons. On occasions it congregates in fairly large flocks, and keeps company with other species of shore-loving and wading birds.

It is a shy species, very difficult to approach. Although it freely mixes with other birds when feeding, yet when disturbed it separates from them and flies only in company with its own species. On the mainland when plentiful it is shot for the market.

Although the nest and eggs of this species have not yet been discovered it is thought there is every probability that they are very similar to those of the Bar-tailed Godwit.

*COMMON SANDPIPER

(*Tringoides hypoleucus*, Linn.)

Male (breeding plumage).—Upper surface bronzy-brown, with central arrow-shaped markings of black, forming bars on the scapulars and inner secondaries; tail feathers bronzy-brown, barred with blackish-brown and tipped with white; wing coverts like the back, but regularly barred with blackish; greater coverts broadly tipped with white; primary coverts and quills brown, glossed with olive; the secondaries are tipped with white, and have broad white bases; head and neck bronzy-brown, with blackish-brown shaft-streaks; cheeks and under surface white, streaked with brownish; sides of chest and upper breast brown; axillaries white; iris brown; bill blackish; feet greyish-green. Dimensions in mm.:—Length, 200; bill, 27; wing, 103; tail, 50; tarsus, 24.

Female (breeding plumage).—Similar to male, but less heavily marked.

Male and Female (winter plumage).—Upper surface almost uniform bronzy-olive, without central black marks to feathers; under surface less distinctly streaked.

Young.—Upper surface with cross bars of reddish-buff and dusky-brown, giving the upper surface a freckled appearance; under surface almost uniform, scarcely streaked.

Nest.—" A mere hole lined with dry grass and moss, or without lining; situated among herbage upon the banks of a stream, in a gravel bed among pebbles, in irregularities upon the surface of a bare rock (Buller)" (A. J. Campbell).

Eggs.—" Generally four in number, varying in colour from pale clay-colour to greenish-white, with chocolate-brown spots and blotches, as a rule equally distributed, but sometimes more thickly round the larger end, the underlying spots purplish-grey. Axis 1.3-1.6, diameter 0.95-1.05 " (R. B. Sharpe).

Breeding Season.—May and June.

Geographical Distribution.—Tasmania, Australia in general, New Guinea, Africa, India; also throughout temperate Europe and Asia, where it breeds.

Observations.—Like a number of other species the Common Sandpiper, or, as it is called in England, the Summer Snipe, only visits us during the northern winter, arriving here with the other migratory wading birds and departing at or about the same time. Not only does it frequent the sea-shore and the mouths of rivers and estuaries, but also the margins of inland lakes. The Sandpiper almost invariably moves about singly, but on occasions as many as half a dozen may be seen feeding and flitting from place to place in company. I have seen this on the North-West Coast. Its food consists of insects of various descriptions and crustacea gathered from out of the water and under the pebbles of its haunts.

" Shortly after their arrival at their breeding grounds the males are very demonstrative and excessively noisy. In early summer they may often be seen running along the rough stone walls near the water, with drooping wings, as if displaying their charms to the females crouching amongst the herbage below. At this season the cock birds sometimes soar into the air and utter a short trill, as is the case with most other waders " (Seebohm).

*GREENSHANK

(*Glottis nebularius*, Gunner).

Male (breeding plumage).—Upper surface ruddy-brown, with black centres to the feathers; lower back, rump, and upper tail coverts white; two central tail feathers ashy-grey, remainder of tail feathers white barred with blackish; head and neck streaked with black; under surface white; lower throat, fore-neck, and chest spotted with black; bill blackish-brown; legs and feet yellowish-grey. Dimensions in mm.:—Length, 305; bill, 52; wing, 193; tail, 76; tarsus, 55.

Female (breeding plumage).—Similar to male.

Male and Female (winter plumage).—Upper surface ashy-brown, with whitish fringes to the feathers; lower back, rump, and upper tail coverts white; tail feathers white, barred with brown; wing coverts brownish, fringed with white; secondaries ashy-brown, fringed with white; crown and hind-neck greyish-brown, feathers edged with white; forehead, lores, and sides of face pure white; sides of neck streaked with ashy-brown; under surface white; sides of upper breast freckled with brown; axillaries white; iris dark brown; bill, legs, and feet light slate colour.

Nest.—" Sometimes built in a tuft of grass, or concealed amongst the heath and short herbage; it is, according to Mr. Seebohm, very slight, being a mere depression in the ground, lined with a few bits of dry grass or withered leaves" (R. B. Sharpe).

Eggs.—Clutch four; pyriform in shape; texture fine; surface glossy. According to Dr. Sharpe, the ground colour varies from creamy-buff to deep clay-brown; spotted and blotched with deep chestnut and purplish grey, especially about the stouter end. Dimensions in mm. vary from 42 to 51 by 31 to 34.

Breeding Season.—May and June.

Geographical Distribution.—Tasmania, Australia in general, Africa, India, China; migrating to Northern Europe generally, and parts of Northern Asia, where it breeds.

Observations.—To the late Mr. Tom Carr belongs the honour of being the first to record the Greenshank for Tasmania. This specimen was shot down the Tamar in 1892.

My first introduction to this species was in 1904, when staying at Kelso, at the mouth of the Tamar. I there recorded:—" Not far away, and sometimes mingling with the Dottrels, were a number of Greenshanks. Their behaviour was a marked contrast to that of the Dottrels; for, while the latter birds were all hurry and skurry, the Greenshanks took matters very calmly. While some fished in the pools and along their edges, thrusting their long bills into the mud, others slept or preened their feathers. Now and then a small party would leisurely take flight to another and more distant part of the beach. All the while I had the birds under observation there was constant movement, much coming and going. Altogether there must have been some twenty individuals of this species scattered over different parts of the beach. What made their presence all the more interesting was the fact that the species is but an irregular visitor to our shores, there being but few records of previous visits."

Sub-Family—Scolopacinæ.

*LITTLE STINT (Red-necked Stint)
(*Limonites ruficollis*, Pallas).

Male and Female (winter plumage).—Forehead and above the lores white; crown of the head and back ashy-brown, with dark shaft-streaks to the feathers; lower back, rump, and upper tail coverts blackish-brown; sides of lower back and upper tail coverts white; tail feathers smoky-brown; wing coverts rather dark brown, the greater coverts tipped with white; primary coverts blackish-brown, tips edged with white; quills dark brown, with white shafts; secondaries dark brown, tips fringed with white, also base of inner web white; lores dusky-brown; ear coverts light brown; cheeks, throat, and under surface white; sides of neck brownish; under wing coverts white; bill, legs, and feet black. Dimensions in mm. :—Length, 147; bill, 17; wing, 95; tail, 41; tarsus, 19.

Male (summer plumage).—" Much more mottled on the upper surface than in winter, the centres of the feathers being blackish and the whole of the upper parts overspread with a brighter chestnut colour, with which the feathers are broadly margined; the crown is blackish, washed with rufous and mottled with grey margins; the forehead and eyebrows are shaded with bright rufous, and this colour occupies the whole of the sides of the face, sides of neck, throat, and chest, the chin being whitish; bill and feet black; iris nearly black " (B. M. Cat.)

Female (summer plumage).—Practically similar to that of the male, but slightly less rufous.

Young.—Upper surface blackish, edged with rufous; hind-neck ashy; scapular feathers edged with whitish; fore-neck and chest tinged with buff.

Nest and Eggs.—Unknown.

Breeding Season.—Unknown.

Geographical Distribution.—Tasmania, Australia in general, New Guinea, and the Malay Archipelago; migrating to Burma, China, Japan, and Eastern Siberia.

Observations.—The home of this little Sandpiper is Eastern Siberia, where it is supposed to breed. By some writers this species is known as the Red-necked Stint, to distinguish it from another species, also called the Little Stint, which breeds in Northern Europe and winters in Japan and Ceylon.

The favourite haunts of the species that visits our shores during the summer are brackish lagoons, arms of the sea, and the shores of rivers flowing into the ocean. In such places it feeds on all manner of marine insects and crustacea. The Little Stint never visits us in any numbers, as it does Rottnest Island, off the coast of Western Australia.

During December, 1909, Mr. H. Stuart Dove observed individuals of this species on the West Devonport beach.

~ *SHARP-TAILED STINT (Marsh Stint)

(*Heteropygia acuminata*, Horsf.)

Male (breeding plumage).—Crown of the head bright sandy-rufous, streaked with black; lores and eyebrow white, streaked with blackish; back and shoulders sandy-rufous, streaked with black; lower back, rump, and upper tail coverts dusky-black; tail feathers ashy-brown, fringed with white; lesser wing coverts dull brown; greater coverts dusky-brown, tipped with white; primary coverts blackish, inner tipped with white; quills brown, shafts white for the most part; secondaries with narrow whitish fringe near the tips; sides of the face white streaked with dusky; ear coverts tinged with rufous; under surface white, with a tinge of rufous, spotted minutely with blackish on the throat, fore-neck, and chest; sides of the body distinctly spotted; under wing coverts white; bill blackish-brown; legs and feet olive-greenish. Dimensions in mm. :—Length, 175; bill, 27; wing, 136; tail, 51; tarsus, 30.

Female (breeding plumage).—Similar to male.

Male and Female (winter plumage).—Head very slightly tinged with rufous; upper surface almost uniform brownish; under surface white, with the lower throat and chest ashy-fulvous, sparsely streaked with blackish; flanks slightly washed with brown.

Young.—Crown of the head distinctly rufous, streaked with black; back almost black, intermixed with rufous, many of the feathers having whitish edges; wing coverts broadly margined with sandy-rufous; quills brown; under surface mostly white, tinged with buff to sandy-buff in parts; feathers on the lower throat, sides of neck, and sides of breast with black shaft-streaks.

Nest and Eggs.—Unknown.

Breeding Season.—Unknown.

Geographical Distribution.—Tasmania, Australia in general, New Zealand, New Guinea, Malay Archipelago; migrating through China and Japan to Eastern Siberia and Alaska, where it is thought to breed.

Observations.—Some years the Marsh Stint or Tringa is fairly plentiful in different parts in the northern half of the island, at least. It is nomadic in its habits during the short time it is with us.

During March, 1909, a large flock suddenly appeared on the marshes in the Bracknell district, where they had never before been seen. After remaining a few days the flock disappeared as suddenly as it had come. On several occasions small flocks have been noted on the Town Point reclamation area at Launceston.

Mr. H. Stuart Dove informs me that on 27th October, 1909, he saw a party of five feeding on the mud-flats close to Launceston.

Early in December in the same year the same observer saw a party of eight individuals of this species on the beach at West Devonport.

Marshy districts and the edges of streams are frequented by

this species; it may also be seen in small flocks hunting along the ocean beaches. Aquatic insects and their larvæ, also other insects, constitute its principal food.

*CURLEW STINT
(*Ancylochilus subarquatus*, Gmelin).

Male (summer plumage).—Upper surface deep brown to dark reddish-brown, with black centres and whitish edges to the feathers; lower back dull greyish-brown; sides of lower back and upper tail coverts white, the latter tinged with rufous, with a few black bars; tail feathers ashy-brown, fringed with white; wing coverts dark brown, the latter tipped with white; primary coverts and quills dark brown, the brown fringed with white; the secondaries fringed with white; under surface rich chestnut, the feathers more or less edged with white; sides of body and flanks white, sparsely barred with black; bill, legs, and feet black. Dimensions in mm. :—Length, 190; bill, 33; wing, 132; tail, 49; tarsus, 29.

Female (summer plumage).—Similar to male, but not so richly coloured.

Male and Female (winter plumage).—Upper surface and wing coverts ashy-brown, slightly mottled with blackish; rump and upper tail coverts white; tail feathers ashy-brown, fringed with white, and a subterminal bar of blackish; quills blackish-brown; under surface white, with fine markings of dusky-brown on sides of face and neck, also on lower throat and fore-neck.

Young.—" Similar in general colour to the winter plumage of the adult, and distinguished by the absence of rufous colour in the plumage of the upper surface; on the under surface the streaks on the fore-neck are almost obsolete, and a fulvescent shade overspreads the fore-neck and chest, in some specimens even extending to the breast itself " (B. M. Cat.)

Nest, Egg, and Breeding Season.—Unknown.

Geographical Distribution.—Tasmania, Australia in general, New Guinea, Africa, India, and so northwards to the Arctic regions, where it is supposed to breed.

Observations.—But few individuals of this species visit our shores in company with other birds of northern breeding species. Mud-banks and shingly beaches of rivers and estuaries are the favourite haunts of the Curlew Stint. In such localities little parties may be seen feeding in company, when the tide is out, on the edges of the shallow pools left by the receding waters, while others are busily engaged in procuring food on the mud-flats.

" This fine Stint, though it is fond of frequenting sand-banks and fore-shores left bare by the tide, is frequently found on salt-marshes near the lagoons and estuaries on which it has taken up its winter abode; and I have seen a little flock on dry, rising ground, a few hundred yards away from the water's edge. It associates in Ceylon with the Long-toed Stint and the Little Stint, but when found in such company is generally single or in a small troop of three or four. When collected in small flocks of six to two dozen or more, it is almost always accompanied by other species, and feeds gregariously in close company, the whole walking nimbly about as they pick up their food. It does not run about as much as its smaller relatives, feeding more after the manner of a Sandpiper than a Stint " (Col. Legge).

SNIPE
(*Gallinago australis*, Lath.)

Male.—Crown of the head brownish-black, with a median line of buff; back dark brownish-black; four central tail feathers blackish-brown, tipped with white; lateral feathers barred with dark and lighter brown, also tipped with white; scapulars mottled with deep sandy-buff, the feathers margined with pale buff; wing coverts dark brown, tipped with pale buff; quills dark brown, tips fringed with white; sides of the neck, breast, and flanks washed with pale reddish-brown and mottled with spots of deep brown— on the flanks the spots become bars; centre of the abdomen white; under tail coverts buff, barred with dark brown. Dimensions in mm. :—Length, 292; bill, 67; wing, 169; tail, 65; tarsus, 46.

Female.—Similar to male.

Nest.—" On the ground amongst the grass of marshy uplands " (A. J. Campbell).

Eggs.—" Clutch four; pyriform, or pear-shaped; texture of shell comparatively fine; surface glossy; colour warm stone-grey, boldly blotched and spotted, especially round the upper quarter, with rich umber and dull or cloudy purplish-brown; some of the heavier markings have the appearance of having been wiped on with a brush. Somewhat large compared with the size of the bird, and, except for their larger size, come nearest in likeness to those of the Turnstone (*Arenaria interpres*). Dimensions of a clutch in inches:—(1) 1.77 x 1.2, (2) 1.73 x 1.22, (3) 1.71 x 1.22, (4) 1.7 x 1.21 " (A. J. Campbell).

Breeding Season.—The eggs described by Mr. Campbell were obtained for him in Japan in May, so we may infer that that month and June constitute the chief breeding months.

Geographical Distribution.—Tasmania, Australia in general, New Zealand (accidental); migrating to Japan to breed, *via* Formosa and intermediate localities.

Observations.—Although during the time the Snipe is in Tasmania it is scattered over a wide area, in no locality is it anything approaching plentiful.

In Widowson's " Present State of Van Diemen's Land," written somewhere about 1830, it is stated that " Snipe are found in great abundance from September to March in the lakes and wet

11

valleys. They are precisely like the Snipe of England, but not near so wild." Jas. Bischoff, in his "Sketch of the History of Van Diemen's Land" (1839), states that Snipe were found in the Circular Head district, but fails to mention whether plentifully or not. Some twenty-five years ago, Colonel Legge, in the course of an article published in the P.R.S. of Tasmania, says:—"It is a singular fact that the Snipe is decreasing in numbers in Tasmania; the country is doubtless not as suited to its habits as in former years, when swamps and favourite marshy feeding grounds were in their primeval state; but there are many tracts of land fit at the present time to hold numbers of Snipe, and to which one would think that they would stray on their arrival. Nevertheless, they fail to appear in them, and the common lament of the sportsmen is that the Snipe are getting scarcer."

The conditions to-day are far worse than they were a quarter of a century ago, and sportsmen complain that some years they never see a Snipe. Mr. Thos. Haley, than whom there is not a better sportsman on the East Coast, informs me that he has not seen a Snipe for years. The whole thing is very puzzling, for there are still a number of localities ideal in their way for Snipe—localities where the birds would be very little disturbed.

The beginning of September may be taken as the average time when the bird arrives, and the end of February to the beginning of March that of its departure. Mr. W. L. Sidebottom tells me that it practically, if not always, arrives and departs during a moonlight night.

The marshy ground round and about the Western Tiers is said to be the most likely locality to find Snipe nowadays.

Mr. Campbell mentions that on the 27th July, 1897, three birds were shot at Melton—an extraordinarily early date. A correspondent to the "Nature Notes" in a recent issue of the *Argus* writes:—"The earliest Snipe I shot in Australia during 40 years' experience was on 16th June, 1908, at Lake Corop, and the latest was at a swamp near Kentbrook, Heywood Forest, on 7th March, 1906."

ORDER—GAVIÆ: SEA-BIRDS.

FAMILY—LARIDÆ (8 species).

*CASPIAN TERN

(*Hydroprogne caspia*, Pall.)

Male (*breeding plumage*).—Forehead, crown, and nape glossy greenish-black; mantle pale French grey; tail greyish-white; quills dark grey to slate colour; entire under surface white; bill vermilion-red; legs and feet black. Dimensions in mm.:—Length, 505; bill, 79; wing, 419; tail, 153; tarsus, 41.

Female (breeding plumage).—Similar to male. Dimensions slightly less.

Male and Female (winter plumage).—The black on the crown of the head and nape is streaked with white; bill orange-red, tipped with horn colour.

Immature.—Less white on crown and nape than in winter plumage of adults; wings and tail more or less washed with brownish-grey.

Young.—"Similar, but feathers of the mantle and tail mottled and barred with brownish-black " (B. M. Cat.)

Nest.—A slight depression in the ground among pig-face weed, &c.; usually situated on the rocky summit of an islet.

Eggs.—Clutch two to three; oval in shape; texture coarse; surface slightly glossy; colour light olive-brown, blotched and spotted with roundish markings of umber and dull greyish-black. Dimensions in mm. of a clutch :—(1) 59 x 42, (2) 60 x 40, (3) 61 x 41.

Breeding Season.—September to January.

Geographical Distribution.—Seas of Tasmania, Australia, and New Zealand, also many parts of the coasts of Europe, Asia, and America.

Observations.—This almost cosmopolitan species may be seen in small numbers round the coast of Tasmania and the shores of many of the islands in Bass Strait. Small parties may be seen about the mouth of the Tamar at almost any time; it comes up the river as far as George Town.

The Caspian Tern may readily be distinguished by its habit of carrying its bill downwards at right angles to its head when flying over the water on the look-out for food; it does not move its head from side to side, but keeps it practically motionless. This Tern is a very graceful diver. When about to take the plunge the wings are closed, and the body falls like a stone into the water; on a still day the splash can be heard for some distance. The body just goes beneath the surface, and that is all; very little time is wasted in the water. Round our coast it generally moves in pairs, but round the coast of India and about the Persian Gulf it congregates in colonies, oftentimes of considerable size. Dr. Sharpe mentions that it is said to rob other birds' nests, devouring both eggs and young. The Caspian Tern is an extremely noisy bird, uttering its harsh, cackling, screeching notes constantly, especially when either eggs or young are in the nest, thereby attracting attention to the fact.

*CRESTED TERN (Bass Strait Tern)

(*Sterna bergii,* Licht.)

Male (breeding plumage).—Forehead greyish-white, becoming black at the back of the head; back, throat, and all the under surface white; wings and tail grey; bill yellow; feet black. Dimen-

sions in mm. :—Length, 490; bill, 67; wing, 345; tail, 182;
tarsus, 27. The dimensions of individual birds vary considerably.

Female (breeding plumage).—Similar to male.

Male and Female (winter plumage).—Crown mottled with
white; otherwise practically similar to summer plumage.

Young.—" Forehead and lores dull white, closely streaked with
brownish-black; crown and nape more boldly streaked with black;
mantle mottled with black and buffish-white; primaries chiefly
dark brownish-grey, the shafts brown; tail feathers dark grey,
tipped with white; under parts chiefly white; the neck and throat
streaked with brown; bill olivaceous-yellow " (B. M. Cat.)

Nest.—A shallow depression is made in the sand or shingle
among the pig-face or short herbage. Fairly large colonies are to
be found on the small islands to the south of Tasmania. The nest
on Little Acteon is in a slight depression among the shingle, overgrown with herbage, just above high water mark, a few herbs
and strips of seaweed being the only lining in the bottom.

Eggs.—Clutch two; oval, with one end somewhat pointed;
texture coarse, and faintly glossed; ground colour usually stone-
grey, irregularly streaked, spotted, or blotched with dark sepia or
black, sometimes chestnut-brown and purplish-brown. Dimensions in mm. of a clutch :—(1) 61 x 43, (2) 62 x 42.

Breeding Season.—November principally.

Geographical Distribution.—Seas of Tasmania and Australia;
also the greater part of the Western Pacific Ocean, up to Japan,
Indian Ocean, Arabian and Red Seas, and the east and west coasts
of South Africa.

Observations.—Discussion has arisen at various times as to
whether the Crested Tern found in Australian waters is distinct
from the bird found in the Indian Ocean and elsewhere. Gould
made two species of them, but Mr. Howard Saunders, the eminent
authority on sea-birds, recognizes but one species.

Although the Crested or Bass Strait Tern is to be observed in
some numbers round the northern coast of Tasmania, yet it is
not nearly as plentiful as round the southern coast, where it
nests in fairly large colonies on some of the small islands, notably
the Acteons.

On several occasions, especially during rough weather, I have
seen this species fishing in company with Gannets in sheltered
bays on the North-Eastern Coast of Tasmania. Occasionally a few
may be seen about the mouth of the Tamar, but not as frequently
as the Caspian Tern.

*WHITE-FRONTED TERN (Southern Tern)

(*Sterna frontalis*, Gray).

Male and Female (breeding plumage).—Lower forehead and
lores white; crown of the head and nape black; upper surface
very pale grey; under surface white, flushed with a delicate pink

CRESTED TERNS NESTING.

From " THE EMU."

Photo. by A. J. CAMPBELL.

when alive; bill black; legs and feet reddish-brown. Dimensions in mm.:—Length, 420; bill, 55; wing, 284; tail, 180; tarsus, 20.

Male and Female (winter plumage).—Similar to summer plumage save that there is more white on the forehead and the crown is mottled with the same colour.

Young.—Forehead, crown, and nape greyish-black, mottled with white; practically the whole of the upper surface buffy-white to grey, mottled with greyish-black; under surface white.

Nestling.—"Covered with buffy-white down, tinged with fulvous on the head and neck and mottled with grey on the back" (Buller).

Nest.—A slight depression on the ground among the herbage growing near the sea-shore. Breeds in colonies.

Eggs.—Clutch two usually; inclined to oval in shape; texture fine; surface faintly glossy; colour stone-grey, boldly blotched and spotted with umber and dull grey. Dimensions in mm. of a clutch:—(1) 46 x 32, (2) 45 x 31.

Breeding Season.—November and December.

Geographical Distribution.—Seas of Tasmania, Australia, and New Zealand.

Observations.—In certain favoured localities the Southern or White-fronted Tern is moderately plentiful round the coast of Tasmania, especially about some of the small rocky islets, on which it breeds. No prettier sight can be witnessed than a flock of this species fishing; the graceful motions and clear-cut way in which the fish are captured are very interesting.

On its general habits round New Zealand the late Sir W. Buller wrote:—"This elegant species is extremely abundant on our coasts, flocks of a hundred or more being often met with on the sand-banks at the river mouths in association with Gulls and other shore birds of various kinds. The term 'Sea-Swallow' as applied to this Tern is a very appropriate one, for on watching the evolutions of a flock of these birds one is forcibly reminded of a flight of Swallows coursing in the air. Their aerial manœuvres are truly beautiful, and the apparent ease with which they dip into the water and capture their finny prey cannot fail to interest an observer. They usually alight on the sandy beach near the edge of the water, and stand so closely packed that 30 or 40 may be obtained at a single shot. They shuffle about with a constant low twittering, and occasionally stretch their wings upwards to their full extent, presenting a very pretty appearance. When fired at, or otherwise alarmed, the whole flock rises simultaneously in the air, crossing and recrossing each other as they continue to hover over the spot, producing at the same time a perfect din with their sharp cries of 'Ki-ki-ki.' Some years ago, when exploring among the shoals and sand-banks of the Great Kaipara Heads or Basin, I observed thousands of these birds, and in this wild and unfrequented part of the coast they were so fearless that they coursed about our boat within a few feet of our heads. The discharge of a gun among them only tended to increase their apparent interest in us."

SOOTY TERN
(Sterna fuliginosa, Gmel.)

Male (breeding plumage).—Forehead and upper part of lores white; head and nape deep glossy black; entire upper surface and wings blackish-brown, the latter white along the outside edges; outer webs of lateral tail feathers white; under surface white; bill, legs, and feet black, slightly tinged with red. Dimensions in mm. : —Length, 430; bill, 51; wing, 300; tail, 191; tarsus, 24.

Female (breeding plumage).—Similar to male.

Male and Female (winter plumage).—Similar to the above save that the crown is flecked with white.

Immature.—"Brownish-black above, darker on the upper wing coverts; outer tail feathers nearly as sooty-black as the rest of the rectrices, except towards the tips; tarsi and toes reddish-brown" (B. M. Cat.)

Nest.—None formed, the egg being laid on the sand or on the ground under bushes. Breeds in large colonies.

Eggs.—Clutch one; stout oval in shape; texture fairly fine; surface slightly glossy; colour warmish white to pinkish, blotched and spotted, especially about the stouter end, with chestnut and dull purplish-brown. Dimensions in mm. of odd examples :—(1) 50 x 35, (2) 50 x 36, (3) 50 x 36.5.

Breeding Season.—November to January.

Geographical Distribution.—Seas of Tasmania (?) and Australia; "also tropical and juxta-tropical seas, wherever suitable islands and reefs exist; occasionally wandering to Maine, in North America, and to Europe, even as far as England. Almost unknown on the South American side of the Pacific; otherwise very generally distributed" (B. M. Cat.)

Observations.—It is somewhat doubtful whether this Tern really does come as far south as the Tasmanian seas, but at the same time it is quite probable stragglers do come down. Mr. A. J. Campbell states that he has seen eggs of this species supposed to have been taken in the Furneaux Group, but he was unable to obtain confirmatory evidence.

In an interesting account of this Tern on Ascension Island, Captain Sperling writes :—"Leaving Comfortless Cove about the middle of the day, I walked two dreary miles of cinders and ashes, uncheered by a symptom of vegetation, before I noticed flocks of Terns converging from various parts of the ocean to a spot apparently about a mile in front of me; but as yet I observed nothing of the 'fair.' At length, on turning slightly to the left, and surmounting a low ridge, the whole scene was disclosed. A gradual incline of a quarter of a mile terminated in a plain of ten or fifteen

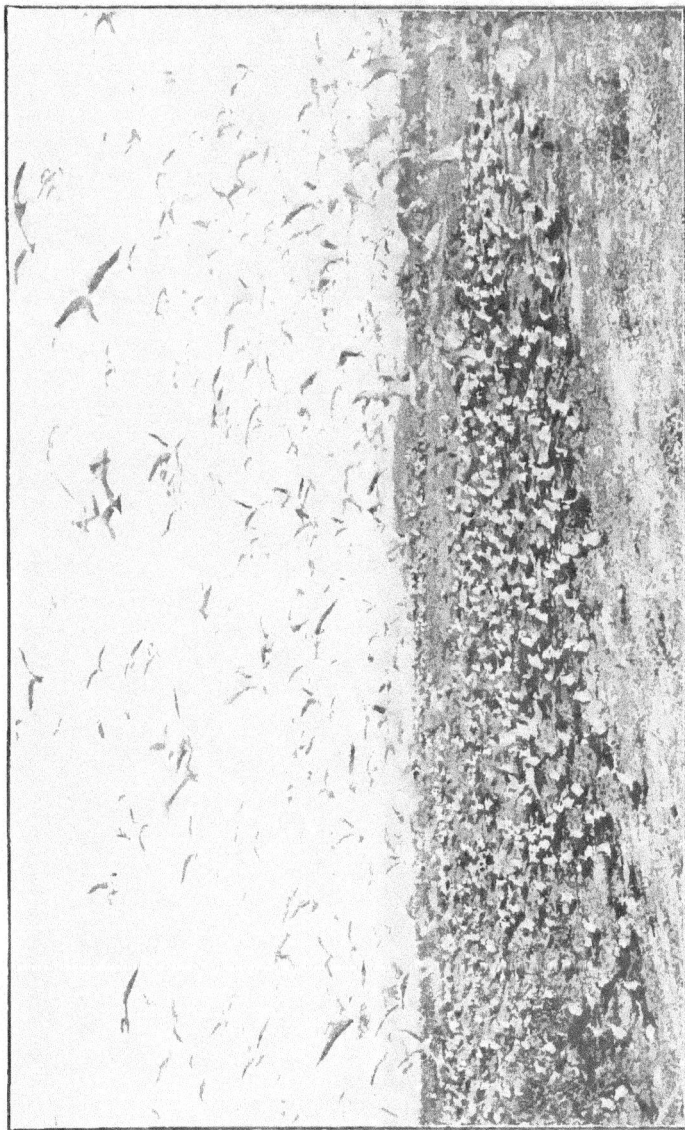

ROOKERY OF SOOTY TERNS.

Photo. by E. M. CORNWALL.

From " THE EMU "

acres in extent, which was literally covered with the birds. The
plain was surrounded by low mountains, except on the side on
which we stood, and, being entirely sheltered from the wind, its
heat under the full blaze of a tropical sun was very oppressive.
No description can give an adequate idea of the effect produced
by the thousands upon thousands of these wild sea-birds, floating
and screaming over this arid cinder-bed, the eggs and young
scattered so thickly over the ground that in some instances it was
impossible to avoid crushing them, and the bleached bones of dead
birds distributed in all directions. During our short walk down
the incline, large flocks of parent birds hovered over our heads,
and assailed us with plaintive cries, regardless of our sticks, with
which we might have killed any number of them; but their
beautiful pure black and white plumage and graceful motions
caused it to appear almost a sin to knock any of them down. On
arriving within the precincts of the breeding grounds, their
numbers increased; large flocks were arriving in endless succession
from seaward; clouds of birds rose from the ground, and joining
those already attending us, their wheelings and gyrations almost
made us giddy. I sat down on a lump of cinder, and the society,
being at length convinced that my policy was not aggressive, went
on with the ordinary routine of incubation. There were young of
all sizes, from the little callow ones just hatched to the nearly
fledged birds, that fluttered and crawled like young Pigeons.
There were also lots of eggs exposed on the bare ground; but in
most instances the old bird sat on its solitary treasure, hissing
defiance as I approached, and fighting if I attempted to remove it."

*WHITE-FACED TERNLET (LITTLE TERN)
(*Sterna nereis*, Gould).

Male and Female (breeding plumage).—Forehead and lores
white; spot in front of each eye, crown, and nape black; back,
shoulders, and wing coverts pale pearl-grey; rump greyish-white;
tail white; quills brownish; under surface silvery-white; bill bright
yellow; legs and feet dull yellow. Dimensions in mm.:—Length,
238; bill, 36; wing, 186; tail, 88; tarsus, 15.

Male and Female (winter plumage).—Crown marked with
white, otherwise similar.

Immature.—Crown greyish-white; nape black; tail greyish-
white; rest of plumage practically similar to winter plumage.

Young.—Crown and nape mottled with dull brownish-black;
back barred with ash and tipped with dull white; slight mottling
of ashy-grey on tail feathers.

Nest.—Merely a slight depression in the sand or shingle.

Eggs.—Clutch two usually; oval in shape; texture fine; surface
faintly glossy; colour warm stone-grey, moderately marked with

dark umber and grey. Dimensions in mm. of odd examples :—
(1) 35 x 24.5, (2) 36 x 25.

Breeding Season.—November to January.

Geographical Distribution.—Seas of Tasmania, Australia, and New Zealand.

Observations.—So far as I am aware, this species is a some-what rare bird round our coast, its home being chiefly in sub-tropical and New Zealand waters.

Of its general habits the late Sir W. Buller wrote :—" It is very active in its movements, flies high, turns in the air with facility, and dips into the water after its prey in a very adroit manner. Its note is a harsh scream. During the breeding season it is very clamorous, especially when its nesting ground is invaded, or even approached."

Sub-Family—Larinæ.

*SILVER GULL

(*Larus novæ-hollandiæ*, Steph.)

Male.—Head, neck, tail, and under surface white; back and secondaries pearl-grey; first and second primaries, basal three-quarters black, then a long white patch on the inner web, and subterminal black patch and a narrow tip of white; third primary, greater part of inner web black, then as first and second quills; fourth and fifth quills, large subterminal black patch and a narrow white tip; under tail coverts grey; bill crimson-lake; iris silver-white; eyelid coral-red; legs and feet lake-red. Dimensions in mm. :—Length, 410; bill, 35; wing, 804; tail, 124; tarsus, 50.

Female.—Similar to male.

Young.—Mottled with brown on the back and wings; tail with subterminal band of brown; iris brown.

Immature.—Very little grey on back.

Nestling.—Heavily mottled with brown on the upper surface; under surface white.

Nest.—Somewhat flimsy, and constructed of grass, sea-weed, and sometimes of different kinds of vegetable *débris*. It is placed in a colony, either on a bold headland or an isolated rock.

Eggs.—Clutch two to three. In a majority of cases they are inclined to oval in shape; texture of shell coarse; surface glossy; the ground colour varies from light greyish-green to olive; the markings vary very considerably in number, size, and shape, ranging from small spots to blotches or wavy lines; in colour they are umber, olive-brown, and dull grey. Dimensions in mm. of a full clutch :—(1) 53 x 40, (2) 52 x 39, (3) 55 x 40. A clutch of two laid by a pair of birds in semi-captivity are distinctly pyriform in shape; the ground colour of one is bluish, sparingly spotted except round the stouter end with the usual colours; the other is light

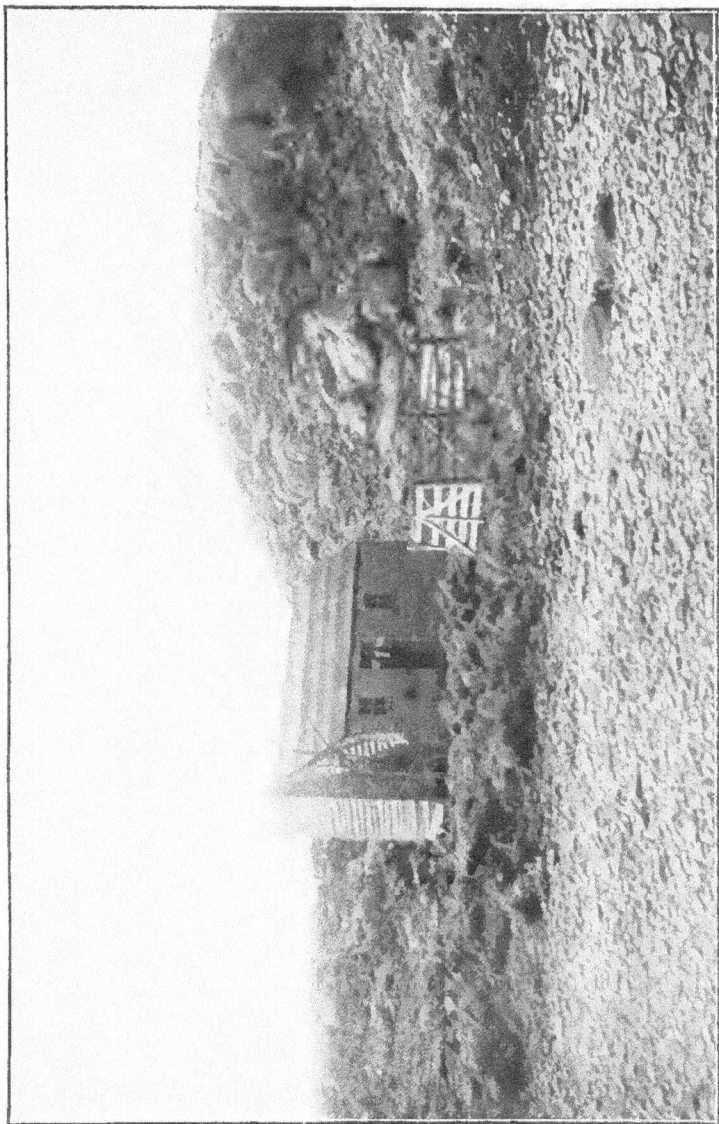

THE HUT, NINTH ISLAND.

Photo by J. G. LITTLER.

olive, well spotted and blotched all over. Dimensions in mm. : —
(1) 56 x 38, (2) 54 x 37.

Breeding Season.—September to December.

Geographical Distribution.—Seas of Tasmania and Australia
to New Caledonia.

Observations.—Of the various species of sea-birds frequenting
the coast of Tasmania, the Silver Gull is the most familiar. It
frequents the sea-shore and the mouths of rivers rather than the
open ocean. It congregates oftentimes in immense flocks,
especially at low tide, along the beach or on reefs and shoals. At
Devonport it is to be seen in hundreds at low tide on the sand-
banks just below Wood's Slip, left bare by the receding tide. As
the tide comes in they move off to the mouth of the harbour and
out to sea. Some go up the river towards Latrobe and search for
food along the shores of the sedge-grown sand-banks, where I am
given to understand many nest. Round Launceston wharves and
on the mud-flats of the Tamar large flocks may be seen every day
in the year. The same may be observed about any of the rivers
and harbours round the island.

Every winter the low-lying lands up the valley of the North
Esk become flooded for longer or shorter periods. To these
swampy flats the Silver Gulls resort in hundreds, and feed on the
young grass-grubs and worms that have been washed out. Every
evening, shortly before sunset, the birds may be seen winging their
way harbourwards, following the course of the river all the while,
from St. Leonards to the wharves. At the Great Lake a flock has
been firmly established for some time; they breed on a rocky islet
in the middle of the lake.

Regarding the general habits of the Silver Gull nothing need be
said, as they are so well known, both when flying in the wake of
a vessel and darting down and squabbling over scraps thrown into
the water or when quietly feeding about any of our rivers.

As a domestic pet for picking up noxious insects in gardens,
this species is held in high estimation.

*PACIFIC GULL

(*Gabianus (Larus) pacificus*, Lath.)

Male.—Head, neck, and under surface white; the feathers of
the under surface are distinctly flushed with rosy-pink, which
lingers for some hours after death; mantle and surface of wings
deep black; scapulars slightly tipped with greyish-white; secondaries with broader white tips and dark lead coloured upper parts;
primaries black, rather paler on the inner webs, and with white
tips from the fifth upwards; tail coverts white; tail feathers white,
with broad subterminal band of black; irides white; bill yellow,
tip reddish-orange; legs and feet saffron-yellow. Dimensions in
mm. :—Length, 615; bill, 59; wing, 450; tail, 182; tarsus, 65.

Female.—Similar to male.

Immature.—Forehead and under surface practically white; head and neck mottled with brown; upper surface nearly black; tail coverts white; tail almost white, slightly mottled.

Young.—" Head and hind-neck nearly uniform dark brown; feathers of the mantle and tail coverts rather paler brown, with buffish edges; primaries sooty-black, with pale tips to the inner quills; rectrices dark brown, with whitish extreme tips; under surface brown; paler on the abdomen; under wing coverts dark brown; bill nearly black, ochraceous near the base of the upper mandible; tarsi and toes yellowish-brown. At a subsequent stage the forehead and throat are streaked with greyish-white and brown, while the general tone of the plumage is lighter. The next year dull white is the prevailing colour on the under parts; some black shows on the mantle; the throat and head are very boldly streaked with brown; some white begins to show at the base of the tail, and the coverts are nearly white; bill greenish basally " (B. M. Cat.)

Nest.—Well constructed either of grass and stalks of plants or of pieces of pig-face weed; it is placed under the shelter of rocks, tussock-grass, or salt-bush, generally on islands or islets.

Eggs.—Clutch two to three; oval in shape; texture coarse; surface slightly glossy; colour light olive-brown, sometimes dark olive-brown, spotted and blotched with umber and dull grey, some of the markings appearing as though under the surface. Dimensions in mm. of two clutches :—A—(1) 78 x 56, (2) 80 x 55, (3) 73 x 54; B—(1) 71 x 57, (2) 78 x 55.

Breeding Season.—October to December.

Geographical Distribution.—Coasts of Tasmania, New South Wales, Victoria, Queensland, South and Western Australia.

Observations.—Next to the Silver Gull, this species is perhaps the most familiar sea-bird found round our coasts. At no time, however, does it congregate in as large flocks as the previous species, on whose eggs and young it wages relentless war during the breeding season.

The general habits of the Pacific Gull closely resemble those of the preceding species as far as gathering food from river flats, sea beaches, and following steamers for the sake of the scraps thrown overboard. It also wanders up the valley of the North Esk in winter and feeds, in company with Silver Gulls, Ravens, and Starlings, on the grubs and worms washed out of the ground by floods.

Three years elapse before it attains adult plumage.

On Ninth Island, where there are large rookeries of White-faced Storm-Petrels (*Pelagodroma marina*), I found that the Pacific Gull was responsible for the death of great numbers of this dainty little Petrel, for on moonlight nights it could both be seen and heard " hawking " over the rookeries, and every now and then pouncing down on a bird. It is a noble bird on the wing, reminding one much of the Swamp-Hawk (*Circus gouldi*) in the manner in which it sails in great circles, and, in small companies, hawks backwards and forwards over the same ground. When progressing at what might be termed an ordinary rate of speed, it beats the air with its wings 100 times in 80 seconds (actual count). When sailing directly in the eye of the wind on motionless wings, and wishful of changing its course either to the right or the left, the tips of the wings are slightly depressed and the body brought round by a slight lateral movement of the head and tail, but not the faintest semblance of a flap is given. Its cry is a very harsh single note, which frequently might be mistaken for a short, sharp bark uttered by a terrier dog. At other times a somewhat long drawn out note, sounding like "Oh-ah," is uttered in doublets, especially when hawking in couples over Petrel rookeries.

FAMILY—STERCORARIIDÆ (2 species).

SKUA

(*Megalestris antarctica*, Less.)

Male.—Crown of the head very dark brown, almost black; rest of upper surface dark brown; under surface slightly paler; iris dark brown; bill, legs, and feet black. Dimensions in mm. :— Length, 595; bill, 54; wing, 410; tail, 170; tarsus, 80.

Female.—Similar to male.

Young.—Faint wash of rufous on upper surface, also on wing coverts.

Nest.—A depression in the moss or grass, with a little lining in the shape of a few grass-stems.

Eggs.—Clutch two; varying in shape from pointed oval to pyriform ; texture of shell coarse; slight gloss on surface; colour varies from olive-green to olive-brown; in a pair one is usually olive-green and the other olive-brown, both sparingly blotched with dark olive-brown or dull brown and greyish-black. They may be distinguished from those of the Pacific Gull by being less marked and slightly smaller. Dimensions in mm. of a pair :—(1) 75 x 53, (2) 78 x 55.

Breeding Season.—August to November.

Geographical Distribution.—Tasmania and Australian seas; also Southern Ocean in general, ranging as far north as Madagascar.

Observations.—Of this species in the Antarctic, Dr. E. A. Wilson says :—"They live here, as Skuas do elsewhere, largely by harassing other birds until they disgorge. We saw one dipping at a Whale-bird (Prion). Fear was a thing apparently unknown to them, for in the open ocean we watched them chasing even the largest Albatross, and no sooner did the sailing flight of the Skua change for its bee-line swoop than the Albatross would immediately drop to the water, there to remain until either its tormentor was gone or the coveted food in its stomach had passed beyond recall."

The Antarctic Skua, or Sea-Hen of sailors, is more plentiful in southern Tasmanian waters than in northern. As a matter of fact, it is rarely seen round the northern coast. Gould records having seen this species somewhat plentifully about Storm Bay, near the mouth of the Derwent. Whale-Birds or Prions seem to be a favourite article of diet, the unfortunate birds being swallowed whole.

The Rev. A. E. Eaton, who accompanied the British Transit of Venus Expedition to Kerguelen Island, writing of this Skua, says, *inter alia*:—" Every marsh near Royal Sound used to have its pair of Skuas. Many were destroyed within a radius of four miles from the ships; and before the expedition sailed from the island it was impossible to walk far without coming across dead bodies of the poor creatures. The cause of this useless slaughter was the menacing aspect of the birds, who swoop with fierce impetuosity directly towards the face of anyone approaching their domain, rising just in time to clear his head, and uttering short despairing cries. They did not feign to be crippled quite so much as the Skuas of Spitzbergen, but preferred intimidation as a means of averting danger near their nest. When they thought they had succeeded in making the enemy retreat they celebrated their triumph by standing face to face upon the ground, with their wings extended vertically so as to almost meet above their back, whilst they chanted a pæan, consisting of a dozen notes or so delivered in the tones of a Carrion Crow. . . . If Blue Petrels were turned loose in the daytime, they almost invariably chased by Skuas and killed on the wing before they had flown half a mile. Petrels of one sort or another seem to constitute the staple diet of these Skuas. They hunt for them in the evening when it is becoming dusk, flying rapidly along the hillside close to the ground, ready to pounce upon any that they may see emerging from the mouths of their burrows. Again in the early morning they are upon the wing to waylay Petrels returning late from sea."

RICHARDSON SKUA

(*Stercorarius crepidatus*, Banks).

Male.—" Crown, nape, and sides of the head dull greyish-brown; neck all round, breast, and sides of the body greyish-white; shoulders and all the upper surface dark olivaceous-grey of different shades; primaries and tail feathers blackish-brown, the former with white shafts; inner surface of wings, axillary plumes, and abdomen ashy-grey, tinged with brown; some of the under tail coverts uniform ashy-grey, others white barred with grey; irides black; bill dark brown; tarsi and toes greyish-black, the claws darker " (Buller). Dimensions in mm. : —Length, 420; bill, 30; wing, 300; tail, 140; tarsus, 40.

Female.—Similar to male.

Immature.—" Streaked and mottled with various shades of brown on the upper surface; mantle chiefly umber; upper tail coverts barred with dark brown, white, and rufous; under surface more or less barred with brown on a paler ground " (B. M. Cat.)

Nestling.—" Sooty-brown above, paler below " (B. M. Cat.)

Nest.—" Constructed rather carelessly of grass, moss, and fragments of heather, and situated on the ground amongst heather in marshy or uncultivated moorland (Butler) " (A. J. Campbell).

Eggs.—" Two in number; ground colour dark chocolate-brown, varying to light clay colour, the darker eggs more strongly marked with deep brown or blackish, the spots being distributed over the greater part of the egg, and the grey underlying markings very indistinct. The pale eggs have the spots collected round the larger end, the rest of the egg being rather free from markings. Axis 2.3-2.55, diameter 1.5-1.65 " (R. B. Sharpe).

Breeding Season.—June and July.

Geographical Distribution.—Seas of Tasmania, New South Wales, Victoria, and New Zealand; also off the southern coast of Africa, Indian Ocean, Persian Gulf, and ranging northwards to Arctic and sub-Arctic regions to breed.

Observations.—To Mr. A. J. Campbell belongs the honour of having first recorded this species for Australia. In 1883 he noticed individuals about Port Phillip Bay when returning from a trip to Tasmania.

ORDER—TUBINARES : TUBE-NOSED SWIMMERS.

FAMILY—PROCELLARIIDÆ (5 species).

Sub-Family—Oceanitinæ.

*YELLOW-WEBBED STORM-PETREL (WILSON'S PETREL)
(*Oceanites oceanicus*, Kuhl).

Male.—Upper surface sooty-brown, tinged with leaden-grey; upper tail coverts white; tail black; primaries and secondaries black; throat same as back; rest of under surface a shade lighter; a patch of white feathers on each side of the vent; "bill entirely black; feet and toes black, the webs black at the outer border, and black also along the sides of the outer digits, but otherwise bright orange from the base of the first phalange to a point level with the second phalange; claws black; iris dark brown " (Edward Wilson).

Dimensions in mm. :—Length, 190; bill, 15; wing, 152; tail, 65; tarsus, 35.

Female.—Similar to male.

Nestling.—" Covered with a uniform greyish-black down; bill black; legs bluish, tinged with faint yellow; webs of toes bright yellow; toes faint black; nail black " (R. Hall).

Nest.—" A shallow indentation beneath a slope, or within a crevice, lined with twigs " (Hall).

Eggs.—Clutch one; elliptical in shape; texture fine; surface without gloss; colour white, with a zone of fine purplish-brown spots round the stouter end. Dimensions in mm. :—31.5 x 22.

Breeding Season.—The Scottish Antarctic Expedition obtained their first egg on the South Orkneys on 11th December; Dr. Wilson, with Nat. Ant. Expedition, the first egg at Cape Adare on 9th January; while Mr. Robert Hall found eggs on Kerguelen Island in February.

Geographical Distribution.—Seas of Tasmania, Australia, and New Zealand, down to the Ice Barrier in the Antarctic, and up through the Atlantic to Labrador; and in the Indian Ocean to the Arabian Sea.

Observations.—The statement made by Gould that this Petrel is one of the most plentiful in the Australian seas holds good to this day. Almost anywhere in Tasmanian waters may this extremely graceful little bird be seen flitting from wave crest to wave crest. " Its food, consisting of minute crustaceans, is picked up from the surface of the water while on the wing. Flitting about from wave to wave the little Petrel delicately treads the water to steady itself for a moment while it picks up a tiny morsel " (E. A. Wilson).

Dr. Wilson's account of the finding of the first nest is very interesting. He says:—

" The birds were to be seen hovering round the mouth of crevices in the rocky side of the cliff, often settling close by for a few seconds, and then sailing in short circles round it, reminding one strongly of the movements of a House-Martin at its nest under the eaves of a country barn. Two of these crevices could not be reached, but soon we saw a bird hover round and settle upon a large boulder. Hunting about for a burrow underneath, we caught the sound of twittering, and traced it to a kind of mouse-hole. This, by dint of long and tedious picking with a sheath-knife, we enlarged until it admitted an arm up to the shoulder. The work was laborious, as the floor of the burrow was hard black ice and grit, but eventually we reached the nest. At the end of the little tunnel was a chamber containing a very comfortable nest, thickly lined with Adelia Penguins' feathers, and in it a somewhat remarkable collection. First we brought out an adult male alive, then an adult female; then two eggs, one clean and newly laid, the other old and rotten; and under all another dead and flattened adult *Oceanites.* Outside, as we worked, a fourth bird was hovering, which, when shot, proved to be an adult male. It has long been known that with this species the nesting burrow is often used by more than a single pair. The fresh egg was preserved, the rotten one fell to pieces, and the three birds were preserved.

" The burrows are not very difficult to discover, for one's attention is drawn to them by the habit the bird has of hovering round the entrance in the evening hours, and settling there without actually going in, and also sometimes by the twittering of the bird within. They are often quite inaccessible without a rope, even when located, but on the other hand they may be almost on level ground.

" The flight of the bird is peculiarly attractive in these barren wastes of snow and rock, chiefly perhaps from its resemblance to the flight of the familiar Martin, for it flits here and there exactly as though in search of insects on the wing. Occasionally it sails on outstretched wings. The power of flight must be very wonderful, for it seems to spend its lifetime on the wing."

*GREY-BACKED STORM-PETREL
(Garrodia nereis, Gould).*

Male.—Upper surface, including head and neck, dark ashy-grey; rump and upper tail coverts a little lighter; tail feathers ashy-grey, with a terminal bar of black; primaries and secondaries black, shaded with ashy-grey; throat and chest dusky-brown; rest of under surface white; bill, legs, and feet black. Dimensions in mm. :—Length, 180; bill, 12; wing, 130; tail, 69; tarsus, 30.

Female.—Similar to male.

Young.—" Differs from the adult in having hoary-white margins to the feathers of the back and scapulars, as well as the upper wing coverts and tail coverts, the latter thus showing a dusky-black subterminal bar " (F. Du Cane Godman).

Nest.—The nests discovered by Dr. Kidder on Kerguelen Island were placed under overhanging clumps of grass and " Kerguelen tea " (*Acæna ascendens*) in low, swampy ground near the sea." Mr. Percy Seymour informed the late Sir W. Buller that the nests were placed in burrows resembling rat-holes, about 15 inches deep.

Eggs.—Clutch one; oval in shape; texture fine; surface slightly glossy and finely pitted; colour white, some specimens with a distinctly freckled patch of reddish and lilac on the apex, others almost devoid of markings. Dimensions in mm. :—34 x 24.

Breeding Season.—November to January.

Geographical Distribution.—Seas of Tasmania, Australia, New Zealand, and the Southern Ocean in general.

Observations.—The Grey-backed Storm-Petrel was first discovered and procured by Gould in 1839 between Hobart and Sydney. Later he found it between the coast of New South Wales and New Zealand, off the coast of which it breeds. During the Transit of Venus Expedition to Kerguelen Island, it was found by both the British and American naturalists, but only by the latter were nests found. Dr. Kidder, of the American party, states that it becomes very fat during the breeding season, and is strictly crepuscular in its habits.

In New Zealand individuals have been captured inland, where they have been blown by strong gales.

*WHITE-FACED STORM-PETREL
(*Pelagodroma marina*, Lath.)

Male.—Forehead and a line above the eyes white; crown of the head dark ashy-grey; back and shoulders and sides of the neck dusky-grey; rump and upper tail coverts light ashy-grey; tail feathers black; primaries and secondaries black; sides of the face, throat, and under surface white; irides black or nearly so; bill, legs, and feet black, middle of webs yellow. Dimensions in mm.: —Length, 205; bill, 19.5; wing, 155; tail, 76; tarsus, 41.

Female.—Plumage similar to male. Dimensions in mm.:— Length, 200; bill, 17; wing, 152; tail, 69; tarsus, 39.

The above dimensions were taken from a pair of birds captured in the same burrow.

Young.—" Covered with a sooty-black down. The first feathers resemble those of the adults, but the grey feathers of the mantle are fringed with white and the greater coverts and secondaries are edged with white at the tips, the grey of the upper and under tail coverts being barred with white. These markings are retained by the young bird after it has become full grown and lost the down " (R. B. Sharpe).

Nest.—A rat-like burrow underground, frequently curved, and from 18 inches to 2 feet long; the nesting chamber is circular, and on the floor are placed a few fragments of weeds and tussock-grass. Situated in a rookery on an islet covered with short herbage. On parts of Ninth Island burrows of this species are in close proximity to those of Mutton-Birds and Little Penguins.

Eggs.—Clutch one; elliptical in shape; faint gloss on surface; colour white, with minute reddish dots, especially round the larger end. Dimensions average about 38 mm. x 25 mm.

Breeding Season.—November to January.

Geographical Distribution.—Seas of Tasmania, Australia, New Zealand, and the Southern Ocean generally, ranging northwards to the South Indian Ocean, Canary Isles, British Isles (accidental), and off the coast of Massachusetts.

Observations.—This dainty little Petrel is to be found breeding on a number of islands in Bass Strait, notably Petrel, Three Hum-

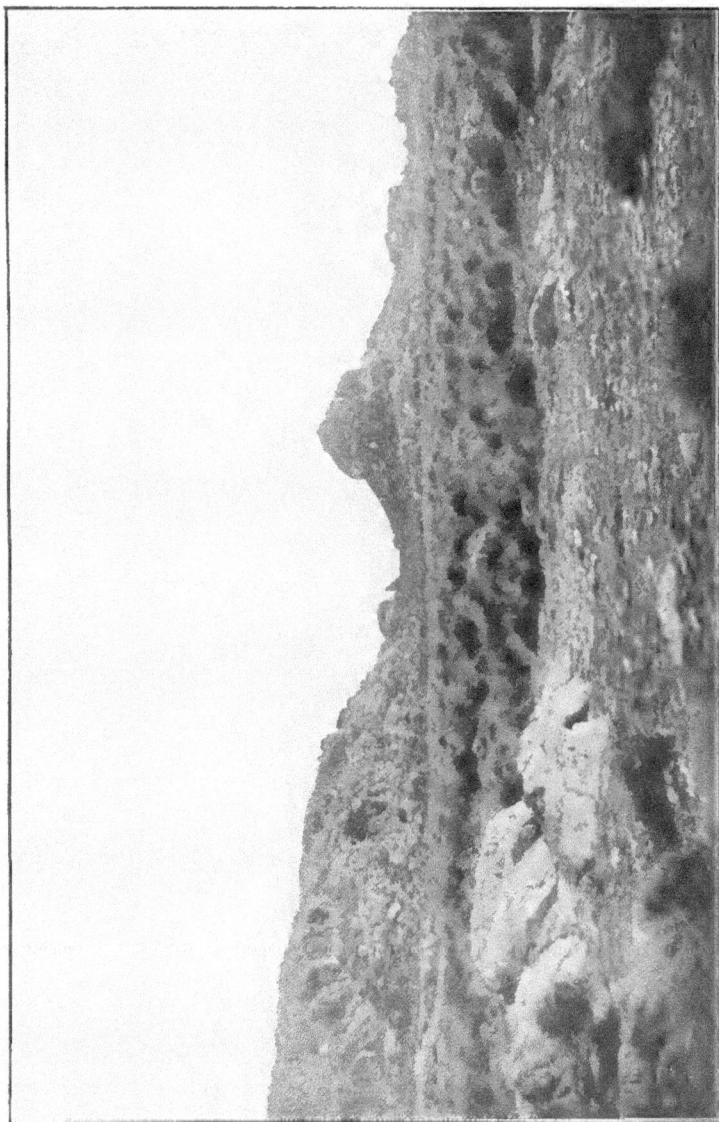

WHITE-FACED STORM-PETREL ROOKERY, NINTH ISLAND.

Photo. by J. G. LITTLER.

mock, several islets of the Hunter Group, and others. Its food, as far as we know, consists of minute animalculæ gathered from the surface of the ocean.

During a visit, extending over nearly a fortnight, paid to Ninth Island, on the North-East Coast of Tasmania, in September, 1909, I had exceptional opportunities for observing the White-faced Storm-Petrel. Before going to the island I had been informed that large numbers of this species nested there. So, naturally, I expected to witness some interesting sights when the birds came in to clean out their burrows. Nor was I disappointed. On arriving on the island on the 22nd September, a keen search was made for evidences of the burrows of this tiny Petrel. I was not long in discovering signs that the birds had commenced to come in to clean out their homes in preparation for the breeding season. How long prior to my arrival they had been coming in it was impossible to say. As I afterwards discovered, not only were the burrows driven under the tussock-grass almost everywhere, but also in the soft soil on the top and sides of the island. An investigation showed that in these latter places the burrows were from 2 feet 6 inches to 3 feet in length; many were curved, some almost forming the letter L. The nesting chamber was some 6 inches in diameter, with a few fragments of vegetable *débris* on the floor.

It was my custom every evening, after watching the Little Penguins landing on some part of the island, to spend some hours on the various rookeries armed with a powerful acetylene lamp, watching the various birds. I found that by walking slowly and as noiselessly as possible, I could move with impunity, and observe the birds cleaning out their burrows, courting, fighting, &c. I found that the first White-faced Storm-Petrel arrived each evening punctually at 6.50. By 8 o'clock the majority of the birds had arrived and were in their burrows hard at work " spring cleaning." It was a very pretty sight watching them alight and seek out their homes; they cannot walk after the manner of ordinary birds, but flit over the ground, just tipping it with their toes. They gave one the impression of being full of springs. As soon as a bird arrived at the entrance of its burrow it would come to a stop and dart suddenly out of sight. Even with hundreds of birds of this species round, not a sound was heard while they were on the wing, but when in their burrows a mouse-like squeaking, only slightly louder, could be heard. With many hundreds of birds underground, the noise was distinctly audible. From the 22nd to the 25th, Storm-Petrels were only fairly numerous; then a curious thing occurred— not a single bird put in an appearance for three nights. On the 29th they reappeared in vast numbers, and continued every night while I was on the island.

No prettier sight can be imagined than hundreds, perhaps thousands, of these dainty creatures passing and repassing in the rays of the lamp, coming from darkness into light and disappearing again into darkness as they flitted over the rookeries. They looked for all the world like giant moths, and appeared as thick as flakes in a snow-shower on a calm day.

Again and again 1 caught individuals in my hands as they flew past, to be released again. It was found that after being held in one's hand for a few seconds and then the fingers slowly opened, the birds would remain either quietly resting or poised with out-stretched wings for quite an appreciable time. On suddenly turning the lamp on to any bird on the ground, it was always possible to pick it up without any attempt at escape on its part. As to the number of birds in the various rookeries, it was impos-sible to arrive at any estimate, beyond that the number must have run into some thousands. Not all the birds left at dawn, for in several instances pairs were found in their burrows during the day.

Pacific Gulls are not the only enemies they have to contend against on Ninth Island, for a couple of domestic cats run wild, in high condition, were seen. Scores and scores of dead Storm-Petrels in various stages of disruption were scattered about the rookeries, and in several places among the rocks cn the hill-side were heaps of bones and feathers. Penguins also account for a number, for they peck them as they search for their burrows, and one peck means death.

*BLACK-BELLIED STORM-PETREL

(*Cymodroma melanogaster,* Gould).

Male.—Upper surface sooty-black, glossed with leaden-grey; lower rump and upper tail coverts white; tail black; wing coverts sooty-brown; quills black; throat sooty-black, shaded with grey and slightly mottled with white; lower throat, chest, breast, abdomen, and under tail coverts sooty-black—the last have white bases; sides of breast, abdomen, also flanks, white; bill, legs, and feet black. Dimensions in mm. :—Length, 190; bill, 12; wing, 165; tail, 67; tarsus, 37.

Female.—Similar to male. Some of the feathers on the back however, have greyish-white fringes.

Young.—Some of the feathers on the back have greyish-white fringes; chin more or less mottled with white; also a few black-tipped feathers on breast and abdomen.

Nest.—Crevice in a rock.

Eggs.—According to Dr. F. Du Cane Godman, an egg taken on Kerguelen Island by the *Challenger* Expedition is dull white, with a faint pinkish shade at one end, sprinkled with dots of the same colour, which are also seen over the rest of the egg; there is a slight indication of purplish dots, which are, however, scarcely perceptible; axis 1.45 in., diameter, 1.03 in. Another egg in the British Museum is from Falkland Island, and two others from Chatham Islands.

Breeding Season.—In all probability similar to that of other Storm-Petrels.

Geographical Distribution.—Seas of Tasmania, Australia, New Zealand, and Southern Ocean in general, and northwards off the coast of Africa and in the Indian Ocean.

Observations.—Gould met with this species on several occasions in Australian waters. He found it very abundant in the South Pacific and Indian Oceans, especially off the islands of St. Paul and Amsterdam.

Dr. Edward Wilson states that during the voyage of the *Discovery* the species was constantly seen in the South Atlantic during September and October.

Practically nothing is known of the general habits of the Black-bellied Storm-Petrel.

*WHITE-BELLIED STORM-PETREL
(*Cymodroma grallaria*, Vieill.),

Male.—The upper surface resembles that of the Black-bellied Storm-Petrel save that the dorsal feathers have hoary-white margins; breast and abdomen pure white; under tail coverts black, lightly fringed with white. Dimensions in mm. :—Length, 175; bill, 12; wing, 165; tail, 78; tarsus, 35.

Female.—Similar in plumage to male.

Nest and Eggs.—Unknown.

Breeding Season.—Unknown.

Geographical Distribution.—Seas of Tasmania, Australia, Southern Ocean in general, and northwards to off the coast of Florida.

Observations.—This species is described as being scarce in Australian waters. Dr. E. A. Wilson observed several in the wake of the *Discovery* in the Southern Indian Ocean, but none in the South Pacific or Atlantic. He records having seen them "dropping to touch the water with one foot and steadying themselves while they daintily took their minute crustacean food from the surface of the water."

FAMILY—PUFFINIDÆ (21 species).

WEDGE-TAILED PETREL
(*Puffinus chlororhynchus*, Less.)

Male.—Upper surface sooty-brown; tail black; primaries and secondaries blackish-brown; throat ashy-grey; remainder of the under surface, including under tail coverts, dull ashy-brown; bill, legs, and feet yellowish flesh colour. Dimensions in mm. :— Length, 445; bill, 41; wing, 295; tail, 131; tarsus, 48.

Female.—Similar to male.

Nest.—A burrow driven obliquely into the ground for 2 to 5 feet.

Eggs.—Clutch one; oval in shape; texture somewhat coarse; surface slightly glossy and minutely pitted; colour pure white. Dimensions in mm. of odd examples :—(1) 62 x 39, (2) 60 x 40.

Breeding Season.—November and December.

Geographical Distribution.—Seas of Tasmania, Australia, New Zealand, and northwards to the Society Islands; there are also a few records for the Indian Ocean.

Observations.—The Wedge-tailed Petrel closely resembles the familiar Sooty Petrel or "Mutton-Bird." It breeds on several islands off Australia, but to the best of my knowledge has not been recorded from any of the Tasmanian islands in Bass Strait.

Of this species on Rat Island, Mr. A. J. Campbell records :— "About half an hour after sundown they commence moaning and get uneasy in their burrows, and shortly afterwards birds may be seen swiftly cutting the air in many directions. The moaning and infant-like cries of the Wedge-tailed Petrel are a curious experience. After a ramble one quiet night I noted in my pocket-book next morning that the whole island seemed groaning and travailing in pain with the noise of Mutton-Birds. About half an hour before sunrise they disappear underground, when all is quiet as far as they are concerned. The attitude of this Petrel upon the ground resembles a Duck upon water—a squatting posture. When walking they are assisted by their wings, which gives the birds a waddling or lame gait. The eggs, like those of the Noddies and other birds, are excellent eating, not at all fishy in flavour, as may be supposed."

ALLIED PETREL

(*Puffinus assimilis*, Gould).

Male.—Upper surface, including head, slaty-brown to black; tail black; quills black; sides of the face and cheeks white; sides of the neck mottled black on white; entire under surface pure white; "bill dark horn colour; tarsi and toes greenish-yellow, webs yellowish-orange" (Gould). The colours of the bill and feet have been variously described by different authors. Sir W. Buller (Hauraki Gulf) describes them as "bill bluish-black; feet greenish-grey, with yellow interdigital webs, marked with black on the outer edge." Specimens procured by the *Scotia* Expedition from Gough Island had "basal half of bill blue, distal part and nasal tubes black; front of tarsus and toes greyish-blue; posterior portion of tarsus and sides of toes black; webs yellowish." Dimensions in mm. :—Average length, 270; bill, 24; wing, 184; tail, 65; tarsus, 38.

Female.—Similar to male.

Nest.—A rabbit-like burrow, driven obliquely into the ground.

Eggs.—Clutch one; broad oval in shape; texture of shell somewhat fine; surface minutely pitted; with or without a faint trace of gloss; colour pure white. Dimensions in mm. vary from 48-50 x 35-37.

Breeding Season.—October and November.

Geographical Distribution.—Seas of Tasmania, Australia, and New Zealand; also the Atlantic Ocean as far as Madeira.

Observations.—The Allied Petrel does not breed off the Tasmanian Coast, but does so in some numbers on the Abrolhos Islands, Western Australia. In its general economy it closely resembles the other members of the genus *Puffinus.*

FLESHY-FOOTED PETREL
(*Puffinus carneipes*, Gould).

Male.—Upper surface, including head, sooty-black; tail black; quills darker black than upper surface; ear coverts slightly tinged with ashy-grey; whole of the under surface sooty-brown; cheeks and throat only tinged with grey. The bill is variously described as being "fleshy-white, the culmen and tips of the mandibles brown," "flesh-colour with a yellowish tinge," "the tip brownish-black," "dark brown," "yellow horn colour, brownish-black at the tips of both mandibles and along the culmen to the opening of the nostrils." The feet are likewise variously described as being "yellowish flesh colour," "dull flesh colour," "pale flesh colour," and "flesh colour." Dimensions in mm.:—Length, about 485; bill, 40; wing, 310; tail, 113; tarsus, 55.

Female.—Similar to male.

Nest.—A burrow some 4 to 8 feet in length.

Eggs.—Clutch one; inclined to oval in shape; texture somewhat coarse; surface slightly glossy and minutely pitted; colour pure white. Dimensions in mm.:—66 x 43.

Breeding Season.—November and December.

Geographical Distribution.—Seas of Tasmania (?) and probably the southern coast generally, Western Australia, New Zealand, and northwards to Japan.

Observations.—It is somewhat doubtful whether this species really does frequent Tasmanian waters. It obtains its vernacular name from its flesh-coloured feet. Although it ranges to Japan, it has never been found breeding there, nor yet in the intervening area. According to the late Sir W. Buller, the Fleshy-footed Petrel breeds in large colonies off the coast of New Zealand.

SHORT-TAILED PETREL (Mutton-Bird)
(*Puffinus tenuirostris*, Temm.)

Male.—Upper surface, including head, sooty-black; tail black; quills black; some of the wing coverts and secondaries shaded with brown; under surface sooty-brown, the feathers faintly edged with ashy-grey; irides brown (practically invisible at night time); bill black; legs and feet, outer edges black, inner and webs much paler. Dimensions in mm.:—Length, 410; bill, 34; wing, 280; tail, 82; tarsus, 49.

Female.—Plumage similar; dimensions vary but little.

Nest.—An obliquely driven burrow, ranging in length from 1 to 7 feet, largely depending on the nature of the soil. The burrows are so close together on some rookeries as to honeycomb the ground.

Eggs.—Clutch one; shape varies from oval to slightly elongated oval; texture fairly coarse; surface minutely pitted and faintly glossy; colour pure white at first, but usually soon becoming nest-stained. Dimensions in mm. of examples from different rookeries: —(a) 73 x 47, (b) 80 x 58, (c) 72 x 44, (d) 75 x 57. Should the burrows be robbed at the beginning of the season another egg is laid.

Breeding Season.—Birds arrive to scratch out their burrows about the 20th September; eggs laid about 25th November, varying only a day or two each year. Young birds are able to fly end of April or beginning of May.

Geographical Distribution.—Seas of Tasmania, Australia, and New Zealand; also northward to Japan and eastward to Samoa.

Observations.—So much has been written about this interesting Petrel that I shall make my notes as brief as possible.

Only those who have witnessed a flight of Mutton-Birds can have any conception of the vast numbers in which they move. On two occasions I have been fortunate enough to witness gigantic fights during the daytime. The second and more remarkable occasion was on the 2nd October, 1909, when, standing on the top of an island off the north coast of Tasmania, I watched a stream of birds go by that lasted all the morning, and must have numbered hundreds of thousands. One of the earliest accounts of the vast hordes of birds to be seen during certain seasons in Bass Strait is by Flinders, who, accompanied by Ross, was, in December, 1798, in the neighbourhood of Three Hummock Island. According to calculations made by him, the birds numbered some 132,000,000. Since that time many more or less full accounts have appeared in various publications concerning the vast numbers seen in Bass Strait and vicinity.

When on Ninth Island in September, 1909, I had the good fortune to witness the incoming of a flight of birds for the purpose of cleaning out their burrows in preparation for the laying season, which commences on or about the 25th November every year. The first bird of the season put in an appearance at 6.30 p.m. on the evening of the 29th. It was observed that the birds did not at once enter their burrows on alighting, but rested on the ground outside for some time as though worn out. The mouths and throats of a couple of individuals secured for taxidermical purposes were full of a pasty substance of the appearance and smell of semi-masticated tinned salmon. It is generally thought that the food

PORTION OF MUTTON-BIRD ROOKERY, NINTH ISLAND.

of this species consists of "whale food," an oily substance consisting of animalculæ, found floating on the surface of the water. Both birds appear to assist in the task of cleaning out the burrows. When the burrows have all been cleaned out and some fresh ones scratched—do not get within the line of fire when a Mutton-Bird is making the sand fly—the birds disappear and do not return until the laying season.

During the camp-out of the Australasian Ornithologists' Union on Phillip Island in November, 1902, I had the opportunity of witnessing the birds coming in to lay—an experience even more remarkable than that of seeing them coming in to scratch out. The din made by some thousands of birds is something that once heard can never be forgotten. It is, as Donald Macdonald has remarked, incessant, variable, but always harsh and unearthly. Its uncanniness baffles description.

As the first streak of dawn appears the birds emerge quietly from their burrows, and as they cannot rise directly from off the ground, start out from the edge of a cliff or some slight eminence so as to get the wind under their wings. The departure is as silent as the arrival is clamorous.

I omitted to mention that the birds commence to come in for laying purposes just a few minutes after sunset. Just at this time of the year heavy gales usually blow, which are known as "Mutton-Bird gales." Only one bird of a pair goes to sea in the morning, as a rule, the other remaining in the burrow.

On Phillip Island, which is under the jurisdiction of Victoria, egging is allowed, and some 20,000 or more eggs are taken every season of a few weeks, the bulk finding their way to the Melbourne market, where they are sold as fresh duck eggs. They are all right as an article of diet so long as they are not boiled. The eggs are raked out of the burrows by means of a piece of looped wire at the end of a stick. It takes a good deal of practice to locate and draw an egg out.

On the Tasmanian islands egging is forbidden under a penalty, only the birds being taken. A few years since, however, this was not so. The Mutton-Birding season lasts from 20th March until 20th May. The principal "birding" islands are Chappell, Babel, Little Dog and Big Dog Islands, Green Island and Little Green Island. Vigorous, but unfortunately unavailing, protest has been made within late years by white and half-caste residents on some of the islands regarding the damage done to a number of rookeries by sheep and cattle. The owners of these animals are supposed to remove them off the rookeries in time for the birds to get their homes in order for the nesting season. Unhappily, the stock is too often left on, in defiance of the regulation, until after the birds return, and they, finding the burrows trampled in as fast as they clean them out, leave in despair, perhaps never to return. It is a matter for regret that the bulk of the residents of the Strait islands should be to a great and increasing extent deprived of their only harvest in the year owing to the greed and selfishness of a few non-resident holders of grazing licences.

Any article dealing with Mutton-Birds would be incomplete without some reference to their economic value. In 1905 I was engaged in making some investigations on this subject, and feel I cannot do better than reprint the result of my inquiries. The figures given may be taken as a criterion for other years. As I previously remarked, the season opens on the 20th March each year :—

" For some time previous men arrive on the scenes of their future operations from Launceston, the North-West Coast, the largest islands in the Strait, and from other places. They rebuild their temporary huts and get everything ready so that there will be no hitch when the real work commences. Empty casks by the dozen, for putting the birds in, either accompany the men or are sent down almost immediately. The *modus operandi* of ' birding ' is briefly as follows :—The young bird is dragged out of its burrow and has its neck dislocated by a smart jerk. Then some fifty or more birds are strung on a spit, care being taken that their heads are upwards, else the oil will run out of their mouths. The next operation is to pluck, then scald the body, to remove all feathers and down, after which the feet are cut off. After the bodies have been allowed to cool on the grass for some time they are cleaned, the head and neck removed, and finally salted or pickled in the barrels brought for the purpose. Birders always retain a certain number of birds for their own home consumption. On my turning up the Government year-books and other likely and unlikely publications, I found that no attempt had been made to ascertain the number of birds imported into Tasmania. In my perplexity I applied to Mr. Geo. D. Gardner; he very good-naturedly and at some considerable trouble compiled me some statistics for last season. He estimates that some 555,000 birds were captured last year. Of this number 475,000 were landed in Launceston, 10,000 each at Beaconsfield and George Town, and the balance consumed on the islands. The whole of those received in Launceston are not consumed locally, many casks being sent to the various mining fields and the larger townships. I am given to understand that practically no Mutton-Birds are captured on the islands lying off Hobart, nor are they brought direct into that place from any of the other islands. The same authority informed me that these birds are practically unknown in Sydney. The birds are sold wholesale at so much per 100, and retail at so much per dozen. For the last three years the prices were :—1902, 10s., 11s. ; 1903, 11s., 12s. 6d. ; 1904, 14s. per 100. Last year was a bad year, owing to the continuous wet during the hatching season, consequently the number of birds caught was much below the average, and the selling price as much above. The birds are retailed at eight a shilling in the beginning of the season, then falling to twelve for the same money. Of course, on the West Coast, and other far-away places the prices are much higher. The wholesale price has been down as low as 6s. per 100, but, as a large importer remarked to me, there is nothing in them at that price. Mutton-Birds captured last season represented £3,885—no inconsiderable amount. The fat and oil are worth about a shilling a gallon, and are used for many purposes. Saddlers utilize good quantities. Up to the last few years the feathers were a wasted asset, on account of their very strong odour. I am informed that a German on one of the islands now collects them and sends them to Germany, where the odour is extracted, and they are used for many purposes."

Further details concerning this very interesting species may be found in A. J. Campbell's "Nests and Eggs," *The Emu*, P.R.S. of Tasmania, and in my series of articles in *The Weekly Courier* of 1905.

FORSTER PETREL

(Puffinus gavia, Forster).

Male.—Upper surface, including head, sooty-black; tail and quills black; cheeks, sides of throat, and sides of neck dull ashy, mottled with white; throat and under surface pure white; a patch of sooty-black in the region of the thighs; "bill dark grey, lighter and more yellowish-grey on the under mandibles; tarsi and toes pinkish flesh colour, stained with blackish-brown along the front of the tarsus and on the outer edge of the toes; the webs darker; iris brownish-black" (W. Buller). Dimensions in mm. :—Length, about 345; bill, 34; wing, 215; tail, 62; tarsus, 45.

Female.—Upper surface similar to male, but the ashy-brown on the sides of the neck extends down the sides of the breast; centre of the throat mottled with ashy-brown; sides of the body smoky-brown.

Nestling.—Covered with thick down, slate coloured on the upper and white on the under surface.

Nest.—A burrow some 3 feet long, with a fairly large nesting cavity at the end. Breeds in colonies or rookeries.

Eggs.—"Clutch one; oval in shape, or more pointed at one end; texture of shell comparatively fine; surface slightly glossy; colour pure white. Dimensions in inches:—2.2 x 1.55" (A. J. Campbell).

Breeding Season.—October chiefly.

Geographical Distribution.—Seas of Tasmania (doubtful), New South Wales, South Australia, and probably other parts of Australia, also New Zealand.

Observations.—Some doubt exists as to whether this species should really be included among the sea-birds frequenting our waters, but as it is found off the coast of South Australia and New

South Wales there is little doubt that some individuals, at least, wander further south. New Zealand waters are a stronghold, it breeding in large numbers on islands off the coast. It was in Queen Charlotte Sound that Forster's Petrel was first discovered, during Captain Cook's voyages.

The late Sir Walter Buller wrote of this species :—

" They congregate in flocks, often of considerable size, and fly in a compact body, generally in a zig-zag course, with a very rapid movement of the wings and not far above the water. Their flight is peculiar, too, in this respect, that they appear all to turn at the same moment, like a company of soldiers, showing first the dark plumage of the upper surface and then the white under parts, as they simultaneously dip towards the water.

" Their habits are sociable, and flocks may often be seen in the daytime disporting themselves in the sea, making short flights just above the surface, then flopping into the water, splashing and chasing one another in their playful gambols, and when tired of their fun rising in a body and rapidly disappearing from view as already described. On one occasion I saw a flock of several hundreds thus amusing themselves in the bright sunshine (though the bird is more nocturnal than diurnal) as our ship was steaming through the narrow ' French Pass ' in Cook's Strait.

".They seemed to scatter at night, for as darkness approached I have noticed numerous single examples, as if the flocks of the daytime were dispersing over the surface of the ocean in quest of their food. They fly low but swiftly, and with a note resembling the native name by which the bird is called, but somewhat prolonged, as ' Paka-ha-a-paka-ha-a.' During the breeding season I have seen very large flocks of them between Whale Island and the mainland, some of them hovering on the wing, hundreds together in ' schools ' or flocks, and others scattered far and wide over the surface, floating in a listless manner, as if resting after the hunting exploits of the night.''

*BROWN PETREL (GREAT GREY PETREL)

(*Priofinus cinereus,* Gmelin).

Male.—Crown of the head dusky-black; rest of the upper surface ashy-grey, with faint hoary-grey margins to the feathers; tail black, with ashy-grey on the inner webs; wing coverts and quills dusky-brown; sides of the neck slate-grey; entire under surface pure white; sides of the body ashy-brown. There is considerable difference in the colouration of both the bill and the legs in individuals from different localities. Dimensions in mm. :— Length, 500; bill, 50; wing, 332; tail, 106; tarsus, 56.

Female.—Similar to male.

Nest.—According to Mr. Campbell, on Macquarie Island burrows are formed under tussock-grass, mostly high upon the mountain sides.

Eggs.—Clutch one; roundish oval in shape; texture somewhat coarse; surface very slightly glossy; colour pure white. Dimensions in mm. :—70 x 50.

Breeding Season.—November and December.

Geographical Distribution.—Seas of Tasmania, Australia, New Zealand, and Southern Ocean in general.

Observations.—This large and powerful Petrel is somewhat numerous in southern seas. During the voyage of the *Magenta* a number were observed in Bass Strait. The flight of this species is very powerful, and resembles in some ways that of an Albatross. Of the diving powers of the Great Grey Petrel Dr. E. A. Wilson remarks that they "drop suddenly beneath the surface of the water with their wings spread to seize some scrap of food. They unhesitatingly go completely under, and reappear with their wings still spread."

Ascension Island is considered to be the most northern point reached by this bird.

*SILVER-GREY PETREL

(Priocella glacialoides, Smith).*

Male.—Crown of the head white; nape and hind-neck slightly shaded with pearly-grey; tail pearly-grey; back and wing coverts pearly-grey; quills blackish; secondaries pearly-grey; under surface of body pure white; shade of pearly-grey on lower flanks; "bill rarely pink, blackish at the tip of both mandibles and maxilla; iris rich brown; legs, toes, and webs all flesh-grey, with a strong pink tinge" (E. A. Wilson). Dimensions in mm. :— Length, about 460; bill, 45; wing, 330; tail, 115; tarsus, 48.

Female.—Similar to male.

Nest and Eggs.—Unknown.

Geographical Distribution.—Seas of Tasmania, Australia, New Zealand, Southern Ocean in general, and ranging northwards to the Columbia River, on the Pacific Coast of America.

Observations.—Much mystery attaches to the site of the breeding grounds of this delicately marked Petrel, whose range over the Southern Ocean is very wide. Strong suspicions are held that Kerguelen Island contains a rookery or two, but nothing definite has been discovered. Mr. W. Eagle Clarke, of the Scottish Expedition, looks upon Laurie Island as a probable breeding ground, while Dr. Wilson, who accompanied the National Antarctic Expedition, considers the Balleny Islands a probable nesting place. He further adds :—"It may be that the basaltic rocks of Scott Island, discovered in Ross Sea by the relief ship *Morning,* are a breeding place for this Petrel and for the Antarctic Petrel too. From its position this is quite likely, and from the large

number of birds seen in the neighbourhood in January one might
well be led to think that the eggs and young of these two birds
may at some future date be found there."

Those who have had opportunities of seeing this handsome
Petrel in any number in the southern seas state that it flies higher
and rests more frequently than the smaller species.

*SPECTACLED PETREL

(*Majaqueus æquinoctialis*, Linn.)

Male.—Upper surface sooty-brown; tail and quills nearly
black; under surface, except the chin, which is white, a shade
paler than upper surface. Dimensions in mm.:—Length, about
560; bill, 52; wing, 365; tail, 115; tarsus, 59.

As Dr. Du Cane Godman points out ("Monograph of the
Petrels," pp. 171, 172), there is some difference in the markings
of Australian specimens of this species and those from more
northerly latitudes. In some birds there is a band of white (varying in width) across the crown, and in others the cheeks are white,
and this white extends nearly right round the occiput; this band is
in addition to the one on the crown of the head. The white on the
chin is also variable in extent.

Female.—Similar to the male. Dr. Godman remarks that the
female procured in Tasmanian waters examined by him had no
white on the cheeks.

Nest.—A burrow on the sloping sides of a hill. According to
the Rev. A. E. Eaton, the nesting chamber is spherical in shape
and rather large; the nest itself is composed of mud and pieces of
plants arranged in the form of an inverted saucer, 3 or 4 inches
high, slightly hollowed out on the top, a space being left between
its base and the sides of the chamber.

Eggs.—Clutch one; elongated oval in shape; texture coarse;
surface slightly glossy; colour pure white. Dimensions in mm.:—
86 x 52.

Breeding Season.—November to January.

Geographical Distribution.—Seas of Tasmania, New South
Wales, Southern Ocean in general, and north to off the southern
coast of South Africa.

Observations.—Seldom does this species come into purely
Tasmanian waters, but it is very plentiful almost everywhere in
the South Atlantic. "The wings in flight have a very angular
look. The bird is of a quarrelsome disposition, fighting greedily
for scraps, and displaying the most ungainly spread of feet and
straddled legs as it splashed with its rivals into the water" (E.
A. Wilson). The Rev. A. E. Eaton, who accompanied the Transit
of Venus Expedition to Kerguelen Island, states, *inter alia*:—"In
Kerguelen Island a hole similar to a deserted rabbits' earth,
excavated in wet ground, with water standing (in early summer)

an inch or two within the entrance, especially if it be in a slope near the sea, may be regarded as a burrow most likely to be that of a White-chinned Petrel. If it is occupied by the birds there will probably be some green shoots of *Acæna*, clipped off from plants near its mouth, dropped by them in the water. During the season when the birds are pairing, before their egg is laid, they make an extraordinary cackle in the nest-chamber; the sound of approaching footsteps, or a thump upon the ground some distance from the nest, and even a shout at the mouth of the burrow, will cause them to commence in the daytime. During the night this call is uttered by the female sitting on her nest or in the entrance of the tunnel, and she can be heard at a distance of a quarter of a mile when it is calm."

BLACK PETREL

(Majaqueus parkinsoni, Gray).

Male.—Similar in plumage to the previous species, but smaller, and also lacks the white band on the head and the white chin. Dimensions in mm. :—Length, about 460; bill, 50; wing, 335; tail, 105; tarsus, 55.

Female.—Similar to male.

Nest.—A burrow, either in loose soil or under the roots of trees, or even under stones.

Eggs.—Clutch one; stout oval in shape; texture coarse; surface glossy; colour pure white. Dimensions in mm. :—69 x 49.

Breeding Season.—November and December.

Geographical Distribution.—Seas of Tasmania, New South Wales, Victoria, and New Zealand.

Observations.—The Black Petrel is an infrequent wanderer to Tasmanian waters. Round the coast of New Zealand, however, it is very numerous, and breeds in great numbers in certain parts of the North Island and on small islands off the coast. The Maoris make great inroads not only among the young birds, but also the old ones, which are captured in large numbers by lighting fires on calm nights and thus decoying them to their destruction.

*GREAT-WINGED PETREL (Long-winged Petrel)

(Œstrelata macroptera, Smith).

Male.—Both the upper and lower surfaces are sooty-brown ; the back is tinged with grey; tail black; quills also black; "the primaries dull ashy at the base of the inner web, not forming a white base " (Godman); "bill and feet black " (Buller). Dimensions in mm. :—Length, about 385; bill, 34; wing, 300; tail, 45; tarsus, 41.

Female.—Similar to male.

Nestling.—"Covered with dingy slaty-grey down; the black

feathers first appearing on the head and in four or five parallel series on the cheeks. The down is long, thick, and fluffy, especially on the under parts; and the bill and feet are perfectly black" (W. Buller).

Nest.—"A hole or burrow, usually at the base of a cliff. In companies, sometimes four or five pairs of birds having nests within the same cavern, each nest being placed at the end of a separate burrow, having a varying length, with an oval chamber at the farther end. These burrows are generally about 3 feet in extent (one, however, measured 4 feet) and the nest or egg chamber is decidedly smaller than that formed by the Black Petrel (*M. parkinsoni*) and had a few dry leaves on the floor" (Buller).

Eggs.—Clutch one; roundish oval in shape; texture fairly coarse; surface faintly glossy and minutely pitted; colour pure white. Dimensions in mm.:—85 x 48.

Breeding Season.—September.

Geographical Distribution.—Seas of Tasmania, New South Wales, Victoria, New Zealand, and ranging over the Southern Ocean generally.

Observations.—During the non-breeding season the Great-winged Petrel may frequently be observed in Tasmanian waters. It may at once be identified by its great stretch of wing, reminding one of a gigantic Swift.

"These Petrels are common on the coast of New Zealand. I saw them in large flocks out at sea, where they remain from March to August; in the latter month they come ashore to their old breeding places, which they use annually as long as they are not molested. These birds breed in colonies; their burrows are sometimes very close to one another; on the Little Barrier Island (or Hauturu Island) I measured a piece of ground thirty-six feet in circumference in the centre of which were six burrows. Their breeding resorts are always on the cliffs along the coast—and some were very difficult to approach—dug out by these Petrels in hard sandy formation or clay. . . .

"After sunset thick clouds of these Petrels swarm round the cliffs, uttering the melancholy sound 'Ohi! ohi!' from which the native name is 'Ohi.' Each one circles round its burrow several times before it goes down to it; and then they stop for a moment before entering. These birds go to and from their burrows several times a night. When the young is hatched, the female stops for a few days with her chick in the burrow; after that both parents leave every morning before sunrise, and fly to their haunts on the ocean. Returning after sunset, they circle round their burrows, then swoop down to the entrance and call; when answered by the young bird they enter. If both birds come to the burrow together, one stops outside until the other reappears. When feeding the young they make a whimpering noise" (A. Reischek).

*WHITE-HEADED PETREL

(Œstrelata lessoni, Garnot).

Male.—Head white, a patch of black in front, round, and behind the eye; neck and back light ashy-grey; the feathers on the back have hoary-grey margins; centre tail feathers ashy-grey, remainder mostly white; shoulders and wing coverts inclined to slaty-black; quills blackish, tinged with grey; entire under surface pure white; sides of chest light ashy-grey; sides of body faint ashy-grey; "bill black; tarsus and half the toes and webs fleshy-white; tips of toes and their webs black " (Gould). Dimensions in mm. :—Length, about 460; bill, 38; wing, 300; tail, 145; tarsus, 42.

Female.—Similar to male.

Nest.—A short burrow, the entrance of which is usually strewn with green shoots of *Acæna.*

Eggs.—Clutch one; inclined to oval in shape; texture fine, surface glossy; colour dull white. Dimensions in mm. :—70 x 49.

Breeding Season.—The Rev. A. E. Eaton found young in the burrows in September, and Mr. R. Hall found eggs in December and January, both on Kerguelen Island.

Geographical Distribution.—Seas of Tasmania, Australia in general, New Zealand, and South Indian Ocean generally.

Observations.—Very little is known of the habits of this fine species, whose wing powers, according to Gould, far exceed those of any of its congeners. There are but few records of the White-headed Petrel being seen in Tasmanian waters.

SOFT-PLUMAGED PETREL.

(Œstrelata mollis, Gould).

Male.—Crown of head slaty-brown; feathers round eye and a patch below same black; upper surface slaty-grey; rump a shade darker than back; tail ashy-grey; shoulders and wing coverts blackish-brown; throat and whole of under surface pure white; sides of neck ashy-grey; centre of upper fore-neck barred with wavy lines of dark ashy-grey; sides of body sparsely barred in a similar manner; bill black; tarsus flesh colour. Dimensions in mm. :—Length, 315; bill, 25; wing, 220; tail, 92; tarsus, 32.

Female.—Similar to mâle.

Nest.—A rabbit-like burrow in the ground.

Eggs.—Clutch one; inclined to oval in shape; texture fairly coarse; surface slightly glossy; colour pure white. Dimensions in mm. :—69 x 41.

Breeding Season.—January, probably.

Geographical Distribution.—Seas of Tasmania (doubtful), Australia in general (possibly), New Zealand, Southern Ocean, South Atlantic and South Indian Oceans.

Observations.—A certain amount of doubt exists as to whether the Soft-plumaged Petrel is really found in Tasmanian waters. So far as I am aware there are no records of this species having been observed round our coasts, but, taking into consideration the fact that Petrels in general are great ocean wanderers, there is no reason to doubt that, occasionally at least, it comes to within close proximity of the Tasmanian coast.

Those who have observed this bird in its haunts state that it is a very rapid flier and generally moves at a considerble height above the surface of the water.

*BROWN-HEADED PETREL (SOLANDER PETREL)
(Œstrelata solandri, Gould).

Male.—Head black; cheeks and sides of face dark brown; upper surface black, tinged with grey; tail feathers blackish, tinged with ashy-grey; under surface dusky-brown, shaded with slaty-grey; "slightly mottled with white spots on the throat and with larger ones on the breast, mostly concealed" (Godman); bill, legs, and feet black. Dimensions in mm.:—Length, 460; bill, 38; wing, 300; tail, 135; tarsus, 30.

Female.—Probably similar to male.

Nest and Eggs.—Unknown.

Geographical Distribution.—Seas of Tasmania and Australia in general.

Observations.—Nothing is known of the habits of this species, the type specimen of which was secured by Gould in Bass Strait on 13th March, 1839, and is now in the British Museum.

Dr. F. Du Cane Godman is inclined to think that this Petrel is but the dark phase of some other species, possibly *Œ. lessoni.*

*WHITE-WINGED PETREL
(Œstrelata leucoptera, Gould).

Male.—Forehead white, mottled with black; head and hind-neck blackish; sides of face white, spotted with black in front of and below the eye; feathers immediately surrounding the eye black; back dark slaty-grey, edged with black; rump and upper tail coverts light slaty-grey; tail feathers slaty-grey, blackish on the inner web; shoulders slaty-grey; wing coverts and quills black; under surface white; sides of neck and upper breast black, with a faint ashy tinge. "Bill black; tarsus and basal half of the interdigital membrane fleshy-white, remainder of the toes and interdigital membrane black" (Gould). Dimensions in mm.:—Length, about 310; bill, 27; wing, 216; tail, 92; tarsus, 30.

Female.—Similar to male.

Nest and Eggs.—Unknown.

Geographical Distribution.—Seas of Tasmania and Australia in general; also among the Fiji Islands and Duke of York Islands. *Observations.*—The White-winged Petrel was discovered by Gould on Cabbage-tree Island, at the mouth of Port Stephen Harbour, in New South Wales, on which island he was informed it bred abundantly. Mr. A. J. Campbell states that it does not do so now.

"Gould describes it as one of the most beautifully formed species of the genus, and says it is easily distinguished by its white abdomen and under wing coverts, which show to great advantage when the bird is seen on the wing from below; it seldom, however, rises higher than the vane of the ship" (Godman).

Sub-Family—Fulmarinæ.

*GIANT PETREL

(Macronectes gigantea, Gmelin).

Male.—Head dark brown, slightly mottled with black; back slaty-brown, the feathers having pale brown edges; tail feathers dark brown; wing coverts slaty-brown; quills blackish-brown. "Throat dull white, mottled with bars of brown on the lower throat" (Godman). Rest of under surface slaty-brown; iris brown; bill pale yellowish horn colour; legs and toes grey, tinged with yellow. Dimensions in mm.:—Length, about 840; bill, 102; wing, 535; tail, 197; tarsus, 95.

Female.—Similar to male.

Young.—When in down they are light greyish in colour, when fully fledged the feathers are dark brown mottled with white.

Nest.—A hollow scratched in the ground, in which are placed a few stems of grass.

Eggs.—Clutch one; inclined to oval in shape; texture very coarse and granulated; surface rough and without gloss; colour dull white. Dimensions in mm.:—99 x 65.

Breeding Season.—September to November.

Geographical Distribution.—The seas round Tasmania and the most of Australia; also New Zealand, Southern Ocean in general, ranging as far south as 78 deg. S. lat., and as far north as 30 deg. S. lat.

Observations.—This Giant Petrel, which has a close superficial resemblance to the Sooty Albatross, is a very familiar bird to all those who "go down to the sea in ships." The following quotations extracted from the writings of those who have had exceptional opportunities for observing it in its haunts may not be without interest:—

Dr. Wilson writes:—"Of the Giant Petrel, the 'Nellie,' or 'Stink-pot'—call him which you will—we saw far more in milder

13

climates than we have seen since we entered the ice.   At Cape
Adare it is true that we saw a number, and among them all
varieties of shade, from the white albino to the chequered grey
and the dark individuals, of which some were dark all over, even to
blackness, and others had light-coloured heads and necks, contrasting with their darker bodies.   It is strange that we should
have found here a dozen or so of this albino variety, for a white
Giant Petrel was considered a great rarity by the members of the
Southern Cross Expedition, nor was more than one seen there
during the whole time of their stay at Cape Adare.   The Nellie
has never been found nesting so far south of the Circle, but breeds
freely at most of the islands that lie a short way north of it.
Variability is its marked characteristic, far more so than it is of
the Skua, whose changes bear some relation to the age of the
individual.   It appears, however, that the variations in the Giant
Petrel are independent of sex and age, and it may result in some
way from the safety it enjoys from enemies that it has no need in
the economy of life to maintain any definite colouring, and therefore individual variation has full play."

Howard Saunders, in his "Antarctic Manual," writes:—
"The Giant Petrel, which approaches the larger species of
Albatross in size, was observed by Dr. M'Cormick soaring over
Possession Island, Victoria Land, and the *Belgica* found it a
constant attendant in the ice-pack.   The 'Nelly,' as sealers call it,
is, in fact, the Vulture of the sea, visiting every spot where carcasses and refuse of seals and Penguins, or any other means of
subsistence, can be found.   Its breeding and habits on Marion
and Kerguelen Islands have been described by Moseley and others,
and the bird probably nests on Heard Island.   Webster found it on
Deception Island, South Shetlands, from January to March; and,
as regards South Georgia, where the eggs are laid in the beginning
of November, the practical Weddell remarks that these are inferior
to those of other species.   The beak of this voracious bird is very
powerful, and assertions have often been made by sailors that it
will attack a drowning man and accelerate his death.   Dr.
M'Cormick states that when, after leaving Kerguelen, the boat-
swain of the *Erebus* fell overboard and could not be saved, the
Giant Petrels swooped at him as he struggled to keep afloat, and
it is doubtful if they did not actually strike him with their bills;
while Mr. Arthur G. Guillemard states that a sailor who was
picked up had his arms badly lacerated in defending his head from
the attacks of an 'Albatross,' which may have been this Giant
Petrel."

Mr. Borchgrevink, in "First on the Antarctic Continent," says:
—"The Gigantic Petrels also visited Camp Ridley.   They were
very scarce during the summer.   We did not find one of their nests,
and their visits to the peninsula were always short and interrupted,
and, to a great extent, I ascribe their visits to Robertson Bay and

our peninsula to strong gales at sea, which drove them towards shore for shelter. In fact, during the strongest gale we had in the autumn, they arrived at Camp Ridley the day before the gale commenced, and left immediately after it was over. So I, at least, came to look upon their arrival as the sign of an approaching gale. These large birds, which in their flight much resemble the Albatross, vary somewhat in their colour—perhaps as much as the *Lestris*—from dark brown to light faded brown; and albinos are occasionally seen. I secured one of these latter, and Captain Jensen secured another. We had both of us great difficulty in securing a specimen. A noble, rare bird as he is, he seemed to soar about higher and more lonely than the rest, and remarkable was it that an albino, although of exactly the same species as the dark one, was seldom or never seen in its company. Whether this is because the others combine against him and hunt him because of his whiteness, or because he, in modest ignorance of his value, seeks his own sphere, I do not know, but certain is it that he willingly or compulsorily soars about in higher regions than the rest."

Mr. Burn-Murdoch, who was on the *Balaena* on the "Edinburgh to the Antarctic" Expedition, gives the following note on the species :—" A number of Nellies, or Giant Petrels, come circling over us as we slowly drift from our shelter to leeward. They gorge themselves with the ' cran ' (scraps of seal's flesh cut off the blubber—this name is also given to the carcass of the seal when it is skinned and the blubber has been stripped off), that is constantly being thrown over our sides, then fly back to the sea and sit beside their Penguin friends. Strange, ugly birds they are, the apparent coarseness of their build, and their grey-green, clumsy beaks and rough brown feathers, give the impression that nature has turned them out in a very wholesale fashion. Some of them are apparently white, and a few of the same kind of bird, I believe—perhaps one in twenty—are pure white, all but one or two brown feathers. The different stages of colouring are rather like those of the Gannet. We call them ' scavengers.' "

*CAPE PETREL (Cape Pigeon)

(*Daption capensis*, Linn.)

Male.—Head and hind-neck black; sides of shoulders and sides of neck black; central upper tail coverts white, conspicuously spotted with black; tail feathers white, with a broad terminal black band; marginal wing coverts black; inner wing coverts white, spotted similarly to shoulders; primaries black, with inner webs white; outer secondaries white; inner also white, tipped with black; chin black; throat white, mottled with black; rest of under surface white.

Female.—Similar to male.

Nestling.—According to Mr. W. Eagle Clarke "it is slate-grey above, paler and more sooty on the under side."

Young.—" Covered with greyish down above and greyish-white below; bill black " (R. Hall).

Nest.—On Kerguelen Island, according to Mr. R. Hall, the nests are placed in holes in stony parts of the cliffs about 50 feet above sea level, no lining of grass or weeds being used. On Laurie Island nests were found composed of stones and earth, and placed on exposed ledges of cliffs, frequently in colonies, but sometimes isolated.

Eggs.—Clutch one; oval in shape; large for the size of the bird. Dr. Godman states that the eggs obtained on South Orkney Islands averaged 62.35 x 43.11 mm. Average dimensions in mm. of three examples presented to the British Museum by Dr. W. S. Bruce:—61 x 41.

Breeding Season.—December.

Geographical Distribution.—Seas of Tasmania, Australia, New Zealand, Southern Ocean in general, to lat. 65 deg. south, ranging north to European waters.

Observations.—Round the southern coast of Tasmania this species is more or less plentiful during the greater part of the year, but is not at all plentiful at any time in northern waters. To all those who have voyaged from Australia to the Cape it is a very familiar object skimming over the waters in the wake of the steamer in company with Albatrosses and other ocean wanderers, or else moving in great flocks over the face of the waters.

" It feeds upon minute crustaceans, most of which appear to be coloured with bright orange pigment, that is so marked a feature in those animals. They are freely ejected in a mucoid orange-coloured mess when the bird is caught and handled, and the same objectionable habit is said to be indulged in when the birds are disturbed upon their nests " (E. A. Wilson).

Mr. W. Eagle Clarke gives the distance of ejection as " 6 or even 8 feet."

" This Martin among the Petrels is extremely tame, passing immediately under the stern and settling close down to the sides of the ship if fat of any kind or other oily substance be thrown overboard. Swims lightly, but rarely exercises its natatorial powers except to procure food, in pursuit of which it occasionally dives for a moment or two. Nothing can be more graceful than its motions while on the wing, with the neck shortened, and the legs entirely hidden among the feathers of the under tail coverts " (Gould).

*BLUE PETREL

(*Halobæna cærulea*, Gmelin).

Male.—Forehead, sides of face, and ear coverts white; feathers on the forehead mottled with black; crown of the head and neck slaty-black; back, rump, upper tail coverts, tail,

BIRDS OF TASMANIA.   181

shoulders, and wing coverts greyish-blue; tail feathers broadly tipped with white; outer webs of primaries black, inner hoary-white; inner primaries and secondaries greyish-blue; whole of under surface pure white; sides of chest greyish-blue. " Bill dull blackish-brown, with a stripe of blue-grey along the lower part of the lower mandible; tarsus and toes delicate blue; interdigital membrane fleshy-white, traversed with red veins " (Gould). Dimensions in mm. :—Length, about 280; bill, 27; wing, 212; tail, 92; tarsus, 32.

Female.—Similar to male.

Nest.—According to the testimony of the Rev. A. E. Eaton and Dr. Kidder, of the British and American Expeditions respectively, the burrows on Kerguelen Island were excavated beneath clumps of *Azorella.* The winding burrows terminated in large, dry chambers lined with fine roots, fibres, twigs, ferns, and leaves of the Kerguelen "tea."

Eggs.—Clutch one; roundish oval in shape; texture fairly fine; surface without gloss; colour white. Dimensions in mm. :— 48 x 36.

Breeding Season.—October and November.

Geographical Distribution.—Seas of Tasmania, Australia, New Zealand, and Southern Ocean to 70 deg. south lat.

Observations.—Gould on his first voyage to Australia observed the Blue Petrel in large numbers off the coast of Tasmania. Some authorities place this species among the Prions, which bird it closely resembles, but may be readily distinguished by its square tail and white tips to its tail feathers.

" The resemblance between this Petrel and the *Prion desolatus* extends even to their ' coo.' Their calls underground are so much alike that on hearing one it is difficult to state to which of the two species the bird cooing should be referred without digging it up for inspection, and their tone is very similar in sound to the cooing of some foreign doves. But their calls during flight are very different from one another " (A. E. Eaton).

*BROAD-BILLED DOVE-PETREL (PRION)

(*Prion vittatus,* Gmelin).

Male.—Crown of the head blue-grey, the grey being somewhat pronounced; back blue-grey; patch of black in centre of rump. " Sides of the rump, upper tail coverts, and tail feathers blue-grey, the centre ones with a broad black bar, disappearing towards the outermost feathers, which have black ends and black shafts " (Godman). Wing coverts like the back; primaries blackish; secondaries greyish; cheeks and under surface white; sides of the chest blue-grey; under tail coverts light blue-grey. Dimensions in mm. :—Length, 290; bill, 32; wing, 215; tail, 100; tarsus, 34.

Female.—Similar in plumage to male, but, according to Dr. Godman, slightly smaller in size.

Nest.—A small burrow on the summit of small islets or a hole in the face of a cliff on the sea-shore.

Eggs.—Clutch one; roundish oval in shape; texture fairly fine; surface without gloss and minutely pitted; colour pure white. Dimensions in mm. of four specimens in the British Museum average 48 x 34.

Breeding Season.—September.

Geographical Distribution.—Seas of Tasmania, Australia, New Zealand, Southern Ocean down to at least 61 degrees south lat.; also South Pacific Ocean.

Observations.—Prions, or " Whale-birds," are extremely difficult to separate into species, even when handled.

" Of the genus Prion four species are recognized. They are alike in plumage and markings. There is very little difference in the dimensions except in the bill and in the development of the lamellæ at the base of the upper mandible, but with respect to these characters great individual variation is displayed. *Prion vittatus* has the largest bill, its sides being distinctly bowed and graduating towards the tip. *P. banski* has a bill bowed on the sides, but is smaller. I have, however, examined some specimens which could not be referred with certainty to either *P. vittatus* or *P. banski,* but were intermediate between the two. *P. ariel* and *P. desolatus* have the sides of the bill straighter, but as in the case of *P. vittatus* and *P. banksi,* it is not always possible to separate the two species definitely " (F. Du Cane Godman).

But little is known of the habits of the Broad-billed Prion, or, for the matter of that, of any others of the genus. Usually consorts in small parties, or even immense flocks.

*BANKS DOVE-PRION

(*Prion banski,* Gould).

Male.—Head dark ashy-blue; back, rump, upper tail coverts, and tail feathers ashy-blue; centre tail feathers broadly tipped with black, outer ones with narrow white tips; primary coverts and primaries black; inner primaries and secondaries pearly-grey; sides of the face and whole of under surface white; the bill has been variously described as being " turquoisene lead colour," " blue and slate colour," " bluish-grey "; legs blackish. Dimensions in mm.: —Length, 255; bill, 27; wing, 200; tail, 90; tarsus, 30.

Female.—Similar to male.

Nest.—A burrow in the side of a hill.

Eggs.—"Clutch one; roundish or broad oval in shape; texture of shell comparatively fine; surface without gloss; colour pure white. Dimensions in inches :—(1) 2.01 x 1.38, (2) 2.0 x 1.4, (3) 1.98 x 1.49, (4) 1.97 x 1.45, (5) 1.97 x 1.42, (6) 1.87 x 1.32 " (A. J. Campbell).

Breeding Season.—End of November and December.

Geographical Distribution.—Seas of Tasmania, Australia, New Zealand, Southern Ocean to 74 deg. S. lat.; also South Indian Ocean.

Observations.—Very little is known concerning the habits of this Prion, but they are doubtless very similar to those of the other species of the genus.

Macquarie and Auckland Islands at present appear to be the only localities where it has been found breeding.

*DOVE-LIKE PRION
(*Prion desolatus*, Gmelin).

Male.—Similar to previous species except that the blue-grey is slightly paler; the head is also the same colour as the back; " bill bluish-grey, darker on the sides, and inclined to black at the base; legs and feet light blue, tinged with green in front, the webs whitish-grey; iris brownish-black " (Buller). Dimensions in mm.—Length, about 265; bill, 26; wing, 185; tail, 88; tarsus, 27.

Female.—Similar to male, but slightly smaller.

Nest.—A rat-like burrow underground or in a crevice of a rock; the floor of the egg-chamber is lined with a little herbage or seaweed.

Eggs.—Clutch one; inclined to oval in shape; texture fairly fine; surface slightly glossy; colour pure white. Dimensions in mm. :—46 x 36.

Breeding Season.—November and December.

Geographical Distribution.—Seas of Tasmania, Australia, New Zealand, Southern Ocean down to the Ice Barrier, and as far north as 30 deg. S. lat.

Observations.—The Dove-Petrel is occasionally washed upon the north-western and southern coasts of Tasmania after a severe storm.

" In boisterous weather it appears to suffer more than any other oceanic species from the fury of the tempest, and the sea-beach is sometimes found literally strewn with the bodies of the dead and dying. I have frequently watched them battling, as it were, with the storm, till at length, unable longer to keep to windward, they have been mercilessly borne down upon the sands, and, being unable from sheer exhaustion to rise on the wing again, have been beaten to death by the rolling surf, or pounced upon and devoured by a hovering Seagull " (W. Buller).

On Kerguelen Island, according to the Rev. A. E. Eaton, it is extremely plentiful, and on calm nights the rustling of a multitude of wings as the flocks flew produced a continuous murmur like the sound of distant traffic in a large town.

*FAIRY DOVE-PRION
(*Prion ariel*, Gould).

Male.—" Similar in colour to the other species of Prion, but with a pale crown, hardly differing from the tint of the back; the spot below the eye also paler and less conspicuous; the terminal dark band of the tail wider; the bill much narrower and more compressed, though the unguis is as large as those of the other species; the sides of the mandibles are nearly straight, and the lamellæ feebly developed and quite invisible when the bill is closed " (B. M. Cat.)

Female.—Similar to male.

Nest.—A small burrow underground or in a crevice of a rock.

Eggs.—Clutch one; somewhat oval in shape; texture fine; surface without gloss; colour pure white. Dimensions in mm. :— 43 x 32.

Breeding Season.—October and November.

Geographical Distribution.—Seas of Tasmania, eastern and southern coasts of Australia, New Zealand, and Southern Ocean in general.

Observations.—Of the various species of Prion frequenting the coasts of Tasmania, this one is the most often seen. Among other localities, it breeds on several islets in Bass Strait.

Very little is known regarding the habits of the Fairy Dove-Petrel, but what is known goes to show that it closely resembles the other members of the genus in its natural economy.

FAMILY—PELECANOIDIDÆ (1 species).

*DIVING-PETREL
(*Pelecanoides urinatrix*, Gmelin).

Male.—" Crown and sides of the head, hind-neck, and all the upper surface shining steel-black; the forehead tinged with brown, the sides of the neck dusky, and the scapulars touched with white; throat, fore-neck, and all the under parts pure white; the sides of the body and flanks sometimes stained with grey. Irides and bill black; legs and feet cobalt, tinged with green, the webs bluish-white " (Buller). Dimensions in mm. :—Length, 240; bill, 20; wing, 140; tail, 50; tarsus, 25.

Female.—Similar to male.

Nest.—A short burrow underground or in a crevice in a rock.

Eggs.—Clutch one; roundish oval in shape; texture fairly fine; surface without gloss and minutely pitted; colour pure white. Dimensions in mm. :—38 x 30.

Breeding Season.—July and August in some localities; October and November in others.

Geographical Distribution.—Seas of Tasmania, Australia, New Zealand, and south coast of South America.

Observations.—"In mid-ocean one may see a small Petrel, quite alone, flying fast and straight close over the wave tops, until suddenly, like a stone, it disappears into the water. If the sea is particularly calm it may be seen that its wings flap rapidly for three or four strokes, then follows a quick, short sail; the bird seldom rising more than a foot or two from the surface of the water. Its flight seems to be hurried and in a straight line, coming to an abrupt termination as the bird drops. It is not easy to observe at sea, but its flight is so peculiar that it cannot well be mistaken for any other form of Petrel." The above description of the habits of *P. exsul*, a close ally of *P. urinatrix*, by Dr. Wilson, may be taken as equally applying to the latter species.

The Diving-Petrel is to be found in small numbers in Bass Strait, where it breeds on one of the islands of the Kent Group.

Round the coast of New Zealand it is very plentiful, consorting in flocks.

Its food consists of medusæ and other marine life.

FAMILY—DIOMEDEIDÆ (6 species).

*WANDERING ALBATROSS
(*Diomedia exulans*, Linn.)

Male.—General colour white; feathers of the back and mantle crossed with narrow wavy brown lines; tail white, irregularly spotted with black near the tip; wings blackish-brown mottled with pale brown, edges of wings white; primaries blackish; secondaries browner; breast and sides of body with tiny pale brown markings; under surface of wings and under tail coverts white; "irides rich dark brown; bare eyelids greenish-purple; bill white, with a pinky tinge, yellowish horn coloured at the tip; legs and feet flesh-white, sometimes with a pinky tinge. Total length, 40.5 inches; extent of wings, 40; wing from carpal flexure, 24; tail, 8.5; bill, following the curvature of upper mandible, 7; length of lower mandible, 6; depth of bill at the base, 2.5; bare tibia, 1.5; tarsus, 5; middle toe and claw, 6.5; greatest width of expanded foot, 6.5" (Buller).

Female.—Similar to male.

Young.—"Above dark brown, paler on the neck, with a dark patch on the crown and nape; wing uniform darker brown; forehead, sides of the head, and upper portion of the throat white, under surface whitish, paler on the abdomen; the flanks speckled; under tail coverts brown; under wing coverts and axillaries white" (B. M. Cat.)

Nest.—" Clumps of short grass and moss, trodden down, well matted together, and scooped about with earth and feathers into a conical-shaped mound, with an egg-cavity at the top about the size and depth of a soup plate " (A. J. Campbell).

Eggs.—Clutch one; elongated oval in shape; texture coarse; surface rough and without gloss; colour dull white, with a few dull purplish-brown markings on the apex. Dimensions in mm. :— 125 x 75.

Breeding Season.—December.

Geographical Distribution.—Seas of Tasmania, Australia, New Zealand, Southern Ocean, northwards to South Pacific and South Atlantic Oceans.

Observations.—Much has been written from time to time concerning this great ocean wanderer, a giant among birds. Those who have witnessed the majestic ease and grace with which it wings its way over the waters or circles on outstretched pinions on the look-out for tit-bits cannot but conclude that the Wandering Albatross is the embodiment of grace when on the wing.

Round the southern coast of Tasmania this bird is a somewhat familiar object, wheeling over the blue water, its snowy plumage glistening in the sunlight.

" When on the wing the feet are held together the full length under the tail, and, extending well beyond its longest feathers, give the impression of a markedly wedge-shaped tail with a white terminal border. This, of course, is not the case, for the tail is bordered by black at the extremity and the appearance of white beyond the black is due to the whitish feet " (E. A. Wilson).

*BLACK-BROWED ALBATROSS

(*Diomedia melanophrys*, Temm.)

Male.—General colour white; a slaty patch in front of and behind the eyes; back and wings slaty-black; tail slate-grey; bill dull yellow; legs and feet yellow. Dimensions in mm. :—Length, about 860; bill, 138; wing, 510; tail, 185; tarsus, 78.

Female.—Similar to male.

Young.—Differs from the adult in that the head is grey and the bill dark blue.

Nest.—Constructed of grass, moss, and earth into the shape of a small inverted cone. Breeds in colonies.

Eggs.—Clutch one; inclined to oval in shape; texture coarse; surface without gloss; colour dull white, with a few distinct markings on the apex. Dimensions in mm. :—101 x 67.

Breeding Season.—November and December.

Geographical Distribution.—Seas of Tasmania, Australia, New Zealand, and the Southern Ocean in general.

Observations.—Round the coast of Tasmania this fine Albatross

ROOKERY OF WHITE-CAPPED ALBATROSS.

Photo. by H. P. C. ASHWORTH.

From "THE EMU."

is frequently to be seen either following in the wake of ships or else scouring the ocean for food.

It has been found breeding on Campbell, Auckland, Antipodes, Bounty, Falkland, and Kerguelen Islands.

" Of all the species with which I am acquainted this is the most fearless of man, for it often approaches many yards nearer the vessel than any other; I have even observed it so near that the tips of its pinions were not more than two arms' lengths from the taffrail. It is very easily captured with a hook and line, and, as this operation gives not the least pain to the bird, the point of the hook merely taking hold in the horny and insensible tip of the bill, I frequently amused myself by capturing specimens in this way, and after detaining them sufficiently long to afford me an opportunity for investigating any particular point respecting which I wished to satisfy myself, setting them at liberty again, after having marked many, in order to ascertain whether the individuals which were flying round the ship were the same that were similarly engaged at daylight in the morning after a night's run of 120 miles, and this in many cases proved to be the case. When brought upon deck, from which it cannot take wing, it readily becomes tame, and allows itself to be handled almost immediately; still, I believe that no member of this group can be domesticated, in consequence of the difficulties of procuring a supply of natural food " (Gould).

*WHITE-CAPPED OR SHY ALBATROSS

(*Thalassogeron cautus*, Gould).

Male.—" Head, neck, lower back, upper tail coverts, whole of under surface, under wing coverts, and axillaries white "; a greyish-black mark in front and over the eye; face pale grey; back, wings, and tail greyish-brown; " bill light vinous, grey or bluish horn colour, except on the culmen, where it is more yellow, particularly at the base; the mandible is surrounded at the base with a narrow belt of black, which also extends on each side of the culmen to the nostrils; base of the mandible surrounded by a belt of rich orange, which extends to the corners of the mouth; feet bluish-white; irides brown " (Gould). Dimensions in mm.:—Length, about 890; bill, 152; wing, 560; tail, 230; tarsus, 92.

Female.—Similar to male save that the face is slightly lighter in colour and the culmen dull yellow.

Nest.—Constructed of soil mixed when in the wet state with rootlets and other vegetation and raised a few inches off the ground.

Eggs.—Clutch one; elliptical in shape; texture coarse; surface rough and without gloss; colour soiled white, with a freckled band of reddish-brown about the apex. Dimensions in mm. of odd examples:—(1) 96 x 70, (2) 107 x 69.

Breeding Season.—September and October.

Geographical Distribution.—Seas of Tasmania and Australia except the northern portion.

Observations.—Round the southern coast of Tasmania the White-capped Albatross is frequently to be seen not far from the land. It appears to be more plentiful there than off the immediate northern coast. Gould first detected this species as a distinctive one when lying wind-bound in Recherche Bay.

During the 1909 camp-out of the Tasmanian Field Naturalists' Club on Freycinet Peninsula, several individuals of this species were seen out in the bay. Albatross Island, in Bass Strait, is one of its principal breeding grounds. Owing to the difficulty of landing on the island, the birds are very little disturbed.

*FLAT OR BROAD-BILLED ALBATROSS

(*Thalassogeron culminatus*, Gould).

Male.—Head and neck whitish-grey; a patch of blackish in front of and above the eye; back blackish-brown; tail dark greyish-brown, shafts white; bill blackish, tip pale; legs and feet yellow. Dimensions in mm.:—Length, 920; bill, 129; wing, 510; tail, 197; tarsus, 82.

Female.—Similar to male.

Young.—"Has the head and neck dark grey; the space between the upper mandible and the eyes, as well as a mark above the latter, of a deeper shade; beneath the posterior side of the lower eyelid a light grey mark; the cheeks whitish; bill black, with indications of yellow in the middle portion of its ridge, and with the outer edges of the lower mandible horn-coloured towards the base; legs and feet yellowish-white " (Buller).

Nest.—" Composed outwardly of tussock-grass and mud, lined inside with fine grass and feathers; situated on the top of a rock or a loamy plain. Dimensions in inches :—External diameter at top 12, at base 18; egg-cavity, 10 across by 5 deep (Emerson) " (A. J. Campbell).

Eggs.—" Clutch one; oval in form, smaller at one end; both ends quite blunt; colour inclined to light creamy-white, with a ring of seemingly fine, spattered burnt sienna specks or spots, like those made by drawing a brush of colour across a stick, as a painter does to get the effect of granite. They form a ring about 2 inches broad round the larger end. The centre of the ring runs together in the fine markings, making the colour almost solid, and fading away from the outer edge almost to needles' points. Dimensions in inches :—4.75   x   2.88 " (Emerson). According to Kutter:—(1) 4.25 x 2.75, (2) 4.11 x 2.7 " (A. J. Campbell).

Breeding Season.—December and January.

Geographical Distribution.—Seas of Tasmania, Australia, New

Zealand, Southern Ocean, and ranging northwards to the coasts of Central America.

Observations.—This species was observed by Gould to be plentiful in the seas round Australia. Between northern Tasmania and South Australia he noticed it in numbers. Regarding its general habits, he states that they are very similar to those of the other members of the group, and therefore there was no necessity to repeat what he had already written of other species.

*YELLOW-NOSED (GREEN-BILLED) ALBATROSS.

(Thalassogeron chlororhynchus, Gmelin).

Male.—Head and neck white, with a slight tinge of grey; an indistinct dark grey mark in front of the eye; back dark sooty-brown; rump white; tail dark grey, the shafts white; wings almost black; under surface white; " bill black, culmen yellow passing into blood-orange at the tip, base of the mandible yellow, the tip also slightly yellow; legs flesh colour " (B. M. Cat.) Dimensions in mm. :—Length, 850; bill, 128; wing, 480; tail, 192; tarsus, 77.

Female.—Similar to male.

Nest.—Does not differ from those of the other members of the genus.

Eggs.—" Clutch one; colour dull white, with single yellowish blotches, probably resulting from dirt. Dimensions in inches :—4.0 x 2.28 (Kutter) " (A. J. Campbell).

Breeding Season.—October and November.

Geographical Distribution.—Seas of Tasmania, Australia, New Zealand, and the Southern Ocean generally.

Observations.—Practically nothing is known of the natural economy of the Yellow-nosed Albatross, but which we may suppose is very similar to other species.

Gould, on his way to Australia in 1838, found this species very plentiful at times.

*SOOTY ALBATROSS

(Phœbetria fuliginosa, Gmelin).

Male.—Plumage generally sooty; shoulders and under surface slightly tinged with brown; ring of white, interrupted in front, round the eyes; bill black; along either side of the lower mandibles a line of yellow; " feet dark hazel " (B. M. Cat.); " legs and feet white, with a purplish tinge " (Buller). Dimensions in mm. :—Length, 880; bill, 113; wing, 505; tail, 245; tarsus, 76.

Female. Similar to male.

Immature.—An immature female captured in Bass Strait was similar in plumage to the adult save that some of the feathers on the abdomen were tipped with dirty-white; iris black; bill yellow, tip bluish horn colour; legs and toes black; webs sooty-black. Dimensions in mm.:—Length, 860;. bill, 92.5; wing, 505; tail, 187; tarsus, 82.

Nest.—A low mound constructed of earth and vegetation.

Eggs.—Clutch one; somewhat oval in shape; texture fairly coarse; surface without gloss; colour dull white. Dimensions in mm.:—99 x 40.

Breeding Season.—September to November.

Geographical Distribution.—Seas of Tasmania, Australia, New Zealand, and Southern Ocean in general.

Observations.—At times the Sooty Albatross is very plentiful about Bass Strait, chiefly when heavy weather is being experienced in the Australian Bight or further south.

" The cuneated form of the tail, which is peculiar to this species, together with its slight and small legs and more delicate structure, clearly indicate that it is the most aerial species of the genus, and accordingly we find that in its actions and mode of flight it differs very considerably from all the other species of the Albatross, its aerial evolutions being far more easy, its flight much higher, and its swoops more rapid; it is, moreover, the only species that passes directly over the ship, which it frequently does in blowing weather, often poising itself over the mast-head, as if inquisitively viewing the scene below; at this moment it offers so inviting a mark for the gunner that it often forfeits its life " (Gould).

ORDER—PLATALEÆ.

FAMILY—IBIDIDÆ (2 species).

STRAW-NECKED IBIS

(Carphibis spinicollis, Jameson).

Male.—Crown of the head and fore part of the throat bare and of a dull inky-black, surrounded by a ruff of white feathers; lower hind-neck dusky-black; upper back, mantle, shoulders, and wings black, glossed with steel-green and purplish, crossed with dull black bars; lower back, rump, and upper tail coverts black, almost destitute of gloss; the long upper tail coverts and tail feathers white; wing coverts and quills black, outer webs glossed with dull green; " centre of fore-neck white, with long straw-coloured plumes on each side "; sides of neck and chest black, glossed with green and purplish; breast and abdomen white; bill dull black; legs and feet blackish-brown. Dimensions in mm.:— Length, 725; bill, 204; wing, 372; tail, 135; tarsus, 83.

Female.—Similar in plumage, but dimensions slightly less.

Young.—Upper surface, save hind-neck, dull sooty-black, without gloss; hind-neck and under surface white; sides of chest slightly blackish.

Nest.—A platform of broken-down reeds in a colony in a swamp.

Eggs.—Clutch three to four; roundish oval in shape; texture coarse; surface pitted and slightly glossy; colour dull white. Dimensions in mm. of a clutch:—(1) 62 x 46, (2) 61.5 x 46, (3) 63 x 47, (4) 61 x 45.

Breeding Season.—September to December.

Geographical Distribution.—Tasmania (accidental), Australia in general, and New Guinea.

Observations.—I cannot find any exact data relating to this bird's appearance or appearances in Tasmania.

*GLOSSY IBIS

(*Plegadis falcinellus*, Linn.)

Male (breeding plumage).—Forehead and crown glossy green; back black, glossed with green and bronzy-purple; lower back, rump, upper tail coverts, and tail black, glossed with green and bronzy-green; wing coverts deep chestnut; primary coverts and quills glossy green; neck and under surface deep maroon chestnut; bill, legs, and feet dark brownish-olive. Dimensions in mm. —Length, 560; bill, 128; wing, 284; tail, 98; tarsus, 104.

Female (breeding plumage).—Similar to male, but dimensions slightly less.

Male and Female (non-breeding plumage).—Head and neck more or less striped with whitish and black; no rufous on back or shoulders; rest of plumage practically similar to breeding dress.

Young.—Head dusky-brown, both it and the throat lightly striped with whitish; rest of plumage similar to adults, but more of a uniform oil-green, with metallic reflections.

Nest.—Somewhat bulky, composed of sticks and twigs, placed in the branches of a tree in or near water.

Eggs.—Clutch three to four; oval in shape; texture coarse; surface slightly glossy; colour deep bluish-green. Dimensions in mm. of odd examples:—(1) 50 x 36, (2) 52 x 36.5.

Breeding Season.—October and November.

Geographical Distribution.—Tasmania (accidental), Australia in general, Borneo, Java, Celebes, New Guinea, China, Siam. Afghanistan, Turkestan, Persia, Southern Europe, eastern portion of the United States, South Africa, Egypt, and several minor places.

Observations.—The same remarks apply to this species as to the former one. At the most they are but rare and accidental visitors, in all probability blown out of their course.

ORDER—HERODIONES : HERONS.

FAMILY—ARDEIDÆ (6 species).

*EGRET

(Herodias timoriensis, Less.)

Male (breeding plumage).—Entire plumage pure white, with a bunch of elongated plumes on the back reaching just beyond the tail; "bill beautiful orange; naked space before and behind the eye fine greenish-yellow; legs above the knee pale dull yellow, this colour continued down the centre of the inner part of the tarsi; remainder of the feet and tarsi black " (Gould). Dimensions in mm.:—Length, 760; bill, 110; wing, 385; tail, 158; tarsus, 143.

Female (breeding plumage).—Similar to male.

Male and Female (winter plumage).—Similar to that of the summer but without the plumes; bill yellow.

Young.—Similar to winter plumage of adults.

Nest.—A rough but strong platform of sticks, built in a tree overhanging water; usually a heronry is formed.

Eggs.—Clutch three or four; elliptical in shape; texture coarse; surface slightly glossy; colour light bluish-green. Dimensions in mm. of odd examples:—(1) 55 x 38, (2) 55 x 37, (3) 54 x 37.

Breeding Season.—Commences towards the end of November.

Geographical Distribution.—Tasmania, Australia in general, New Zealand; through the Austro-Malayan Archipelago to North China and Japan.

Observations.—This handsome species is but seldom seen about our rivers, and when seen is unfortunately rarely left un-molested. During the summer of 1892 there was an astonishing influx of birds of this species into the island. Reports as to its occurrence were received from the Tamar, North and South Esk, Midlands, Sorell district, and the basin of the Derwent. Unhappily the birds were not given an opportunity to breed in any of the above localities; but were ruthlessly hunted down. At the present time it is sparingly found at different points on the East Coast.

*WHITE-FRONTED HERON (Crane)

(Notophoyx novæ-hollandiæ, Lath.)

Male.—Forehead, eyebrow, cheeks, and the whole of the throat white; head and neck dark slate colour, especially the former; back and shoulders slaty-grey, with long lanceolate plumes of pale vinous tint; lower back, rump, and upper tail coverts lighter grey; tail dark slaty-grey, the lateral feathers with brownish tips; wing coverts slaty-grey; primary coverts and quills black; long lanceolate plumes on neck and chest deep vinous; abdomen and thighs pale isabelline-grey; lining of wings white; upper man-

NESTS OF WHITE-FRONTED HERON.

Photo. by A. H. E. Mattingley.   From "The Emu."

dible blackish; lower mandible yellow for basal half, balance blackish; legs and feet yellowish-brown. Dimensions in mm. :— Length, 655; bill, 79; wing, 320; tail, 132; tarsus, 99.

Female.—Similar to male.

Young.—Upper surface uniform grey; cheeks and upper throat white; rest of under surface as in adult, but no lanceolate plumes on neck and chest.

Nest.—A platform of stout sticks, with finer ones in the centre, placed in the branch of a tree close to or overhanging water. I have seen nests in lightly timbered country built in trees some considerable distance from water.

Eggs.—Clutch four to five; elliptical in shape; texture fairly coarse; surface moderately glossy; colour pale bluish-green. Dimensions in mm. of a clutch :—(1) 48.5 x 34, (2) 48 x 34, (3) 49 x 33, (4) 47 x 33.5, (5) 49 x 34.

Breeding Season.—September to December.

Geographical Distribution.—Tasmania, Australia in general, New Zealand, and a number of islands in the Malay Archipelago.

Observations.—The Blue Crane is a very common object in almost every part of the island. It frequents the sea-shore, the banks of tidal rivers, edges of lakes, lagoons, and swamps. Oftentimes it is to be seen in flocks of a dozen to twenty individuals, though frequently it is a solitary bird. Not only does it seek its food in pools left by the receding tide, or on the edge of the marshy ground of its haunts, but it also wades knee-deep into the water in quest of aquatic insects, crustacea, fish, &c. Its flight is heavy, with a great flapping of wings; the neck is much constricted the while. In some districts the Crane is shot and eaten; it is said to be very good stewed.

*WHITE-NECKED (PACIFIC) HERON
(*Notophoyx pacifica*, Lath.)

Male.—Head and neck pale vinous-grey to buffy-white; upper surface glossy olive-green, the lanceolate feathers on shoulders maroon tipped with slate; edges of wings white; throat white, spotted with a few black spots; feathers of fore-neck elongated; remainder of under surface blackish, streaked with white; on either side of the upper breast a patch of elongated purplish-red feathers; sides of body and flanks deep slate colour; upper mandible black, basal half of under mandible yellow; legs yellowish-olive; feet black. Dimensions in mm. :—Length, 760; bill, 41; wing, 400; tail, 135; tarsus, 126.

Female.—Similar to male.

Young.—Head grey; upper surface dingy; throat heavily spotted with black; under surface blackish-grey, streaked with white.

14

Nest.—A loosely constructed platform of sticks, placed in a tree overhanging water or standing in a lagoon.

Eggs.—Clutch four to five; oval-roundish in shape; texture coarse; surface slightly glossy; colour light bluish-green. Dimensions in mm. of a small clutch:—(1) 50 x 40, (2) 50 x 39.5, (3) 51 x 40.

Breeding Season.—September and March.

Geographical Distribution.—Tasmania and Australia in general.

Observations.—The Pacific Heron cannot be considered a resident species, though doubtless a few individuals occasionally remain the year through. During the autumn of 1892 several districts in the north of Tasmania were suddenly visited by this handsome species. Specimens were shot at Lake River, Stanley, St. Mary's, and on the River Tamar. During certain months it is sparsely distributed on the North and East Coasts; doubtless there are other localities as well. In addition to the mouths of rivers, the Pacific Heron frequents swamps, in which place it may be seen in company with other wading birds. Its food is very similar to that of the Pacific Crane.

The first record of this species in Tasmania was from Lake Tiberias, March, 1876.

*REEF-HERON

(*Demiegretta sacra*, Gmelin).

Male.—" General plumage slaty-grey, darker on the upper parts, tinged on the lower with brown; a broad line of white down the middle of the throat, and extending in some examples down the fore-neck. The back is ornamented with a number of narrow lanceolate feathers of a bluish-grey colour, overlying the scapulars, and there are a few similar feathers on the lower part of the neck, overlapping the breast; the feathers of the nape are long and silky and of a brighter tint than the surrounding plumage. Dimensions in inches:—Length, 25; bill, 3.5; wing, 11.5; tail, 4; tarsus, 3 to 3.5 " (Buller).

Female.—Similar to male.

Nestling.—" Covered with slate-coloured down " (Buller).

Young.—More sooty-brown than adults; ornamental plumes on head, back, and chest wanting.

Nest.—" Perfectly flat nest of coarse grass-stems in a cranny of rock " (J. D. MacLaine).

Eggs.—Clutch two to four (occasionally); elliptical in shape; surface finely granulated and without gloss; colour delicate greenish or bluish white, depending on how they are examined. Dimensions of a clutch:—(1) 45 x 33, (2) 46 x 33.5, (3) 45 x 32.5.

Breeding Season.—September and the two succeeding months.

Geographical Distribution.—" Coasts of Australia and Tasmania; also New Zealand and other islands of the Pacific up to

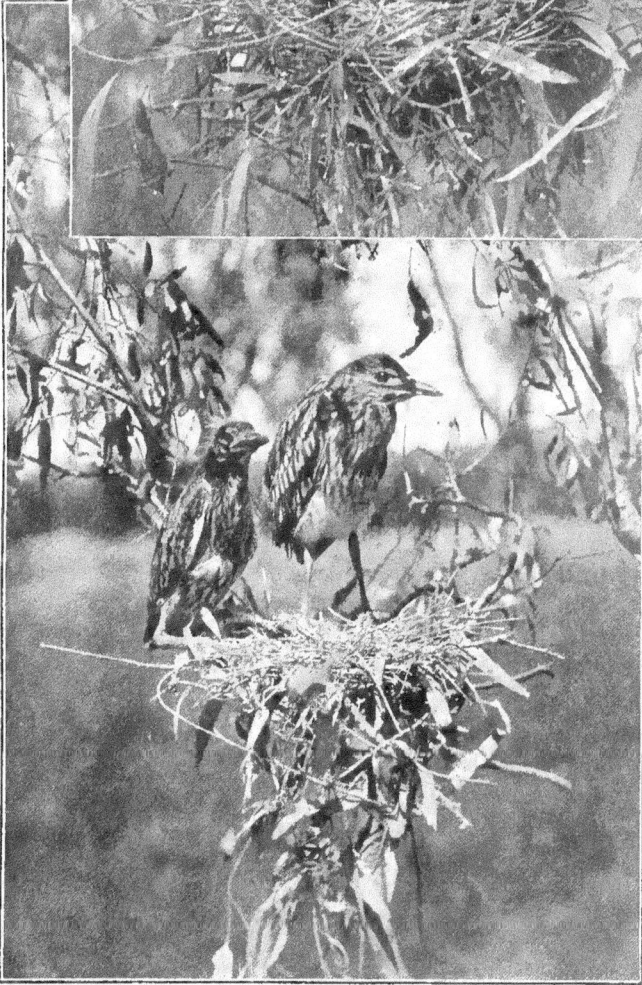

NESTS OF NIGHT-HERON, EGGS, AND YOUNG.

Photo. by A. H. E. MATTINGLEY. *From* "THE EMU."

Corea Bay; coast of Further India and Austro-Malayan Archipelago " (A. J. Campbell).

Observations.—Although found in many places round the coast of Tasmania, some of the islands in Bass Strait must be considered its stronghold as far as Tasmania and its dependencies are concerned. Much discussion has taken place among authorities at various times concerning the blue and white phases of this species. Those who are interested in this matter can find valuable information in Legge's " Birds of Ceylon," Baird, Brewer, and Ridgway's " North American Water-Birds," and the writings of Drs. Finsch and Hartlamb.

*NIGHT-HERON

(Nycticorax caledonicus, Gmelin).

Male.—Head black, with two long white plumes; eyebrow white; upper surface cinnamon or light chestnut; whole of under surface white; bill black; legs and feet yellow. Dimensions in mm. :—Length, 505; bill, 76; wing, 296; tail, 92; tarsus, 90.

Female.—Similar to male.

Young.—Upper surface heavily streaked and spotted with buffy-white, under surface streaked with blackish.

Nest.—Loose platform of sticks, placed in a heronry, in trees standing in water.

Eggs.—Clutch four; oval in shape; texture of shell fairly coarse; surface slightly glossy; colour light bluish-green. Dimensions in mm. of a pair :—(1) 50 x 35, (2) 50.25 x 35.5.

Breeding Season.—September to December.

Geographical Distribution.—Tasmania, Australia in general, New Zealand, and several islands in the Pacific.

Observations.—The Nankeen Night-Heron is a rare species as far as Tasmania is concerned, there being but few localities from which it has been recorded. As its name implies, it is a nocturnal species, seeking its food in swamps and lagoons when most of the other members of the feathered world are steeped in slumber.

Its note is a hoarse croaking one, which can be heard for some considerable distance on a still night. During the daytime it sleeps in lofty trees.

*BITTERN

(Botaurus pœciloptilus, Wagler).

Male.—Head and nape dark brown; back of neck and back dark purplish-brown, varied with buff; tail feathers dark brown, margined and freckled with buff; scapulars and secondaries like back, and mottled on the edges with tawny yellow; " the longer coverts with broad arrow-head marks along their whole extent, and the shorter ones freckled and mottled with different shades of brown " (Buller); quills purplish-brown, with buff markings on inner webs of primaries and both webs of secondaries; throat, sides of neck, and all the under surface tawny-buff, variegated with dark brown, some of the markings zig-zag shape; abdomen and under tail coverts yellowish-buff; irides yellow; bill dark brown; legs and feet pale green. Dimensions in mm.:—Length, 760; bill, 69; wing, 350; tail, 112; tarsus, 103.

Female.—Plumage somewhat duller, but otherwise similar.

Young.—Differs from the adults in being more uniformly yellow; crown of head and ruff pale smoky-brown; quills mottled and barred with rufous; under surface yellowish-buff, distinctly streaked with rufous.

Nest.—The usual situation is in a swamp, when a platform of reeds laid crosswise is built up some few inches above the surface of the water.

Eggs.—Clutch four to five; oval in shape; texture coarse; surface glossy; colour pale olive. Dimensions in mm. of a clutch:— (1) 49 x 36, (2) 50 x 35, (3) 49 x 35.5, (4) 48.5 x 36.

Breeding Season.—October to December or January.

Geographical Distribution.—Tasmania and the larger islands in Bass Strait; also Australia in general, New Zealand, and New Caledonia.

Observations.—Although nowhere plentiful, the Bittern is distributed over a wide area in Tasmania, those districts where there are swamps being frequented. Both by night and by day may its hollow, booming notes be heard issuing from the reedy fastnesses of its haunts. As may be expected, its food consists of fish, frogs, aquatic insects, and molluscs.

Among other places, I have records of this bird from Kelso, Waratah, the country lying between The Tunnel and Lilydale, Noland Bay, lower reaches of the Tamar, Tasman's Peninsula, Gladstone, and Ross.

Of the general habits of the Bittern, the late Sir Walter Buller wrote:—

"It appears to love a solitary life, being always met with singly; it remains concealed during the heat of the day, and at eventide startles the ear with its four loud, booming notes, slowly repeated, and resembling the distant roar of an angry bull. . . . It is interesting to steal up, under cover, and watch this Bittern alternately feeding and reposing in its sedgy haunts. When in a quiescent posture the body is nearly erect, the head thrown back and resting on the shoulders, with the beak pointed upwards, and the contracted neck forming a broad curve with the closed ruff depending, the attitude altogether being rather grotesque. The instant, however, any sound causes it alarm, the whole character of the bird is changed; the neck is stretched to its full extent, and every movement betokens caution and vigilance; unless immediately reassured, it spreads its broad wings and raises itself into the air in a rather awkward manner, with the legs dangling down, but gradually raised to a level with the tail; the flight then assumes a steady course, often in a broad semicircle, and is maintained by slow and regular flappings. If unmolested, it may be observed stalking knee-deep in the water in search of food, with its neck inclined forward, raising its foot high at every step as if deliberately measuring the ground."

ORDER—STEGANOPODES : PELICANS.

FAMILY—PHALACROCORACIDÆ (4 species).

BLACK CORMORANT
(*Phalacrocorax carbo*, Linn.)

Male (breeding plumage).—General colour dark, glossy purplish-black; crown and greater part of the neck covered with long, narrow white feathers; distinct crest of black feathers on nape; tail black; a large patch of white feathers on each flank; bill greyish-brown; legs and feet blackish. Dimensions in mm. :— Length, 905; bill, 65; wing, 340; tail, 178; tarsus, 60.

Female (breeding plumage).—Similar to male.

Male and Female (non-breeding plumage).—No white feathers on head and neck; white patches on the flanks also absent.

Immature.—Upper surface similar to adult, but some brownish feathers mixed with it; under surface mottled with broad brownish-black ends to the feathers.

Young.—Upper surface dull brown, margined with black and faintly glossed; centre of under parts white; sides, flanks, and under tail coverts dark brownish-black.

Nestling.—Covered with thick blackish down.

Nest.—Placed in a rookery and generally roughly constructed of twigs, leaves, and aquatic herbage. The situation of a rookery varies from the tops of stunted bushes or low trees over water to ledges of rock on some sea-girt island. When the nest is situated in this last position it is constructed of seaweed, and is some 4 or more inches thick. There are several rookeries on various islets in Bass Strait.

Eggs.—Clutch three to four; somewhat elliptical in shape, with the shell coarse; no gloss on surface; greenish-white in colour; the surface is more or less coated with lime, but laid on more evenly than on the eggs of the White-breasted species. Dimensions in mm. of a clutch:—(1) 57 x 39, (2) 59 x 37, (3) 58 x 39.

Breeding Season.—June to November.

Geographical Distribution.—Tasmania, Australia in general, New Zealand, Chatham Islands, the Austro-Malayan region, parts of Asia, Africa, Europe, South Greenland, the Faroes, Iceland, and the Atlantic coast of North America.

Observations.—The Black Cormorant is, perhaps, the most plentiful of its genus, not only being found in numbers off the coast, at the mouths of rivers emptying into the sea, bays, and islets, but also about inland rivers and lakes. It is the *bête noir* of fishermen, though hardly more so than the other species.

Much discussion has ensued at various times, especially recently, as to whether the Cormorant, treating all species as one, is as black as it is painted. The conclusion one arrives at, after reading all the correspondence, is that in inland waters the Cormorant may be voted a pest; while, as to the coast, man in his wisdom has decided that but little damage is done. I have no intention of entering into a discussion on the subject, but would like to call attention to the fact that the Cormorant is not the only enemy against which imported trout have to contend. It is a well-known fact that eels are very destructive to ova and young fry; then there are the large trout, who develop decided cannibalistic tendencies and wreak great havoc among the young of their own kind. A writer in *The Emu* has asserted that it is only the weak and deformed fish that fall victims to the Cormorant.

The following word picture of the Black Shag is from the pen of the late Sir W. Buller:—"It walks with awkward, waddling gait, supporting itself in part with its tail, which is moved alternately to the right and left at every step. It has a very fœtid odour; and a person approaching a flock of these birds on the leeward side is made sensible of this at a hundred yards or more. Its usual attitude on the beach is one of repose, with the body inclined forward, the tail resting full length on the ground, and the head drawn in upon the shoulders. When disturbed it instantly stretches up its neck, listens and watches attentively for a second or two, and then, after a few ungainly steps, shoots its white ordure along the sands, then rises into the air with laboured flapping of its wings, and flies off in the direction of the sea, into which it speedily plunges."

LITTLE BLACK CORMORANT

(*Phalacrocorax sulcirostris*, Brandt).

Male and Female (breeding plumage).—All the upper and under surface save the upper back, wing coverts, and shoulders, which are ash-coloured margined with black, are brownish-black, glossed with dull brown; on the sides of the head and scattered about the neck are a few narrow white feathers; behind the ears is a rather long tuft of white feathers; bill lead colour, with a line of black down the centre; legs and feet black. Dimensions in mm.:—Length, 640; bill, 42; wing, 255; tail, 123; tarsus, 41.

Male and Female (non-breeding plumage).—Similar to the above, but without the white plumage on head and neck.

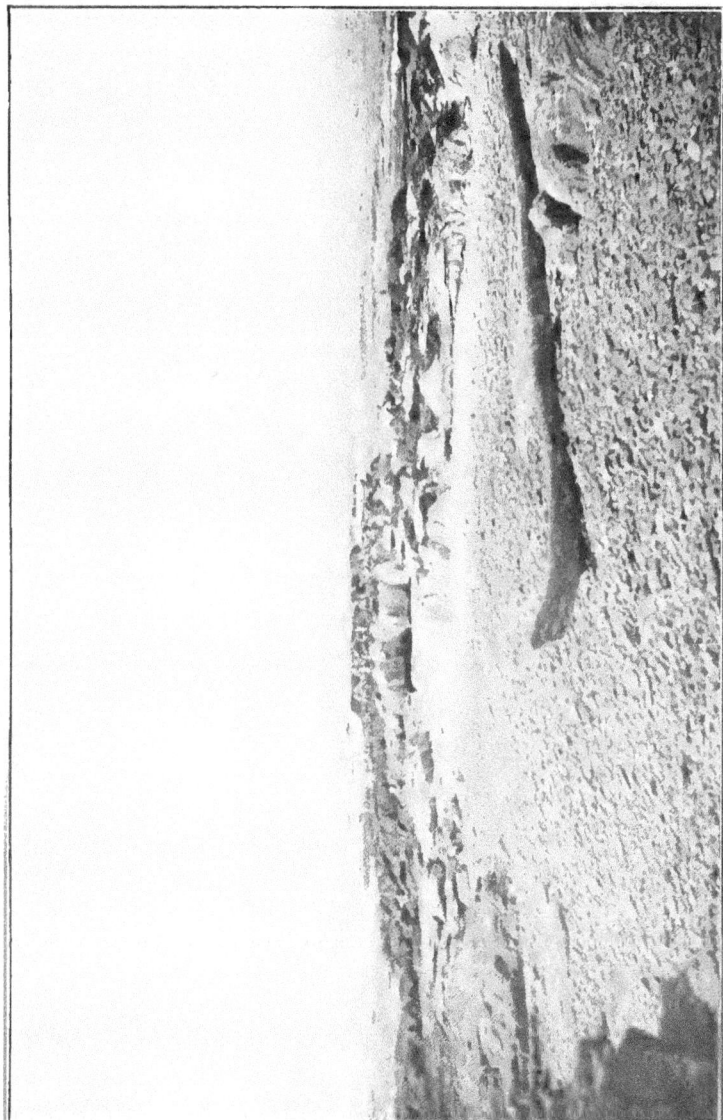

GENERAL VIEW OF CORMORANT ROOKERY, NINTH ISLAND.

Immature.—Head, neck, and under surface brownish-black; rest of plumage brownish-grey.

Nest.—Constructed of sticks and placed in a low tree over water.

Eggs.—Clutch three; somewhat oval in shape; texture coarse; surface without gloss; colour greenish-white, with a limy coating. Dimensions in mm. of odd examples :—(1) 49 x 33, (2) 50 x 35.

Breeding Season.—August to December.

Geographical Distribution.—Tasmania, Australia, New Zealand, New Caledonia, and portion of the Austro-Malayan Archipelago.

Observations.—This species was first recorded for Tasmania by Mr. A. E. Brent in 1890. In 1893 he again saw several more of the same species.

A few individuals have been seen in the River Tamar within the last twelve months. Altogether, the Little Black Cormorant is somewhat rare in Tasmania.

WHITE-BREASTED CORMORANT

(*Phalacrocorax gouldi*, Salvad.)

Male and Female (breeding plumage).—Crown, neck, back, rump, upper tail coverts, and flanks black, glossed with dull steel-blue; sides of the upper back, shoulders, and wing coverts glossed with dull green; quills and tail feathers brownish-black; sides of the head and under surface white; on both the upper surface and the flanks are a few scattered white plumules; iris green; bill legs, and feet black. Dimensions in mm. :—Length, 695; bill, 58; wing, 300; tail, 110; tarsus, 54.

Male and Female (non-breeding plumage).—Differs from the above in that the white plumules are absent.

Nest.—A fairly large structure of seaweed and marine *débris*, placed in a rookery on the tops of flattish rocks on an island or islet, close to the water. The rookery of this species and that of the Black Cormorant are sometimes adjoining.

Eggs.—Clutch two to three; long oval in shape; shell coarse and without gloss; colour varies from greenish to bluish white; surface roughly coated with lime, and soon becoming nest-stained. Dimensions in mm. of a clutch :—(1) 62 x 37, (2) 57 x 37, (3) 60 x 38.

Breeding Season.—August or September to November. Frequently eggs have been found in June and July on some of the islets in Bass Strait.

Geographical Distribution.—Tasmania and the greater part of Australia; also Louisiade Archipelago.

Observations.—It is a matter for debate as to whether this species or the Black Shag is the more plentiful in and around Tasmania. Those whose business or pleasure has taken them

among the islands and islets dotting Bass Strait during the latter
months of the year cannot but have observed rookeries of the
White-breasted Cormorant on many of them, showing out conspicuously on account of the rocks being "whitewashed."
Along many of our rivers flocks of this species may be seen perched
on piles or on the dead branches of trees overhanging or close to
the water.

During my trip to Ninth Island, in September, 1909, I had
good opportunities for observing this Cormorant. On a rocky
isthmus running out from the south-east corner of the island was a
large rookery, with incubating operations in full swing. There were
between 100 and 150 nests, the majority containing eggs. The
rookery was divided into two parts, the portion on the landward
side containing eggs absolutely fresh; some of the nests farthest
inland were only just ready for their reception. The nests towards
the extremity of the isthmus contained eggs somewhat incubated.
They were bulky structures of variously coloured seaweed; the egg-
cavity occasionally contained fragments of tussock-grass, but
usually no lining other than fragments of sea *débris* was used.
The nests were placed about 2 feet apart, on top of the rocks,
which were heavily limewashed, as was the surrounding shingle.
After taking some photographs of the sitting birds—for they
allowed one to approach to within three yards on this my first visit
—and the nests, a few clutches of eggs were secured, then the
birds left in peace.

On again visiting the rookery, a few days later, it was found
that the Silver Gulls (*Larus novæ-hollandiæ*) had played havoc
among the eggs. Later on I watched through my field-glasses
these Gulls quietly drop down among the nests and steal eggs
from unprotected nests right under the noses of birds sitting hard
by. From observations it was found that the Cormorants were
afraid of the Gulls, and would not return to protect their nests
while any of these impudent robbers were close by.

On other parts of the island remains of extensive rookeries
were evident.

It was noted that when this Cormorant was in full flight its
wing action much resembled that of the Black Duck (*Anas super-
ciliosa*). When disturbed from the rookery they would fly some
few hundred yards from the shore and settle in a compact mass in
the water, with their bodies sunk low and necks erect.

LITTLE CORMORANT

(Phalacrocorax melanoleucus, Vieill.)

Male and Female (breeding plumage).—Upper surface shining
black, glossed with greenish; on the sides of the head and neck
longish white feathers, forming a kind of mane; the feathers
on the forehead form a short crest, in which a few white feathers

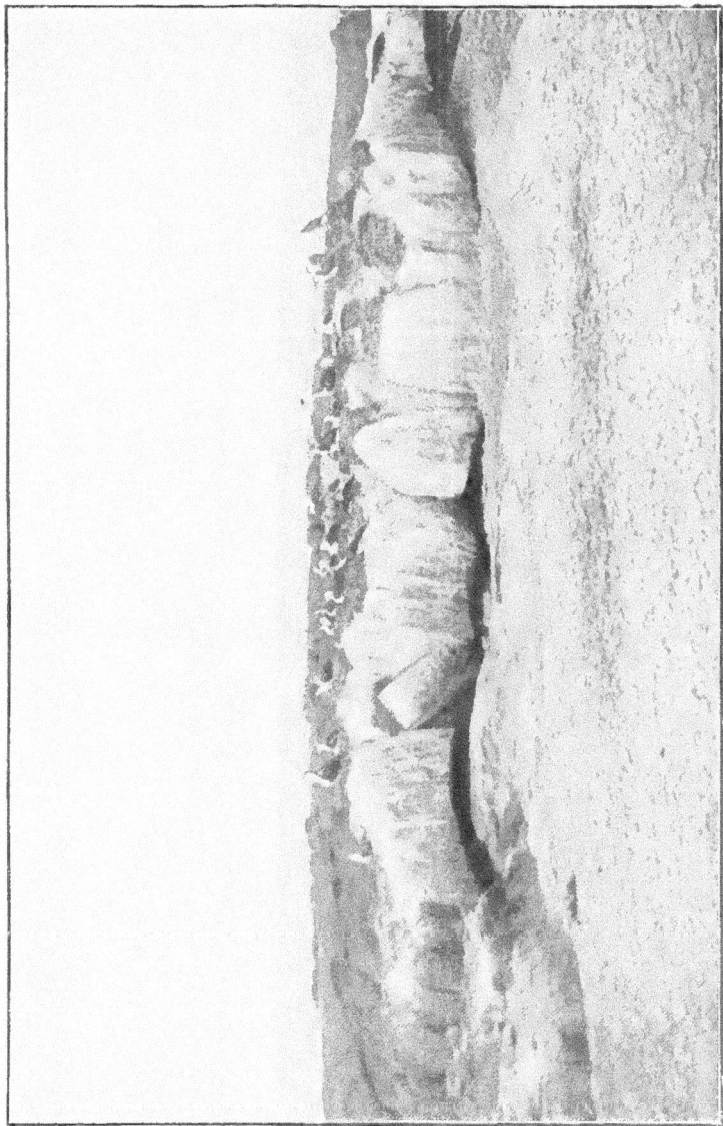

PORTION OF CORMORANT ROOKERY, NINTH ISLAND.

are mixed; shoulders and wing coverts shining greyish-black; under surface white; under tail coverts sooty-black; bill yellow; legs and feet black. Dimensions in mm.:—Length, 585; bill. 29; wing, 228; tail, 152; tarsus, 36.

Male and Female (non-breeding plumage).—Crest almost absent and without white feathers; feathers forming lateral mane short.

Young.—Feathers of upper surface margined with brownish to brownish-white; those of under surface somewhat yellow-brown towards the tips.

Nest.—Constructed of sticks and lined with leaves; placed in the branches of a low tree in water. Breeds in colonies.

Eggs.—Clutch three to four; inclined to oval in shape; texture coarse; surface without gloss; colour bluish-white, irregularly coated with lime. Dimensions in mm. of a clutch:—(1) 47 x 30, (2) 46 x 30, (3) 47.5 x 31.

Breeding Season.—August or September to November.

Geographical Distribution.—Tasmania, Australia, New Zealand, New Caledonia, and northwards to some of the islands of the Austro-Malayan Archipelago.

Observations.—The first Tasmanian recorded specimen of this Cormorant was shot in November, 1874, at Brown's River. Since the above bird was recorded the Little Cormorant has spread to many districts, but in no one is it at all plentiful. So far as I am aware, it has not been found breeding on any of the islets in Bass Strait. It may be found about inlets, rivers, and lakes, frequently fishing in lonely solitude.

FAMILY—SULIDÆ (1 species).

*GANNET

(Sula serrator, Gray).

Male.—Crown of the head and back of neck deep sienna-yellow; primaries, secondaries, and two central pairs of tail feathers brownish-black, with white shafts; rest of the plumage white; irides olive-white; bill dark pearl-grey; naked space round the eyes bluish-grey; bare skin down the centre of the throat blackish; legs and feet dark brown, with a stripe of greenish-yellow down the centre of the tarsi and toes. Dimensions in mm.:—Length, 905; bill, 90; wing, 470; tail, 248; tarsus, 54.

Female.—Similar to male.

Young.—When first hatched are naked and slaty-black in colour; later they are clothed in white down and have the bill and feet black. Later the plumage becomes brown, dark on the upper surface, light on the lower. Gradually the brown disappears and white takes its place.

Nest.—Constructed on the ground, of scraped-up earth and vegetable *débris*, well trodden together; the height of the nest is some 4 inches, and the egg-cavity about 1½ inches. The largest rookeries in Australia are in Bass Strait, and notably the one on Cat Island.

Eggs.—Clutch one; elongated oval in shape; texture coarse; surface under the chalky coating slightly glossy, otherwise without gloss; the whole egg is covered with a thick, rough coating of lime, more or less nest-stained; under the coating the shell is bluish-white. Dimensions in mm. of odd examples:—(*a*) 79 x 46, (*b*) 84 x 44.

Breeding Season.—October to January.

Geographical Distribution.—Seas of Tasmania, Australia, and New Zealand.

Observations.—The Gannet is one of the most conspicuous and handsome of sea-birds; it is plentiful practically all round the coast of Tasmania. The gigantic rookery on Cat Island, which has recently been proclaimed a "sanctuary," has been several times visited and described by ornithological enthusiasts. Nearly 3,000 birds are said to nest on this island. The sight during the breeding season is one never to be forgotten. When the males of the sitting birds come in from the sea it is a pretty sight to watch them caress in most loving fashion. It is a matter of difficulty to estimate from what height the Gannet plunges when fishing; however, it enters the water with a splash that sends the spray up all round, and completely disappears from view for a few seconds. When on the wing it is rather an imposing bird, and is a very powerful flier. Sometimes it will soar to a great height and wheel round and round after the manner of an Eagle.

During heavy weather Gannets gather in the bay off Bridport in numbers, and may be seen busily fishing in company with Terns of various species. A few pairs also come a few miles up the Tamar, especially when fish are plentiful in the river.

Unfortunately, yachtsmen consider this bird fair game, and a large number are shot round various parts of the coast, especially during the holiday season, and their bodies either allowed to drift away unheeded or else they are taken aboard for a few hours and then cast away as worthless.

FAMILY—PELECANIDÆ (1 species).

*PELICAN

(*Pelecanus conspicillatus*, Temm.)

Male and Female (breeding plumage).—Plumage chiefly pure white; on the back of the head and neck is a fairly long crest; the feathers of the inner lesser wing coverts, the median wing coverts,

GANNET ROOKERY, CAT ISLAND.

From "THE EMU."

Photo. by C. L. LEMPRIERE.

and the chest are elongated and of a pale straw colour; sides of rump, upper tail coverts, tail, shoulders, and outer lesser wing coverts brown; quills and their coverts black; basal half of primary shafts white on the upper surface; " gular pouch and mandibles yellowish-white, the latter stained with blue, which gradually increases in depth to the tip; apical half of the cutting edges of the mandibles yellow, gradually increasing in depth to the tip; nail of both mandibles greenish-yellow; irides dark brown; eyelash indigo-blue; orbits pale sulphur-yellow, bounded by a narrow ring of pale indigo-blue; legs and upper part of the metatarsi yellowish-white; feet, webs, and lower part of the metatarsi pale bluish-grey, the two colours blending with each other at the middle of the metatarsi; nails dull yellowish-white " (Gould). Dimensions in mm.:—Length, 1,520; bill, 445; wing, 625; tail, 190; tarsus, 127.

Male and Female (non-breeding plumage).—Crest and straw-coloured feathers absent.

Nest.—Either a flat construction of dry herbage, or else a shallow depression scratched in the ground; placed in a small rookery in an elevated position on a small island, or else on the shore of an inland lake.

Eggs.—Clutch two to three; elliptical in shape, with the shell coarse in texture; surface fairly glossy; colour white, more or less heavily and unevenly coated with lime; the shell soon becomes much nest-stained. Dimensions in mm. of a clutch:—(1) 105 x 60, (2) 92 x 59. In no instance did a clutch number more than two in a number of nests examined in a moderate-sized rookery in Bass Strait.

Breeding Season.—September and November usually.

Geographical Distribution.—Tasmania, Australia in general, and New Guinea.

Observations.—Thanks to the attentions of " pot-hunters," the Pelican is far more scarce round the coast of Tasmania than it was a few years since. At various times I have seen solitary individuals fishing some distance up rivers emptying into the sea. On several small islets lying off the Tasmanian coast there are small rookeries of this species.

ORDER—PYGOPODES : DIVING BIRDS.

FAMILY—PODICIPEDIDÆ (3 species).

*BLACK-THROATED GREBE

(Podicipes novæ-hollandiæ, Steph.)

Male and Female (breeding plumage).—Forehead, crown, and back of the neck black, glossed with green; a dark chestnut band, commencing behind the eyes, runs down either side of the neck;

back sooty-black, washed with grey; sides of the lower back and rump white, tinged with rufous; wing coverts similar to back; quills brown; inner primaries and secondaries more or less white; cheeks, chin, throat, and upper part of the fore-neck black; upper parts of the chest, sides, and flanks more or less smoky-black; rest of under surface glossy white. Dimensions in mm.:— Length, 236; bill, 24; wing, 106; tarsus, 34.

Male and Female (non-breeding plumage).—Cheeks and entire under surface white.

Young.—Upper surface more or less striped with black and brownish-white; under surface white.

Nest.—"A floating structure, composed usually of aquatic weeds piled up in rounded form, the top being almost level with the surface of the water—in some instances the eggs are in the water—and stranded among rushes or submerged fallen reeds, &c., or anywhere in flooded country. Sometimes these nests are placed near or amongst those of the large Tippet Grebe " (A. J. Campbell).

Eggs.—Clutch four to six usually; elliptical in shape; texture fine; surface glossy; colour pale bluish-white, which is obscured by a thin coating of lime. Dimensions in mm. of a clutch:—(1) 33 x 25, (2) 34 x 25, (3) 33.5 x 26, (4) 32 x 24.

Breeding Season.—September to January.

Geographical Distribution.—Tasmania, Australia in general, New Guinea, Java, and New Caledonia.

Observations.—According to Mr. A. J. Campbell, the Black-throated Grebe "is the most plentiful of the three species inhabiting the Australian region." This may be so on the mainland, but as far as my own observations go it does not hold good for this island. Owing to its retiring habits, this species is but seldom seen save by those who lay themselves out to do so.

A rather curious habit of this bird is mentioned by Mr. A. J. North, and which doubtless has been noticed by many others; that is, the bird while sitting covers herself over with the outer portions of the nest until only her head and neck are visible. When leaving the nest the eggs are covered over, the bird diving immediately and reappearing some 10 or 15 yards away.

*HOARY-HEADED GREBE

(*Podicipes poliocephalus,* Jard. and Selby).

Male (breeding plumage).—"Head covered with long, fine hair-like white feathers; throat, occiput, and upper surface dark-brown; bill black, with light tips; tarsi blackish-olive " (Gould). Under surface silvery-white; inner primaries and secondaries almost pure white. Dimensions in mm.:—Length, 252; bill, 20; wing, 108; tarsus, 33.

Female (breeding plumage).—Similar to male. Dimensions the same.

NEST OF BLACK-THROATED GREBE.

Photo. by A. H. E. MATTINGLEY.

From "THE EMU."

Male and Female (non-breeding plumage).—Head destitute of long hair-like feathers; rest of plumage practically similar to summer coat.

Young.—Similar to non-breeding plumage of adults.

Nest.—Very similar to that of the previous species.

Eggs.—Clutch four to five usually; elliptical in shape; texture fine; surface glossy; colour greenish-white, obscured by a thin limy coating. Dimensions in mm. of a clutch:—(1) 39 x 28, (2) 38 x 27.5, (3) 38.5 x 28, (4) 39 x 27.

Breeding Season.—October to January.

Geographical Distribution.—Tasmania, New South Wales, Victoria, South-West and North-West Australia, and South Queensland.

Observations.—This species is fairly plentiful in different parts of the island, both on tidal rivers and inland waters. I have records of it from a number of widely separated localities. Like other members of the genus, it is very shy, quickly taking flight at the slightest semblance of danger.

*TIPPET GREBE

(Podicipes cristatus, Linn.)

Male and Female (breeding plumage).—Forehead and crown black; feathers on each side of the crown elongate, and forming a long double crest; feathers on the upper part of the neck elongate, forming a ruff; lower part of hind-neck deep ashy-brown; back blackish-brown; " lesser wing coverts forming a wide white band along the edge of the wing "; humeral feathers white; primaries blackish; lores, space in front of the eye, cheeks, chin, and throat white; tinged with rufous, becoming rich chestnut on the long feathers on the hinder part of the head; rest of under surface silvery-white, save the sides and flanks, which are dark ash; irides crimson; culmen blackish, base of lower mandible dull carmine, tip pale horn colour; legs and feet yellowish-brown. Dimensions in mm.: —Length, 530; bill, 50; wing, 172; tarsus, 54.

Male and Female (non-breeding plumage).—Head, neck, and back dark ashy-brown; sides and flanks similar; rest of plumage similar to breeding plumage.

Young.—Similar to above, save that the head and neck are striped with dark ash-brown.

Young in down.—"General colour of the upper parts whitish-brown, shading into white on the head and neck; longitudinally striped with deep smoky-brown; rather large patch of the latter colour on each side of the crown, immediately behind the bare red patch on the forehead; base of the fore-neck and rest of the under part white " (B. M. Cat.)

Nest.—Composed of aquatic herbage, and so constructed that the top is nearly on a level with the surface of the water; placed among rushes, &c., in large lagoons.

Eggs.—Clutch five to seven; somewhat elliptical in shape; texture fairly fine; surface glossy; colour greenish-white; obscured by a limy coating. Dimensions in mm. of odd examples:—(1) 50 x 34, (2) 50.25 x 35, (3) 50 x 34.5.

Breeding Season.—November and December.

Geographical Distribution.—Tasmania, Australia in general; also New Zealand, Africa, Asia, Central and Southern Europe.

Observations.—Although fairly well distributed, the Tippet Grebe, which is a very handsome species when in full breeding plumage, does not appear to be as plentiful as the preceding species. Very much the same localities are frequented. Its general habits and shy, retiring disposition are very similar to those of the other species. Of this bird in New Zealand, Mr. W. T. L. Travers writes:—"Both the male and female Grebe assist in the labour of incubation, although I believe that the chief part of the task devolves upon the female, and that she is only relieved by her partner for the purpose of enabling her to feed. Before the actual work of incubation commences the eggs are usually covered with pond-weed during the absence of the birds from the nest; but afterwards the nest is but seldom, if ever, left by both except under unusual circumstances."

Henry Seebohm says:—"Its food is entirely procured in the water, and consists of water-beetles and other aquatic insects, small fish, small frogs, and molluscs. The seeds and tender shoots of aquatic plants are also to be found in its stomach, but, instead of small stones or gravel, numbers of its own feathers plucked from the ventral region are mixed with its food. It is not known that this curious habit, which is more or less common to all the Grebes, is intended to assist digestion, but it has been remarked by many ornithologists in widely different localities."

ORDER—IMPENNES : PENGUINS.

*CRESTED PENGUIN

(*Catarrhactes chrysocome,* Forst.)

Male.—"Crown, sides of the head, throat, and hind part of neck black; rest of the upper surface bluish-black, each feather having a narrow central streak of pale blue from the base of the upper mandible on each side; broad line of pale golden-yellow passes over the eyes and is continued beyond in a crest of fine-pointed feathers extending nearly 2 inches beyond the head; the black feathers of the crown between these side crests are lengthened acuminate and slightly rigid; upper surface of the flippers glossy bluish-black, the feathers, which are lanceolate and

BIRDS OF TASMANIA. 207

closely imbricated, being margined and tipped with pale blue,
along the inner edges a narrow band of white. The under parts of
the body are silvery-white, contrasting sharply on the sides with
the dark plumage of the upper surface, and tapering up on the
fore-neck to a point about 3 inches below the angle of the lower
jaw; under surface of flippers bluish-grey, with the central portion
outwardly and a continuation towards the root silvery-white; tail
feathers long, narrow, very rigid, and perfectly black; the coverts
greyish-white, with black shafts, and tipped with blue; irides
yellowish-brown; bill rich nut-brown, darker on the lower
mandible, blackish at the base and horn-coloured at the tip; feet
yellowish-white with darker webs, claws dark brown with black
points, the soles blackish-brown. Total length, 27 inches; length
of flipper, 8.5; tail, 4; bill along the ridge 2.75, along the edge of
lower mandible 2.75; tarsus, 1.5; middle toe and claw, 3.5;
hind toe and claw, .75 " (Buller).

Female.—Similar to male.

Young.—" Differs from the adult in the character of the crests;
instead of the broad superciliary band of golden-yellow there is a
narrow line of pale yellow, beyond which there are a number of
narrow straggling feathers, forming, so to speak, occipito-lateral
crests " (Buller).

Nest.—A shallow depression either in the ground or among
shingle, sometimes scantily lined with a few bits of grass, or not
lined at all.

Eggs.—Clutch two; round, with one end somewhat compressed; texture coarse; surface without gloss; colour greenish or
bluish white, with a limy coating. Average dimensions in mm.
of several eggs :—60 x 48.5.

Breeding Season.—On Tristan da Cunha the birds commence
in July or August, Falkland Islands end of October, Kerguelen
Island the same, Macquarie Island a little later.

Geographical Distribution.—" Terra del Fuego, Falkland
Islands, South Georgia, Cape of Good Hope, Tristan da Cunha,
Prince Edward, Marion, Crozette Islands, Kerguelen Island, St.
Paul Island, Tasmania, South Australia, Campbell, Antipodes
and Bounty Islands, New Zealand Group " (B. M. Cat.)

Observations.—This dweller on the lonely islands of the
Southern Ocean is very seldom seen round the coast of Tasmania.
A few specimens have been taken round the southern coast, and
one or two in Bass Strait.

The following is taken from Professor Moseley's account of his
experience with this Penguin on Inaccessible Island :—

" Many of the droves of Penguins made for one landing-place,
where the beach surface was covered with a coating of dirt from
their feet, forming a broad track leading to a lane in the tall grass
about a yard wide at the bottom and quite bare, with a smoothly
beaten black roadway; this was the entrance to the main street

of this part of the 'rookery,' for so these Penguin establishments are called. Other smaller roads led at intervals into the rookery to the nests near its border, but the main street was used for the majority of the birds. The birds took little notice of us, allowing us to stand close by, and even to form ourselves into a group for the photographer in which they were included. This kind of Penguin is called by the whalers and sealers 'Rock-hopper,' from its curious mode of progression. The birds hop from rock to rock with both feet placed together, scarcely ever missing their footing. When chased they blunder and fall among the stones, struggling their best to make off. With one of the Germans as guide, I entered the main street. As soon as one was in it, the grass being above one's head, one was as if in a maze, and could not see in the least where one was going to. Various lateral streets led off on each side from the main road, and are often at their mouths as big as it; moreover, the road sometimes divides for a little and joins again; hence it is the easiest thing in the world to lose one's way, and one is quite certain to do so when inexperienced in Penguin rookeries. The German, however, who was our guide on our first visit, accustomed to pass through the place constantly for two years, was perfectly well at home in the rookery, and knew every street and turning.

"It is impossible to conceive the discomfort of making one's way through a big rookery, haphazard, or across country as one may say. I crossed the large one here twice afterwards, with the seamen carrying my basket and vasculum, and afterwards went through a still larger rookery at Nightingale Island. You plunge into one of the lanes in the tall grass, which at once shuts the surroundings from your view. You tread on a slimy, black, damp soil, composed of the birds' dung. The stench is overpowering, the yelling of the birds perfectly terrifying—I can call it nothing else. You lose the path, or perhaps are bent from the first in making for some spot on the other side of the rookery. In the path only a few droves of Penguins on their way to and from the water are encountered, and these stampede out of your way into the side alleys. Now you are, the instant you leave the road, on the actual breeding ground. The nests are placed so thickly that you cannot help treading on eggs and young birds at almost every step. A parent bird sits on each nest, with its sharp beak erect and open ready to bite, yelling savagely ' Caa, caa, urr, urr,' its red eye gleaming and its plumes at half-cock and quivering with rage. No sooner are your legs within reach than they are furiously bitten, often by two or three birds at once—that is, if you have not got on strong leather gaiters, as on the first occasion of visiting a rookery you probably have not. At first you try to avoid the nests, but soon find that is impossible; then, maddened almost by the pain, stench, and noise, you have recourse to brutality. Thump, thump, goes your stick, and at each blow goes

LITTLE PENGUIN IN NEST, WITH YOUNG.

From "THE EMU."

Photo. by T. G. CAMPBELL.

a bird. Thud, thud, you hear from the men behind as they kick the birds right and left off the nests; and so you go on for a bit— thump and smash, whack, thud, ' Caa, caa, urr, urr,' and the path behind you is strewed with the dead and dying and bleeding. But you make miserably slow progress, and, worried to death, at last resort to the expedient of stampeding as far as your breath will carry you. You put down your head and make a rush through the grass, treading on old and young haphazard, and rushing on before they have time to bite.

" The air is close in the rookery, and the sun hot above; and, out of breath and running with perspiration, you come across a mass of rock fallen from the cliff above, and sticking up in the rookery; this you hail as ' a city of refuge.' You hammer off it hurriedly half a dozen Penguins who are sunning themselves there and are on the look-out, and, mounting on the top, take out your handkerchief to wipe off the perspiration, and rest awhile, and see in what direction you have been going, how far you have got, and in what direction you are to make the next plunge. Then when you are refreshed you make another rush, and so on.

" If you stand quite still, so long as your foot is not actually on the top of a nest of eggs or young, the Penguins soon cease biting at you and yelling. I always adopted the stampede method in rookeries, but the men usually preferred to have their revenge, and fought their way every foot.

" Of course, it is horribly cruel thus to kill whole families of innocent birds; but it is absolutely necessary. One must cross the rookeries in order to explore the island at all, and collect the plants or survey the coast from the heights."

*LITTLE PENGUIN
(Eudyptula minor, Forst.)*

Male.—Upper surface varies from slate-blue to bright slate-blue, each feather having a brownish-grey base and black shaft-streak; chin, throat, fore-neck, and rest of the under surface silvery-white; the feathers on the throat and fore-neck have brownish bases, whilst those on the chin, breast, and lower parts are pure white; flippers greyish-black, narrowly edged with white on the inner margin; tail white, but very seldom found that colour; iris yellowish or silver-grey, acording to the light; bill black; legs and feet white, tinged with pink. Dimensions in mm.:— Length, 425; bill, 39; wing, 75; tarsus, 19.

Female.—Similar in colouration, but less bulky in build. Dimensions in mm. :—Length, 400; bill, 35; wing, 65; tarsus, 18.

Young.—" Down on upper surface grey and fluffy; on under surface dull white and somewhat close in texture " (J. R. M'Clymont).

Nest.—When a short burrow is not scraped out beneath tus-

15

sock-grass or on the side of a gentle slope, a slight hollow either
between or under rocks is formed, and a small quantity of dry
grass and weeds placed therein. Very large rookeries are to be
found on several small islands in Bass Strait.

Eggs.—Clutch two; vary from pyriform to roundish in shape;
texture of shell coarse; surface slightly glossy; colour white,
slightly tinged with green. The eggs soon become nest-stained.
Dimensions in mm. of two clutches :—A—(1) 58 x 40, (2) 59 x 41;
B—(1) 54 x 47, (2) 55 x 45.

Breeding Season.—September to January.

Geographical Distribution.—Off the coasts of Tasmania, New
South Wales, Victoria, South and Western Australia, and New
Zealand.

Observations.—The birds from which the above measurements
were taken were secured from the same burrow, and had paired
up. When two Little Penguins are in a burrow, it is always a
matter of ease to separate the sexes, the male being much stouter
in build. When the pair are teased, the female remains silent at
the extreme back of the burrow, while the male boldly attacks
the stick or whatever is thrust in, hissing loudly the while. Another point of difference exists in the bills. That of the male is a
stout, formidable weapon, while that of the female is much
slimmer and weaker in appearance. I have found the above
differences constant in the great hordes of Penguins that were
under continuous observation for just short of a fortnight on
Ninth Island, off the Tasmanian coast, during the latter part of
September and the beginning of October, 1909. A distinct variation in colouration is discernible among the members of any flock
examined, but this variation cannot be taken as being in the
slightest manner specific. On arriving on Ninth Island on the
22nd September, 1909, I found but few burrows occupied either by
a single bird or by a pair. During my stay the birds increased
until there must have been a few thousand on the island every
night and a couple of hundred during the day. A pair that had
taken up their abode among the stones of the foundation of the
hut, and were kept under the closest observation, never left their
retreat for sixty hours. During the day they remained silent, but
towards evening the male would commence to croon, and later on
both birds joined in the general discord reigning over the island.

It was found that the first bird came up from the sea at 6.30
p.m., the party at each landing-place first consisting of about a
dozen birds. These would sit on the rocks preening their feathers.
At 6.35 the first real contingent would arrive, at 6.40 the second,
and at 6.45 the third and last. When all the birds had landed
and more or less preened themselves, a commencement would be
made over the rocks to the rookeries on the top or sides of the
island. On no occasion were any birds seen to move inland until
the last bird of the last batch was up on the rocks. Also night

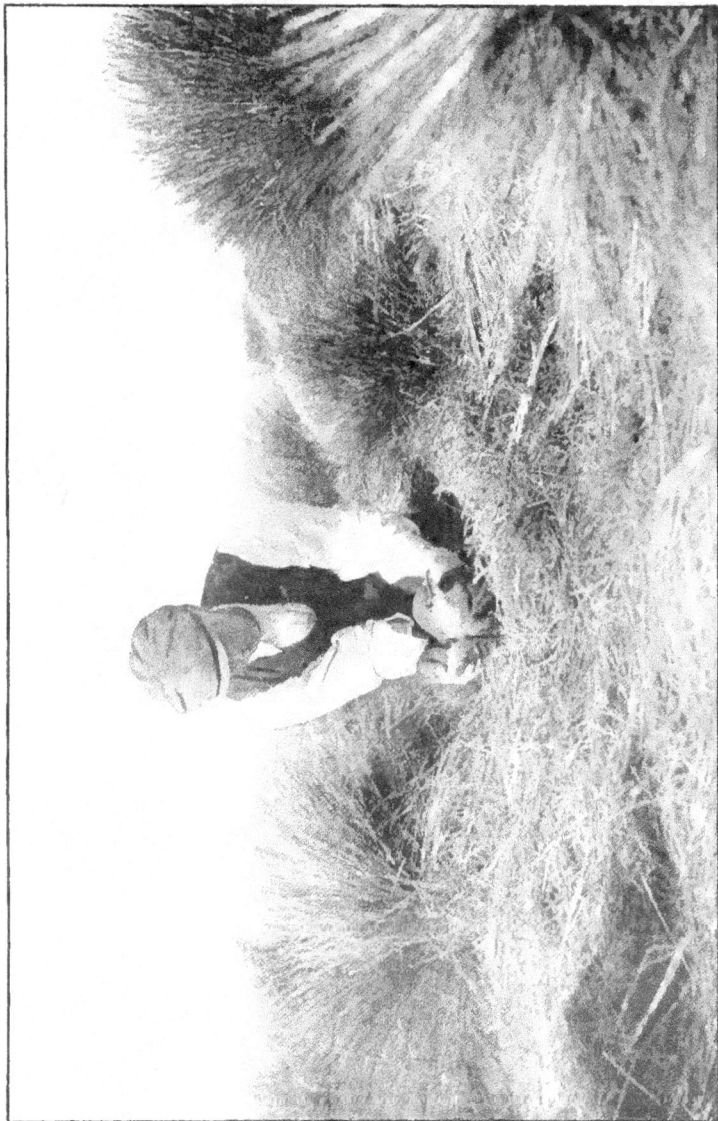

THE AUTHOR, WITH PAIR OF LITTLE PENGUINS, NINTH ISLAND.

Photo. by J. G. LITTLER.

after night, rough or smooth, the various batches arrived punctually to the minute. On a calm evening the birds could be seen moving through the water some five or six hundred yards from the shore, where they would show as a ripple on the surface. As the birds came closer their heads could be distinguished just above the surface. It was usual for them to wait until a roller washed them on to the low rocks at their landing-places; then, before the backwash had time to carry them away, they would rapidly scramble to safety, using feet, flippers, and bills. One evening a party of birds were slightly late, and they seemed to know it, for the speed with which they came through the water was truly astonishing—they gave one the impression of miniature torpedoes. So well did they make up for lost time that they were but a few seconds behind schedule time.

On some evenings no sound was uttered by the birds either when moving through the water or after landing and on their way towards the rookeries. On other occasions a short, sharp barking note was uttered. To see what would happen, a batch was driven back into the water one evening. They tumbled in like so many Ducks, and uttered a note closely resembling the quacking of those birds. They were soon ashore again, however.

Penguins when first issuing from the water have the appearance of the proverbial drowned rats, but they dry rapidly. Almost invariably progress was made to the rookeries in silence. I noted that by 6.50 p.m. a few birds had commenced calling. A variety of notes is uttered by both sexes, varying from mewing to bleating and squeaking. The male bird utters a deeper note than the female. When the former is courting, and uttering deep notes, the female is giving vent to hoarse purring sounds. These sounds are varied by different birds. By 7 p.m. a rookery would be in full swing, some birds courting, some scratching out their burrows, others quarrelling, and others again merely making a hideous noise. I observed that during the early part of any night but a small proportion of the birds in any one rookery would be giving tongue. Occasionally a female would resent the attention of a male; then a battle royal would result, with much noise and little damage. In several instances a bird was observed to enter a burrow already occupied by a pair; result—well, the intruder would come out of that burrow in record time and scuttle away as fast as its short legs would carry it.

Between midnight and 4 a.m. every Penguin on the island seemed to be in active vocal competition with its neighbour, but by 5 a.m. silence reigned supreme, the majority of the birds having quietly waddled down the rocks the same way as they had arrived the previous evening, and swum out to sea, disappearing from view in a few minutes, while the few that remained slept. Very rarely was it that a sound broke the silence on a rookery between the hours of 5 a.m. and 6 p.m., even though a couple of hundred birds might be underground. The curious fact was noted on the 25th September that up to 9.30 p.m. hardly a Penguin had uttered a sound, though present in vast hordes.

*FAIRY PENGUIN
(*Eudyptula undina*, Gould).

Some doubt exists as to whether this is a valid species or not. The author of that part of the 26th volume of the British Museum Catalogue dealing with the Penguins places *E. undina* as a synonym of *E. minor*.

Gould described the species from specimens procured off the North Coast of Tasmania. Of it he says:—"I invariably found the young of that species (*E. minor*), while still partly clothed in the downy dress of immaturity, to exceed considerably in size all the examples of this species (*E. undina*), even when adorned in the adult livery and possessing the hard bill of maturity. There can be no question, therefore, of the two birds being distinct."

The rookery on Waterhouse Island from which he obtained examples no longer exists, all the birds having been either killed or driven off.

The late Sir Walter Buller, who believed in the validity of the species, stating it to be as plentiful if not more so than the preceding species round the coasts of New Zealand, writes:— "Dr. Finsch refused to admit any specific distinction. Dr. Coues, also, in writing of Gould's types in the Museum at Philadelphia, says:—"These specimens are slightly smaller than average *minor*, bluer than usual, but not bluer than No. 1338, for example, and with rather weak bills. . . . I cannot distinguish these specimens even as a variety."

Judging from their writings, both Messrs. A. J. Campbell and D. Le Souëf consider the Fairy Penguin to be a good species. Personally, I am inclined to bracket *E. minor* and *E. undina* together.

ORDER — CHENOMORPHÆ.

Sub-Order—Anseres : Geese, &c.

FAMILY—ANATIDÆ (15 species).

Sub-Family—Cygninæ.

BLACK SWAN
(*Chenopsis atrata*, Lath.)

Male.—Upper surface brownish-black, the feathers tipped with greyish-brown; under surface a little paler; primaries and secondaries pure white; "bill pinky-scarlet, crossed near the tip with a broad band of white; the extremities of both mandibles are also white; irides scarlet; eyelash and lores pinky-scarlet; feet black" (Gould). Dimensions in mm.:—Length, 1,023; bill, 677; wing, 484; tail, 167; tarsus, 92.

Female.—Similar in plumage to male.

Young in Down.—" Upper surface light brownish-grey; under surface white; chin and throat white, changing gradually into the grey tinge of the cheeks; bill and lores brownish-black; nail of the bill white; feet dull greyish-brown; later on the cygnets get greyish also on the under parts" (B. M. Cat.)

Nest.—A large open structure composed of aquatic herbage, bark, sticks, &c.; the lining is usually grass, leaves, a few feathers and a little down. The site generally chosen is on the edge of a swamp among the rank grass.

Eggs.—Clutch four to six generally; elliptical in shape and coarse in texture; surface glossy; dull greenish-white in colour, but soon becoming nest-stained. Dimensions in mm. of a clutch:—(1) 115 x 73, (2) 111 x 71, (3) 102 x 65, (4) 106 x 68, (5) 108 x 65, (6) 108 x 66.

Breeding Season.—August to December generally, January sometimes.

Geographical Distribution.—Tasmania, several of the larger islands in Bass Strait, and the whole of Australia.

Observations.—Shooting begins 1st February, ends 30th June. During certain times of the year the Black Swan is extremely plentiful on the East Coast; then it is that scores fall victims to the guns of "sportsmen" who are concealed in the reeds between the sea and the lagoons frequented by this bird. Among lovers of the gun exists a great diversity of opinion as to whether the Black Swan should be classed as a game bird and shot as such. I have heard keen sportsmen condemn in no measured terms the shooting of this handsome bird, and declare they would never think of eating one. Yet, on the other hand, there are many who consider Swan-shooting fine sport and the bird delicious for table purposes. Almost every shooting season one sees in the press paragraphs recording the exploits of shooting parties who have killed so many hundred Swans in two or three days. What sense there can be in such wholesale slaughter I know not, for the majority of the birds are, too often, left to rot in the reeds. A few years since a resultless effort was made to have the Black Swan placed on the totally protected list.

Not only does it frequent the coastal regions, tidal rivers, and the larger islands in Bass Strait, but it may also be found in small numbers on several of the inland lakes; this more particularly applies to the non-breeding season. I think I am correct in stating that this species is more plentiful about the northern half of the island than the southern. At odd times small parties of this species come some miles up the Tamar towards Launceston.

The largest flock I have seen recently numbered 14 birds; that was some 12 miles down the river.

I am indebted to Captain W. E. Leggatt, of Stanley, for the following interesting note :—

" During the day the Black Swan keeps to the salt water, and feeds over the sandy mud-flats which are covered by the tide. It is timid, and approaches no nearer the shore than the depth of water allows, swimming in as the tide flows and retreating with the ebb, keeping always in such a position that it can comfortably reach the bottom with its bill. At the least strange sound it raises its head above water and looks about, and if all is not quiet moves out from the shore. It is very sensitive with regard to hearing, and it is almost impossible to approach within a couple of hundred yards of it if you are to windward, so that it is always necessary to keep to leeward if you wish to approach close, and then great care must be taken that you do not expose yourself in any way.

" Black Swans generally keep together in large flocks; it is seldom that one sees a couple at any distance from hundreds of others. If the tide, when receding, leaves large banks uncovered, the Swans, after having obtained sufficient food, generally bask in the sun on these banks and go to sleep. Towards evening they make a move towards the river mouths and creeks, and stay in there all night, and so by getting up early one has a good chance of obtaining an easy shot at them by taking up a position at the mouth of a river and waiting for them to swim by.

" The Black Swan does not like rough water, and always moves as the wind changes, so that it may feed peacefully under the lee of some bank or point. When moulting it loses all the white feathers from its wings and is unable to fly. If pursued when in that condition it can travel at a great speed by swimming, and then, using its wings as in flying, flap itself along the top of the water, but if closely followed and made to keep this up for some time it soon gets exhausted. •

" At ordinary times it has great difficulty in rising from the ground unless facing the wind, and even then covers a good space before it rises clear.

" They are as·a rule easily killed, a single grain of large shot in the head or neck being quite sufficient to cause death.

" The above remarks apply to the North-West Coast, to which portion of Tasmania my experience with this bird has been confined."

Sub-Family—Anseranatinæ.

PIED GOOSE

(*Anseranas semipalmata*, Lath.)

Male.—" Head, neck, mantle, wings, tail, and thighs black; back, rump, breast, abdomen, upper and under tail coverts, scapulars, and smaller upper wing coverts white; 'irides blackish-brown; bill reddish-brown; feet yellow' (Gould). Total length, 35 inches; wing, 18.5; tail, 8; bill, 3.25; tarsus, 3.62 " (B. M. Cat.)

Female.—Similar to male.

Nest.—A bulky structure of dead aquatic herbage, placed among growing herbage in a swamp or lagoon.

Eggs.—Clutch nine to eleven usually; oval in shape; texture coarse; surface glossy and pitted; colour yellowish-white. Dimensions in mm. of odd examples:—(1) 76 x 57, (2) 75 x 57, (3) 75.5 x 56, (4) 76 x 56.75.

Breeding Season.—October to December.

Geographical Distribution.—Tasmania (casual) and Australia in general.

Observations.—In June, 1888, a paper was communicated to the Royal Society of Tasmania by the late Mr. A. Morton on Mr W. F. Petterd's account, relating to the recent shooting of a Semipalmated Goose in the Lake district, near Cressy. It was one of a small flock that had recently been seen near Launceston. I know of no other instance of this species having been seen in Tasmania.

Sub-Family—Cereopsinæ.

CAPE BARREN GOOSE

(Cereopsis novæ-hollandiæ, Lath.)

Male.—Upper surface brownish-grey, the feathers margined with a lighter shade, crown of the head much lighter; some of the feathers of the shoulders and wing coverts have a dark spot near their tips; the tail portions of the quills, and under tail coverts inclined to blackish; under surface brownish-grey; "bill black; cere lemon yellow; irides vermilion; eyelash dark brown; legs reddish-orange; toes, webs, claws, and a streak up the front of the legs black" (Gould). Dimensions in mm.:—Length, 850; bill, 49; wing, 512; tail, 201; tarsus, 90.

Female.—Similar to male.

Young.—"They assume the plumage of the adults at an early stage, but have the greenish-yellow cere must less conspicuous " (Gould).

Young in Down.—" Sides of the head and upper parts brown, under parts whitish-grey; throat white; a broad white band on each side of the head, and another on each side of the back as far as the sides of the rump " (B. M. Cat.)

Nest.—Usually constructed on the ground, among salt-bush or tussock-grass, of grass and herbage, the lining being down,

Eggs.—Clutch four to six; elliptical in shape; texture coarse; surface glossy; there is always a thin coating of limy matter over the shell, which is white. Dimensions in mm. of a full clutch :—

(1) 90 x 60, (2) 89 x 57, (3) 88 x 58, (4) 91 x 60, (5) 87 x 59, (6) 88 x 57.

Breeding Season.—Erratic, as eggs may be found in June as well as in September and the following months.

Geographical Distribution.—Coasts of Tasmania, especially the northern; several of the larger Bass Strait islands; also Victoria and South and Western Australia.

Observations.—Shooting begins 1st February, ends 30th June. Discussion has arisen at various times in the pages of *The Emu* as to whether the Cape Barren Goose is decreasing, increasing, or holding its own. Although great diversity of opinion exists on this subject, it is conceded by those most competent to judge that the bird is at least holding its own, and is in no immediate danger of extinction. Unfortunately, the bird is not a favourite one with pastoralists on some of the Bass Strait islands, on account of its voracious appetite and its fouling the grass so that sheep will not feed after it.

Mr. A. J. Campbell states, on the authority of Mrs. Robinson, of Green Island, that—"Each bird possesses its own mate. Should a goose in captivity lose her mate, the probability is that she joins a wild flock and never returns. Should a gander lose his wife, he entices a wild bird to dwell with him. An old bird never mates with a young one, nor do young from the same clutch pair or breed. The birds do not lay until they are two years old. The Geese have a voracious appetite, their chief food being herbage. They eat nearly all day, and frequently by night, quickly digesting their food. Sheep will not graze after them, as in the case of the domesticated Goose."

In *The Emu* for July, 1907 (vol. vii., p. 36), there appeared a note by Mr. T. Hurst, of Caulfield, Victoria, to the effect that during a visit to Launceston he had seen, a few miles down the Tamar, a flock of between 20 and 30 Cape Barren Geese. This being contrary to my experience, I set to work to discover whether this species was in the habit of coming up the river frequently, as stated by Mr. Hurst, but was unable to discover a single person who had within the last 30 years seen a Cape Barren Goose inside Tamar Heads. I interviewed master mariners, yachtsmen, sportsmen, and professional fishermen, the majority of whom had a knowledge of the river extending over some twenty to twenty-five years, and some longer. In no instance were two persons questioned at the same time, nor did I tell them for what purpose I required the information. Mr. Frank Murray, who has a large property abutting on the river, a few miles from Launceston, informed me that some time since, when in Adelaide, he was given a pair of "Chinese Geese," which he stated resembled Cape Barren Geese to a certain extent. The Geese were allowed their liberty on his property, and in course of time bred freely, until he had quite a large flock. Sportsmen and others travelling up and down the river appreciated the Geese greatly, in one morning alone seven being shot before daylight. Mr. Murray has now shot the flock right out, owing to their wandering habits, and being tired of providing " Cape Barren Geese " for river sportsmen.

Sub-Family—Chenonettinæ.

*WOOD-DUCK (MANED GOOSE)
(*Chenonetta jubata*, Lath.)

Male.—Head and neck reddish-brown; lengthened plumes down the back of neck brownish-black; back grey, tinged with black; lower back, rump, and upper tail coverts black; tail glossy black; shoulders grey, broadly margined with black on the outer webs, and narrowly on the inner with the same colour; lesser wing coverts grey; a glossy green band across the secondaries, which are tipped with white; greater wing coverts also tipped with white; primary coverts and primaries brownish-black; breast grey, mottled with black and white; abdomen and under tail coverts glossy black; sides and flanks greyish-white, very finely vermiculated with black; bill olive-brown; legs and feet blackish-brown. Dimensions in mm. :—Length, 504; bill, 30; wing, 274; tail, 98; tarsus, 42.

Female.—Head, hind-neck, mane, and fore-neck pale reddish-brown; sides of the face, chin, and part of the throat finely speckled with white; back greyish-brown; green band on wings somewhat inconspicuous; breast brown, each feather barred and tipped with white; sides and flanks light brown, the feathers broadly barred and tipped with white; abdomen and under tail coverts white; bill more brown than in male; legs and feet blackish-brown.

Young.—According to Mr. A. J. Campbell, they are sooty-brown above, with two stripes along the face; under surface dull white.

Nest.—Within a hole or hollow spout of a tree, either near or standing in water.

Eggs.—Clutch nine to twelve; oval in shape; texture fairly fine; surface glossy; colour creamy-white. Dimensions in mm. of portion of a clutch :—(1) 55 x 39, (2) 55 x 38.5, (3) 54.5 x 39, (4) 54.25 x 38.

Breeding Season.—August to January.

Geographical Distribution.—Tasmania and the whole of Australia.

Observations.—At a meeting of the Tasmanian Royal Society, September, 1864, the late Mr. Morton Allport reported that he had seen a Maned Goose on the Plenty River; this was the first record for Tasmania. Again, in October, 1867, Mr. Allport stated that the species was, and had been, plentiful about the upper reaches of the Derwent. In 1874 a specimen was received at the Hobart Museum from Macquarie River. I have no knowledge of any specimens of this species being taken of late years.

It is of this bird that Gould states :—" It seldom if ever visits Van Diemen's Land."

Sub-Family—Anatinæ.

PLUMED WHISTLING-DUCK

(Dendrocycna eytoni, Gould).

Male.—Crown of head, hind-neck, and breast pale reddish-brown; sides of the head and neck pale grey, becoming white on the throat; feathers of the back and wings brown, the edges of the former pale ochreous; upper tail coverts whitish-buff, edged with greyish-brown; tail brown; quills also brown; lower breast and sides reddish, regularly barred with black, bars very distinct on the sides; abdomen and under tail coverts white, slightly tinged with buff; bill yellowish-brown, with a patch of black in the centre; legs and feet flesh-brown. Dimensions in mm. :—Length, 428; bill, 39; wing, 249; tail, 74; tarsus, 57.

Female.—Similar to male.

Nest.—On the ground, among herbage, away from water.

Eggs.—Clutch ten to twelve probably (A. J. Campbell); roundish in shape; texture fine; surface glossy; light creamy-white. Dimensions in mm. of odd examples:—(1) 49 x 39, (2) 48 x 38.5, (3) 48.5 x 38, (4) 49 x 38.

Breeding Season.—September to the end of the year.

Geographical Distribution.—Tasmania (casual), the whole of the mainland; also New Zealand (accidental).

Observations.—The first record of this Duck is in the P.R.S. of Tasmania, May, 1871, wherein is the report of a specimen having been received from Richmond. Again, in June, 1872, another specimen was received, this time from Bridgewater. It was also reported that several specimens had been seen at Sorell. I can find no record of it having been seen within recent years.

SHIELDRAKE OR MOUNTAIN-DUCK

(Casarca tadornoides, Jard.)

Male.—Head and upper neck glossy greenish-black; in old examples the feathers at the base of the bill and round the eyes become brownish; a white ring separates the upper neck from the lower, which, together with the upper breast and back, are reddish-brown; back, scapulars, and under surface black, finely waved and freckled with pale fulvous; upper tail coverts and tail black, glossed with green; wing coverts white; primaries and primary coverts black; speculum on secondaries glossy green; outer web of tertiaries rich chestnut, inner dark grey; under tail coverts black; under wing coverts and axillaries white; bill black; legs and feet greyish-black. Dimensions in mm.:—Length, 695; bill, 48; wing, 368; tail, 148; tarsus, 58.

Female.—Plumage duller and dimensions less than male; head and upper neck brownish-black; feathers round base of the bill mottled with white.

Young.—According to Mr. A. J. Campbell, the young in down are marked on the head, along the back, and across the wings with dark grey, tending to black, the rest of the upper surface and underneath parts being whitish.

Nest.—Usually within the hollow spout of a tree, close to water. The nesting hollow is lined with down and fine grass.

Eggs.—Clutch ten to twelve usually; roundish-oval in shape; texture fairly fine; surface greasy to the touch; colour creamy-white. Dimensions in mm. of a portion of a clutch :—(1) 68 x 49, (2) 67 x 49, (3) 67.5 x 49.5, (4) 70 x 50, (5) 69 x 48, (6) 68 x 48.

Breeding Season.—August to October generally.

Geographical Distribution.—Tasmania, New South Wales, Victoria, South, Western, and North-West Australia.

Observations.—Shooting begins 1st February, ends 30th June. This handsome Duck is somewhat rare in Tasmania, the Lake district appearing to be its stronghold. I have both seen and have records of it from several other parts of the State. In no locality is it anything approaching plentiful.

Mr. George Russell, of Cressy, informs me that as a table bird it is almost worthless, many people refusing to touch it at all, its flesh being very "strong."

BLACK DUCK (Wild Duck)

(*Anas superciliosa*, Gmelin).

Male.—Crown of the head and nape and a band from the forehead through the eyes to the occiput black, slightly tinged with brown; superciliary stripe and a band from the base of the upper mandible through the cheeks, chin, and throat clear pale buff; a blackish-brown band from the gape to the ear coverts; back, rump, upper tail coverts and tail brownish-black, the feathers, especially the scapularies, narrowly edged with ochreous-buff; wings brownish; speculum on the secondaries glossy green; anteriorly and posteriorly is a band of black; outer web of outer tertiaries black; whole of under surface brownish-black, the feathers margined with yellowish-buff, under wing coverts and axillaries white; bill dull bluish-red; legs and feet yellowish. Dimensions in mm. :— Length, 568; bill, 52; wing, 264; tail, 98; tarsus, 40.5.

Female.—Hind-neck, upper back, and scapulars distinctly

brownish; margins of feathers on the under surface tinged with
rufous; other parts similar to male. Dimensions in mm.:—
Length, 605; bill, 53; wing, 263; tail, 124; tarsus, 45.

Young.—Plumage in general paler than in adult; margins to
feathers distinctly brighter.

Nestling.—" Upper parts dark olive-brown, with produced hair-
like filaments of paler brown; sides of the head and under parts
of the body pale yellowish-brown, lightest on the abdomen; from
the base of the bill on each side a dark band passes beyond the
eye and another in a curve below it; there are markings of fulvous
white on the edges of the wings, and on each side of the back there
are two irregular spots of the same about an inch apart. Irides
black; bill and legs plumbeous, the nail of the former brown "
(Buller).

Nest.—Either placed on the ground among herbage, or else
in a hole in a tree or in a stump. It is formed of grass, lined with
down.

Eggs.—Clutch ten to twelve; elliptical in shape; texture fairly
fine; surface glossy and greasy; colour light greenish-white.
Dimensions in mm. of a portion of a clutch:—(1) 57 x 41, (2) 57
x 40, (3) 56 x 40, (4) 57.5 x 42, (5) 56.5 x 40.5, (6) 58 x 41.5.

Breeding Season.—August or September to December.

Geographical Distribution.—Tasmania, King Island, whole of
the mainland; also New Zealand, Polynesia, Timor, and Java.

Observations.—Shooting begins 1st February, ends 30th June.
Of the various species of Ducks inhabiting Tasmania, the Wild
Duck is the best known, and one of if not the highest esteemed,
both as a game and table bird. Owing to the persistency with
which it has been hunted of late years, it has become very shy,
calling forth great patience and ingenuity on the part of gunners
to circumvent it. On several of our larger rivers " flatties " are
much used, these often being decorated with reeds and rushes to
conceal the gunner. Owing to its semi-nocturnal habits, it is the
custom in districts where this bird frequents lagoons to do most
of the shooting at night, a clear moonlight night being considered
the best. When arriving at its feeding ground, and before settling
down, it always circles round to reconnoitre, and then descends in
an oblique direction.

" In its habits, it differs in no respect from the other members
of its group. In the water it swims low, with the neck erect and
the head gently swayed to and fro; when at rest it either floats
on the surface with the head drawn closely in, or it reposes on the
bank very near to the water's edge, often selecting a jutting point
of land, as affording a more unobstructed view and less danger
of surprise; and when the banks are soft and muddy it takes up
its station on a log of wood, bare rock, or other projecting object "
(Buller).

On the Tamar and Derwent Rivers especially, and in other

NEST OF BLACK DUCK.

Photo. by C. P. CONIGRAVE.

From "THE EMU."

localities, I have seen large flocks of Black Duck, Teal, and Shoveller all feeding together or resting on the mud at low tide. As the tide rises the flocks scatter into small parties and a sharp look-out is kept for possible enemies.

At St. Helens, Swansea, and other places along the East Coast, the Black Duck is at times extremely plentiful, but often very difficult of approach.

TEAL
(*Nettion castaneum*, Eyton).

Male.—Head and neck dull glossy green; mantle and back black, the feathers margined with chestnut; rump, upper and under tail coverts black, glossed with green; tail brownish-black; scapulars and wings dark olive-brown, the former narrowly margined with chestnut; the last row of upper wing coverts white, with a slight tinge of reddish; wing speculum glossy black, along the upper edge of which is a metallic green band glossed with coppery-red; secondaries tipped with reddish-white; breast and abdomen chestnut, with black spots; on the lower flanks a whitish-buff band; under wing coverts olive-brown; axillaries white; " bill bluish lead colour, nail and the edges of the upper mandible black; the under mandible crossed near the tip by a band of reddish-flesh colour; irides hazel; feet lead colour, with the membranes of a somewhat darker hue " (Gould). Dimensions in mm. : —Length, 470; bill, 339; wing, 228; tail, 115; tarsus, 34.

Female.—Crown of the head dark brown, almost black, some of the feathers streaked with buff; sides of the head whitish, more or less streaked with blackish; chin and throat whitish, unspotted; back, rump, and tail blackish-brown, the feathers of the upper back margined with pale rufous; wing coverts uniform dark greyish-brown, the last row white; speculum on the secondaries velvety-black, tipped with white, three middle secondaries metallic green on the outer web; primaries dark brown; under surface reddish-grey, the feathers having a large central mark of black; towards the vent the central mark becomes brownish; under wing coverts brown, axillaries white. Dimensions in mm. :—Length, 462; bill, 37; wing, 200; tail, 101; tarsus, 30.

Young in Down.—" Upper parts brown; the upper part of the head darker; sides of the head, fore-neck, and lower parts whitish, with a rufescent tinge; a dark brown band from the lores through the eyes backwards; a small dark spot at the gape; two whitish rufescent spots on the back at the base of the wings and two more on the sides of the rump " (B. M. Cat.)

Nest.—" Usually in a hollow tree, but occasionally on the ground in grass or other herbage in the vicinity of water; furnished with a plentiful supply of down. Should the nest be on the ground, fine grass is sometimes intermixed with the fuscous-coloured down, each particle whitish in the centre, and with light-coloured tips, apparently slightly darker than the nest down of the Grey Teal. Dimensions (inside), 5 inches across by 2½ inches deep " (A. J. Campbell).

Eggs.—" Clutch nine to ten usually, thirteen maximum; elliptical in shape; texture of shell fine; surface glossy and greasy; colour rich cream. Dimensions in inches of odd examples :—(1) 2.04 x 1.5, (2) 1.9 x 1.45. Of four from a set :—(1) 2.14 x 1.5, (2) 2.1 x 1.49, (3) 2.09 x 1.52, (4) 2.08 x 1.48 " (A. J. Campbell).

Breeding Season.—According to Mr. A. J. Campbell, it extends from June to December.

Geographical Distribution.—Tasmania, some of the larger islands in Bass Strait, and Australia in general.

Observations.—Shooting begins 1st February, ends 30th June. Doubtless there are but few who are aware that two species of Teal exist in Tasmania, most being under the impression that the species so much in evidence in a number of localities during the " open " season is the only one found here. The species under review is on the mainland frequently called the Mountain-Teal. It is a scarce species in Tasmania, or at least the males are but seldom procured. I have inspected specimens from the Lake district, and am informed on good authority that it frequents several localities on the North-East Coast; doubtless it is also to be found in the southern portion of the island.

To verify my own observations concerning the two species, I forwarded to Mr. A. J. Campbell a set of questions, which I now give, with his answers appended thereto, thinking they may be of interest :—

Question.—Does the male of the Chestnut-breasted Teal retain its black head and neck and chestnut breast during the non-breeding season ?

Reply : Yes. [I believe that once the male of this species dons his full livery he never throws it off; but I also believe that many males breed before they have attained full livery.]

Question.—Is the breeding plumage of both sexes of the Grey Teal similar to the non-breeding plumage ?

Reply.—Yes.

Question.—Are there any outward differences between the female of the Chestnut-breasted Teal and the female of the Grey Teal ?

Reply.—None, except in weight—Chestnut, 1½ lbs.; Grey, 1 1/16 lbs.

Question.—Are both sexes of the Grey Teal similar in appearance ?

Reply.—Yes.

GREY TEAL

(*Nettion gibberifrons*, Mull.)

Male.—Upper part of the head dark brown, with the edges of
the feathers reddish or greyish; sides of the head paler, thickly
streaked with black or brown; chin and throat white; upper
parts brown, the feathers edged with pale reddish; feathers of the
lower back and rump almost uniform, with edges scarcely paler;
feathers of the under parts light fulvous on the margins, with
obscure brown spots in the centre, especially on the breast and
the sides of the body, each feather having a broad central mark
of blackish-brown; sides and under tail coverts darker than the
rest of the under parts; wing coverts dark greyish-brown, with
an olive lustre, the greater series white, forming a band broader
outwardly than inwardly; speculum on the secondaries velvety
black, tipped with a white band, but the three middle secondaries
metallic green on the outer web; primaries and tail feathers dark
brown; under wing coverts dark brown; axillaries white; irides
yellowish-brown; bill bluish-black; legs and feet lead colour,
tinged with yellow. Dimensions in mm.—Length, 462; bill, 37;
wing, 200; tail, 101; tarsus, 30.

Female.—Somewhat smaller and less distinctly marked than
the male. I have seen individuals with the markings on the under
surface scarcely distinguishable.

Nest.—A hole in a tree or in the hollow spout of a limb is
usually chosen, but occasionally a situation among herbage is
resorted to. The nest is always well furnished with down.

Eggs.—Clutch nine to twelve usually; elliptical in shape;
texture fine; surface glossy; colour light creamy-white. Dimensions in mm. of a portion of a clutch:—(1) 46 x 34, (2) 45.5 x 34,
(3) 45 x 33, (4) 46 x 33.5, (5) 44 x 33.

Breeding Season.—September to the end of the year.

Geographical Distribution.—Tasmania, King and other of the
larger islands in Bass Strait, the mainland in general, New Zealand, and a number of the islands of the Austro-Malayan region.

Observations.—Shooting season begins 1st February and ends
30th June. Here we have the Teal so well known to all shooters,
whether on rivers, lakes, or lagoons. It is widely distributed
throughout the island, and, in company with the Black Duck,
frequently congregates in large flocks on many of our rivers. As
a consequence, it is one of the most familiar species of Duck to
be seen in poulterers' windows during the season.

SHOVELLER

(*Spatula rhynchotis*, Lath.)

Male.—Crown of the head, base of the bill, and chin brownish-
black; a crescentic white band between the bill and the eyes;

rest of the head and neck bluish-grey; back brownish-black, the feathers edged with fulvous; rump and upper tail coverts glossy black, tail black, the outer feathers narrowly margined with whitish; "shorter scapulars brown, with white crescentic bars and rufous edges; the longest scapulars have a central greyish-white stripe, but the upper ones glossy black, while the lower ones have the outer webs light blue, like the upper wing coverts" (B. M. Cat.); upper wing coverts light blue, with the last row broadly white; speculum glossy green; primaries and outer secondaries brownish-black; inner secondaries long, black glossed with blue, some with a terminal whitish central stripe; feathers of lower neck and upper edge of breast more or less often very slightly white, centred with blackish-brown and edged with fulvous; rest of breast and abdomen bright rufous-chestnut, with black bands; in old males the black markings practically disappear, leaving only the bright reddish-chestnut; flanks brighter, broadly barred with black; under tail coverts black glossed with green; a patch of white on the lower flanks; marginal under wing coverts pale brown, edged with white; bill purplish-black; legs and feet bright saffron. Dimensions in mm. :—Length, 503; bill, 62; wing, 244; tail, 108; tarsus, 31.

Female.—Crown of the head blackish-brown, slightly streaked with ochreous; neck ochreous, streaked with black; back and shorter scapulars blackish-brown, tipped and edged with reddish-brown; longer scapulars as in male, with central streak almost absent; rump and tail blackish, with narrow rufescent edges; upper wing coverts paler blue, white band on wing, and speculum less distinct than in male; chest and throat sandy-buff; rest of under surface pale brown, the feathers with black centres, more distinct on chest than on abdomen. Dimensions in mm. :—Length, 462; bill, 58; wing, 226; tail, 88; tarsus, 34.

Young.—Very similar to female.

Nest.—A slight hollow in the ground among herbage is usually selected, and this is lined with grass and down.

Eggs.—Clutch seven to nine usually; roundish-oval in shape; texture fine; surface glossy and greasy; colour light creamy-white, tinged with green. Dimensions in mm. of a clutch :—(1) 50 x 38, (2) 50.25 x 28.5, (3) 51 x 39, (4) 50 x 37.5, (5) 51.5 x 38, (6) 52 x 38.5, (7) 51.5 x 39.

Breeding Season.—September to November.

Geographical Distribution.—Tasmania, King, and several other of the larger islands in Bass Strait, Australia in general; also New Zealand.

Observations.—Shooting begins 1st February, ends 30th June. The Blue-wing or Shoveller is a very showy species, especially the male, and although not nearly so plentiful as the Black Duck or the Grey Teal, yet it congregates in fair numbers on several of our tidal rivers, and therefore often falls a victim to the fowler's gun. When on the wing it moves with great rapidity, the noise made by its wings being very pronounced.

PINK-EARED DUCK
(*Malacorhynchus membranaceus*, Lath.)

Male.—Crown greyish-brown; sides of the head and chin whitish; a patch on the sides of the head and a line from either eye, uniting at the occiput and passing down the back of the neck, blackish-brown; a patch of rose-pink, oblong in shape, immediately behind the dark patch surrounding the eye; back, scapulars, and upper wing coverts greyish-brown, minutely freckled with whitish points; rump and upper tail coverts dark brown; the latter with a dark band at the base; tail brown, minutely tipped with white; the secondaries with a terminal band of white; primaries dark brown, the inner ones tipped with white; neck, breast, and under surface greyish-white, thickly barred with brown, narrow on the neck, broader on the breast and flanks, almost disappearing in the centre of the abdomen; under tail coverts buffy-white; "irides dark reddish-brown; bill varies from greenish-grey to bluish-olive; tip of the lower mandible white; tarsi and toes emerald-green in some specimens and yellowish-brown in others; webs dark brown " (Gould). Dimensions in mm.:—Length, 429; bill, 68; wing, 185; tail, 66; tarsus, 32.

Female.—Plumage similar; dimensions slightly less.

Nest.—The deserted nest of some bird such as the Raven or Heron is frequently appropriated and thickly lined with down.

Eggs.—Clutch seven to nine, oval in shape; texture fine; surface glossy; colour creamy-white. Dimensions in mm. of odd examples:—(1) 45 x 32, (2) 47 x 33, (3) 46 x 32, (4) 47 x 32.5.

Breeding Season.—August to November.

Geographical Distribution.—Tasmania and the whole of Australia.

Observations.—Shooting begins 1st February, ends 30th June. The Pink-eared Duck, which on the mainland is known to shooters and dealers by the name of Widgeon, is somewhat scarce in Tasmania. I can obtain but few records of specimens having been secured within the past few years. To my knowledge individuals have been secured in the Longford district, the Lakes district, Lakes Sorell and Crescent, the vicinity of Noland Bay; and it has been seen as a very rare visitor on both the Tamar and Derwent Rivers.

FRECKLED DUCK
(*Stictonetta nævosa*, Gould).

Male.—Whole of the upper surface, wings, and throat blackish-brown; crown of the head almost black, minutely freckled and

16

spotted with irregular buffish-white marks; no speculum on the wings; primaries plain brown; under surface whitish, tinged with buff, especially on the chest, where the colour approaches rich chestnut; under wing coverts white, more or less freckled with brown; axillaries pure white; bill greenish-grey, nail black; legs and feet bluish-green. Dimensions in mm.:—Length, 550; bill, 57; wing, 232; tail, 75; tarsus, 41.5.

Female.—Similar to male.

Nest.—Among herbage on the ground.

Eggs.—Clutch nine to twelve probably; lengthened ellipse in shape; texture of shell fairly fine; surface greasy to the touch; colour light greenish-white. Dimensions in mm. of odd examples in the Launceston Museum:—(1) 52.5 x 40, (2) 55 x 41.

Breeding Season.—October to December.

Geographical Distribution.—Tasmania, New South Wales, Victoria, South and Western Australia, and Queensland.

Observations.—Shooting begins 1st February, ends 30th June. The Freckled Duck is an extremely rare species in Tasmania; there are but few records of it having been obtained here. It is occasionally seen on the Macquarie River and about Noland Bay, on the North-East Coast; also on the Great Lake.

In Victoria this species is frequently called the "Monkey-Duck" by shooters.

Sub-Family—Fuligulinæ.

WHITE-EYED DUCK (WIDGEON)

(*Nyroca australis*, Gould).

Male.—Head, neck, and breast rich chocolate; feathers on the back and shoulders dark brown, edged with olive-brown; rump dark brown; tail brown; wings brown, glossed with olive; quills brown; secondaries mostly white; primaries centrally white, together forming a conspicuous bar on the wings; across the centre of the under surface is a broad band of brownish-white; rest of abdomen brown; under tail coverts white; bill, basal two-thirds black, rest bluish-red, with the nail black; legs and feet pale bluish-lead. Dimensions in mm.:—Length, 490; bill, 48.5; wing, 225; tail, 63; tarsus, 34.

Female.—Similar, but slightly duller, and dimensions slightly less.

Young.—Male.—"Has a chestnut-brown plumage, much lighter, and the feathers at the back margined with pale brown; it has also less gloss on the head and the brownish-white of the under parts mottled with brown" (Buller).

Nest.—The situation of the nest varies from a hollow in a tree to the ground among herbage, where it is composed of grass, feathers, and down.

Eggs.—"Clutch eleven to thirteen; elliptical in shape, texture of shell comparatively fine; surface glossy and greasy; colour light creamy-white. Dimensions in inches of a pair:—(1) 2.27 x 1.67, (2) 2.26 x 1.64 " (A. J. Campbell).

Breeding Season.—September to November.

Geographical Distribution.—Tasmania, Australia, New Zealand, New Caledonia, and several other islands in the South Pacific.

Observations.—Shooting begins 1st February, ends 30th June. Among shooters the Widgeon is much sought after, it being considered by many a better table bird than some of the commoner species. On account of its rapid flight, it is one of the most difficult birds to shoot; this, combined with its comparative scarcity, does more to make it a desirable bird in the eyes of shooters than its problematical superiority of flavour. On the Tamar, Derwent, and other rivers it may be found in small numbers feeding in company with Teal, Black Duck, and Shoveller; in addition to rivers it frequents a number of the lakes and larger lagoons.

Sub-Family—Erismaturinæ.

BLUE-BILLED DUCK
(*Erismatura australis*, Gould).

Male.—Head, neck, and throat black; back, chest, and flanks rich chestnut; wings and tail brownish-black; under tail coverts brownish-grey, with dark brown markings; bill bluish to bluish lead colour. Dimensions in mm.:—Length, 395; bill, 45; wing, 158; tail, 70; tarsus, 39.

Female.—Uniform blackish-brown, with transverse zig-zag lines of chestnut-brown; the under surface is more greyish-brown, the feathers being tipped with yellowish.

Nest.—"Not unlike that of a Musk-Duck, well concealed in the herbage of a marsh or swamp, and lined with grass and down " (A. J. Campbell).

Eggs.—Clutch two to nine or ten (Gould); four or five (Campbell); six (J. C. FitzGerald, quoted by A. J. Campbell); fairly oval in shape; texture of shell coarse; surface slightly glossy; colour light greenish-white. Dimensions in mm. of odd examples:—(1) 66 x 47, (2) 70 x 49, (3) 68 x 48.

Breeding Season.—August to December.

Geographical Distribution.—Tasmania, New South Wales, Victoria, South and Western Australia.

Observations.—This little-known Duck is found in various parts of the island, but is scarce everywhere. I have records of it from the river Tamar, Piper's River, and Lakes Crescent and Sorell. The first recorded Tasmanian specimens (a pair) were secured at Cambridge, May, 1892.

*MUSK-DUCK

(*Biziura lobata*, Shaw).

Male.—Crown of the head and nape brownish-black; back, wings, chest, and flanks blackish-brown, crossed by very narrow freckled lines of buffy-white; quills and tail feathers blackish-brown; sides of the head and neck freckled with buffy-white and black; abdomen blackish-brown, with broad buffy-white margins to the feathers; towards the under tail coverts the margins almost disappear; "bill and large lobe beneath the chin greenish-black; legs and feet dark leaden-grey, inside of the tarsi greenish-grey" (Gould). Dimensions in mm.:—Length, 658; bill, 40; wing, 246; tail, 152; tarsus, 38.

Female.—Plumage similar, save that the narrow buffy-white bars on the upper surface are more distinct, lobe much smaller or even absent. Dimensions in mm.:—Length, 565; bill, 33; wing, 186; tail, 99; tarsus, 35.

Young in Down.—"Upper parts, head, neck, upper part of the breast, sides, and flanks uniform dark brown, scarcely lighter round the face at the base of the bill; lower breast, abdomen, and under tail coverts whitish" (B. M. Cat.)

Nest.—Usually a hollow in the ground among rushes or grass, or the centre of a slight elevation in a swamp, is chosen. The nesting hollow is lined with down.

Eggs.—Clutch two to three; elliptical in shape, with both ends somewhat pointed; texture of the shell coarse; surface slightly glossy and rough; colour greenish-white, more or less soiled. Dimensions in mm. of a clutch:—(1) 84 x 54, (2) 85 x 51.

Breeding Season.—October to December or January.

Geographical Distribution.—Tasmania, round and on several of the larger Bass Strait islands, New South Wales, Victoria, South and Western Australia, and South Queensland.

Observations.—At one time and another much printers' ink has been expended in controversy over this Duck's ability or otherwise to fly. A proof positive that it does so is furnished by Mr. C. H. Hamilton (*Emu*, vol. i., p. 147), who records being with a friend when he shot a Musk-Duck at dusk one evening in mistake for a Black Duck; it was flying high and very fast.

The largest flock of this species I have ever seen numbered twenty-four birds (actual count), on the River Tamar. On some of the inland waters it is moderately plentiful, but very shy.

As is well known, this Duck, when disturbed but in no immediate danger, will submerge itself until only the eyes and nostrils are showing above water.

APPENDIX.

EXTRACT FROM THE TASMANIAN GAME PROTECTION
ACT 1907, being "An Act to consolidate and amend the
Laws relating to the Protection of Game, and for other
purposes."

1. This Act may be cited as "The Game Protection Act 1907."

2. (1) The Acts mentioned in the Schedule (1) are hereby
repealed.

3. In this Act, unless the context otherwise determines—

"Imported game" means and includes Wonga Wonga
Pigeon (*Leucosarcia picata*), Pheasants, Partridges,
and Grouse, whether the same are alive or dead, and
any other bird or animal which the Governor by
proclamation as hereinafter provided declares to be
imported game.

"Mutton-Bird" means the Short-tailed Petrel (*Puffinus
tenuirostris*).

"Native game" means and includes Wild Ducks (other
than Musk-Ducks), Teal, Widgeon, Quail, Plover,
Black Swans, Wattle-Birds, Cape Barren Geese,
Bronze-winged Pigeons, and Brush Bronze-winged
Pigeons, whether such birds are alive or dead, and any
other bird, whether such bird is alive or dead, which
the Governor by proclamation as hereinafter provided
shall declare to be native game.

"Quail" includes the bird usually called the Californian
Quail.

"Tasmania" includes the dependencies thereof.

4. It shall be lawful for the Governor, by proclamation, to
name any other bird or animal which shall be included in the term
"imported game" or "native game"; and after the publication
of any such proclamation in the *Gazette*, and after the expiration
of the period mentioned in such proclamation for the commencement thereof, the bird or animal so named shall be included in the
term "imported game" or "native game" as the case may be.

Imported Game.

5. If any person kills or takes any imported game, or uses any dog, gun, net, snare, or other engine or instrument, for the purpose of killing or taking any such game, he shall for every head of imported game so killed or taken, and for every such offence of so using any dog, gun, net, snare, or other engine or instrument, incur a penalty not exceeding Ten Pounds.

6. If any person buys or sells, or knowingly has in his house, possession, or control, any imported game, except live game kept or to be kept in a mew or breeding place, every person shall, for every head of imported game so bought or sold, or found in his house, possession, or control, incur a penalty not exceeding Ten Pounds. Nothing herein contained shall extend to any dead imported game brought into this State.

7. If any person wilfully takes out of the nest, or destroys in the nest, the eggs of any imported bird of game, or knowingly has in his house, possession, or control any such eggs, every person shall for every egg so taken or destroyed, or found in his house, possession, or control, incur a penalty not exceeding Five Pounds; but this provision shall not extend to the owner of any mew or breeding place for game in respect of eggs in or taken from the nest in such mew or breeding place, or to any person in respect of any eggs taken from the nest and given to such person by such owner.

Native Game.

8. The following shall be deemed to be the breeding seasons for native game; that is to say :—

> For Wild Ducks, Teal, Widgeon, Plover, and Black Swans, from the first day of July in every year to the last day of January in each succeeding year, both days inclusive.

> For Cape Barren Geese, from the first day of June to the last day of December in each year.

> For Bronze-winged Pigeons and Brush Bronze-winged Pigeons, from the first day of July in every year to the last day of February in every succeeding year, both days inclusive.

> For Wattle-Birds, from the first day of August in every year to the thirtieth day of April in every succeeding year, both days inclusive.

> For Quail, from the first day of July in every year to the thirtieth day of April in every succeeding year, both days inclusive.

9. It shall be lawful for the Governor from time to time by proclamation to declare that any native game described in such proclamation shall not be killed, taken, or captured during any

time, to be stated in such proclamation, in such parts of Tasmania
as may be described and set forth in such proclamation; and every
person acting in contravention of such proclamation shall be liable
to the like penalty as if he had offended against the next section
of this Act.

10. If any person kills, takes, or captures, or has in his
possession or control (whether on his own land or on that of
any other person), any native game during the breeding season
of such game, such person shall for every head of native game
so killed, taken, or captured by him, or so found in his possession
or control, forfeit and pay a penalty not exceeding Two Pounds;
but nothing in this section contained shall apply to any person
keeping native game in a mew or breeding place for breeding
purposes, or to any person in whose possession or control any dead
native game is found, and who proves that the same was not
killed during the breeding season of such game.

11. Whoever at any time—

(1) Kills or attempts to kill or destroy any Wild Ducks,
Teal, Widgeon, Black Swans, or Cape Barren Geese,
with any device or instrument known as a swivel or
punt gun, or with any gun other than such guns as are
habitually raised at arms' length and fired from the
shoulder, or

(2) Uses or attempts to use any decoy duck (whether arti-
ficial or not) or similar device, for the purpose of taking
or killing any Wild Ducks, Teal, or Widgeon, shall be
guilty of an offence against this Act.
Penalty : Five Pounds.

12. Whoever takes or wilfully destroys the eggs of any native
game shall be guilty of an offence against this Act.
Penalty : One pound for every egg taken or wilfully destroyed.

13. Whoever takes or wilfully destroys the eggs of any Mutton-
Bird shall be guilty of an offence against this Act.
Penalty : One pound for every such egg taken or wilfully
destroyed as aforesaid.

14. Whoever, without the written consent of a police magistrate or two justices, buys, sells, or offers for sale any of the birds
enumerated in the Schedule (2) of this Act, whether dead or alive,
shall be guilty of an offence against this Act for every such bird
so bought, sold, or offered for sale : Provided that this section shall
not apply to Pheasants, Partridges, or Grouse in a mew.
Penalty : One pound.

15. Whoever shoots at or wilfully kills any of the birds
enumerated in the Schedule (2), or takes or destroys the nest or
eggs, or takes the young of any of the birds enumerated in the
said Schedule, without the written consent of a police magistrate

or two justices, shall be guilty of an offence against this Act: Provided that this section shall not apply to Pheasants, Partridges, or Grouse in a mew.

Penalty : One pound.

16. Notwithstanding anything to the contrary contained in this Act, the Governor may, in writing, authorize any person at any time to kill, capture, or destroy any native game or imported game, or any bird or any animal or the progeny thereof which is protected by this Act or by any proclamation issued hereunder, or to take and keep the eggs of any protected bird, provided that the Governor is satisfied that any such person requires any such native game, imported game, bird or the eggs thereof, or any such animal or the progeny thereof, for a scientific purpose.

17. The Governor is hereby empowered from time to time, by proclamation, to reserve any lands of the Crown as and to be hunting grounds for Mutton-Birds, and also for acclimatization purposes, and any such proclamation to revoke.

LICENCES.

23. (1) No person—

(1). Shall kill, take, or capture any Mutton-Bird unless he holds a licence for that purpose.

28. Nothing in this Act contained shall be deemed to authorize any person holding any licence issued under this Act to kill, take, or capture Mutton-Birds, except during the prescribed time. . .

31. (1) The Governor may from time to time make regulations for the following purposes, or any of them ; that is to say :—

i. For the protection of Mutton-Birds.

ii. Prescribing the time during which and the purpose for which the Mutton-Bird may be killed or captured.

SCHEDULE (2).

1. Albatross, Black-browed (*Diomedia melanophrys*).
2. Albatross, Flat-billed (*Thalassogeron culminatus*).
3. Albatross, Green-billed (*Thalassogeron chlororhynchus*).
4. Albatross, Sooty (*Phœbetria fuliginosa*).
5. Albatross, Wandering (*Diomedia exulans*).
6. Albatross, White-capped (*Thalassogeron cautus*).
7. Avocet, Red-necked (*Recurvirostra rubricollis*).
8. Barn-Owl, Tasmanian (*Strix castanops*).
9. Bittern (*Botaurus pœciloptilus*).
10. Blackbird (*Turdus merula*).
11. Brown-tail (*Acanthiza diemenensis*).
12. Caterpillar-eater, White-shouldered (*Lalage tricolor*).

13. Chat, White-fronted (*Ephthianura albifrons*).
14. Cockatoo, Black (*Calyptorynchus xanthonotus*).
15. Cockatoo, Gang-Gang (*Callocephalon galeatum*).
16. Crake, Little (*Porzana palustris*).
17. Crake, Red-backed (*Porzana tabuensis*).
18. Crake, Spotted (*Porzana fluminea*).
19. Cuckoo, Broad-billed Bronze (*Chalcococcyx lucidus*).
20. Cuckoo, Bronze (*Chalcococcyx plagosus*).
21. Cuckoo, Channel-bill (*Scythrops novæ-hollandiæ*).
22. Cuckoo, Fan-tailed (*Cuculus flabelliformis*).
23. Cuckoo, Narrow-billed Bronze (*Chalcococcyx basalis*).
24. Cuckoo, Pallid (*Cuculus pallidus*).
25. Curlew, Australian (*Numenius cyanopus*).
26. Diamond-Bird (*Pardalotus punctatus*).
27. Diamond-Bird, Allied (*Pardalotus affinis*).
28. Diamond-Bird, Forty-spotted (*Pardalotus quadragintus*).
29. Dove, Ground—The Ground-Bird (*Cinclosoma punctatum*).
30. Drongo (*Chibia bracteata*).
31. Duck, Musk (*Biziura lobata*).
32. Egret, White (*Herodias timoriensis*).
33. Fantail, Tasmanian (*Rhipidura diemenensis*).
34. Finch, Fire-tailed (*Zonæginthus bellus*).
35. Flycatcher, Leaden (*Myiagra rubecula*).
36. Flycatcher, Satin (*Myiagra nitidia*).
37. Gannet, Australian (*Sula serrator*).
38. Godwit, Barred-rumped (*Limosa uropygialis*).
39. Goldfinch (*Carduelis elegans*).
40. Goose, Maned (*Chenonetta jubata*).
41. Goshawk, White (*Astur novæ-hollandiæ*).
42. Grass-Bird (*Megalurus gramineus*).
43. Grebe, Hoary-headed (*Podiceps nestor*).
44. Grebe, Little (*Podiceps novæ-hollandiæ*).
45. Grebe, Tippet (*Podiceps cristatus*).
46. Greenshank (*Glottis nebularius*).
47. Grouse (*Lagopus scoticus*).
48. Gull, Little (*Larus novæ-hollandiæ*).
49. Gull, Pacific (*Larus pacificus*).
50. Hawk-Owl, Brown (*Ninox boobook*).
51. Hawk-Owl, Spotted (*Ninox maculata*).
52. Heron, Night (*Nycticorax caledonicus*).
53. Heron, Pacific (*Notophoyx pacifica*).
54. Heron, Reef (*Demiegretta sacra*).
55. Heron, White-fronted (*Notophyx novæ-hollandiæ*).
56. Honey-eater, Black-headed (*Melithreptus melanocephalus*).
57. Honey-eater, Crescent (*Meliornis australasiana*)
58. Honey-eater, Fulvous-fronted (*Glycyphila fulvifrons*).
59. Honey-eater, Minah, Garrulous (*Manorhina garrula*).
60. Honey-eater, Strong-billed (*Melithreptus validirostris*).

61. Honey-eater, White-bearded (*Meliornis novæ-hollandiæ*).
62. Honey-eater, Yellow-throated (*Ptilotis flavigularis*).
63. Ibis, Glossy (*Geronticus australis*).
64. Kingfisher, Blue (*Alcyone azurea*).
65. Kingfisher, Great, or Laughing Jackass (*Dacelo gigas*).
66. Kingfisher, Sacred (*Halcyon sanctus*).
67. Lark, Magpie (*Grallina picata*).
68. Lyre-Bird (*Menura superba*).
69. Lyre-Bird, Albert (*Menura alberti*).
70. Lyre-Bird, Victoria (*Menura victoriæ*).
71. Magpie, White (*Gymnorhina hyperleuca*).
72. More-pork or Frogmouth (*Podargus strigoides*).
73. Owlet Nightjar (*Ægotheles novæ-hollandiæ*).
74. Oyster-catcher, Sooty (*Hæmatopus unicolor*).
75. Oyster-catcher, White-breasted (*Hæmatopus longirostris*).
76. Parrakeet, Ground or Swamp (*Pezoporus formosus*).
77. Partridge (*Perdix cinerea*).
78. Pelican (*Pelecanus conspicillatus*).
79. Penguin, Crested (*Catarrhactes chrysocome*).
80. Penguin, Fairy (*Eudyptula undina*).
81. Penguin, Little (*Eudyptula minor*).
82. Petrel, Atlantic (*Pterodroma atlantica*).
83. Petrel, Black-bellied Storm (*Cymodroma melanogaster*).
84. Petrel, Blue (*Halobæna cærulea*).
85. Petrel, Cape (*Daption capensis*).
86. Petrel, Diving (*Halodroma urinatrix*).
87. Petrel, Giant (*Ossifraga gigantea*).
88. Petrel, Grey (*Priofinus cinereus*).
89. Petrel, Grey-backed Storm (*Garrodia nereis*).
90. Petrel, Long-winged (*Pterodroma macroptera*).
91. Petrel, Silver-grey (*Priocella glacialoides*).
92. Petrel, Solander (*Pterodroma solandri*).
93. Petrel, Spectacled (*Majaqueus equinoctialis*).
94. Petrel, White-bellied Storm (*Cymodroma grallaria*).
95. Petrel, White-faced Storm (*Pelagodroma marina*).
96. Petrel, White-headed (*Œstrelata lessoni*).
97. Petrel, White-winged (*Œstrelata leucoptera*).
98. Petrel, Yellow-footed Storm (*Oceanites oceanicus*).
99. Pheasant (*Phasianus colchicus*).
100. Pigeon, Superb Fruit (*Lamprotreron superbus*).
101. Pigeon, Topknot (*Lopholæmus antarcticus*).
102. Pigeon, Wood (*Columbus palumbus*).
103. Pipit, Australian (*Anthus australis*).
104. Plover, Double-banded Sand (*Ægialitis bicincta*)
105. Plover, Hooded Sand (*Ægialitis monacha*).
106. Plover, Red-capped Sand (*Ægialitis ruficapilla*).
107. Plover, Southern Stone (*Burhinus grallarius*).
108. Prion, Banks (*Prion banksi*).

109. Prion, Broad-billed (*Prion vittatus*).
110. Prion, Dove (*Prion desolatus*).
111. Prion, Fairy (*Prion ariel*).
112. Rail, Pectoral (*Hypotænidia philippinensis*).
113. Rail, Short-toed (*Hypotænidia brachypus*).
114. Robin, Dusky (*Petrœca vittata*).
115. Robin, Flame-breasted (*Petrœca phœnicea*).
116. Robin, Pink-breasted (*Petrœca rhodinogastra*).
117. Robin, Scarlet-breasted (*Petrœca leggei*).
118. Sandpiper, Common (*Tringoides hypoleucus*).
119. Shrike-Thrush, Whistling (*Collyriocincla rectirostris*).
120. Sea-Eagle, White-bellied (*Haliaëtus leucogaster*).
121. Skylark (*Alauda arvensis*).
122. Spinebill (*Acanthorhynchus tenuirostris*).
123. Stilt, Banded (*Cladorhynchus pectoralis*).
124. Stilt, White-headed (*Himantopus leucocephalus*).
125. Stint, Curlew (*Tringa subarquata*).
126. Stint, Marsh (*Tringa acuminata*).
127. Stint, Red-breasted (*Tringa ruficollis*).
128. Summer-Bird (*Graucalus parvirostris*).
129. Swallow, Australian (*Hirundo neoxena*).
130. Swallow, Tree (*Petrochelidon nigricans*).
131. Swallow, Wood (*Artamus sordidus*).
132. Swift, Spine-tailed (*Chætura caudacuta*).
133. Tern, Bass Strait (*Sterna poliocerca*).
134. Tern, Black-billed (*Sterna frontalis*).
135. Tern, Caspian (*Sterna caspia*).
136. Ternlet, White-faced (*Sterna nereis*).
137. Thickhead, Grey-tailed (*Pachycephala glaucura*).
138. Thickhead, Olivaceous (*Pachycephala olivacea*).
139. Thickhead, Yellow-breasted (*Pachycephala gutturalis*).
140. Thrush (*Turdus musicus*).
141. Thrush, Ground (*Geocichla macrorhyncha*).
142. Turnstone (*Strepsilas interpres*).
143. Warbler, Reed (*Acrocephalus australis*).
144. Warbler, Rush (*Calamanthus fuliginosus*).
145. Wattle-Bird, Brush (*Acanthochæra mellivora*).
146. Whimbrel (*Numenius phæopus*).
147. White-eye (*Zosterops cærulescens*).
148. Wren, Blue, or Long-tailed Warbler (*Malurus gouldi*).
149. Wren, Brown Scrub (*Sericornis humilis*).
150. Wren, Emu (*Stipiturus malachurus*).
151. Wren, White-breasted Scrub (*Acanthornis magna*).
152. Yellow-tail (*Acanthiza chrysorrhœa*).

An inspection of the above list will show that it requires considerable amendment in various ways to make it an ideal one.

VERNACULAR INDEX.

————◆————

17

www.ingramcontent.com/pod-product-compliance
Lightning Source LLC
Chambersburg PA
CBHW020822270326
41928CB00006B/412